Introduction to
Computing
and Algorithms
SECOND EDITION

Russell L. Shackelford
Georgia Institute of Technology

McGraw-Hill, Inc.
College Custom Series

New York St. Louis San Francisco Auckland Bogotá
Caracas Lisbon London Madrid Mexico Milan Montreal
New Delhi Paris San Juan Singapore Sydney Tokyo Toronto

McGraw·Hill

A Division of The McGraw·Hill Companies

Introduction to Computing and Algorithms

Copyright © 1997, 1996 by McGraw-Hill, Inc. All rights reserved. Printed in the United States of America. Except as permitted under the United States Copyright Act of 1976, no part of this publication may be reproduced or distributed in any form or by any means, or stored in a data base retrieval system, without prior written permission of the publisher.

McGraw-Hill's College Custom Series consists of products that are produced from camera-ready copy. Peer review, class testing, and accuracy are primarily the responsibility of the author(s).

Cover Photo: *Globe and Keys*, copyright © 1993 by Barry Rosenthal/FPG International Corp.
Cover Photo: *Pat's Hands* by Jessica L. Weber
1 2 3 4 5 6 7 8 9 0 BBC BBC 9 0 9 8 7 6

ISBN 0-07-057936-9
Editor: Judy T. Ice
Cover Designer: Maggie Lytle
Printer/Binder: Braceland Brothers, Inc.

Preface

Overview

This book, and the introductory course that it represents, are results of our efforts at Georgia Tech's College of Computing to simultaneously accomplish two things:

1. Correct some of the well-known problems of CS introductory courses;
2. Respond to a broad audience of students who require a computing foundation.

We designed the new introductory course in 1991-92 and implemented it in 1992-93 as a part of our redesign of the lower division CS curriculum. The course has proved a success, with enrollments skyrocketing from approximately 100 students per year in 1992-93 to more than 1500 in 1995-96. Soon, it will be part of Georgia Tech's core curriculum and enrollments will stabilize at about 2000 students per year.

Thus, we have been gaining experience with both a new approach to introductory computing education and new class management techniques required by the rapid increase in enrollments. Along the way, we have instituted processes that allow us to track both student performance and student opinion. As a result, we know more about the effects of our efforts than would otherwise have been the case. This allows us to have some insight about the consequences of some of the risks we took in designing the new course. I will return to the question "what have we learned?" after I summarize what we are doing pedagogically and why.

Course Goals

The design of this book reflects our original goals for the new introductory course:

Goal 1: Provide a course that is a true "introduction to the field"

Within academia, traditional computer science introductory courses have been an aberration. Unlike introductory courses in other disciplines, traditional introductory CS courses have failed to provide any substantive coverage of the conceptual and intellectual foundations of the discipline. Instead, we have always had students "do programming" from the very beginning of study without providing them with any foundation. Small wonder, then, that CS faculty complain that others think computer science is "nothing but programming." It would seem only natural that people think precisely that when the introduction that CS departments offer is called "Introduction to Programming" and features no other substantive subject matter.

What subject matter is relevant for an introductory course in computing? One possible approach is to use the introductory course as an opportunity to give students a tour of the various sub-disciplines within computer science, e.g., "If it's week 4, it must be Database." We rejected this approach because our goal is to introduce students to the important ideas of computing, not to the current organization of CS departments. We find the "tour" approach to be lacking in conceptual content and irrelevant (and therefore probably boring) to students who are not CS majors.

The approach we have taken is to acknowledge that the central concept that underlies computer science is the algorithm and thus we make algorithms the central object of study. This approach calls for the introduction of basic ideas, including both essential algorithm constructs and certain foundational aspects of theory, tailored to students at the freshman level.

Goal 2: Introduce a broad population of students to key ideas from computer science

Over the last decade, it has become clear that computing is having a radical impact on virtually all aspects of science, commerce, and communication. In this respect, computing is unlike other disciplines. Computing affects everybody, and does so in at least two ways. At the level of tools, computing is transforming how things are done in nearly every domain of human endeavor. At the level of conception, computing is providing the intellectual framework that underlies cutting-edge research in virtually every discipline. Both the tools and the ideas of computing are essential to the much ballyhooed "paradigm shift" that is sweeping through modern society.

We believe that, as computer science educators, we should broaden our perspective to appreciate this important fact. To the world at large, the differences between *Pascal* and *C++*, or between *UNIX* and *Windows*, are small matters. In contrast, the widespread acceptance of the "algorithmic model" of phenomena is a very significant event in the history of human knowledge and understanding. Throughout the natural sciences and the behavioral sciences, the current state of the art is to model phenomena in algorithmic terms and to generate algorithmic simulations to test and refine those models. Algorithms provide the basis for the new "rules of the game" across the spectrum of theoretical and empirical study. We believe that any well-educated college graduate should have been exposed to the basic tenets of "algorithmic thinking." They should also have experiences which encourage them to add this mode of thinking to their "repertoire of ways to think." The algorithm-oriented agenda found in this book is not for CS-majors only. It is offered as "foundational 21st Century knowledge" for a broad population of students from across the family of academic disciplines. Computing will increasingly shape their lives. As well-educated citizens of the future, they need to know about computing's central ideas and its limitations.

Goal 3: Provide conceptual content to complement software-use skills

The immense impact of computing has made it necessary for all college students to possess basic computer-use skills. At many colleges, there has been rising demand for basic instruction in the use of computers and of standard software applications. Often, this has resulted in the creation of pre-programming courses focused on "the computer as a tool", i.e., teaching students to use word processors, spreadsheets, etc.

We emphatically agree that an introductory computing course should include this focus, but we do not agree that such a focus is sufficient. In our view, "application use" is primarily a skills issue and thus is properly the focus of a lab agenda. It is lacking in substantive content and one can therefore question whether it is inappropriate as the basis for a college-level course. To us, offering college credit for learning how to use a spreadsheet is uncomfortably analogous to an Electrical Engineering department offering college credit for learning how to solder, or a Mechanical Engineering school giving academic credit for a course in welding.

Thus, our "Introduction to Computing" course features a two-pronged approach. The lecture-and- homework component focuses on conceptual tools for constructing and analyzing algorithms, while the lab-and-project component focuses on a variety of standard software applications. This book supports the lecture-and-homework agenda, which we believe should be essentially the same regardless of institutional specifics. Labs, on the other hand, will naturally vary somewhat, based on institutional mission and on local computing resources. Our lab agenda is implemented in an environment of generic PCs and PC-based software, with *telnet* access to centralized *UNIX* resources. In principle, it can be implemented in a range of local environments. Our lab agenda consists of five modular components:

- *Communications Tools and Facilities,* a four week module which introduces e-mail, newsgroups, text and graphics editing, desktop publishing, and HTML;

- *Data Processing Tools and Facilities,* a four week module which introduces databases, spreadsheets, and equation solvers;

- *Problem Solving,* a three week module which focuses on the use of the above tools and facilities in discipline-specific problem solving;

- *A Taste of Programming,* a three week module which prefaces the second course by introducing the basics of *Java,* including component construction and rapid prototyping, in a way that is intended to be stimulating and fun;

- *Lab Skills Evaluation:* a "show me you can do it" lab-based final exam which occurs during the last week of class.

Further information about our lab agenda, environment and materials may be obtained upon request.

Goal 4: Prepare students for programming

The complaints of faculty who teach traditional "Introduction to Programming" courses seem remarkably similar. Students in such courses can be counted upon to ignore good practices of software design and implementation, to doubt the value of documentation, to evidence poor abstraction in the design of their programs, to show a strong tendency to "hack" solutions, all the while largely ignoring faculty's words of wisdom about how to "engineer" a good program that will do the job properly. These and similar teaching-and-learning problems are ubiquitous. In our view, each of them is a natural consequence of the traditional "intro to programming" approach that (a) blurs together design and implementation issues, (b) presents students with program implementation tasks too early, and (c) focuses lecture on the language-specific implementation of generally-applicable constructs and techniques.

We believe that the traditional approach errs by giving students information on what they are trying to do in a narrow language-specific context (thus defeating effective abstraction). At the same time, it puts students in programming situations in which they must satisfy algorithm execution requirements (thus implicitly focusing the student on implementation, not design). The results are predictable: students quickly lose all sense of design and abstraction as they "wrestle with a compiler at 2 a.m." Any trace of an "engineering" attitude is quickly replaced by desperate prayers such as, "let's try putting a semicolon here and, oh please, let it work!" We believe that overcoming such problems requires that we separate the treatment of (a) effective design and abstraction from (b) implementation and testing. Our experience tells us that if we fail to separate them, the latter is guaranteed to overwhelm the former.

Thus, we make sure that the foundational issues of abstraction and design are treated in an informal environment (pseudocode and picture drawing) where a human audience determines grades without allowing the student near a compiler. In this context, clarity of design and implementation is more important than syntax compliance and algorithmic accuracy. Once students have a foundation in design and implementation, we then (and only then) add the requirement that the computer must be satisfied. We insist that students focus on logical abstraction and design in the first course ("Introduction to Computing") so that they enter the second course ("Introduction to Programming") knowing what they are trying to do. Essential algorithmic concepts and techniques are introduced in the first course, which in turn liberates lecture in the second course to focus on effective design, implementation, and debugging skills and strategies.. In short, we think that the secret to preparing students for programming is to simply give them some preparation. We believe that to do otherwise (especially at a time when languages such as C++ are sometimes used in intro courses) is unwise and counterproductive.

**The results of
our experience**

We created this course with four main goals: (1) provide a good introduction to the discipline of computer science, such that (2) computing's important ideas are conveyed to a broad range of students, while simultaneously giving students both (3) a broad range of experience with standard software applications, and (4) a good foundational preparation for high level computer programming, including an introduction to the object-oriented paradigm. With four years of experience, what have we learned about our ability to do these things?

I will summarize our findings in terms of the various aspects of our approach which we thought were somewhat risky.

**Risk 1: No
programming?**

There was initial concern that the absence of explicit programming in the first course would cause students to be disgruntled. The assumption here was that students are "champing at the bit" to program, and that any delays would frustrate their desires. Indeed colleagues from other universities who had experimented with some form of this idea cautioned us on this very point. On the other hand, there was opinion to the effect that, since we would be keeping students active doing other related things (such as learning application software and creating algorithms via pseudocode and pictures), students would not object. We proceeded according to plan, and made sure to sample student opinion on this very point during each and every term.

Student opinion is mixed, with about 25% of students perceiving the absence of programming as a negative factor, and a similar number perceiving this same delay as a positive factor. Those students who like the absence of programming feel more strongly about this than do the students who dislike it. Approximately half the class see it as neither a positive nor a negative. As we averaged student responses, adjusting for both polarity and intensity of opinion, we have found the mean, median, and mode all falling directly on "no difference." These results are consistent over different academic terms. They confirm for us that the absence of programming is far from a significant problem, with only 1 of 4 students challenging it, and then usually weakly. Our response has been to develop procedures by which students who are ready for programming may exempt the course; only a small few are able to do so. (It occurs much more frequently that students who already have a programming background complete the first course, then exempt the second one.)

**Risk 2:
Pseudocode that
looks like Pascal?**

There was also concern about the particulars of our pseudocode environment. There was near-universal support for a pseudocode environment that features reliance on pictures and a minimal language with generic features and little punctuation. However, there was disagreement about whether it should be oriented towards procedural or object-oriented abstractions. After consultation with faculty who specialize in the *OO* realm, we initially resolved this by providing a procedural foundation (upon which *OO* implementations are based) with a minimal set of *OO* constructs. This led us to the "*Pascal* like" appearance, with single-inheritance class extensions. The pseudocode differs from *Pascal* in many ways (e.g., parameters, scoping, typing, iteration construct, and other areas where *Pascal* itself is lacking or problematic), but its relatively easy to read *Pascal*-like (and *Ada*-like, and *Modula*-like, and so on) "look and feel" is retained.

On this issue, we expect ongoing evolutionary change. In particular, we expect programming languages such as *Java* to have significant impacts, allowing programmers to exploit both *OO* design and Internet connectivity in ways that may fundamentally change how programmers do things. We are now shifting to *Java* as the programming language used in our second course, and we will be watching for evidence that, with more low-level reusable code available to our students, we can further raise the level of abstraction in the first course in various ways (for example: a de-emphasis on data structure manipulation and greater focus on design and performance analysis). At the moment, however, we believe such a shift in the first course is premature, as most students will still have to be competent in pre-*OO* environments. In such a world, *Pascal*-like features still provide both a good introduction to ideas and good "pre-emptive pedagogy" against the more controversial features of *C* and its extensions. It's likely that future editions of this text will feature evolutionary change in this regard as the impact of *Java* grows.

Risk 3: Can freshmen really do this? There was initial controversy as to whether we were establishing an agenda that was unreasonably ambitious for freshmen. After all, we were moving certain topics down to the freshman level from upper- division theory courses, courses in which the performance of upper classmen was often marginal. If CS juniors and seniors often sought to simply "survive" a theory course, were we not crazy for expecting freshmen to "catch on?" Experience has shown that this fear was not well founded. Both performance data and opinion data indicate that students have no more difficulty with these topics than with other, "more typical" introductory topics.

There appear to be two main factors in our success with introducing theory-related topics early. First and foremost, the pedagogical treatment is explicitly aimed at a broad freshman population, i.e., we use concrete examples and we de-emphasize mathematics. Secondly, it appears that "liberating" this foundational material from the theory courses has, in and of itself, a positive effect. Students evidently approach self-labeled "theory" courses as painful exercises that have little to do with applied issues. By taking the most basic issues, such as order notation, intractability, limits of parallelism, etc., and couching that material in practical, "down to earth" examples, it appears that they are "demystified", i.e., students do not become afraid of these topics. By introducing such concepts from the earliest levels in common-sense ways, it appears that students see the relevance of them and never "learn to fear" these topics.

Risk 4: Can "normal" freshmen do this?

Given Georgia Tech's admission standards, the questions has arisen, "Can a more typical freshmen population master this theoretical material?" Adopting an approach that only a select few could utilize would be inconsistent with our goal of supporting others in achieving high quality computing education.

Our experience leads us to believe that success with the theoretical topics will transfer across many populations. Numerous studies indicate that, for most students, different levels of intellectual ability manifest themselves as "differences of degree," not "differences of kind." Thus, a bright student can reasonably be expected to learn new material faster than a slower student, but rarely will the slower student be unable to grasp the material if given more time. Our experience to date at Georgia Tech has been based on a quarter-system course in which the entire term lasts no more than 10-weeks, with occasional aberrations of as little as 7-weeks. At such an accelerated pace, we believe that, yes, we have indeed been exploiting the "superior horsepower" of our students to grasp things quickly. However, as we transition from a quarter- to a semester-system implementation, we are not adding new material. Instead, we are simply distributing the same "10 weeks worth" of topical coverage across a 15 week term. Thus, the pace of absorption is slowed by one third. Since we already focus on concrete examples and de-emphasize mathematics, we believe that this expansion of the time window by 50% will be adequate to meet the needs of most freshmen.

Risk 5: Curricular implications

Originally, there was concern about the suitability of such a course for the rest of the CS curriculum. How would an algorithm-based, non-programming "Introduction to Computing" course, followed by a second course in "Introduction to Programming" impact the rest of the curriculum? In our case, this proved not to matter. We implemented this sequence at the same time as we redesigned the rest of the lower division CS curriculum.

We see, however, no reason for such an approach to have troublesome consequences for others who offer a more standard curriculum. In such an environment, the standard two "Intro to Programming I and II" courses are replaced by "Introduction to Computing" followed by a single, more intensive "Introduction to Programming." Experience shows that, given the first course, progress in the second course can be more aggressive since students will enter with a conceptual foundation that prepares them for programming. In balance, it is reasonable to expect this change to show a slight weakening of rote "button pushing skill" coupled with a stronger conceptual base and better adaptability to other programming paradigms. In balance, this is a trade that we gladly make, and we expect that other computer scientists will too.

Summary

We are well satisfied with the impacts that this new introductory course has had. Aside from obtaining the improvement effects that we sought, the only other curricular repercussions we foresee for others who adopt it are (1) an increase in enrollment, as more disciplines will appreciate the relevance of such an introductory course for their students, and (2) greater flexibility to experiment with forward-looking curricular structures for the sophomore year and beyond. All in all, we sought to provide a better foundation in computing for undergraduate students, and all indications are that we have largely succeeded.

We hope to support others obtain the kind of curricular benefits that we have seen. Our idea of "supporting others" goes beyond just making a textbook available. We have, over time, developed a number of resources to support the course, and have other resources in the design and/or prototype stages. These range from lecture slides and assignments with detailed grading criteria, etc., to software capabilities for on-line grading and data-capture, student opinion gathering, and data analysis to support both ongoing course optimization and individualization of instruction. Information about the current status and availability of such support resources may be obtained by contacting us directly at *curriculum.support@cc.gatech.edu.*

Table of Contents

Part I:
The Computing Perspective

[this page intentionally left blank.]

Chapter 1: Technology, Science and Culture

What is "computing"? It means many things to different people:

- For older people, it often means a complicated new technology which they do not like and do not understand.

- For many consumers, it means the excuse that's used by a bank or retail company to explain that billing errors or inflexible policies are "not our fault," i.e., they blame it on the computer.

- For writers and clerical staff, it means a word processor that allows them to create, edit, and reproduce documents with far less effort than was required when using mechanical typewriters.

- For automotive engineers, it means the ability to design and build systems which control cars' engines, brakes, and traction with far greater efficiency, reliability, and safety than purely mechanical systems alone can provide.

- For CS majors, it means the challenge of creating computer programs which do whatever the programmer can conceive and implement, as well as the expectation of an attractive, well-paid career.

- For architects and many kinds of engineers, it means computer aided design (CAD) tools which allow them to design and refine their creations in less time and with far greater precision.

- For children and many adults, it means interactive computer games.

- For military people, it means dramatic new abilities to detect enemy activities and to use and control weapons precisely and from safe distances.

- For musicians, it means synthesized sounds and digital representations of music which allow greater flexibility and power in creating and editing musical works.

- For music lovers, it means CD's which offer sound that is clearer and that does not deteriorate with age and use.

We have enumerated some ten different ways that computing impacts the lives of people. We could easily list literally hundreds more, many of which you are aware, some of which you probably aren't. But making a list is not the point. What's important to notice is the impact of computing into virtually all aspects of modern life, from design and engineering work to mundane experiences of ordinary daily life.

Furthermore, as we shall see, the impact of computing is more than just a collection of disparate impacts that come about from computer use. While the use of computers is transforming many things, perhaps the most powerful impact of computing has more to do with the human mind and how we are learning to think about our world than it does with just how we use our machines. This is what we mean by the "computing perspective": the ways in which our ability to understand phenomena and solve problems is changing. In short, the "computing perspective" is an extension of a singular new way of thinking-and-doing that is transforming how we live, how we work, how we conceive of science and knowledge... even how we conceive of reality! Do you doubt this? Stay tuned!

What is the Computing Perspective?

☐ What do we mean by the "computing perspective?" It is a way of looking at the world, and at phenomena in it, *as if* reality were governed by a computer program.

For example, as a medical researcher investigates the human immune system with respect to cancer, the computing perspective enables him to ask questions such as:

- What process enables some people's immune system to recognize the presence of cancerous cells? What "information" are these immune systems picking up?

- How is this process different than the process that causes other people's immune systems to ignore those same kinds of cells? How does their immune system get fooled into "missing the important information?"

- If a person's immune system recognizes the presence of cancer, how does one part of their immune system "send instructions" to another part in order to have the cancer killed?

- How is this process different from the process in other people, when cancer is recognized but not effectively killed? What interferes with one part of the immune system "communicating with" another part of it, thus allowing the cancer to survive?

In asking these kinds of questions, the researcher is, in effect, thinking of the human body as if it were a computer governed by a computer program. In some people, the "program" processes "information" about cancer more effectively than does the "program" of others. Some cells "react to information" by "sending information" to other kinds of cells. And so on.

Of course, this is not to say that the immune system *is* a computer program, nor that the cells *are* computers; instead, it means that it is useful to think of them "as if" they were. Nor does it mean that medical researchers are particularly knowledgeable about computing. Instead, we refer only to a way of understanding phenomena that is consistent with computing, i.e., that we understand phenomena in terms of "processes," "algorithms," and "information." The medical researcher may not be *aware* that he is applying a computing model, but he is "thinking that way" nonetheless.

This perspective, this "way of thinking," is radically transforming how researchers are going about understanding a wide range of phenomena, from cancer to traffic jams, from psychological illnesses to corporate management, from basic science to philosophy. The goal of this course is to help you learn how to view reality from the computing perspective and to help you gain a firm foundation in the basic intellectual constructs which are part of it. We do not expect you to understand it now; by the end of this course, you should.

What is Technology?

☐   By the word "technology" we mean *ways of externalizing human abilities into the things we make.* Thus,

- a bowl is technology which externalizes our ability to hold things in our hands;

- a steamroller is technology which externalizes our ability to mash things down;

- an alphabet is technology which externalizes our ability to communicate words;

- an automobile is technology which externalizes our ability to walk from one place to another.

In each case, technology serves as a tool for externalizing our own capabilities into the things we make.

*Technology
and Human
Evolution*

There are countless obvious ways in which technology allows us to do the things we have always done in more convenient ways. In addition, technology allows us to do things we could never do before, e.g., go to the moon. Beyond these obvious impacts, however, technology appears to be intimately related to the ways in which human consciousness changes and evolves.

The word "evolution" is often used to refer to gradual changes in the *physical* properties of species. Rarely do we think of the evolution of *mental* properties, e.g., our way of perceiving the world, solving problems, etc. Yet history tells us that the capabilities of human perception and thought *have* changed in significant and powerful ways throughout Western history. Furthermore, technology seems to be intimately connected with the ways in which human consciousness evolves.

In the case of computing technology, it allows us to approach phenomena with new insights about the order and the behavior of things, to think of things in ways that we could not conceive of fifty years ago. Think about it: right now, you are taking an introductory course in computing and computer science. Sixty years ago, even the brightest college students would not have a clue as to what such a course would do. The words "computer science" *would not make any sense to them.*

To understand what is new about the computing perspective, to understand how technology is changing the way that our society and the people in it understand reality, we must have some sense of the history of such things. We cannot fully appreciate the significance of what is going on now unless we can see how it differs from what came before. In addition, looking at history allows us to notice certain patterns in the relationship between technology and consciousness, patterns which we can perhaps apply to help us understand the changes we are now witnessing in the world.

*Paradigmatic
Change*

☐ The word *paradigm* means "a form or model evidencing a single theme or pattern." When we talk about *cultural paradigms* or *scientific paradigms*, we refer to the set of *shared assumptions*, the shared way of "making sense of the world" that a society holds to be true.

Ancient tribal peoples and modern scientists have radically different "views of the world." Their beliefs about the nature of reality are different because the cultures from which they come have vastly different paradigms. If you are the product of a modern Western (or "Westernized") culture that produces modern scientists, your beliefs about the world are probably more similar to the scientist's than to the ancient tribesman's.

☐ Throughout Western history, we find a pattern in which advances in knowledge cause the existing paradigm to crumble. When this happens, a period of cultural chaos and confusion ensues until such time as a new paradigm emerges. Once a new paradigm is established, things settle down and stability returns. Relative stability continues until future knowledge shows the new paradigm to be inadequate, thus causing it to crumble, and the cycle repeats itself. This is the process by which human experience contributes to better and better models of reality, better theories, and new ways of understanding.

It appears that technology plays a powerful role in this cycle of paradigmatic stability and paradigmatic change. In particular, it seems that new technology for human communication, i.e., *media*, is related to paradigmatic change in two ways:

- new media tends to emerge just before an old paradigm start to crumble;

- new media tends to embody key attributes of the new, emerging paradigm.

One could debate whether new technology *causes* paradigmatic shifts or whether new technology is just one *expression* of human consciousness as it is evolving. Either way, history shows that new media technology can tell us a lot about the cultural paradigmatic shift that comes with it.

Below, we present a summary of the different paradigms as they occurred in Western culture, and of the technological forces which helped shape the transitions between them. (Non-western cultures are not included because the author does not know very much about them.)

Paradigm:
The Age of
Tribal
Consciousness

People of various times lived with what we might call "tribal consciousness." In history and sociology books, they are called "tribal cultures" or "pre-literate societies." With respect to technology, the pertinent factor is that they did not have any alphabet, any "technology" which allowed them to write down their observations, their thoughts, their stories. For this very reason, there is much that we do not know about them. With no written language, they could not leave written works for us to decipher. Instead, all we know is what we can tell from archaeological research. As scientists encounter the remains of their towns and villages, they can deduce a great deal about their style of life. However, there is no written word; these people cannot "talk" to us in the same way that a written language allows. The only means of such people had of "writing down" their stories, beliefs, and customs was drawing or painting. Drawings on cave walls, in burial crypts, or on bowls and tools were not "art" to these people. Instead, it was their most advanced "communications technology."

What did these people believe? What forces governed the world for them? How did they understand "the nature of reality"? As best we know, virtually all such preliterate cultures present a shared pattern of beliefs and assumptions about reality.

> ☐ As best we know, they all had what we might call "mythological belief systems," i.e., they believed in multiple gods and goddesses. Such gods were closely related to what we would call "aspects of nature," i.e., the wind, the sun, the moon, and so on.

In many such cultures, they had elements of human form. Such gods and goddesses did not "live in heaven." Nor was there a "satan" who lived in hell. Rather, they were all embedded in the world, often transforming themselves back and forth from spiritual form to human and/or animal form.

In many cultures, these gods and goddesses were capricious, i.e., they acted on whim and mood. Thus, the people might suffer if the gods were angry or displeased. This idea of the gods being angry did not imply any moral sense, i.e., a god might be angry because of a spat with another god or goddess, and this might cause unfortunate consequences for the people without the people having done anything "wrong." Thus, the people tried to honor and appease the gods, to make sacrifices to the gods in an effort to stay in the gods' good favor.

Tribal cultures existed all over the earth and over a wide span of years, from thousands of years ago in Europe to less than a hundred years ago in much of the Third World. Yet the structure of their beliefs, the structures which governed their subjective experience, had much in common. Such peoples lived in a very *literal* world. Their history was told by oral stories and song and by primitive drawings. They lived in a world together with their gods and goddesses. They were governed more by the mood and whim of the gods than by any strict dichotomy of values into "good" and "evil." All they knew came to them from verbal stories and from direct first-hand experience. They lacked the ability to communicate over distances or over time, and they appear to have lacked the ability to think abstractly in terms of principles and forces that we associate with science.

What is noteworthy about these traits? They traits seem to be mostly consistent across cultures that lack a means of writing their language, irrespective of their location in either time or space. Regardless of whether the culture resided 6000 years ago near the Mediterranean or only 80 years ago in Micronesia doesn't seem to make any difference: it is the absence of written communications technology, e.g., an alphabet (or something like one), that appears to be the necessary and sufficient condition for these traits. As we shall see, the arrival of "alphabet technology" in a culture signals a radical change in each of these traits, as people begin to live differently, think differently, solve problems differently, and understand reality differently.

Transformation:
Abstract
Media
Technology

☐ An alphabet is but one form of written language. Of natural human written language forms, it is the most artificial and abstract because each letter in an alphabet has no literal meaning unto itself. The letter "s" doesn't mean anything at all, it is just a symbol for a particular sound.

The letters of a word simply signify a series of sounds, and they take on meaning only when the sounds they signify correspond to the sound of a word. Thus, the string of letters "kllajh" has no meaning whatsoever in English, while the string of letters "textbook" has meaning. Even the letters "mayohnaiz" can have meaning to you because, despite the fact that it is not really a word, you can use the letters to construct the sound of a meaningful word.

☐ What is fascinating about this abstract quality of alphabets is that the very presence of an alphabet in a culture appears to signal the development of increasingly abstract thinking, problem-solving abilities, and models of reality.

The alphabet in its pure form was an invention of the Ancient Greek culture. Prior to Ancient Greece, several cultures took strides towards the alphabet, such as various Semite cultures and the Phoenicians. Other cultures developed written language based on "pictographs" or "ideographs," i.e., a system of symbols wherein each symbol *does have* some literal meaning [1]. Such systems tend to include a very large number of symbols [2] and are not nearly as flexible and adaptable as are alphabets. Some cultures developed writing systems which were a hybrid, featuring elements of pictographic, ideographic, and alphabetic symbology.

[1] The traditional Chinese and Japanese writing systems are based on pictographs and include literally thousands of different symbols. Some historians wonder if the difference between the dominance of the alphabet in Western culture and the dominance of the pictograph in Eastern culture might contribute to the dramatic differences in cultural consciousness between the cultures. In recent times, modern derivatives of the traditional Oriental written languages have evolved which function more like alphabets. These were developed largely to support the needs of business and commerce.

[2] The large number of characters in the traditional Japanese symbol set is what lead to the development of the Fax machine. How? Because it was more efficient to develop a technology to simply transmit a picture of the symbols than it was to transmit the long codes required by the large number of symbols (each of which requires a unique code). Why? Think about it: how many binary digits are required by a 26-letter alphabet? And how many binary digits are required by a 4000-character pictograph system?

With the Greeks, we find a purely abstract alphabetic system emerging as the dominant mode of meta-verbal communication. And with this change, we find a number of fascinating phenomena, all of which concern the ability to *engage in abstraction*.

☐ By "abstraction," we mean "an essence considered apart from any specific embodiment" or "the expression of a quality apart from a particular object."

It is with the Ancient Greeks that we find the Western foundations of the ability to abstract. The Greeks provide us with the fathers of philosophy (Plato, 427-347 B.C., and Aristotle, 384-322 B.C.), mathematics (Pythagoras, 582-500 B.C.), geometry (Euclid, *c.* 300 B.C.), engineering (Archimedes, 287-212 B.C.), astronomy (Ptolemy, A.D. 139-161), and anatomy and medicine (Galen, A.D. 130-201), to name but a few. In effect, the Greeks supplied us with the fathers of virtually every field of human knowledge.

All of their accomplishments share a central quality: *abstraction*. Plato was able to look at worldly phenomena, human phenomena, and conceive of "virtue," "truth," and other fundamental abstractions. Pythagoras and Euclid were able to look at the material world and conceive of the abstract relationships of numerical values and geometrical forms. Aristotle was able to engage in abstraction with respect to both philosophical and biological phenomena, and laid the foundation for empiricism. Galen was able to conceive of the organs of the human body in term of abstract functional properties. And so on.

While some of their specific abstractions have proved to be incorrect, it is nevertheless true that the Greeks provided the roots of virtually every field of Western human knowledge, from science and engineering to mathematics and philosophy. Moreover, virtually all of their foundational contributions feature the same singular theme. They were able to consider phenomena from a new perspective: they were able to engage in abstraction. Thus, while the Greeks made many different important contributions, it might be more fitting to say that they made exactly one crucial contribution and applied it to many particular phenomena: *they contributed the ability to engage in abstraction.*

This represents a perceptual and cognitive watershed in Western history. The very same phenomena that had previously been understood as being due to "the whim of the gods" was now being understood in terms of abstract qualities and orderly relationships. This amounts to a radical change in the"view of the world," the ways in which people were able to perceive and conceive of themselves, their experiences, and the world around them. And, as with any radical change, the early "abstracters" were treated as heretics and traitors. Indeed, Plato's teacher, Socrates, was forced to commit suicide in order to stay true to his beliefs simply because what he was saying went "against the grain" of the then-established "world view" or paradigm.

While we cannot say that the alphabet *caused* such cultural changes, we can say that its emergence did go hand in hand with the new perceptual and cognitive abilities evidenced by the Greeks.

> ☐ *The abstract alphabetic symbol system gained dominance at the same period of history as did the ability to engage in abstraction.*

Similarly, if we consider other cultures from around the globe and from across historical periods, we find the same pattern: if a culture doesn't feature an alphabet, neither will its people feature the ability to engage in the kind of logical abstraction featured in Western thought.

Indeed, some historians suspect that this relationship between the alphabet and the cognitive/perceptual capability for abstraction explains many minor historical mysteries. For example, historians have long puzzled over the fact that, despite a rich and sophisticated culture, the American Indians never invented the wheel. Why? Perhaps it is because they lacked an abstract symbol system and thus never developed the ability to look at a log and abstract the qualities of a "tool for rolling." Of course, this remains a mystery. While there may be a causal relationship here, we do not know that there is. We can only say that the "technology of abstract media" and the "cognitive and perceptual ability to engage in abstraction" go hand in hand.

Paradigm:
The Age of
Absolute
Abstraction

Over a period of a just a few hundred years (very fast relative to the pace of change in ancient times), the cognitive/perceptual ability to abstract transformed nothing less than the dominant view of reality and the forces which govern it. This is perhaps most apparent with respect to religion. By the latter years of the Roman Empire, the mythological view of reality was effectively replaced by a monotheistic ("one God") view. The particulars of this transformation illustrate the impact of abstraction.

> ☐ The mythological belief system which saw reality governed by multiple gods and goddesses was replaced by one which saw reality governed by a struggle between one God and one Satan. The difference here is more profound than simple the change from multiple gods to a single God. What we see here is the emergence of a belief system, a paradigm, a way of conceiving of reality, that *requires* the mental ability to abstract.

Most obviously, we find the abstractions of "good" and "evil" tied to particular divine forces. A single God represents all that is good, while Satan embodies all that is evil. The gods and goddesses no longer lived on the Earth among the people. Instead, as the abstractions of good and evil took form as God and Satan, they also had their seats of power localized in unseen abstract places, i.e., Heaven and Hell.

This is a dramatic shift from the locus of good and evil in the previous mythological belief system. To the preliterate cultures, there was no such dichotomy. All the various gods and goddesses each personified mixed patterns of what we might call good and evil (remember, people of tribal consciousness did not have these abstract concepts). All gods and goddesses were variously kind and cruel, noble and petty, generous and selfish. In short, the divine forces of mythology embodied all that was human, both the higher and lower sides of human existence. Thus, *all* of humanity was reflected in the divinity of the gods and goddesses.

In contrast, the monotheistic view which took hold imposed dichotomy everywhere... even *inside* each person! No longer were all sides of human existence divine. Instead, the higher side of humanity, the good, was divine and consistent with the wishes of God, while the lower side of human existence was satanic, sinful, and contrary to God's wishes.

> ☐ Thus, the structure of the meaning of mundane life changed radically. Instead of being at the mercy of whimsical and capricious gods and goddesses, people came to see the Earth as a "holy battleground" wherein the struggle between God and Satan was being fought. Evil deeds were the work of Satan or his agents, while Good deeds were evidence of being in God's grace. This view implies an inner dichotomy within people, with each person seeing his or her own wishes, acts, urges, and wants as being evidence of the presence of either Divine or Profane forces within.

In modern psychological terms, this signals a shift in the basis of internalized control of behavior. In tribal consciousness, the basis for social mores and taboos is *shame* ("I am embarrassed before the tribe"). With the abstraction of good and evil into divine forces, *shame* is replaced by *guilt* ("I have done something terribly wrong").

The transformation of mythological gods and goddesses into a single good God and a single evil Satan, and the movement of divine forces out of the Earth to Heaven and Hell, signaled a fundamental transformation of the relationship between people and their divine forces. One no longer made sacrifice to appease a capricious god or goddess; instead one prayed for the gift of strength to see and do God's will and to resist the temptations of Satan. This model of divine power, both Holy and Profane, became primarily a dichotomy of male traits, as the goddesses of mythology were not replaced by any female aspects of either the new One True God or of Satan. Even the conception of One God as a Holy Trinity included no female images.

As this view of reality achieved dominance, it was not thinkable to question the basic tenets. It was an authoritarian belief system. One did not question what God's plan was. His plan was announced by The Church, and one only questioned his/her ability and commitment to conform to it. Any questioning of this paradigm was viewed as heresy which was dealt with harshly (just as Socrates discovered in an earlier era when he violated the paradigm of his time).

For many hundreds of years, this view of God and the world was dominant in an absolute way. Virtually all phenomena came to be viewed as an expression of a supernatural plan. The world worked according to God's Plan, with never-ending interruptions caused by the agents of Satan. Thus, there was no need for questioning or thought about the nature of reality. All was given by God. The only reason for questioning and investigation was in reference to one's ability to do God's wishes. The wishes of God were not the capricious wishes of the gods and goddesses. Instead, they were empowered by the abstraction of Good in never ending opposition to the abstraction of Evil. In short, they carried the weight of absolute authority based on the abstractions of Right and Wrong, Good and Evil.

☐ As you might expect, this world view contributed to a stagnant period with respect to developments in science, mathematics, and philosophy. Since all was given by God, there wasn't much need to question or explore. This stagnation in science was not because there were no "smart people." Rather, during this time, smart people were engaged in a different activity as determined by their paradigm: they were searching for an understanding of God's Will, for therein lay truth and the secrets of the world.

There are several features of the *consciousness of absolute abstraction* that should be noticed. It appears to occur only after the evolution of an abstract written language system. For example, the Judaic culture featured a monotheism with absolute values for many, many generations prior to the rise in Europe of the dominant Christian view. The Judaic culture also featured an abstract symbol system quite early, from which the Greek alphabet derived, although the particulars are shrouded in the mysteries of pre-history.

This structure of beliefs, which shaped subjective experience, have certain features. People lived in a very *absolute* world, with rather rigid conception of Right and Wrong and with a strong denial of the lower aspects of human experience. They lived in a world apart from any *physical* connection to God, yet were governed by His Will with respect to strict dichotomy of values into good and evil. The educated members of society had the ability, via writing, to communicate over distances and over time, and the ability to think abstractly in the terms of principles and forces. However, this ability was focused almost exclusively on trying to understand God's will, not on empirical investigation concerning phenomena in the world.

Transformation: Mechanical Media Technology

The state of media technology in Western culture remained largely stagnant until the mid-1400's when Johannes Guttenberg (*c.*1400-1468) developed the printing press. The idea of a printing press seems rather ordinary to us today, but its place in history is extremely significant. To understand why, we must consider what properties of technology were embodied in the printing press.

First and foremost, the printing press is a machine. The workings of a simple printing press involve the movement of a lever, which in turn moves a gear, which in turn moves a plate, which in turn brings paper in contact with inked typefaces of alphabetic letters. Such a machine made it possible to produce writings in mass quantities, whereas before each and every copy of a writing had to be written by hand.

More was changed than just the economics of reproducing writings. For the first time, to was possible to produce things that were effectively identical. Prior to this time, everything was produced by hand and, as a result, was effectively unique. No two copies of a given document (or a bowl or a nail) were identical; each had its own unique attributes that were accidental and unavoidable side effects of the made-by-hand production process. With the advent of the printing press, Western technology developed the capability for virtually identical production.

In sum, we find communications technology introducing two new qualities: mechanical means of reproducing communications, and the capability to produce items that were virtually "the same."

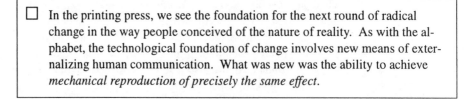

☐ In the printing press, we see the foundation for the next round of radical change in the way people conceived of the nature of reality. As with the alphabet, the technological foundation of change involves new means of externalizing human communication. What was new was the ability to achieve *mechanical reproduction of precisely the same effect.*

Just as the establishment of the Greek alphabet went hand-in-hand with the then-new capability for abstract thought, the development of the printing press appears to go hand in hand with (or precede?) the development the human ability to engage in what we shall call "mechanical thinking."

This relationship between media technology and consciousness is the crux of the insight offered by historian Marshal McLuhan: "the Medium is the Message." By this he meant that the *technology of communication* is the "real" message of an era, much more so than the content of the various messages conveyed via the technology. The transformation that followed the printing press is a prime example.

☐ Less than 100 years after the invention of mechanical media technology, i.e., the printing press, a radical "mechanistic model" of the universe was proposed, first by Copernicus (1473-1543). He challenged the conventional belief that the sun and moon rotated around the earth, correctly claiming that the earth revolves around the sun in an annual orbit, and that the earth rotates on its axis every 24 hours. His view was taken up by Kepler (1571-1630) who discovered that the orbits of the planets were elliptical, not circular, by Galileo (1564-1642) who first used a telescope for observation and who formulated the mathematical law of falling bodies, and by Newton (1642-1727) who applied the same law to both planetary motion and falling bodies.

While the view of reality proposed by these men proved correct, it was not readily accepted. Copernicus was ridiculed for lunacy and absurd notions. He was opposed both by the conservative Church and by radical reformers alike. His views contradicted the Bible, went again "common sense" observations, and could not readily be proved. Yet he confined himself to technical papers and thus suffered only ridicule. Galileo openly opposed the authorities on these points of science, and was eventually forced to formally renounce what he knew to be true under threat of the gravest penalty.

Of these men, only Galileo truly believed in a mechanistic model of the universe; yet the work of all four signals the beginning of a new way of thinking about the universe, the world, problem solving, and life itself. By the end of the 1600's, mainstream Western thought had embraced the mechanistic model which had seemed so heretical less than 200 years before.

Paradigm: The Age of Mechanistic Thinking

☐ Just as development of the ability to think in abstract terms led to a new conception of the workings of the universe and of the role of divinity in it, so too did the development in Renaissance Europe of the human ability to think in mechanical terms. By the end of the 1600's, it was widely accepted that speculation and empirical investigation was proper science, not heresy. And, while the monotheistic nature of God continued, God's role was redefined.

Rather than being the authoritarian "determiner of earthly events," God was now seen as more of an "engineer of the universe." That is, the universe was still rooted in divine creation, but that divine creation was the creation of a large machine. God created the "machine of the universe" and then largely "let it operate"[3]. It became Man's role to solve the puzzles and mysteries of the detailed workings of that machine.

Once this view solidified, the great body of modern scientific knowledge was rapidly discovered. Many areas of knowledge that had been part of philosophy became sufficiently organized and "filled in" as to be considered "science" as distinct from philosophy. The "natural science," e.g., physics, chemistry, and biology, quickly gained solidity and were split from philosophy. Together, the natural sciences shared the tenets of the "empirical method," a set of rather mechanistic precepts which governed how scientific research should be conducted. Great strides were made in mathematics, including geometry, trigonometry, and calculus. With these subjects achieving validity in their own right, philosophy effectively "lost" these subjects and became increasingly focused on matters of religious, social, and psychological experience.

During this time, God became an increasingly hidden and private God, mostly irrelevant to the workings of the natural world and instead relevant only to matters of human interaction, introspection, morals, and ethics. During this time, the American and French Revolutions established major Western societies which defined matters of religion as private and separate from the matters of government. To modern Americans, this seems an obvious development aimed at protecting freedom. In the course of history, however, this was an extremely radical change. Only 200 years before the American Revolution, God, Church, and government were effectively *synonymous* with respect to both social governance and the "nature of reality."

Throughout the 18th and 19th centuries, and continuing through much of the 20th century, the mechanistic model of reality became more and more engrained in Western consciousness. Developments in technology during this period focused almost exclusively in the development of machines that could amplify the human ability to manipulate physical forces through the deployment of fossil-fueled energy. Knowledge of human anatomy evolved considerably, mainly as a result of conceiving of the human body as a machine with various functional components.

With the advent of farm machinery, the typical workplace ceased to be the farm or the village and became instead the factory. The factory was, at core, itself a machine. Workers were components of the factory-machine just as were the cogs and gears of

---

[3] We say "largely let it operate" because there were and, according to some, still are, occasional Divine interventions in the workings of this machine. These interventions are known as "miracles". This is effectively the operational definition of "miracle" for ecclesiastical purposes.

plant equipment. Unlike machinery, workers didn't cost very much were thus "used up" and disposed of. For much of this time, children were viewed as cheap little workers, and were treated as disposable machine components, "just like adults, only better": they cost less and took up less space.

People increasingly modeled their life in a mechanical way, with a series of life stages, each leading to the next (early childhood, then school, then job and family, then retirement), much as one part of a machine would transfer force to another part. Strife and sacrifice were accepted as elements of the early stages in the hope that retirement would provide happiness. For many, healthy children and happiness in retirement became the intended product of one's life, much as the document was the product of the printing press.

> ☐ By the latter half of the current century, many people were either uninterested in God or else very confused and fuzzy about exactly what God meant to them and their lives. For most religious people, God became a resource for private reflection, prayer, and perhaps a sense of local community with fellow churchgoers. For some others, God became little more than an object to which they directed prayer and hope in times of personal trauma. For many, mechanistic science became the de facto religion, i.e., the "true story" about the workings of the universe, and of life within it. Mechanistic Age societies came to expect their members to believe in scientific truth, and left religion to be a personal matter that is either effectively absent from peoples lives or else is a matter of private "personal belief and philosophy."

Transformation: Electronic Media Technology

New technologies do not establish new dominant modes of human consciousness overnight. It takes a matter of some generations. In the case of the alphabet, it took several hundred years for its essential contribution (abstraction) to dominate cultural conceptions about reality. In the case of the printing press, it took a couple hundred years for its essential contribution (mechanistic thinking) to achieve dominance. In discussions of such eras, the boundaries are a bit fuzzy, especially at the time; only in retrospect can we look back and identify watershed events and remarkable people. Socrates was driven to suicide. Galileo was forced to recant under threat of death. Only in retrospect did they achieve their status as great and revolutionary thinkers.

> ☐ In the case of electronic media technology, the period of transition is now. It is as if we were alive during the time between the arrival of the alphabet and the dominance of abstract thought, between the arrival of the printing press and the dominance of mechanistic thought.

In fact, it may well be that the people who history will later judge as equal in stature to Socrates and Galileo are alive right now. Such a person might be in this class. *You* might be such a person. Because the transition in consciousness is a current one, we cannot say who history will judge to be the "big guns." However, we do know the facts of the history of electronic media technology, and we can make reasonable guesses about the paradigm shift that accompanies it.

The watershed events in the development of electronic media technology began in the 1800's. The telegraph emerged in the 1830's (enabled via the code developed by Samuel Morse), the telephone in the 1870's (by Alexander Graham Bell and Thomas Edison). Both inventions had an important impact: they provided technology which allowed virtually instantaneous communication over great distances.

However, there is an important difference between the two. Telegraphic communications was based on the transmission of increasingly abstract signals: Morse code is an abstract binary aural system which is superimposed onto the abstract alphabetic symbols, i.e., it *adds* a layer of abstraction. Telephone communication is quite different. By transmitting the sound, not only of the words but also of the speaker's actual voice, it *removes* layers of abstraction.

> ☐   At the same time that telephony was emerging, so was the ability to record and replay sound (Thomas Edison). Taken together, these electronic media provided the ability to transmit *literal representations* of the human voice across both time and space. Telephones allowed people to communicate via literal media, not abstract media, over obstacles of distance, while sound recording allowed the literal sound of the spoken word to survive over time.

During the 1920's and 1930's, radio took these new capabilities even further. Both live and recorded sounds could be immediately *broadcast* to the population as a whole. By the 1940's and 1950's, television integrated monochromatic *literal visual images* with sound into broadcast technology. In the 1960's, the monochromatic visual images were replaced by full color images. In the 1970's, the home VCR made it possible for ordinary people to record, edit, and distribute integrated color-and-sound images.

This is, of course, not news to you. But have you considered the implications of these developments for the evolution of the ways in which think, the things in which we believe, the values which influence how we live our lives?

Think about it. If the development of abstract media is a metaphor for (or perhaps a causal factor in) the transformation from tribal consciousness to absolute religious consciousness, and if the development of mechanical media is a metaphor for (or casual factor in) the transformation from an absolute religious consciousness to a mechanistic scientific consciousness, what might we suspect about the implications of electronic media which instantaneously communicates literal color-and-sound images?

Well, we might safely suspect that radical transformative change is afoot! But what kind of changes? How will electronic media transform the ways in which we understand the world, make sense of reality, govern society, and experience mundane daily life?

> ☐ The major obstacle to gaining clarity about such things is that we seem to be *in the midst* of whatever the transformation is and thus can have no perspective on it. Only in hindsight do these things become clear. At the same time, what we know of the history of such things suggests a few things that we might look for if indeed a major transformation is afoot.

Hallmarks of a Paradigm Shift

Before we consider what the nature of the transformation might be, can we be sure that such a transformation is going on? History tells us that a certain kinds of phenomena tend to follow the invention of new communications medium. As we use technology to externalize new parts of ourselves, we see clusters of change. Do we see these kinds of changes occurring with the advent of electronic media? If so, where?

New Models of Reality

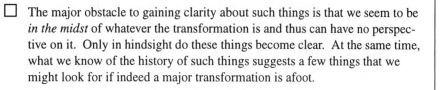

> ☐ If the impact of previous media technology is any guide, then we might expect that fundamentally *different models of reality* would emerge relatively early in the transformation. These would be conceptions of reality (analogous to Greek *abstraction* or Renaissance *mechanism*) which go beyond the established paradigm. We would expect these conceptions to be initially seen as foolishness or heresy, and to be later adopted as the basis for a new paradigm. Thus, we might ask if we find evidence of *fundamentally new conceptions* of the nature of reality.

Indeed, if we look at developments in science shortly after the advent of "instantaneous literal media" (the telephone), we see a number of such developments. Einstein's Theory of Relativity, Freud's Theory of the Unconscious, and various fundamental work on bacterial infection and general physiology, all occurred close in time.

What is important about these developments is that they all went beyond the mechanistic model of reality, they all initially met with the severest opposition, and they all have (in general, if not in particular) proved to be correct, i.e., dominant. In each case, the assumptions, beliefs, scientific work, and daily practice of modern societies have been pervasively affected.

Regardless of whether you understand Einstein's theory, you believe that atomic bombs and nuclear power plants are real things of tremendous. Regardless of your opinion of the particulars of Freud's theory, you accept the notion that behavior is sometimes influenced by various unintended psychological factors and motivations. Regardless of your knowledge of physiology, you believe that a surgeon should clean his hands and his instruments before operating on a patient.

What you may not realize is that each of these developments went directly "against the grain" of the established mechanistic model of reality that was the order of the day. In each case, we are not talking about physical forces acting on tangible matter. Instead, we're dealing with invisible forces and processes, phenomena that can not readily be observed and that do not readily lend themselves to study via the traditional "scientific method." The degree of conceptual innovation, and the degree of transformative effect, of these and similar developments did as much to "set the world on its ear" in recent times as did the work of Plato and Galileo in their times.

New
Organizations
of Knowledge
With the alphabet, during the period of transformation from the tribal paradigm to the paradigm of abstraction, we find the creation of Philosophy and the Academy. Philosophy originally referred to all of knowledge, i.e., math, science, ethics, etc., were all parts of philosophy. The academy was an institution of study and inquiry. Inquiry and abstract thought replace mythological thinking.

With the printing press, during the period of transformation from the paradigm of absolutism to the paradigm of mechanistic thinking, we find the creation of the natural sciences and of the modern university. Mathematics and the sciences "split off" from philosophy and became disciplines unto themselves. Philosophy remained the locus of all other academic study. Mechanistic methods and reproducible results replaced theological inquiry as society's path to truth.

> ☐ With electronic media, we again see new areas of knowledge gaining the status of independent disciplines. Just as the rise of mechanical consciousness led to the development of natural sciences (biology, chemistry, physics) and their split from philosophy, so too did the advent of electronic media coincide with the birth of the human sciences (psychology, sociology, anthropology, management, etc.) [4].

Just as the natural sciences before them, the human sciences split away from philosophy and became disciplines in their own right [5]. The new human sciences initially adopted the methodology of the natural sciences. After a century of producing much data and little information, recent years have seen a search for new models and methodologies that are more useful than the mechanistic ones. While it's not clear what the new "knowledge paradigm" might be, the inadequacies of the old mechanistic paradigm are increasingly visible to scientists from all fields.

Chaos and Strife   Another transformative phenomena we might expect to see is a period of great uproar and strife in politics, war, and social structure. These things appear to be the hallmarks of transformative periods, as any inspection of the history of ancient times and the Renaissance/Reformation will show. Clearly, the 20th century has been filled with major, even cataclysmic wars (the First and Second World Wars), political upheavals (e.g., Communism and Fascism), and upheavals in social structure (civil rights and anti-war demonstrations, decolonization around the globe, the epidemic of family deconstruction and divorce in Western societies, etc.).

Changes in Power   We would also expect to see a fundamental shift in *the nature of boundaries* of power and influence. In ancient times, the tribe gave way to the city-state and then, after the alphabet to the church-state. In the Renaissance, the church-state gave way to the emergence of nations. In modern times, we find an analogous shift: the deconstruction of *the importance of* national boundaries, sometimes via explicit political acts, e.g., European unification, and more pervasively via the increased influence of both high personal mobility and boundary-crossing technology (e.g., CNN) as well as the emergence of multinational corporations to whom international boundaries are largely an unfortunate annoyance.

Changes in Art: We would also expect to see fundamental changes in the worlds of art, music, and
Old Technology   other forms of human expression. Throughout history, new media technology not
becomes "Artistic   only improves on previous technologies, it also relegates them to the status of an art
Media"   form. Prior to alphabet, painting and sculpture were not art, they were communications media. With the advent of the alphabet, painting and sculpture became obsolete as effective communications media and became artistic media instead. Similarly,

[4] The fact that the human sciences have not yet achieved the sort of fundamental breakthroughs that were evidenced by the natural sciences after they adopted the mechanistic model of reality can be attributed to the fact that the human sciences initially tried to adopt that same mechanistic model with which the natural sciences began. This model appears to be not very useful for the phenomena which the human sciences are attempting to understand, i.e., they have not yet developed a model that is adequate to the study of their subject matter. Instead, the human sciences were "new" sciences that adopted the "old" model. Corrections are currently underway.

[5] Unfortunately, the loss of both the natural sciences and the human sciences leaves philosophy with rather little to do. As a result, most academic "departments of philosophy" behave as if they were "museums of philosophy".

prior to the printing press, calligraphy was not an art form, it was media; after the printing press, calligraphy became art.

With the advent of the electronic media, we would expect mechanical media to become art. Do we find this occurring in the world around us? Most certainly, in several ways. We find it in such phenomena as the invention of the "coffee table book," i.e., large books whose purpose is not one of conveying information but rather one of providing an attractive visual presence regardless of particular content. Prior to electronic media, books were not art; they were society's most advanced medium. In recent years, they have become increasingly incapable of providing cutting edge information because the information they contain is "old news" by the time a book can be written, edited, published, and distributed. Thus, the role of the book has shifted towards art, witness the aforementioned "coffee table book." In the same vein, the preponderance of books sold are not sold for informational purposes but rather are fiction: novels, a form of artistic expression.

We see other evidence of mechanical phenomena becoming art forms:

- Some styles of modern architecture present the mechanical systems of the building as part of its visual design. Rather than hiding the plumbing and ventilation systems, they accentuate them.

- Arts and crafts shows increasingly feature artists who create toy mechanical devises.

- Old machines, previously seen as antiquated "junk," are now valued as objects d'art and items of decor, e.g., old treadle sewing machines, antique farm implements, etc.

In sum, there seems to be ample phenomena which suggest that we are indeed in the midst of a major transformation in our culture's model of reality:

- Institutions and social structures that are based on established cultural assumptions are faltering,

- Scientific conceptions which transcend the established paradigm are widely and increasingly accepted, and

- A new medium (electronic) has replaced the established media (mechanical) as the source of most of our information and entertainment.

Given that a major transformation is indeed underway, what can we surmise about its nature and its outcome?

*Essential
Features of the
Emerging
Paradigm*

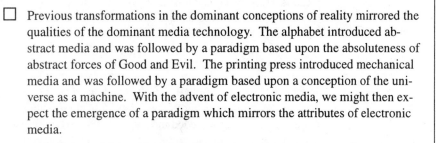

Previous transformations in the dominant conceptions of reality mirrored the qualities of the dominant media technology. The alphabet introduced abstract media and was followed by a paradigm based upon the absoluteness of abstract forces of Good and Evil. The printing press introduced mechanical media and was followed by a paradigm based upon a conception of the universe as a machine. With the advent of electronic media, we might then expect the emergence of a paradigm which mirrors the attributes of electronic media.

What are these attributes? First, electronic media operates via *intangible* forces and matter. Whereas physical forces, such as gravity, friction, and applied force, can be perceived directly via direct human perception and sensation, the workings of electronic devices are hidden from us. While we can feel electric shocks given significant current, we cannot observe television signals or radio waves directly via first-order observation. We can only observe them indirectly via second-order observation, i.e., scopes, meters, etc.

This same difference, between the directly observable and the indirectly observable, also characterizes the subject matter of the radically new scientific developments that occurred near the beginnings of of the 20th century. Neither Einstein's atomic particles, nor Freud's unconscious processes, nor the bacteria and genetic material of physiology and biochemistry can be directly observed. *Thus, we might expect the emerging paradigm to be one that addresses intangibles, things which cannot be directly seen or measured.*

Secondly, mechanical devices operate as a result of a causal chain of moving parts, i.e., a lever moves a gear which turns a roller which moves a plate, etc. Each moving part acts upon the next moving part in the "chain of events" that is designed into the machine. Inside of television set, there is no such "chain of events." Instead, there is a synergistic (various things happening concurrently) process which produces a combined effect (picture and sound). The effect does not appear to the human senses to be a causal, step by step process but rather an instantaneous, synergistic effect. *Thus, we might expect the emerging paradigm to be one that addresses synergistic instantaneous phenomena.*

Thirdly, the result of mechanical process is some material product (a printed page) or material effect (movement of a car). The output of electronic media is not a material product or effect but instead a continuum of sensory stimuli, continuous sounds and moving images, signals not things. *Thus, we might expect the emerging paradigm to be one that focuses on a "currency" of signals (i.e., information), not of things.*

> ☐   In sum, and in contrast to the mechanistic paradigm's focus on the tangible, causal, time-ordered manipulation of physical matter via physical force, we might expect that the emerging paradigm will focus on *the intangible, synergistic, instantaneous manipulation of information.*

In fact, these are precisely the attributes of an emerging set of new demands that face society. People increasingly focus upon immediate, synergistic, intangibles. For example, the criteria for a good marriage used to be "an effective partnership for survival"; now, it appears to be "the mutual subjective satisfaction of both parties." People used to be satisfied with a "steady job"; now, it appears that people require "a satisfying job and a pleasant relationship with co-workers and boss." In virtually all aspects of modern life, people seem to apply criteria different from that of their ancestors, criteria that now include the instantaneous satisfaction of intangible needs.

The Central Theme of the New Paradigm

Recall that "paradigm" refers to a "single model or theme." We've seen what themes (*tribalism, absolutism, mechanism*) dominated previous periods of paradigmatic stability. How can we identify the "central theme" of the emerging paradigm? Earlier, we observed that one effect of new media technology is the inclusion of the old medium as art. While the *media* of art includes old technology, the *vision* of art is something quite different. If we consider fundamental changes in the content and technique of artists, we find other fascinating correlations with the development of new technology. By tracing the progress of artistic vision, we can find clues to the emergent paradigm.

Artistic Vision and Paradigms

Preliterate tribal cultures typically produce paintings and sculpture which to our eyes appear quite primitive. Human figures are not well formed or detailed. Often, they appear similar to the art work of a child in today's world.

When we look at the art the classic ancient civilizations (Greek and Roman) who had an alphabet, we notice technique improvements of a particular kind. In sculpture, the transformation is dramatic. Greek and Roman sculpture evidences technique equal to any sculptor of modern times. Human forms are not only well formed and detailed, they are also often quite *ideal*. It would be difficult to find real people who are quite as well formed, quite as *perfect* as the human figures in classical sculpture. It is as if the ancients were able to consider the mass of humanity around them and "abstract out" the shape of the perfect eyes, the perfect arms, the perfect legs, etc. This is, of course, consistent with the abstract alphabetic media technology of their culture. As the culture gained abstract media, it also evidenced the artistic ability to form ideal abstractions of human form.

However, the ancients did not succeed so well in drawing and painting technique. While their sculpture was perfect, their two-dimensional art remained flat and life-less. They could not make their figures "come alive." They could not even create realistic perspective. Look at pre-Renaissance paintings and you will see that the art-ists didn't know how to put foreground and background figures in perspective, create a dynamic sense of action and life, or even of paint facial features in a way we would call "realistic." In short, ancient drawing and painting appears primitive to us today.

Art took a momentous stride forward at just about the time that the printing press was invented. Suddenly, artists gained the ability to draw and paint in a way that we would call realistic. There is no reason to think that the printing press "caused" art-ists to make a technical breakthrough. Yet nonetheless, beginning in Italy and spreading rapidly throughout Europe, artists learned the technique of "perspective." In all probability, many of you were taught a key "trick" of this technique in art class as children. To achieve an accurate sense of depth and proportion, one simply picks a point on the imaginary horizon of the scene being drawn, then draws lines to it from the various figures in the foreground. These lines are then used to scale objects in be-tween the foreground and the imaginary horizon. Notice that there is nothing very mysterious or difficult about this technique. In fact, it is a rather *mechanical* trick. Even little children can master it. Also notice that it was not discovered until the be-ginning of the "age of mechanical thinking."

Thus, as with the ancients, the new *artistic techniques* of the Renaissance presented the same quality as did the new technology that was emerging at that time. In Renais-sance Europe, the mechanical technique of drawing in perspective spread like wildfire, becoming a standard technique of artists far faster than mechanical thinking developed sufficiently to allow the Scientific and Industrial Revolutions to occur.

This relationship between artistic technique and transformative technology was no-ticed by Marshal McLuhan. He began referring to artists as "probes from the future." To the extent that he is right, we might wonder what "message" we might get from developments in the art world of the last 100 years.

The Message of Modern Art   The most radical transformation in artistic technique since the Renaissance devel-oped in the late 1800's and early 1900's, i.e., shortly after the development of initial forms of electronic media technology. We find it in the movement towards what has been called "abstract art." From early "cubism" through the apparently-random color dollops of Jackson Pollack, painters moved radically away from realistic forms and instead created art that was harder and harder for most people to understand. The subtle nuances of literal representations were abandoned, first in a movement to abstract angular shapes, then in a movement that abandoned the notion of repre-sentational shape altogether. The net effect was to take art away from the comprehension of "most people" into an increasingly abstract domain.

Paradigm	Media Technology	Art	Religion
Preliterate	Spoken word, sculpture, drawing	none	Multiple gods and goddesses. Divine forces incorporate both good and bad traits.
→ Alphabet →	Abstract symbol system	New art media: Sculpture ———————— New technique: Ideal forms	Heresy: Postulating abstract principles (Socrates)
Absolutism	Handwritten documents	Content: Divinity	One God, one Satan, good and bad separated. Divine forces control events.
→ Printing Press →	Mechanical reproduction of physical objects	New art media: Calligraphy ———————— New technique: 2D Realism	Heresy: Positing laws of natural forces (Copernicus, Galileo)
Mechanistic Thinking	Mechanically reproduced books, documents	Content: Real world (portraits, landscapes, still lifes, action scenes, etc.)	God as "Engineer of the Universe." Religion as part of family and community.
→ Electronic Media →	Instantaneous transmission of sensory signals	New art media: Mechanicals ———————— New technique: Abstract content	Heresy: Positing forces that cannot be directly measured, (Einstein, Freud, Curie)
Computational Models	Literal audio/visual images	Content: Subjective meaning	God as source of elemental forces, e.g., Big Bang. Religion as personal matter.

After several hundred years of mastering the techniques of making things appear realistic, artists went in a radically new direction: they were using abstraction not as the *medium* of communication (ala the alphabet) but rather as the *content* of their work. If artists are, as McLuhan said, "probes from the future," what might we glean from this? We might conclude that they are inadvertently telling us that the essential quality contributed by electronic media is the ability to *externalize abstraction*.

New Technology: "Abstraction Devices"

☐ As it turns out, devices for "externalizing abstraction" is precisely what computers are. Computers allow us to externalize our ability to create abstraction outside of ourselves. Before computers, only people could "abstract" (and only then if they had an alphabet). With computers, we are building little electronic boxes into which we *build* abstractions.

World View	Knowledge, Science	Organization
Playground of the gods.	Appease the gods via ritual, homage, sacrifice, etc.	Tribe
Technology externalizes human expression, i.e., the ability to convey thoughts, observations over time & space	Creation of Philosophy as field of all knowledge	City-State
The Holy Battleground	Comprehend the Divine Plan	The Church
Technology externalizes the human body, i.e., the ability to physically manipulate matter by applying physical force	Creation of the Natural Sciences, Math, and their split from Philosophy	"Divine Right" Kingdoms
A Physical Machine Governed by Natural Forces and Laws	Master the manipulation of physical matter via application of physical forces	Secular Nations
Technology externalizes the nervous system, e.g., instantaneous information via real-time feedback system	Creation of the Human Sciences and their split from Philosophy	Super-governments (Fascism, Communism, Socialism)
A Network of Complex Processes	Master the manipulation of informational processes via algorithms	Complex network of global corporations and regulatory governments

When we say this, what do we mean by abstraction? Go back to the basic definition: by abstraction we mean, "expression of a quality apart from any specific embodiment." This, as it turns out, is what computer scientists and software engineers attempt to do when they create algorithms.

Algorithms are the "logical recipes" that underlie computer programs. To put it another way, a given computer program expresses an algorithm in some particular programming language. The goal of an algorithm is to externalize some capability that has heretofore required a human mind. The goal is to allow an electronic box to perform what *used to require* a person's mental work such that the box does the work *for* the person.

There's nothing new about trying to build our capabilities into the things we make: that is what all technology is about. What *is* new is *what* we're externalizing. With the alphabet, we learned to externalize our words into symbols that would tell our stories for us. With mechanical media, we learned to externalize the capabilities of our bodies into machines that would do physical work for us. With computers, we are learning to externalize the capabilities of our mind.

The Emerging Dominance of the Computational Model

The social, political, and scientific upheaval that signals the transformation of society's view of reality from one paradigm to another goes back a century. However, it is only quite recently that the shape of the new paradigm has become clear. As recently as 30 years ago, many astute observers had noted the symptoms of a paradigm shift, but no one was particularly clear about the foundation for the new paradigm.

> ☐   It is only in the last decade or two that it has become evident that *computational models* are addressing the needs of researchers and scientists from a broad spectrum of fields. To many researchers, the emerging dominance of computational models is already apparent. Many others still adhere to the old ways of thinking-and-doing to which they are accustomed, and have yet to realize the shape of things to come. In contrast, you are just starting out, are just now preparing for your careers. There is no reason for you to be confused about this trend. If you are astute, you will recognize it and plan accordingly.

Today, researchers on the cutting edge of virtually every discipline rely on some form of algorithmic model of whatever phenomena they happen to study. From economics to medical research, from social theory to financial analysis, from basic science to city planning, from weapons development to models of human psychology, virtually all cutting edge research relies on computing to provide two crucial things:

- An algorithmic conception of the phenomena they are trying to study.

- A means of simulation and experimentation.

> ☐   In practice, it doesn't matter *which* field of research you might be interested in, the above holds true. In other words, *the computational model has replaced the mechanistic model as the guiding light of modern science, knowledge, and understanding.*

Thus, if you imagine that you might want to be a scientist or researcher, then the computer will be one of your most basic, most necessary, and most powerful tools. If you are not interested in the career of a researcher, the situation doesn't change much. Virtually every conceivable kind of professional (engineer, scientist, manager, writer, musician, executive, salesman, etc.) relies on computing tools for essentially the same reason: computing offers the state of the art with respect to communication, analysis, creation, decision, and management support tools. In short, there is no way out. *If* you want to be at the forward edge of your profession, *whatever that profession might be*, you will both be using computers and be influenced by computational models of whatever phenomena your work focuses on.

This does not mean that you will have to *program* computers. It does mean that you will use them and, if your work has particular requirements, you may have to effectively *communicate with* a programmer in order to obtain the kind of computational tools you require. Thus, at minimum, it is advisable for you to have a solid foundation in understanding computation and how "computer people" think and solve problems.

Apart from the practical demands of a career, computing provides the model which is proving most useful for understanding complex phenomena of virtually any kind. Thus, irrespective of your career goals, you should understand that computing is increasingly providing "the rules of the game." In order to be a well-educated citizen of the 21st century, you will have to understand the basic foundations of computing. This means that you need to be able to see the world from the point of view of the "computing perspective."

Food for Thought:

Is Consciousness Changing?

It is easy to assume that the human mind has stayed pretty much the same, and that we are mentally different from our ancestors only in terms of better education, more knowledge, etc. However, there is growing evidence that this is not the case. Instead it appears that there is ongoing evolution of human consciousness, i.e., fundamental changes in how we perceive the world, how we think about things, how we go about solving problems, and how we respond and react to the meanings in our lives. For example...

Psychiatry and clinical psychology had their beginnings near the beginning of the 20th century. There was a large "cast of characters" who were the founders of these fields. The most famous of them is Sigmund Freud. While there is much of Freud's work that has been criticized, there are many ways in which he laid the foundations for even those psychiatrists and psychologists who now disagree with much of what he said. Part of the criticism of Freud is due to a very interesting phenomena: the kind of symptoms that Freud and others encountered around the turn of the century no longer present themselves. Thus, modern theorists and practitioners cannot reproduce some of his findings simply because they do not see the same kinds of patients.

The Case of "Anna O."

One of the cases that helped Freud become famous was the case of "Anna O." Anna was a woman whose arm became paralyzed for no apparent reason, and no physiological problem could be found. Freud figured out that there was indeed a cause, a psychological one. Here's the story:

Anna's father was ill and bedridden, and it fell to Anna to be responsible for his care. This responsibility dominated her life and, as a loving daughter, she felt no resentment or anger about this. She wanted to care for her father as best she was able. Freud learned that Anna had terrifying nightmares in which she stabbed her father. With the onset of the nightmares, the arm that (in the dream) held the knife became suddenly paralyzed (in real life).

Freud was able to help her understand that, despite her genuine love for her father, she was nevertheless resentful that caring for him consumed her whole life. As Anna became able to understand and accept her resentment, and to see that she could be resentful about the consequences of her father's illness yet still be loving towards him, her paralysis ended. Rather than "block out" the emotion from her awareness, which led to unconscious symptoms, she learned to integrate it into her conscious self, which led to a disappearance of the symptoms.

Freud called this kind of illness a "conversion reaction", an illness in which physical symptoms (such as paralysis) arise with no physical cause in order to safeguard the person from unconscious urges, urges which are so terrifying to the person that he or she blocks them from consciousness. Numerous similar cases were documented in that era and became a mainstay of the early psychoanalytic literature.

There is no doubt that such cases did in fact occur. Yet today, in modern society, such symptoms no longer exist. In fact, the only place where such symptoms have been found in recent decades is in very isolated pockets of Appalachia, places where people lived and worked much as they did a hundred years ago, places where modern society had not "gotten in". It would appear that contact with "modern society" seems to eliminate conversion reactions!

Psychological Wounds of War

Similar changes in mental and psychological processes were noted by the U.S. and British armies. For the last hundred years, there have been soldiers who suffered psychological wounds of war, sometimes so severe as to be disabling. Yet the particular symptoms have evolved over time. In World War I, the diagnosis was "Shell Shock"; in World War II and Korea, it was "Battle Fatigue"; in Vietnam it was "Post Traumatic Stress Syndrome".

These are *not* different labels for the same phenomena. Rather, the various labels apply to very *different* sets of symptoms. "Shell-shocked" soldiers were often catatonic (as if in a trance), i.e., their entire being "shutdown". Soldiers suffering from "battle fatigue" were visibly "nervous wrecks", i.e., as if their nervous system "shorted out". Soldiers suffering from "post traumatic stress syndrome" appear at first glance to function normally, yet they find themselves unable to deal with the stresses of relationships and responsibility, either withdrawing into passivity or lapsing into violent behavior when confronted with social demands.

More fascinating still, British Army doctors observed the shift from "shell shock" to "battle fatigue" during the First World War, with the different symptoms corresponding to differences in social class. Officers, who at that time came only from the upper classes, evidenced "battle fatigue", while the enlisted men, i.e., soldiers from the lower or working class, evidenced "shell shock". Why this difference? There was no difference in the trauma to which they were subjected. Some suspect that the difference is related to the fact that the upper classes had exposure to electronic media while the lower classes did not.

In my psychological work, I witnessed changes in symptoms from the early 70's to the early 80's, i.e., a shift from "neurosis" to "personality disorders" (these are not different labels for the same phenomena; they refer to different phenomena). While not so dramatic or obvious as the ones mentioned above, the evolution in symptomatology I saw led me to try to understand why it was occurring. The changes are not reducible to individual or cultural factors such as education, intelligence, or insight. However, they did seem to conform to age group, i.e., older people fit the expected patterns while younger people did not. It was as if these differences were due to "changing times". And, my research led me to conclude that there was some relationship between these kinds of changes and technology. This is when I first became interested in computer science. If electronic technology was to shape our lives and the minds of our children, I wanted to understand it. Computer science was, and still is, at the forefront of new electronic technology.

Since that time, I've observed many things which suggest that people today evidence subtly different consciousness, depending upon the kind of electronic media that was pervasive during their formative years. For example....

An Informal Technology-Consciousness Test Here's a simple test you can perform by observation with members of your family or other people you know. There's certainly nothing scientific about it, but its results can be interesting. It concerns generational differences in the ability to successfully program a VCR to record a program on some channel at a later date or time. To perform the test, select people you know from each of the following three age groups:

(1) those born before World War II, i.e., those who "grew up on" radio;

(2) those born between the end of World War II and the beginning of the Vietnam War, i.e., those who "grew up on" black-and-white television;

(3) those born after the Vietnam War, i.e., those who "grew up on" color television.

Present each person with a model of VCR which does not support "onscreen programming" and with which the person has no experience. Assign the "programming task" to each person, then simply observe what happens. What I have observed is:

- Most males from Group 1 cannot complete the task, with or without a user manual. Often, signs of extreme frustration (including extensive cussing) ensue.

- Most males from Group 2 can indeed complete task, but only with the assistance of a user manual. Signs of moderate annoyance (including mild cussing) sometimes ensue.

- Most males from Group 3 can complete the task without either a user's manual or any cussing. Minimal to zero signs of annoyance or frustration are evident.

Exceptions to this pattern seem to correlate mainly with technical experience, i.e., Group 1 males who have considerable experience with technical things, either through their work or hobbies, perform more like Group 2 males. Similarly, technically-oriented Group 2 males may perform like Group 3 males. I have never seen any Group 1 male perform like a Group 3 male.

I have found that females sometimes conform to these categories and sometimes do not. In the cases where they do not, they generally fit the description of the males from the next-older group (but without as much cussing), i.e., many Group 2 females will fail, ala Group 1 males, and many Group 3 females require the manual ala Group 2 males.

There are various possible ways to explain this gender difference. Some have speculated that females in American society are raised to be less comfortable with certain kinds of tasks and thus have been "trained to fail" in certain areas. Others have speculated that there are innate gender-specific differences in "styles of relating" which make it easier for females to do some things (relate to people) and harder for them to do others things (relate to objects). I don't know what the truth is. What do you think?

Exercises   1.1. A quote from the book *Mindstorms* by Seymour Pappert: "[Critics] fear that more communication via computers might lead to less human association and result in social fragmentation." In what ways do you agree and/or disagree? Why?

1.2. In what ways do you see electronic media of any kind, including but not limited to interactive computing, contributing to "decay and deterioration in our social fabric"? How might these negative effects be countered?

1.3. In what way do you expect to see "high technology" (of any form) make the strongest impact on our society in the next 20 years? In what way will such changes be positive? In what ways will they be negative?

1.4. Given the power of modern technology (i.e., computer databases, electronic surveillance, blood/urine/hair tests, etc.), it is now possible to monitor and investigate aspects of individual behavior in ways that couldn't have been imagined 200 years ago. In light of these technological developments, do you believe that the U.S. Constitution's *Bill of Rights* is sufficient to protect the citizenry from privacy intrusions by government and/or corporate entities? If you favor "leaving the *Bill of Rights* alone," explain how/why you think it is adequate to modern society and why you don't want it modified. If you favor modifying the *Bill of Rights*, in what ways do you think the *Bill of Rights* should be updated and why?

1.5. Let us assume that "traditional values and ethics" evolved during a time when life was far different than today: when people had far less choice, when people had their "place in the world" determined for them, and when personal happiness was not a prime criteria for major life decisions. Let us further assume that we are today witnessing a weakening of such "traditional values and ethics" in our society, as individual choice and personal satisfaction play larger roles in life decisions. (We am not asking whether you like or dislike such changes, we are only assuming that they are occurring "for better or worse.") Finally, let us assume that there must be some shared system of "values and ethics" in order for our society to function and flourish. Given these assumptions, what do you think will be the central tenets of a new system of "post-industrial values and ethics"? In what ways will a new ethical system differ from the old?

1.6. Imagine a new political party that is tied to any existing party. We will call it the "Systems Party." It is based on the proposition that (a) society is a large and extremely complex "interactive system" much like an enormous computer system, and (b) it should be managed as such, with explicit decisions about costs, benefits, optimization targets, performance thresholds, etc. What do you expect the strengths and benefits of this party would be? What do you expect the weaknesses and dangers of this party would be?

1.7. In recent years, there has been a sharp upturn in interest and funding for research and implementation in computer graphics, hypermedia, and data visualization. Scientists from across the board are increasingly interested in graphic representations of their data, and computer users are more and more "sold" on graphical user interfaces (such as the *Mac* and *Windows* interfaces). This trend is compatible with Marshal McLuhan's thirty year old claim that the alphabet is becoming an obsolete symbol system, outmoded for effective communication purposes, i.e., is archaic media. If McLuhan is right, then perhaps recent declines in reading skills and habits are signs of progress; if he is wrong, then such declines are signs of societal decay. Which do you think is the case?

1.8. Technology of various kinds has served to make many aspects of traditional gender roles obsolete. The caricature of males as aggressive, violent, and forceful may have once been appropriate for survival, but is now "antisocial." The caricature of females as motherly, nurturing, and home-oriented was once dictated by various factors, but is now considered "oppressive," or at least "quaint." Are there ways that traditional characterizations are positive? Are valid? Do you perceive any ways in which the "new equality" is itself a form of "oppression" that invalidates who men and women "really are"?

1.9. List what you perceive as the top three threats to society. For each one, consider whether the issue might be related to a shift from "mechanical" to "electronic" consciousness.

1.10. Consult your own subjective experience of (a) reading books, (b) watching television, and (c) interacting with a computer. Describe the difference in the "kind of subjective experience" each media provides when you engage it.

Chapter 2: The Algorithmic Model

Introduction

We use the term "computing perspective" to refer to a way of looking at the world as it would be seen through the eyes of a computer scientist. You do not have to be a computer scientist to do this, but you do need to know a handful of the basic fundamental concepts which help the computer scientist see things in a certain way.

Computers are devices which do only one kind of thing: they carry out *algorithms* to process information. To computer scientists, the notion of "algorithm" is the most important of all concepts, the central unifying concept of computing, the "mode of thought" that is at the core of the computing perspective.

☐ What is an *algorithm*? An algorithm is a "recipe of action" or something very much like a computer program, i.e., *a set of instructions which govern behavior step-by-step.* Any precise set of instructions which adequately specifies behavior, step-by-step, and which is not ambiguous, can be considered to be an algorithm.

Algorithms need not have anything at all to do with computers. Years before computers were invented, your great grandmother carried out an algorithm every time she followed a recipe to make an apple pie.

☐ What is the difference between a *computer program* and an *algorithm*? An algorithm is the "set of logical steps," apart from their expression in any given programming language. A computer program is an *expression of an algorithm in some programming language.*

There might be several different computer programs, each written in a different programming language, that follow the same logical steps. They all would express the same algorithm, but they would not be the same program. Similarly, there might be various recipes for apple pie, one written in English, one in French, and one in Japanese. If they each describe the same series of steps, they would be different recipes which all express the same algorithm.

While there is nothing about the idea of algorithms that requires "data" (witness the baking of apple pies), *using* algorithms and computers to simulate and model phenomena does require data. Why? Simply because data is the only thing that computers can process.

Thus, whenever a scientist or engineer makes use of a computer model of whatever phenomena he or she might be studying, it is necessary that they represent that phenomena in terms of data that the computer can manipulate. If someone is trying to model a baseball season, all the players are represented by some collection of data describing their performance at bat and in the field. Similarly, if you go to Home Depot to buy kitchen cabinets, an employee will input the dimension of your kitchen into the computer, will use a mouse to indicate whatever arrangement of cabinets and appliances you are considering, and will then show you an onscreen picture of how your kitchen will look from various angles of view. Obviously, the computer does not have itty-bitty refrigerators and sinks inside it; instead, numerical representations of your kitchen and its layout are used to generate perspective pictures for you.

Since we are concerned with algorithms and their power when combined with computers, we will thus be jointly concerned with both algorithms and data. From the computing perspective, algorithms *always* act upon data, and there is no practical way to consider one without the other. Algorithms obtain data from the real world (via data file, keyboard, or other sensor), manipulate it internally, then return data to the real world via some output device (monitor screen, printer, or other receiver of information).

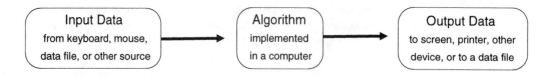

The coupling of *algorithmic thinking* with the *algorithm execution abilities of computers* has lead to an historically unprecedented "tight coupling" of:

- Abstraction: what is it you want to investigate or accomplish?

- Design: how are you going to do it?

- Implementation: making your idea work.

- Experimentation: try out your idea to see what happens.

- Evaluation: how well did your idea perform? How does it need to be refined?

In a large and growing body of disciplines, the "state of the art" is to conceive of phenomena in algorithmic terms, implement computer-based models of that phenomena, and use the resulting "simulated world" for experimentation and exploration. This approach is revolutionizing what can be known, predicted, designed, built and governed.

An Example Algorithm

We shall soon be concerned with the various kinds of abstraction that go into creating good algorithms. First, however, we must cover the basics.

An algorithm contains a series of simple but precise instructions that combine to solve a problem. Before we look at each requirement in more detail, let's see an example of an algorithm that solves the problem of registering for classes[6]:

```
1.  Make a list of courses you want to register for, in
    order of priority.
2.  Start with an empty schedule:  number of hours sched-
    uled = 0.
3.  Choose the highest priority class on the list.
4.  If (the chosen class is not full AND its class time
    does not conflict with classes already scheduled)
    then register for class:
    4a. Add the class to your schedule.
    4b. Add the class hours to the Number of hours sched-
        uled.
5.  Cross the class off of your list.
6.  Repeat steps 3 through 5 until the number of hours
    scheduled is >= 15, or until all classes have been
    crossed out.
7.  Stop.
```

[6] Note that this is a very simple algorithm - it does not guarantee a full course load. For example, if the second class on your list is held at a time that conflicts with all other courses below it on the list, then the algorithm will only schedule the first two classes. An algorithm that would solve this problem is too complicated to present at this point.

Notice how indentation is used to show that steps 4a and 4b are components of instruction 4. Indentation is important in making algorithms easily readable, and we will give some guidelines for indenting as we go along.

Flow Charts

In order to clearly see what an algorithm does, it sometimes helps to have a pictorial representation of the "flow of control," or "which steps are executed in what order." Such a picture is called a flow chart. Each symbol in a flow chart represents a certain kind of instruction. For example, most instructions are symbolized by rectangles, and instructions that involve decisions are symbolized by diamonds. To get a feel for flow charting, look at the flow chart of the registration algorithm (next page). Flow charts provide a picture of the algorithmic steps. The data manipulation instructions are represented by boxes, the control structures are represented by diamonds. Flow charts are especially useful when you are trying to develop an algorithm. Drawing a picture of your intended algorithm can give you an intuitive feel for what it is doing at each step, and where there might be inefficiency or errors.

Properties of Algorithms

☐ Well designed algorithms always have two key properties: "precision and simplicity" and "levels of abstraction."

Precision and Simplicity

Algorithms need to be very *precise*. This is because no matter who carries out an algorithm, the result should always be the same (given identical input). In line 6 of our example, for instance, it would not have been appropriate to say "Repeat steps 3 through 5 until Number-of-hours scheduled is *about* 15," because that lends itself to various different interpretations. One person might think that it means a range of 13-17 hours, another might decide that 11 hours is close enough. And a computer would not able to estimate at all - it only understands definite, precise instructions.

In addition, each step of an algorithm must be *simple*. A general rule of thumb is that each step should carry out one basic instruction. For example, in the case of registration, the entire task is broken down into many elementary steps, none of which takes very long to complete or involve multiple complex instructions.

Levels of Abstraction

While each element of an algorithm must be simple, "simple" is a relative term. Many things that are elementary to a college student are not elementary to a first-grader. Hence, we have the notion of *levels of abstraction*. Every algorithm must be written based on the knowledge appropriate to the processor. For instance, instruction *4a* of the registration algorithm says "add the class to your schedule." The details of adding a class are not specified at all. This is because it is assumed that the

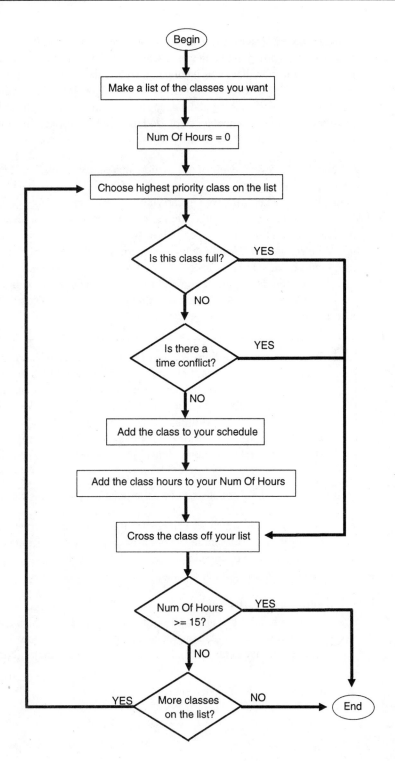

student who is registering knows how to add a class, and that this is a fairly basic procedure such as filling in bubbles on a scantron form. Since this instruction does not present all the particular steps involved in adding the course, we would consider it to be at a fairly "high" level of abstraction. If this algorithm was written for use by someone who knew nothing about such forms, then step 4a might be broken down into multiple, more elementary steps, and the level of abstraction would be "lower." In writing any algorithm, care must be taken to choose the correct level of abstraction.

"Higher" and "lower" levels of abstraction are relative terms. The highest level is the level of algorithm purpose, e.g., "registering for classes." The next lower level contains the logical steps involved in carrying out that purpose (e.g., those steps we labeled with integers in the algorithm given above). Below that level would be the particular instructions which specify how to carry out each of those logical steps, and so on. In computing, the lowest level concerns the electric current sent throughout the circuits of a computer. This level is so low that it is effectively automated; unless you are an electrical engineer, you will never have to deal with it. For most situations, the lowest level of abstraction is that which specifies a single individual instruction, e.g., an arithmetic operation.

> ☐   Well designed algorithms will be organized in terms of *levels of abstraction*.
> This means that we want to be able to refer to each of the major "logical
> steps" without being distracted by the many details that make up each one.
> The simple detailed instructions that make up each step are hidden inside
> "modules" (or "subalgorithms" or "subprograms"). This allows us to think
> in high-level logic; we "hide the details" of each high-level step inside a
> module, then refer to that module by name whenever we need it

Designs based on levels of abstraction are crucial in at least two ways:

- It is the means by which we can create algorithms that instruct computers to do complex things. Without levels of abstraction, any significant computer program would be so cluttered up with tiny details that it would be practically impossible for a person to understand.

- It allows us to easily substitute one set of particulars for another, i.e., we can "plug in" modules that are equivalent in their effect but which achieve that effect in different ways. By isolating details in a modular design, we can readily make selective improvements without having to undertake a major redesign.

Algorithm Components

Any computing algorithm will consist of, at most, five kinds of components: *Data structures*, *Data manipulation instructions*, *Conditional expressions*, *Control structures*, and *Modules*. We describe the usefulness of each below.

Data structures Data is information used by an algorithm. This includes input and output data, as well as any interim data generated by the algorithm for its own internal use. Data structures are "containers" for data values. In most circumstances, we want a data structure to be variable, i.e., a given data structure's contents can and will change as the algorithm acts upon it. In some circumstances we want a data structure's contents to be fixed, e.g. we probably don't want the algorithm to be able to change the value of *pi*. Thus, we have "variables" and "constants." Inside a computer, each data structure (variable or constant) will occupy some location in memory.

To use data, we must have a way of distinguishing one piece of data from another, and a way of referring to a given piece of data over and over again. This is easy: we simply give each data structure a name. While we can choose whatever names we like, the names should be *descriptive* of the data. Thus, if we are using a data structure to hold the sum of several other values, it would be better to call that variable "Sum" than "Fred." Similarly, we would want the constant that holds the value 3.14159 to be called "Pi," not "Ethel." In computer jargon, the names we make up for data structures (and for other purposes) are called "identifiers."

In addition to naming data, we also need to organize our data in a manner that will help us solve the problem at hand. As we shall soon see, how we organize our data can go a long way towards making the algorithm either simple to write or needlessly complicated to write. This is why we must design data structures to suit the task at hand. Creating complex data structures that we can easily reference via meaningful names is one of our key opportunities to create useful abstractions. We shall discuss tools for doing this in Chapter 5.

> ☐ Data structures are entities which allow us to do four things:
> (1) identify data by name,
> (2) refer to a piece of data over and over if we need to,
> (3) organize data to best suit the task at hand, and
> (4) achieve effective "data abstraction," i.e., separating the details of the data from the logical use of the data.

The three key requirements are:

(a) we choose descriptive identifiers to name data structures,

(b) we design data structures to hold data in organized, accessible structures that makes it easy for our algorithm to "get at" their contents.

(c) we design them such that modifications to our data structures are easy to make and do not require wholesale changes to the algorithms which use them.

Instructions   Algorithms require instructions that allow it to:

- obtain data values "from the real world" and store them in its data structures.

- manipulate those data values, i.e., modify the value of a data structure via arithmetic operations, assign the contents of one data structure to another, etc.

- output the resulting data values "back to the real world."

In order to achieve effective abstraction, we want to group logically related instructions together into "modules" (discussed below).

Conditionals   Algorithms also feature "decision points." The ability of an algorithm to make decisions and then act on them is what makes algorithms (and computers) powerful. If a computer could do no more than simply follow a rote list of operations, then it would be nothing more than an automated calculator, performing one arithmetic operation after another. This is the crucial difference between a computer and a calculator: a computer can make decisions and act on them, while a calculator cannot.

In keeping with the nature of computers, each decision must be a precise and simple decision. All such decisions are based on *conditional expressions* that are "true" or "false" (e.g., "$X = 17$"). If the condition is true, the algorithm does one thing, if not it does something else. However, simple decisions can be used to decide extremely complicated things; as we shall see, this is achieved via abstraction.

The elements of algorithms that govern what happens *after* an algorithm makes a decision are called *control structures*. Without control structures, decisions are of no value. What good is a decision if you cannot act on it? Without control structures, the algorithm is just a rote list of instructions that are executed sequentially, and a computer executing such an algorithm is still nothing but a glorified calculator. Control structures allow an algorithm to *act* on the decisions it makes, i.e., they allow us to specify that certain instructions will be executed if one decsion is reached and that other instructions will be executed if a different decision is reached.

Modules   Algorithms can become very complex, especially if they are adequate for doing something useful. Simply placing all the various components of an algorithm together will produce an algorithm that is hard to understand, hard to repair, and hard to extend. Instead, "modules" (or "subalgorithms" or "routines"; you may consider these terms to be equivalent) are used to group together those instructions and data which are required by a given logical task. This raises the level of abstraction and thus allows clearer thinking, faster repairs, easier modifications and, most importantly, a practical way to solve complex problems.

Seeing Things from the Computing Perspective

☐ To view the world from the computing perspective, it is necessary that you be able to do five things:
(1) conceive of behavior as "expressions of algorithms";
(2) conceive of objects which exhibit behavior as "processes";
(3) conceive of algorithms in terms of "levels of abstraction";
(4) realize that an algorithm's usefulness can be limited by its "complexity";
(5) be willing to temporarily put aside other perspectives.

(1) Conceive of behavior as "expressions of algorithms"

Conceive of behavior? What kind of behavior? *Any* kind: the behavior of objects, plants, birds, chemical reactions, devices, people, *parts* of people (e.g., the immune system or a muscle), corporate or governmental organizations, cockroaches, planets, baseball teams, the weather, *anything* at all.

☐ Conceiving of some behavior as an expression of an algorithm means that you must try to imagine what set of instructions is being carried out by the thing or being that is doing the behavior.

The algorithm you imagine which describes the behavior might be correct or it might be completely wrong, maybe even ridiculous. However, for our purposes, the *correctness* of your guess about the algorithm is less important than your ability to imagine it! Even if your algorithm is wrong, it still might be valuable. If you can come up with an algorithm that is *not* the actual algorithm being carried out in the behavior, but which *does* effectively specify instructions which would reproduce that same behavior, then your imagined algorithm *simulates* whatever the real algorithm might be. Such algorithms can be very valuable in business, in science, and in engineering.

(2) Conceive of things which exhibits behavior as "processes"

In computer science jargon, a *process* is very much like a noun-that-is-doing-something. Thus, a given car-and-driver in a traffic jam is a "process," and the behavior of that car-and-driver is an expression of some "algorithm." Since we are interested in all kinds of behavior, we do not want to get lost trying to categorize all the kinds of things which might be *doing* behavior. So, we simply call them all *processes*.

> ☐   A process is anything that is carrying out behavior specified by an algorithm. Thus, a computer, combined with a computer program which it is executing, is a process; a computer that is turned off is not. Your grandmother-cooking-at-the-stove is a process, while an unused stove is not. Some computers can execute multiple programs at the same time; in such a case, that one computer and the several programs it is executing constitute several processes.

As you engage in studying, or in goofing off instead of studying, you are a process. What algorithm do you carry out when you are a "study process," i.e., what are the specific steps in that "behavior recipe"? What algorithm do you carry out when you are a "goofing-off process"? What steps do those two algorithms have in common? At what point to they diverge into different steps?

(3) Conceive of algorithms in terms of "levels of abstraction"

Given that an algorithm is a series of instructions, or a recipe of actions, the question naturally arises, "how detailed must it be?" The answer is "it depends." For example, my grandmother cooked all her life. If someone gave her a recipe for some kind of pie which required a pie crust, she would know how to create the pie crust without further instruction. My brother has not cooked very much and, if he were given the same recipe, he would require detailed step-by-step instructions about what to do.

Thus, depending on the person, two different "levels of abstraction" are called for. For my grandmother, the instruction "make a pie crust" would be sufficient; it would not have to be tied to a detailed set of directions. For my brother, the same instruction would not be sufficiently detailed. Instead, he would have to consult another recipe, one which describes the steps necessary for making pie crust.

"Levels of abstraction" are important, both in creating new algorithms and in understanding algorithms that already exist. They allow us to "hide the details" of a given activity and refer to just a name for those details. Thus, a pie recipe might say:

```
Prepare blueberry filling
Prepare crust
Fill crust
Top pie with lattice crust
Bake at 350 for 45 minutes
Cool and serve
```

Such a recipe would be clear to an experienced baker, yet those who didn't understand those six steps would have to consult more detailed instructions for each step. My grandmother might only need to consult the algorithm for "prepare blueberry filling," while my brother might have to consult the detailed algorithm for all six steps.

This idea of "levels of abstraction" is important to imagining, creating, understanding, and improving algorithms.

> ☐   We do not want an algorithm to be a giant sequential list of all the steps.

From the human point of view, such a large list of instructions proves to be hard to create, hard to understand, hard to analyze, hard to verify, and hard to repair. (From a technical point of view, there are other problems as well.)

> ☐   Instead, we want a "hierarchy of abstraction" in which the "top level" lists the various "main steps," the main ideas, without cluttering things up with a detailed list of what they mean. The details of each of those main steps are described in their own little separate section.

For a recipe, each section might be its own paragraph or a list. For a computer program, each section may be called a "subprogram" or a "procedure" or a "module." Each of these words means approximately the same thing; there are subtle differences between them but, for now, you may use these words interchangeably.

(4) Understand that an algorithm's usefulness can be limited by its complexity
Any algorithm consists of a series of steps which must be followed to achieve the intended behavior. One person might carry them out faster than another, just as a fast computer would execute a given program in less time than would a slower computer. However, the speed of the processor has nothing to do with the amount of work that an algorithm requires. Regardless of the speed of the processor, the algorithm itself implies that some number of steps will be carried out.

> ☐   There is some amount of work which is called for by the algorithm, irrespective of the speed at which a given processor can do that work. The speed of the processor determines how long it takes to get some amount of work done, but the algorithm determines the amount of work to be done.

When we talk about the complexity of an algorithm, we generally refer *not* to the actual number of steps, but rather to the *rate* at which the work grows for a given input into that algorithm.

For example, imagine two different algorithms for baking an apple pie and that the input into this algorithm is the number of pies that we wish to have baked. Let's say that one recipe calls for 15 specific steps while the other calls for 30 steps. Furthermore, for simplicity, let's imagine that each step takes the same amount of time and effort, and that there is no improvement in efficiency if you choose to bake 10 pies rather than one pie. What can we say about these algorithms? Well, at first glance, we see that the first algorithm is twice as efficient as the second. We can also see that for an input of 10, the first algorithm will mean executing 150 steps, while using the second algorithm will mean executing 300 steps. Intuitively, we can easily judge that the first recipe is to be preferred over the second one, if they both produce good tasting apple pies.

However, the *rate* at which the work grows for each algorithm is the same. In both cases, increasing size of the input increases the number of steps in a *linear* fashion. Thus, the second recipe requires exactly twice as many steps as does the first, regardless of how many pies are to be baked.

Unfortunately, algorithmic complexity is not always so simple. For certain kinds of problems, algorithmic complexity is a major problem. For some kinds of algorithms, the rate of work grows by the square of input size, i.e., baking 10 pies would increase the work by a factor of 100 compared to baking only one pie, and baking 1000 pies would increase the work by a factor of a million!

Worse yet, for certain other problems, the rate of work grows by a exponential factor (i.e., 2 to the Nth power where N is the size of the input). With such an algorithm, baking 10 pies instead of one pie would increase the amount of work by a factor of 2 raised to the 10th power, or about a thousand, and baking only 20 pies would increase the amount of work by a factor of 2 raised to the 20th power, or about a million! (What if the input was 1000?)

Clearly, such algorithms are unattractive. Unfortunately, they are the best we can do with many kinds of real-world problems, such as routing salesmen or packing trucks or scheduling classrooms in an optimal fashion. And, lest you think that raw computer power can compensate for such complex algorithms, there are certain kinds of algorithms which could not be executed by the fastest computer built, nor even by the fastest computer anyone can even imagine, and produce a result within your lifetime!

> ☐ There are many perfectly correct algorithms which are of no practical value simply because they require too much work *regardless of the speed of the computer.*

Furthermore, for many of these problems, we believe that there can be no substantial improvement in the solution algorithm. As a result, as we try to understand the algorithms implied by various behavior, we also try to estimate the complexity of them. Algorithms which are sufficiently complex to be unreasonable to run may have theoretical value, but have no practical value whatsoever. We like to know what those are before we try to solve problems with them!

(5) Be willing to temporarily put aside other perspectives so that you can see things from the computing perspective

The computing perspective provides a new way of looking at the world and of understanding reality. It does not necessarily provide "the right answers," nor is it necessarily the "most useful" way to look at any given phenomenon. However, it does give us a way to perceive, model, simulate, and understand many phenomena that have not previously been well understood. And, it has contributed to important breakthroughs in fields ranging from medicine and psychology to engineering and industrial production. Furthermore, it provides the intellectual framework which underlies advanced research in virtually every single field of modern science and knowledge. As a result, you should learn to see things from this perspective.

> ☐ This does *not* mean that you have to throw away other perspectives or beliefs. It *does* mean that you should *add* the computing perspective to your repertoire of "ways of seeing the world."

Why? This perspective is shaping the world today and will likely continue to do so throughout your lifetime. Regardless of what you will choose as a career, regardless of what you do with your life, the computing perspective will be a powerful force in shaping the world you live in and in shaping your experience of that world. For this reason, it is important that you come to understand it. Our job is to help you do so.

Food for Thought:

Confusing "Models" with "Reality"

Our models of reality represent our *best guesses* about the truth. As such, they are crucial to the development of science and knowledge. We develop a model that appears to be adequate for the purpose of helping us explain or understand something. We then not only test that model, we also use it as a basis for expanding our knowledge. Eventually, we reach the limits of a model by learning enough about reality that we can see that our model is flawed, or incomplete, or inadequate. Then, over time, we develop new models that improve on the old, and so on.

For the last few hundred years, the dominant model in the West has been the Mechanical Model. It views reality as if it were a large and complex machine, and seeks to understand the laws which govern that machine. This model has been the basis for much of the great explosion of industry and science since the Middle Ages.

It enabled our ancestors to make great strides in the Natural Sciences (physics, chemistry, biology, geology, astronomy, etc.), and to overpower certain limits imposed on us by the forces of nature (witness the railroads, the automobile, the airplane, etc.).

The Mechanical Model appears to have been most valuable with respect to Natural Phenomena (the material world of objects and matter) and less adequate to Human Phenomena (the invisible world of processes and experiences). Thus, while the Mechanical Model was adequate, for example, in helping understand much about the *material aspects* of medicine (surgery, setting broken bones, removal of diseased organs), it was not adequate for other, more complex aspects of human health and well-being (infections, immune disorders, psychiatric problems, etc.).

Unfortunately, because we have yet to develop models that are adequate to explain the richness and complexity of life, it is unavoidable that we apply our models to phenomena for which they are not adequate. Thus, despite the inadequacies of the Mechanical Model for certain kinds of health phenomena, it was nonetheless deployed as the basis for certain kinds of treatments. For example, hysterectomies were performed on women who were judged to be overly emotional, lobotomies were performed on people judged to be crazy, and so on.

In retrospect, things were attempted that would never be allowed today. At the time they were attempted, however, they were viewed as the "best shot" we had. If a modern physician were to perform a lobotomy for the purposes of "calming down a disturbed patient," he would be considered a criminal. Yet the very same procedure performed a hundred years ago was not criminal, it was an act of discovery, analogous *ethically* (if not *scientifically*) to the experimental treatments of today.

An unavoidable difficulty is that most people who apply models *don't realize* that they are "filtering reality" through their model. They confuse their "best guesses" with being "the truth." Thus, for some of the early pioneers in psycho-surgery, what they were doing was "clearly the right thing," was the "wave of the future," and so on. Only in retrospect can we clearly see them as advocates of an improper course of action and recognize the pain and human loss that some of their actions caused.

Today, the same sort of issues apply. With the emergence of the Computational Model, we can expect all manner of individuals who are visionary, who see the application of the new model to all manner of phenomena. Some such visionaries will be correct, and the future will judge them to be "ahead of their time." Others will be incorrect, and history will either ignore them or judge them to be "misguided crackpots" or worse. The problem is that we do not know what the future will tell us about who's a genius and who's a crackpot! Thus, we should proceed with care.

You can expect to see all manner of developments that apply the Computational Model to human phenomena. Much of it will imply that "people are like computers," and that the best way to solve human problems is to "develop informational programs," to "enhance people's ability to process information," and so on. There is much about this approach that is very sensible. There will also be many stupid things done. And the stupid things, whatever they might be, will mostly have the same flaw: they will ignore the ways that people are *not* like computers, ignore the ways that people are *not* just "processors of information," ignore the things about people that a Computational Model *cannot even see*, much less adequately explain.

Thus, we urge you to do two things. First, become familiar with the idea of the Computational Model, and to "try it on for size." Why? Because it *is* the wave of the future and *is* at the foundation of the huge strides in knowledge that are being made today. But we also urge you take it all with "a grain of salt," to *think critically* about what you see and hear, and to "be your own judge" about what makes sense and what does not. After all, a model is *only a model*.

Summary   Algorithms are the central unifying concept of computing and have proved to be extremely powerful at extending the range of human knowledge and technique.

Algorithms consist of simple and precise instructions. Well designed algorithms are organized by "levels of abstraction" which allow us to combine the detailed, simple instructions for each "logical step" into "modules." This allows us to see the "high level logic" of the algorithm, and thus solve complex problems, without getting lost in the various details of each step. It also allows us to modify the algorithm with minimal work. There are only five kinds of algorithm elements:

1. *Data structures* which hold data values.

2. Simple, precise *instructions* that allow the algorithm to obtain data values "from the real world" and store them in its data structures, manipulate those data values, and output the resulting data values "back to the real world."

3. *Conditional expressions* which allow algorithms to make *true/false* decisions.

4. *Control structures* which allow an algorithm to act on its decisions.

5. *Modules* which allow effective abstraction for solving complex problems.

In the next section (Chapters 3 through 9), we will discuss the full range of algorithm-building constructs, including *all of the conceptual tools* that are available for constructing algorithms and for designing the data structures on which they operate. By the end of that section, we will have described and discussed *all* the elements that are necessary to design and construct algorithms and associated data. No matter how far you go in the study of computing, no matter how many programs you write, no matter what degree of technical expertise you will achieve, virtually all the programming you ever do will boil down to manipulating the constructs we cover in that section.

Of course, we do not expect you to be masterful immediately. In the weeks to come, you will rapidly gain experience and expertise at mastering all of the constructs. For now, it is important that you just understand them, for they lie at the foundation of all the computing that is done.

Exercises   2.1. What is an algorithm?

2.2. What do we mean by "abstraction"?

2.3. Why do we want "levels of abstraction" in our algorithms? Why is abstraction a good thing? (Focus on 2 or 3 things)

2.4. How do we create our algorithms such that they feature abstraction?

2.5. What's the difference between "higher" and "lower" levels of abstraction. Give examples.

2.6. What is the important difference between a computer and a calculator?

2.7. All algorithmic decisions are made on the basis of *true/false* questions. Are there any kinds of "real life" questions that cannot be resolved in this way? If so, give examples. If not, how might complex "fuzzy" questions be resolved in this binary (*true/false*) paradigm?

2.8. A major approach to the design of algorithms is what is called *top-down design*. Given what we already know about *levels of abstraction*, think about what the term *top-down design* means. Briefly describe what you think it means.

2.9. How would you use *top-down design* as you go about creating an algorithm.

2.10. What do you think will be the limit of what can be accomplished using algorithms? Where, if anywhere, will algorithms prove to be useless?

Part II: The Algorithm Toolkit

[This page intentionally left blank.]

Chapter 3: Basic Data, Operations and Decisions

Chapters 4 through 9 introduce the concepts and constructs which serve as algorithmic "abstraction tools." Before we get into the tools of abstraction, we must first understand the basic building blocks upon which they are built. Thus, in this chapter we will cover the "lower level" tools.

Atomic Data

Sometimes an algorithm needs to work with only single pieces of data, like a few numbers or characters. No organization of the data is necessary because the situation is very simple. We merely need a way to refer to the data unambiguously throughout our algorithm. For this we use "atomic" (or "simple") variables. An atomic variable can be thought of as a named box, or cell, which holds only one individual piece of data, such as a number or a character.

Operators

Assignment Operator

Putting a value into a variable is called *assignment*. We use the *assignment operator* (<-) as a symbol for this operation [7]. This operator is called the "assignment operator" because it is used to assign values to variables. For example:

```
X  <-  3
Y  <-  4
```

The first assignment statement means "place the value 3 into the variable named X." The second assignment means "place the value 4 into the variable named Y."

Whenever a variable name is used on the right-hand side of an assignment expression, it represents the value currently stored in that variable. When the expression is

---

[7] Notice that the symbol for the assignment operator requires typing two keys: the < (less than) and the - (hyphen). Despite the fact that it is two keystrokes, think of it as a single symbol: a left-pointing arrow.

evaluated, the value stored in the data structure is substituted for the name of the data structure. For example, consider:

        Z <- X + Y

Since we have already assigned the value 3 to *X* and the value 4 to *Y*, *X* + *Y* evaluates to 3 + 4. This operation is performed and the sum (7) is placed in a variable named Z.

An assignment statement can be confusing to the untrained eye when the same identifier appears on both the right and left sides. For example, consider:

        Y <- X + Y

This means "add the value of *X* to the current value of variable *Y*, then place the new result in the variable *Y*." Hence, if X is 3 and Y is currently 4, then Y will be 7 after the expression is evaluated.

Arithmetic Operators

Basic operations include the four basic arithmetic operations:addition, subtraction, multiplication, and division. To denote them, we use the following symbols:

- *addition* is denoted by +

- *subtraction* is denoted by -

- *multiplication* is denoted by *

- *division* is denoted by /

In addition, we have two additional arithmetic operators that are related to division:

- *integer division* is denoted by *DIV* (returns a whole number quotient, ignoring any remainder, e.g., *11 DIV 3* returns *3*)

- *modulo* is denoted by *MOD* (returns only the remainder, ignoring any whole-number quotient, e.g. *11 MOD 3* returns *2*)

Precedence Rules

As with standard arithmetic, parentheses are used to govern the order of operations. Unless parentheses indicate otherwise, *precedence rules* govern the order of arithmetic operations as follows:

☐   Multiplication and/or division operations are performed first, as they are encountered in a left to right sequence. Then, addition and/or subtraction operations are performed as they are encountered in a left to right sequence.

For example:

```
A <- 2
B <- 3
C <- 5
D <- 4
X <- A + B * C - D
```

would store the value 13 in variable X. In contrast, the statement:

```
X <- (A + B) * (C - D)
```

would store the value 5 in variable X.

Input/Output For any algorithm, we require some means of getting data from the world to the algo-
("I/O") Operators rithm (input) and some means of returning the results of the algorithm back to the
world (output). For our purposes, there are two "I/O" ("input/output") operations:
read and *print*.

Read is used to obtain input values from "the world outside of the algorithm," i.e.,
from a data file or from a person typing at a keyboard or perhaps some sort of sensor
device (e.g., in an F-16 fighter plane, a signal from a radar receiver). Regardless of
the source of data, we obtain it in our algorithms via the *read* operator using the syntax:

☐ `read(X)`

This statement means "read the next input value and store it in variable X."
In effect, the *read* operator does two things: it both *obtains* the data value
and *assigns* it to the specified data structure.

To read the next three input values and store them in variables "Larry," "Moe," and
"Curley," we could write:

```
read(Larry)
read(Moe)
read(Curley)
```

We can achieve the same effect by using a single *read* operation with those three
identifiers concatenated ("chained together"):

```
read(Larry, Moe, Curley)
```

Print is used to generate output from the algorithm to "the world outside," i.e., to a printer or a computer monitor (screen) or some other device (e.g. in an F-16, the weapons control system). If we wanted to output the three values we just obtained in the example above, we would write:

```
print(Larry)
print(Moe)
print(Curley)
```

or

```
print (Larry, Moe, Curley)
```

In addition to printing out the values stored in data structures, we can also print textual messages (known as a "literals") without having to store them in variables, e.g.:

```
print("This is a textual message")
```

Given a few atomic data structures and these simple operations, we can create algorithms that do simple things, e.g., we can find the average of test scores for three students:

```
algorithm StoogeAverage
begin
    read(Larry, Moe, Curley)
    Average <- (Larry + Moe + Curley)/3
    print ("The average for Larry, Moe,")
    print ("and Curley is: ", Average)
end
```

Note that we use only these two I/O constructs, *read* and *print*, regardless of where we get the data or where we are sending it [8]. For our purposes, do not worry about the details of exactly "where the data comes from" (perhaps *keyboard* or *data file* or *modem*), nor "where it goes" (perhaps *monitor screen*, *printer*, etc.), nor how this is done (you may assume "technical magic"). Similarly, do not worry about the details of formatting the data. We will pretend that "technical magic" allows the *print* construct to "read your mind" and insert spaces and lines wherever you think they are necessary to separate one piece of data from the next.

---

[8] Some students want to know why we do not deal with the "real world" details of managing I/O from various sources. We do this for two reasons: first, we are concerned in this course with important concepts, not annoying technical details; second, in the "real world", proper program design will insure that such annoying details are well encapsulated such that they are hidden from most programmers anyway. Interested students will have ample opportunity to program such "low level" tasks in subsequent courses that are concerned with *systems programming*.

Data Types and Declarations

So far, we have implicitly assumed that atomic data structures can hold any kind of data. This is not the case.

> ☐ Each variable must be of a particular *data type* and can only store data of that type. For our purposes there are four kinds of atomic data: *numbers*, *characters*, *booleans* and *pointers*.

These four are the basic data types. Later, we will see how to build other, more complex data types from these atomic types.

Numbers

Numbers include both integers and real numbers. For our purposes, a single number can be of any magnitude. Thus, the values *5.727198* and *2,319,384,732* are both single numbers. While some computer languages consider reals and integers to be different types, we will consider them to be of the same type, called *number* or (for brevity) *num*.

Characters

Characters are alphanumeric and special symbols (punctuation, etc.) written between quotation marks to distinguish them from variable names and numbers (i.e., "q," "x," "4," "&"). Unlike numbers, which can be of any magnitude, a simple character variable can hold only a single symbol. To store a multi-letter word would require multiple character variables. As you can imagine, requiring a separate variable for each character in a word would be very annoying. We'll see how to overcome this problem soon.

Note that the character "4" (in quotation marks) is viewed differently in an algorithm than the number *4*. The *character* "4" is a *numeral*, a character, just like "a." It has no numeric value and cannot be part of an arithmetic expression. The *number* 4 has numeric value and can be part of an arithmetic expression. Similarly, the character "+" is just a character while the symbol + is an arithmetic operator. For brevity, we often refer to the type *character* as *char* (pronounced either "care" or "char").

Booleans

Booleans are variables that have only a binary capability, i.e., they can store only two possible values, *true* or *false*. As with other atomic variables, a boolean variable can hold only one value at any given moment. With boolean variables, *true* is a single value (not a word of 4 characters) and so is *false*.

Pointers

Pointers are a bit different - they do not contain data of their own, but instead point to other variables which contain data. This is probably a new concept to many of you. If you are not familiar with pointers, you will soon discover that pointers are very powerful tools.

What does it mean when we say that a pointer "points to" other data values? The need for such a data structure may not be obvious when writing algorithms to be executed on paper. This is understandable, because the concept of pointers was developed as a tool for computer programming. Hence, the concept of pointers requires some explanation.

Computer memory is made up of many locations (generally millions), each of which can hold a piece of data. These locations are very similar to the cells to which we have referred, with one difference: in writing algorithms, we create our cells out of thin air by merely giving them a name, whereas the memory cells in a computer physically exist in the computer.

These memory cells are numbered sequentially. When the computer processor needs to access a memory cell, it refers to it by its number, or *address*. When an algorithm is written in a programming language for use on a computer, each variable identifier used in the algorithm is associated with the address of the memory cell which has been allocated for that variable. In modern programming languages, the programmer does not have to worry about any of this [9]. Facilities of the programming language environment keep track of the identifiers used by the programmer and automatically associates these with corresponding memory cell addresses.

Having said all that, we can now explain exactly what a pointer is. It is merely a cell which holds the address of another data cell. By looking at the value of the pointer, the computer finds out where in its memory to look for the data value "pointed to" by the *pointer*.

This is somewhat analogous to telephone "call forwarding" which allows us to change the location to which a phone call is directed. With call forwarding, we can call someone at their home number and our call can be *redirected* to another phone number. In effect, we can reach someone without knowing the phone number of their current location. This is what pointers do: they allow our algorithm to *change the location* to which an identifier refers.

Later, we will show the syntax used for accessing pointers and the data to which they point. For now, we use a pictorial method of showing what pointers do. In the drawing below, we have two variables, *Lucy* and *Desi* which are *pointer* variables (often abbreviated as *ptr*) which point to a *num* variable which holds the value *4*.

---

[9] This saves the programmer from worrying about "low level" details such as addresses and thus moves programming to a "higher" level of abstraction. Thus, modern programming languages which provide this kind of benefit are called "high level" languages: they allow programmers to (among other things) use the abstraction of *identifiers* without worrying about the actual memory address at which they are stored.

```
Lucy ──────▶ | 4 | ◀────── Desi
```

Thus, the algorithm can access the numeric value by referring to *Desi* or by referring to *Lucy*. If we were to assign the value *9* to the variable pointed to by *Desi*, we would also be changing the value to which *Lucy* points:

```
Lucy ──────▶ | 9 | ◀────── Desi
```

Later, if we reassigned the pointer variable *Desi* to point to a different *num* variable, one pointed to by *Ethel*, the algorithm could obtain the value stored in it by referring to either *Ethel* or *Desi*. Thus, at various points in time, *Desi* has not only referred to different *values*, but has also referred to different *cells*.

```
Lucy ──────▶ | 4 |        Desi ──────▶ | 7 | ◀────── Ethel
```

If a pointer is not currently pointing to another cell, we say that its value is *nil*, and we draw it as a blunted line. The value *nil* is not the same thing as "no value." Instead, it *is* a particular value which means "this pointer does not currently point to anything."

```
Fred ──────╫
```

The important idea here is that pointers do not themselves *hold* data values. Instead, they hold *addresses of other locations where data values may be found*, i.e., they allow our efforts to access data values to be "forwarded" to other locations. Pointers are the only kind of data structure that can do this.

☐   *Num, char* and *boolean* variables *always* refer to the same location, i.e., the algorithm can change the *value* stored in *num* or *char* or *boolean* variables, but cannot change the *location* to which they refer. *Pointers* allow us to create variables which can refer to *various locations*.

We will discuss the details of how pointers are used in Chapter 5.

Data declarations   When writing an algorithm, you may use many different variables of various types. It can be very confusing for a reader to know and remember which variable is used for what kind of data. Hence, for clarity, we include lines at the top of each algorithm stating what variable names will be used in the algorithm and what type of data they represent. These lines are called *variable declaration* lines, and they are preceded by the label var to indicate that variable declarations are to follow (see example below).

☐   Many (but not all) computer programming languages require that all variables be declared this way before they are used, and we shall adopt this convention. You must *declare* all your data structures before you use them.

For our purposes, variable declarations will be in the form:

```
<Identifier> isa <Type Name>
```

where the *Type Name* is number (*num*), character (*char*), boolean (*boolean*), or pointer (*ptr*). Observe that we simply concatenate the words "is" and "a" to create a single word, "isa." Example:

```
algorithm StoogeAverage
var
     Larry isa num
     Moe isa num
     Curley isa num
     Average isa num

begin
     read(Larry, Moe, Curley)
     Average <- (Larry + Moe + Curley)/3
     print ("The average for Larry, Moe, and Curley is" )
     print (Average)
end
```

While this algorithm is trivial, it shows the general structure of algorithm:

- First, a header line containing the "algorithm identifier," i.e., the name we choose for the algorithm.

- Then, the declaration of all the data structures.

- Finally, the algorithmic steps are specified, always indented between the words *begin* and *end* to remove any confusion about where the algorithm starts and stops.

☐   Note that the *declaration* of a variable only *creates* the variable. After being declared, each variable must be explicitly initialized to hold a value. Prior to initialization, a variable is considered to be "undefined." This means that we cannot assume that it is empty. Instead, we don't know what value might be in it, but whatever value it holds will be "garbage."

Constants   In addition to the four kinds of atomic variables, there is another kind of atomic data that may be declared: a *constant*. A constant does just what its name suggests: it stores a value that is *not* variable, a value that remains the same throughout the algorithm.

Like variables, constants must be declared before they are used. Whereas variables are declared after the label *var*, constants are declared after the label *const* (see example, below). In an algorithm, constant declarations should occur before variable declarations (the reason for this will become clear in a later chapter).

```
algorithm CircleFacts
const
    PI is 3.14159
var
    Area,
    Circumference,
    Radius  isa num
begin
    read(Radius)
    Area <- PI * radius * radius
    Circumference <- 2 * PI * radius
    print ("A circle with a radius of", Radius)
    print ("has an area of", Area,  "and a")
    print ("circumference of ", Circumference)
end
```

A constant declaration specifies the *value* of the identifier, not the type of data its value may be. Since the value of a constant will, by definition, not change, there is no point in specifying the type of data, only its fixed value. Thus, we use the form:

```
<Identifier> is <Value>
```

Literal values   For the most part, we write algorithms to make use of variables and constants. In most circumstances, it is preferable to use those constructs than it is to "hard wire" information into a program. However, there are occasions where it might be reasonable to build values into an algorithm. In such cases, the hard-wired information is known as a *literal*.

For example, often messages need to be written to the screen, prompting the user for information or supplying other information:

```
algorithm TodaysPay
var
    HoursWorked,
    HourlyRate,
    Pay isa num
begin
    print ("Enter the number of hours you worked today")
    read (HoursWorked)
    print ("Enter how much you make per hour")
    read(HourlyRate)
    Pay <- HourlyRate * HoursWorked
    print ("You earned ", Pay, "today.")
end
```

In this example, all the textual messages are neither variables nor constants. They have no identifier to symbolize them. They are *literal* values. Similarly, in the instruction below, the numbers 5 and 9 are literals.

```
ThisValue <- ThatValue - 5 + 9
```

About Identifier Names   Assigning identifiers to variables and constants gives us our most primitive tool for abstraction: it gives us a chance to *name* a variable in a way that is descriptive of what its value represents. For simple algorithms, you might not see the need for appropriate names and instead prefer to use nonsense names or cute ones. However, as soon as algorithms become complex or useful enough to be read by someone else, cute names become a bad idea. Thus, your identifiers should be descriptive of the data they hold. In other words, if you submit algorithms with identifiers such as "Lucy," "Desi," and "Ethel," you'd best have a good reason!

There are three conventions that we want you to follow concerning identifiers. You may find them annoying, but we will insist that you follow them simply because they make it easier to read and grade the algorithms you submit. With respect to identifiers, the rules are:

- Each identifier must consist of only alphabetic characters, numbers, and/or punctuation symbols. No spaces are allowed.

- Identifiers should be capitalized. Other words in the algorithm are not capitalized. This makes it easy to see which words are identifiers and which are not.

- The *first letter of each variable* identifier should be capitalized, and *all letters of each constant* identifier should be capitalized. This makes it easy to distinguish at a glance which identifiers refer to variables and which refer to constants.

- You may abbreviate words and concatenate them together. If you concatenate words together into a single identifier, capitalize the first letter of each original word, e.g., a variable that will be used to store the "Number of Hours" for which a student has registered might be given the identifier "NumHours" or "NumCreditHrs."

Conditions and Decisions

Look again at the flowchart of the class registration algorithm on page 39. It contains two kinds of instructions. The instructions placed in rectangles specify actions, such as adding a class to one's schedule. The instructions placed in diamonds indicate decision points. The results of those decisions determine the order in which the actions are to be carried out, when the algorithm finishes, etc.

The Basis of Decisions

All algorithmic decisions result in "true/false" (or "yes/no") answers. They are based on the evaluation of conditional expressions, such as:

```
"is the number of hours greater than or equal to 15?"
```

which might be expressed in an algorithm as:

```
NumOfHours >= 15
```

A conditional expression always evaluates to a boolean value, i.e., *true* or *false*. This is crucial, as there can never be any ambiguity: either the number of hours is "greater than or equal to 15" or it is not. The general syntax of such expressions is:

```
<Value>  <Relational Operator>  <Value>
```

In effect, two values are compared according to the *relational operator*. There are six relational operators:

- "greater than," denoted by >

- "greater than or equal to," denoted by >=

- "equal to," denoted by =

- "less than or equal to," denoted by <=

- "less than" denoted by <

- "not equal to," denoted by <>

To make a comparison we need two operand values, one on either side of the relational operator. Each of these can be either an *identifier* which has some value associated with it, *a literal value*, e.g., *15*, or an *expression*, e.g., (X+Y).

Acting on   Once the conditional expression has been evaluated, i.e., reduced to either a *true* or
Decisions   *false* value, a control structure can then determine what happens next. The simplest control structure is the "if-then-else" construct. its general form is shown below:

```
if (condition) then
     do A
     do B
else
     do C
     do D
     do E
endif
do F
do G
```

If the condition is *true*, A and B will be executed and C, D, and E will be skipped. If the condition is *false*, A and B will be skipped and C, D, and E will be executed. Thus, either A and B will be executed or C, D, and E will be. There is no way for all five to be executed in simple sequence.

Also, notice how important the `endif` is. The decision statement begins with "if" and continues through "endif." Regardless of the decision, *F* and *G* will be executed because they follow the *if-then-else* and are not a part of it.

A simple example utilizing the *if-then-else* construct:

```
algorithm PassFail
const
     Passing is 60
var
     Average isa num
     DidPass isa boolean
begin
     read(Average)

     if (Average < Passing) then
          DidPass <- false
     else
          DidPass <- true
     endif
```

```
        if (DidPass) then
             print("At least you passed.")
        else
             print("Geez, how could you fail?")
        endif
    end {PassFail}
```

The *else* part of the *if-then-else* construct is optional. A simple example:

```
    if (cash >= $.60) then
         buy a Coke
    endif
    go to class
```

Since there is no "else" clause, the result of the decision statement will either be that you had enough money, so you bought a Coke, or you didn't have enough money, so you didn't. Regardless of the result, the next instruction is executed. So, whether you have a Coke or not, you still have to go to class.

The Boolean Operators Sometimes a condition can be very complicated. It may contain many small decisions that join together to make one complex condition. Decisions are combined via the *boolean operators*: AND, OR, XOR, NOT.

For example, consider the condition in step 4 of the registration algorithm:

```
    if ((the class is not full) AND
         (it doesn't conflict with already scheduled
             classes)) then
```

This condition contains two parts, joined by the logical AND operator. This means that the condition is true *only if both parts are true*. If one or both parts are *false*, then the condition is *false* and steps 4a and 4b will be skipped over.

When two conditions are joined by the OR operator, the entire expression is *true* when *one or more of the subexpressions is true*. For example:

```
    if ((Today = Saturday) OR (Today= Holiday)) then
         go sailing
    else
         go to work
    endif
```

According to this decision statement, you go sailing if today is a Saturday or a holiday or both.

The XOR (*"exclusive or"*) resolves to *true* if exactly one of its operands is *true* and exactly one is *false*. It resolves to *false* if both operands are *true* or both are *false*. For example, if we pretend that $2 bills do not exist:

```
if (have a Five Dollar bill) XOR (have five Ones) then
     print ("You have exactly $5 in paper money")
else
     print ("You've got either more or less.")
endif
```

The NOT operator acts on a single expression instead of joining two expressions. When placed in front of an expression, it reverses the result of the logical test. For example:

```
if NOT(it is raining) then
     go to the park
else
     stay indoors
endif
```

Without the NOT, "go to the park" would be executed if the condition "it is raining" were true. But the NOT reverses this, so that you go to the park only if it is NOT raining.

One caveat about *if-then-else* instructions: a stumbling block for many people is in figuring out the right logical test, or condition, to make the algorithm do what you want it to do. In many cases you can use just one of the logic operations "AND," "OR," "NOT." But a combination of them may be needed to make complex conditions. Then it is easy to make mistakes, and those mistakes can be tricky to detect. It is imperative to be careful! Consider the following example:

Rita and Jim want to buy a house. The house must satisfy the following criteria: it must be in either Atlanta or Miami, cost no more than $120,000, and be in good shape. Construct a decision statement to make the decision for them.

```
if (((location = Atlanta) OR (location = Miami))
        AND (NOT(cost > $120,000) AND
            (condition = good))then
     buy the house
else
     keep looking
endif
```

Notice how important the parentheses are. Just as in mathematics, parentheses indicate the order in which the expressions are evaluated. The innermost expressions are always evaluated first. In this example, we first evaluate the expression ((location = Atlanta) OR (location = Miami)), and replace the expression with its value (*true* or *false*). We then evaluate the other expressions and replace them by their *boolean* values. The final result is obtained by ANDing the 3 *true/false* values. Since they are ANDed, all three of the values must be *true* for the condition to be satisfied.

Nested Decisions   *If-then-else* decision statements can also be "nested." For example, a possible algorithm for a baseball fan's reaction to the home team's performance:

```
if (pitching = good) then
    if (hitting = good) then
        relax
    else
        hope the other team issues walks & makes errors
    endif
else
    if (hitting = good) then
        hope for lots of homers
    else
        kiss it goodbye
    endif
endif
```

Again, the indentation and placement of the *if, else*, and *endif* keywords are crucial.

Food for Thought:

Algorithmically Stealing Bases and Racing Cars

The Computing Perspective implies that we should take an *algorithmic approach* to whatever problem-solving phenomena is at hand. That is, we should try to understand the things we do, the goals we have, and the means to attain those goals in algorithmic terms. This perspective says that we should be asking questions like "What are the algorithms that are implicit in what we do?", "How can we improve what we are doing by approaching our tasks in terms of algorithms?", and so on.

One the early 20th Century examples of algorithmic problem-solving is the work of Henry Ford. He not only revolutionized the automobile industry, he *created* it as an industry. Prior to Ford, cars were produced in a way more akin to the methods of

Middle Ages craftsmen than to what we would call modern industry. Each car was built individually, much like an artisan produces hand-crafted goods. Ford perfected the assembly line means of production. In doing so, he bridged the gap between the Mechanical Model and the Computational Model.

His assembly line reflected a maturation of the Mechanical Model, in that he developed and refined a means of production that *was itself* a machine. Each worker on the assembly line was, in effect, a cog in that machine: performing a specific function again and again.

In accomplishing this, however, Ford's insight implied the attributes of the Computational Model. How? By *abstracting* out the procedures necessary to efficiently accomplish the task. He saw the production process *as a process*, one to be optimized. And, he saw it as a process *with specific requirements*. In order to sell lots of cars, he needed buyers for lots of cars. So, he outraged other industrialists of the day by paying his workers outlandishly high salaries. Why? So they could afford to buy his cars!

Thus, Ford saw the problem at multiple levels of abstraction: from the *process* of production itself ("How can we create an efficient process for making cars?"), to the larger *requirements* of that process ("How can we create a large pool of buyers for our cars?").

Of course, there was nothing about what he did that could not have occurred earlier. Why didn't someone perfect the assembly line decades, even centuries earlier? Why didn't someone develop the "assembly line algorithm" to make covered wagons or muskets? While there were particular technical problems Ford had to overcome, there is no reason, in principle, that someone could not have done this long before Ford did. But they didn't. Why? Who knows? But observe that Ford's algorithmic conception doesn't emerge until *after* the advent of electronic media.

Throughout the 20th Century we can see numerous examples of the same phenomena: algorithmic approaches that *could* have occurred earlier.... but didn't. One example comes from stock car racing, which emerged in the American South after World War II. It grew out of the real-life racing that occurred during Prohibition between moonshine runners and government agents (Many of the early stock car driving stars "cut their teeth" on Appalachian mountain roads, escaping from the federal "Revenuers" who were in hot pursuit).

In the early 1960's, Henry Ford II tried to purchase the Italian sportscar maker Ferrari, but his offer was turned down. Outraged, he decreed that Ford should invade European racing and beat Enzo Ferrari at his own game. The result was the famous Ford GT40 race cars that dominated the previously invincible Ferrari team at the annual race at LeMans. The Fords won three years in a row before retiring from competition. Ford's strategy included using American racing teams and, as a result, the Europeans were left flabbergasted by a particular strength the Americans teams brought with them from their stock car racing background: the perfected "pit stop."

The race at LeMans is a 24-hour endurance race and involves numerous stops for fuel, tires, rested drivers, and whatever minor repairs might be necessary. While the European racers were not casual or lazy about their pit stops, they had never witnessed what they saw from the American teams. As a GT40 entered the pits, it was literally attacked by a swarm of mechanics and support personnel, each with his own particular job, each climbing over and around the car in a well choreographed frenetic ballet. While European cars would receive the same service, it might take several minutes. The GT40s were in and out in a matter of *seconds*. Furthermore, the Europeans were accustomed to major mechanical failures causing a car to withdraw from the race. They were shocked to see a GT40 coast into the pits with a bad transmission and, instead of being pushed to the back, be attacked by the mechanics. In less than 45 minutes, its transmission had been removed from the car, completely rebuilt on the spot, and reinstalled! It returned to the fray and finished the race.

Again, we see algorithmic thinking applied to what is, on the surface, a mechanical phenomena. True, the car is mechanical. But its efficient servicing is a *human* activity, one that the Americans had abstracted to the extreme: each human function and procedure was isolated from the others, assigned to specific agents, then collectively choreographed to maximize efficiency. As with Henry-the-elder's assembly line, the *human* activities benefited from careful analysis, decomposition, and encapsulation: exactly those things that are essential to algorithmic solutions. And, again, there is nothing about this approach that is dependent on any particular technology. Thus there is no reason why the Europeans could not have developed such solutions during the glory years of European racing in the 1930's. But they didn't. Why? Simply because it *did not occur to them*.

By the 1950's this way of thinking was emerging in American business, as "efficiency experts" roamed through many organizations trying to force optimization behavior on employees. Their lack of success was mainly due to the fact that they did not adequately appreciate the range of human factors involved. Unlike Ford's early assembly workers (who were overpaid according to standards of the time) and Ford's later LeMans mechanics (who were motivated by the competitive environment of racing), office workers had little motivation to optimize themselves for the

good of the gray-flannel organization. The efficiency experts of the '50s were naive about implementing algorithmic human solutions, but they were thinking in
those terms nonetheless.

Algorithmic problem-solving became evident in major league baseball by the
1970's. Earl Weaver, manager of the Baltimore Orioles, brought a computer into
the dugout but only after getting his algorithmic approach refined on index cards.
He carefully tracked each batter's performance against each pitcher, and vice versa,
until he was able to identify the best way to deploy each of his his players, situation
by situation. The result was a platoon system that turned a several mediocre, jour-
neymen players into a "virtual left fielder," a composite player who hit .300 with
38 homers and more than 130 rbi's. How? By decomposing each player's performance into component situational attributes, then recombining them as necessary to
optimize the result. His methods of charting performance are now routine throughout professional baseball.

Another algorithm-induced change in standard baseball practice concerns the "art"
of base stealing. Only a few decades ago, a base stealer was a unique talent, some-
body who had not only speed, but also "the knack." In recent years, base stealing
has become demystified. How? By decomposing the activity into its component
parts. Clock the time it takes each pitcher to go from his wind-up to getting the
ball into the catcher's mitt. Clock the time it takes each opposing catcher to throw
to 2nd base. Clock the time it takes each of your base runners to run from 1st base
to 2nd base. Compare. The decision to steal or not falls out of the equation. As a
result, most catchers are able to throw out far less than half of those who try to
steal. Why didn't teams take this approach in the 1950's, or the 1930's, or the
1890's? All you need is a stopwatch. Well, actually, you need more: you need
"the right way of thinking."

The fact is that *all* of these developments, and many more, *could* have occurred
many years before they actually *did*. They were not dependent on any particular
technology. They were dependent upon a given mental approach, a certain way of
thinking: "process thinking" or "algorithmic thinking."

Of course, none of the people we've mentioned here necessarily *knew* that they
were thinking algorithmically. In all probability, they never even *heard* the word.
But they *were* thinking algorithmically nonetheless, bringing new ideas into daily
practice.

History may well judge the 20th Century to be the time when *algorithmic thinking*
arrived in everyday life.

Summary

The elemental building blocks of algorithms include:

- atomic data types: *numbers, characters, booleans* and *pointers*

- *constants* (to refer to fixed atomic data values by meaningful names)

- *literals* (to "hardwire" textual messages into an algorithm)

- basic operations, including:

  arithmetic (+, -, *, /, DIV, MOD),

  relational, (>, >=, =, <=, <, <>) and

  boolean (AND, OR, XOR, NOT)

- *conditional expressions* which allow algorithms to make *true/false* decisions

- *control structures*, such as the *if-then-else* construct, which allow algorithms to act on their decisions

These are the basic "low level" tools. In subsequent chapters, we will discuss how to use these tools to create effective "higher level" abstractions.

Exercises   3.1. What's the difference between *types* and *variables*?

For problems 3.2- 3.4, give the full variable declaration.

3.2. A variable that keeps track of the number of students assigned to a class.

3.3. A variable that keeps track of a student's grade. Possible values are letters *A, B, C, D*, and *F*.

3.4. A variable that is either *true* or *false* depending on whether the class is a graduate level class or not.

For problems 3.5, 3.6, and 3.7, you may assume that the identifiers all represent variables of the appropriate type.

3.5. What happens as a result of:

```
X <- 5 * 4 - 8 / 2
```

3.6. What happens as a result of:

```
Y <- 5 * ((4 - 8) / 2)
```

3.7. What happens as a result of:

```
if ((3+7) * (20-4) > (5 + 20 * J)) then
     print("Yippee")
endif
```

3.8. Write an algorithm that will read in three numbers from the user and print out the greatest of the three numbers.

3.9. Write an algorithm that will read in two boolean variables and then print "true" if either parameter is *true* or "false" if they are both *true* or both *false*.

3.10. Write an algorithm (in plain English) to describe the process of making a peanut-butter and jelly sandwich. Assume that you are writing this algorithm for someone who has never eaten a sandwich before. Be sure and go into enough detail (e.g., don't just say, "put jelly on bread" - this could mean put the jelly jar on top of the loaf of bread!).

3.11 Write a decision statement and that stores a boolean value in the variable ShouldDivorce. The decision statement should represent your opinion about whether or not a troubled married couple should divorce. Factors might include love, religious beliefs, trust, faith, respect, safety, children, economics, or anything else you think is relevant.

3.12. How would you approach the problem of "teaching effectiveness" from an algorithmic standpoint? In particular, how would you ascertain which topics a given teacher taught well and which he taught poorly? And how would you determine what aspects of a teacher's "teaching style" were effective and which were not? How would you gather this information in a way that could be actually used to help the teacher improve? (We don't want reams of information to be gathered if it's just going to sit in a file cabinet and collect dust!)

Chapter 4: Tools for "Procedural Abstraction"

The algorithms we've been looking at have been quite simple, as we have been illustrating basic features of algorithms and thus we have needed only simplistic examples. However, most algorithms are written to solve complicated problems which can be broken down into subtasks. If an algorithm involves a complicated subtask or subtasks that are used in different places in the algorithm, it is best to write an individual algorithm for that particular subtask. When the main algorithm needs to do the subtask, it calls the mini-algorithm, or *subprogram*, to execute. The subprogram then "does its thing," and returns control to the main algorithm when it is finished.

Each subprogram is a building block, or *module*, which we can use to construct the larrger algorithm. Like the main algorithm, each module may contain both data declarations and instructions.

By doing this properly, we create "procedural abstraction." Recall that abstraction means, "the *expression of a quality apart from any specific embodiment.*" This is what we do via *modular design*: we give a name to a module that describes its purpose and we hide the procedural details of how it carries out that purpose inside that module. Thereafter, we simply refer to the module identifier and obtain the benefits of that module's work without being concerned with the "specific embodiment" of how it goes about its business. This allows us to change the internal details of the module, e.g., from one problem-solving approach to another, in a way that is invisible to those who use that module. Thus, the "specific embodiment" (of the module's implementation) is "apart" (i.e., *decoupled*) from how we "express" (i.e., use) the module. *This is a crucial aspect of good algorithm design.*

> ☐ Algorithms which feature good *procedural abstraction* will evidence a high degree of "modularity." They will feature a number of relatively independent modules which together solve the task at hand. The main algorithm serves to organize and coordinate the various modules, while each module takes care of exactly one logical task. Thus, there will be one main algorithm and as many modules as required, one for each subtask.

Such a modular design creates a "hierarchy of abstraction." At the top level is the main algorithm. It coordinates the overriding logic, the main subtasks, or "logical chunks," of the algorithm. Below it are the various modules, each of which is responsible for of one of those "chunks." Depending upon the complexity of each subtask, those modules may themselves call other modules at the next lower level, and so on.

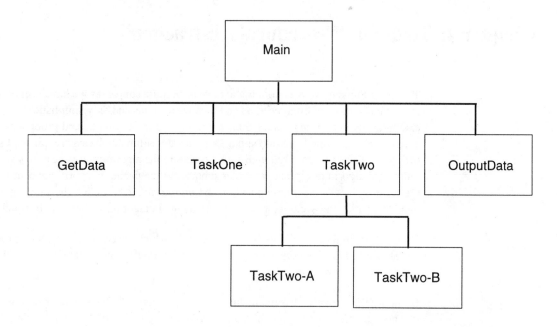

Judging from this diagram, we would expect that Main will primarily consists of instructions calling those modules in the level immediately below it, and will contain relatively few instructions that directly manipulate data (perhaps those needed to initialize variables, etc.). Its work is delegated to those at the level below, and its job is to control and coordinate. According to the diagram, we would expect that Get-Data, TaskOne, and OutputData are all relatively simple and straightforward tasks, as they evidently required no submodules. TaskTwo appears to be more complex, as it has two subordinate modules.

Why modularity? Good modularity in an algorithm accomplishes four things:

1) It *makes the algorithm easier to write*, because we can focus on simple subtasks rather than diving into a complicated problem all at once. In effect, we "chip away" at a problem, solving little bits and pieces at a time, until we find that we've solved the whole thing.

2) It *facilitates the reader's understanding* by breaking the algorithm into readable, more understandable chunks.

3) It *raises the level of procedural abstraction* of the algorithm because annoying details are "hidden" inside modules. By hiding the specific little details of a given logical step in a module, we can consider the larger, more fundamental steps of the algorithm without "getting lost in the details." Then, if we are concerned that the details are not done properly, we know exactly where to look for them.

4) It *saves time, space, and effort* because once a module is written it can be called from many different places in an algorithm.

For example, imagine you have an algorithm that needed to calculate the square root of three different numbers. You could insert steps into the main algorithm to calculate each square root individually, but this would be tedious, time consuming, and error prone. It would be much more efficient to write one module *SquareRoot*, then "call" it once for each number whose square root you need.

By writing the `SquareRoot` algorithm only once, you:

- minimize the number of error possibilities,

- save yourself the effort of duplicating groups of instructions needlessly,

- keep your algorithm smaller, and

- give yourself a module that you can use in future algorithms that might need it.

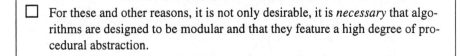

For these and other reasons, it is not only desirable, it is *necessary* that algorithms are designed to be modular and that they feature a high degree of procedural abstraction.

In fact, an algorithm which proved to be perfectly correct but which "glopped" all the small details together into just one large collection of steps would be considered far *less* valuable than a highly modular one which contained major errors!

Two Kinds of Modules.

There are two particular kinds of modules: *procedures* and *functions*. Each module *must* be of one of these two kinds as determined by the kind of tasks it performs.

☐ A *function* resolves to a single value (like a mathematical function). It may not produce muiltiple values, and may not read input or print output.

☐ A *procedure* is a kind of module that is used for varied tasks. It may produce any number of values, and is permitted to have effects on the world outside of itself (such as changing the values of variables of other modules, reading input, and printing output).

These differences allow us to tell ahead of time whether a given task should be implemented as a function or a procedure before we are faced with actually writing it. For example, if we require a module that will calculate the square root of some number, we can see that it should be a function, as it produces a single value. In contrast, a module that determines both the minimum and maximum values found in a list of numbers would have to be a procedure, as it produces multiple values. Similary, a GetData and OutputData modules would have to be procedures because they comminucate with the world outside the algorithm.

Exercises.   For each of the following task desriptions, specify whether the appropriate module should be a *function* or a *procedure*.

4.1.   Reading in 4 pieces of data from the user.

4.2.   Reading in one piece of data from the user.

4.3.   Determining the smallest of several values.

4.4.   Determing the average of several values.

4.5.   Determining whether or not two values are equal.

4.6.   Returning two values such that they are sorted in ascending order.

4.7.   Returning the largest two of serveral values.

4.8.   Deciding whether the value of a given *char* variable is a vowel or a consonant.

4.9.   Determiningthe winner in a contest

4.10.   Determining the winner and the runner up in a contest.

4.11.   Printing the results of a contest.

4.12. Deciding whether to quit or try again.

***Differences in
how they are used***
Not only are functions and proceduresdifferent in what they are allowed to do, they are also different with respect to how they are used.

> ☐ A function is used as an *expression*.
> A procedure is used as a *stand-alone instruction*.

For example, consider the code:

```
begin
    GetData
    ThisVar <- SomeFunction
    SomeProcedure
    ThatVar <- ThisVar + SomeOtherFunction
    AnotherProcedure
    OutputData
end
```

In this "nonsense code," there are four procedure calls: to `GetData`, to `SomePro-cedure`, to `AnotherProcedure`, and to `OutputData`. There are also two function calls: to `SomeFunction` and to `SomeOtherFunction`.

Notice the different usage. A function call is used as an expression, i.e., in places where we might have used particular values. A procedure call is used as a stand-alone instruction. This difference in usage follows logically from the differences in what the two kinds of modules are allowed to do.

Procedures may do all manner of things, and thus we use a procedure call like an in-struction that is shorthand for whatever set of instructions might be contained in the procedure. On the other hand, function calls (like those to mathematical functions) *resolve to a single value*, i.e., they *become* whatever particular value is determined by the calculation they perform. For example, imagine that `SomeFunction` resolves to the value *4*. For the use of this function to accomplish anything, we must *some-how use the value it produces*. In this case we have assigned its value to the variable `ThisVar`. Thus, unlike procedure calls, function calls assume that a single value is returned and, further, that it is returned by the function call itself *becoming* that value.

> ☐ Warning! A typical novice mistake...

Often, students who have no experience with these things make the mistake of calling a function as if it were a procedure. For example,

```
begin
    GetData
    SomeFunction
    SomeProcedure
    OutputData
end
```

In the "nonsense code" above, we have called the function named SomeFunction as if it were a procedure. What is the consequence of this? Imagine that SomeFunction resolves to the value *4*. Using SomeFunction in the way we have shown, above, is equivalent to using the value *4* as a line of code!

> ☐ To use functions correctly, it is necessary to use them *as if* they are a particular value, i.e., as an expression. This is because functions *resolve* to a particular value, i.e., they *become* the value that they calculate. Thus, function call must be used as if they were values.

The Scope of Data

Like the main algorithm, each module may contain its own variables. This fact raises certain questions. If a variable is declared in the main algorithm, can that data be accessed by the various modules which that algorithm calls? If a variable is declared inside a module, can that data be accessed by other modules? By the main algorithm? These questions concern the "scope of data."

> ☐ By "scope of data" we mean "the part or parts of an algorithm that can access a declared data structure."

Various programming languages follow a variety of conventions about this. In some older languages, all data is "global," i.e., every module can access all the data. Experience has shown that this causes many problems. One of them is the problem of *data integrity*: how can we be sure exactly what information is represented by the value of a variable? Data integrity problems arise when variables are "written to" by different modules in an unpredictable way. The problem of data integrity is just another way of saying "we're not sure what a given data value really represents."

As a result of this and other problems, modern languages tend to limit the scope of data. Even when working in a language that does not, good programming technique generally requires that the program be written as if data scope is limited.

> ☐ For our purposes, we will limit the scope of data. To do this, we follow a very simple rule: *The scope of each named variable is limited to the part of the algorithm in which it is declared.*

This means that any named variable can be accessed *only* by instructions in the "begin...end" block which immediately follow its declaration. For named variables declared within a module, the scope is limited to that module. For each named variable declared in the main algorithm, scope is limited to the main algorithm. Thus, variables declared in the main algorithm cannot be accessed by any of the modules, and variables declared in a given module cannot be accessed by either the main algorithm or by other modules. This rule applies to all named variables.

In effect, then, it is as if each module is its own separate algorithm: it uses its own data structures, not those from any other module. Thus, we can rest assured that other modules outside of the scope of that variable cannot "see" it and thus cannot modify it.

This limitation provides several benefits. Chief among them is that, if we become puzzled about how a particular value might have been assigned to that variable, we know where to look: the statements inside its scope.

Parameters

Of course, if we restrict the scope of data in this way, we must have some way for the various modules to communicate with one another, to pass data back and forth as required by the problem. For example, if a *SquareRoot* function is written only once and is then used many times to calculat e the square root of many different numbers, there must be a way of "sending" a value to that function each time it is called so that it knows to take the square root of the appropriate number. Communication between modules is accomplished by the use *parameters*.

Parameters are a special kind of variable which allows values to be passed between the main algorithm and its modules and/or between the various modules themselves.

> ☐ Parameters are similar to other named variables, with one difference: they can send data to or from other modules. They are used *only* when it is necessary to pass information between modules.

Logically, there are three kinds of parameters:

- *Input parameters* allow values to be passed into a module by the calling algorithm. The calling algorithm gives *a copy* of one of its data values to the called module. Such data values may be variables or literals.

- *Output parameters* allow values to be passed from the called module back to a variable in the calling algorithm. The calling algorithm gives the module access to write to one of its variables for purposes of sending its results back, but does not allow that module to see what value was originally stored in that variable.

- *Input/output parameters* allow both *in* and *out* communication. An *in/out* parameter allows values from the calling algorithm to be accessed (i.e., to be read) and modified (i.e., to be written) by the called module.

Procedures may use any combination of these three kinds of parameters. Functions, however, may only have input paramters. This limiation is because finctions may only return a single value, and they do that by resolving to that value; thus there is no legal reason for them to send data back via an out or in/out parameter.

How parameters are specified   When the calling algorithm calls a module by using the module's identifier, followed by any parameters that the module needs. The parameters are given in parentheses. An example of this format is:

```
begin
    ThisVar <- Cube(3)
    ThatVar <- Cube(5)
    OutputData(ThisVar)
    OutputData(ThatVar)
end
```

The first instruction calls the Cube function, passes it the value *3*, then stores the result (*27*) in the variable ThisVar. The second instruction calls the same function, this time passes it the value *5*, and stores the result (*125*) in ThatVar. The third and fourth instructions each call procedure OutputData twice, passing the value of ThisVar the first time and ThatVar the second time.

***Defining* functions *and* procedures**   Of course, the modules must have been written so that they are expecting to receive this information. How do we do this? The *header line* of the module includes both the identifier for the module itself and a specification for all the parameters which the module expects. In this case, each module expectsonly one parameter. In each case, the parameter should be an *in* parameter, as the modules have no need to change the value stored in either of them. Thus, we define these two modules as:

```
function Cube isa num (InValue isa in num)
{purpose: returns the value of InValue raised to
         the 3rd power}
begin
    Cube returns (InValue * InValue * InValue)
end {function Cube}
```

and

```
procedure OutputData (ValueToBePrinted isa in num)
{purpose: prints out the value of ValueToBePrinted with
    an appropriate text message}
begin
    print ("The value is", ValueToBePrinted)
end {procedure OutputValue}
```

As we can see from these examples, the general format for declaring functions and procedures are very similar, but they are *not* identical.

The *similarities* between function and procedure declarations are:

1. The header line of both functions and procedures must specify the kind of module (function or procedure), the identifier of the module (in this case, *Cube* and *OutputValue*), and the appropriate parameters. (In our example each module requires only a single *in* parameter, but any number of parameters are permitted.)

2. Both functions and procedures require a purpose comment which spells out for human readers what the module does.

3. The body of both functions and procedures include as many instructions as required to do their job, all within a `begin ... end` block. (Because our examples are so trivial, only a single line is required for each one.)

4. While not shown above, both functions and procedures may declare their own local constants and variables in the same way that the main algorithm can, i.e., immediately before the `begin...end` block of instructions.

@BODY W/PRE BK = The *differences* between function and procedure declarations are that functions require two things that procedures do not:

1. The header line of a function must include the specification of the *type of data that the function will return*. Thus, the header line of `function Cube` specifies that it will resolve to a *number* value. Procedures do not include such a specification, as they do not resolve to any particular value.

2. The body of function must include an instruction of the form:

```
<ThisFunctionName> returns <SomeValue>
```

which is how the result of the function is determined. Thus, the body of function Cube includes the line:

```
Cube returns (InValue * InValue * InValue)
```

Procedures do not include any such "*returns*" instruction, as they do not resolve to any particular value.

For each parameter variable, we specify its identifier (in our examples, InValue and ValueToBePrinted), then declare both the *type of parameter* (*in, out*, or *in/out*) and the *type of data* it will hold (in this case *num*). (In the example above, we have declared the both parameters to be input parameters that will store numbers.) The module can use its parameter variables in its internal calculations just as if they were declared in the "normal" way.

> ☐ The specification of a parameter in the header line of a module serves as the declaration of that parameter variable. No other declaration is needed or allowed for that identifier.

Once we declare a parameter vaariable to have a given identfier (e.g., InValue and ValueToBePrinted) as, we *need not* and *cannot* use that identifier to declare another variable in the *var* section of the module. We *need not* redeclare InValue because we have *already* declared it as a parameter variable in the module's header line. We *cannot* redeclare it within the module as that would be tantamount to declaring *two different variables* with the same name in the same scope. Declaring multiple uses of an identifier within the same scope is illegal due to the resulting ambiguity about the meaning of the identifier.

Input Parameters   Input parameters are used to send information to the module. If the Cube function is called via:

```
Cube(3)
```

then as the Cube function begins to execute, its parameter variable InValue will be assigned the value *3*. The parameter variable InValue is then used within the function just as if it were a normal variable. The only difference between it and a "normal" variable is that the initial value of InValue was obtained from the calling algorithm via parameter passing.

We can also call our `Cube` module by passing a variable as a parameter, i.e., `Cube(SomeNumVar)` instead of `Cube(3)`. Since `InValue` is an *input* parameter, the calling algorithm sends *a copy* of whatever value is stored in its variable `SomeNumVar` to the `Cube` module. The `Cube` module receives this copy of the original value and stores it in its own variable `InValue`. The module can then do whatever it wants to the value `InValue` without affecting the original value of `SomeNumVar`. This is because `SomeNumVar` belongs to the calling algorithm and, according to our scope rule, the `Cube` module cannot access `SomeNumVar`. Instead, the `Cube` module has received *a copy* of the original value. It can manipulate its copy (`InValue`) but has no way to modify the original copy in `SomeNumVar`.

> ☐ An important feature of *in* parameters is that they allow a module to manipulate a copy of data that "belongs" to another part of the algorithm without any risk of that data being contaminated, i.e., the module that receives an *in* parameter can manipulate its copy but cannot change the value of the original. This security advantage means that *in* parameters should be used whenever they are sufficient, i.e., make *all* parameters *in* parameters unless there is a good reason *requiriing* a parameter to be *out* or *in/out*.

Output Parameters In the function `Cube` example, we assumed that the module would receive a value, calculate its cube, then resolve to the result. There was no need to *send* any data back to calling algorithm, because the function call itself *became* that value. However, procedures may produce more than one value and then must somehow send those values back to the calling algorithm. To accomplish this, procedures can use *output* parameters to pass data the other way.

Output parameters only pass "result data" from the called procedure to the calling algorithm. Consider an example that requires result values to be "sent back":

```
procedure MinMax (A, B, C isa in num,
                  Min, Max isa out num)

{Purpose: accepts three num values, identifies and
    returns the smallest and largest of those three}

begin
    if ((A >= B) AND (A >= C)) then
        Max <- A
    else
        if ((B >= A) AND (B >= C)) then
            Max <- B
```

```
        else
              Max <- C
        endif
    endif
    if ((A <= B) AND (A <= C)) then
        Min <- A
    else
        if ((B <= A) AND (B <= C)) then
              Min <- B
        else
              Min <- C
        endif
    endif
end {procedure MinMax}
```

This procedure accepts three numbers as input and determines which of those three is the largest and which is the smallest. (Is there anything wrong with the algorithm as it is written?) The module itself is declared to have a total of five parameters, all of which are of type *num*: A, B, and C are *input* parameters, and Min and Max are *output* parameters. The module will receive the three data values it requires via the three input parameters, will do its calculation, and will store the results into the two output parameters.

This module might be called via:

```
    MinMax(X, Y, Z, Little, Big)
```

When multiple parameters are passed, the identifiers in the two parameters lists are matched up by their position in the lists (first with first, second with second, etc.). Thus, in our MinMax example X, Y, and Z will send copies of the three original data values *in* to the MinMax module, where they will be received as the A, B, and C, respectively. When the module finishes, the variables Little and Big will receive the appropriate results from the procedure's Min and Max, respectively.

Note that the original values of X, Y, and Z are important, as they provide the original values which MinMax module will use in its calculation. In contrast, the original values of Little and Big don't matter at all. They correspond to the the *output parameters* of the module and thus do not send any data to the module; their initial values are irrelevant. Since the module will send its results back to the calling algorithm via these variables, their original contents will be "written over," i.e., replaced by the module's results.

Output parameters are different than *input* parameters in another respect: the means of communication. Recall that input parameters receive a *copy* of the original value which it can manipulate without affecting the original. In contrast, *output* parameters *do directly manipulate* the original variable. When a variable is passed as an *output* parameter, the called module learns *where* the original variables is. The called module cannot see what the original value is, but whenever it assigns a value to an *output* parameter variable, it is *really replacing the value stored in the original.*

For example, our `MinMax` module cannot discover the original values of `Little` and `Big`, but whenever it assigns a value to `Min`, *that value is actually stored in* `Little`. Similarly, any assignment to `Max` results in the new value being stored in `Big`. In effect, `Min` and `Max` become pseudonyms within the `MinMax` module which really refer to `Little` and `Big`, respectively. `MinMax` is prevented only from seeing the *original* values of `Little` and `Big`. Once it writes values to `Min` or `Max`, it can later refer to those values, modify them further, etc. It is only the *original* values which are invisible to `MinMax`.

Regardless, the *identifiers* `Little` and `Big` are meaningless within `MinMax`. `MinMax` can only refer to the values stored in `Little` and `Big` via the identifiers `Min` and `Max`, respectively. And it can only see what values are in `Min` (*aka* `Little`) and `Max` (*aka* `Big`) *after* it has assigned them values.

Parameter Lists   This example is the first one involving multiple parameters in a parameter list. There are a few particular features of parameter lists which must be noted.

> ☐ The *"formal parameter list"* is the list of parameters that is specified in the definition of the module. This is where the data type (`char`, `num`, etc.) and the kind (*in, out,* or *in/out*) of each parameter is specified.
>
> The *"actual parameter list"* is the list of parameters that is passed to the module whenever the module is called. This is where the actual variables or values to be passed to the module are specified.

Four rules govern the relationship between *actual* and *formal* parameter lists:

> ☐ 1. The number of parameters in the *actual* and *formal* parameter lists must be consistent.

Observe that there are the same number of parameters in the call to `MinMax` as their are parameters declared in the procedure itself. This is absolutely necessary.

In this case, the *actual parameter list* is:

```
(X, Y, Z, Little, Big)
```

and the *formal parameter list* is:

```
(A, B, C isa in num, Min, Max isa out num)
```

The number of parameters in the two list must be the same, i.e., if the formal parameter list "expects" five parameters, the actual parameter list *must* include exactly five parameters, no more, no less.

□   2. Actual parameters are associated with formal parameters based on their position in the the parameter list.

In this case:

- the first *actual parameter* (X) is received as the first *formal parameter* (A)

- the second *actual parameter* (Y) is received as the second *formal parameter* (B)

- the third *actual parameter* (Z) is received as the third *formal parameter* (C)

- the fourth *actual parameter* (Little) is received as the fourth *formal parameter* (Min)

- the fifth *actual parameter* (Big) is received as the fifth *formal parameter* (Max)

Notice that listing the actual parameters in the wrong order leads to error. For example, the calling algorithm presumably wants the largest value of the three to be returned into the variable Big and the smallest of the three to be returned into the variable Little. This is exactly what happen given the actual parameter list we have used. However, if Big and Little were reversed in the actual parameter list, then the Max value would be returned as Little and the Min value would be returned as Big.

□   3. Actual and formal parameters must be of the same type.

In the *formal parameter list*, each parameter is declared to be of a given data type. The corresponding *actual parameter* must be of the same type. In this case, all five formal parameters were of type *num*, so all of the actual parameters had to be of type *num* as well.

□   4. The only time that an actual parameter can be a *literal* or *constant* (rather than a *variable*) is if it is associated with a formal *input* parameter.

This is because *output* (and, as we shall see, *input/output*) parameters require a variable to which they can send results.

```
function IsEven isa boolean (TheNum isa in num)
        {Purpose: returns True if TheNum is EVEN, else False}

begin
    if ((TheNum MOD 2) = 0) then
        IsEven returns true
    else
        IsEven returns false
    endif
end {function IsEven}
```

```
function IsOdd isa boolean (TheNum isa in num)
    {Purpose: returns True if TheNum is ODD, else False}

begin
    IsOdd returns (NOT(IsEven(TheNum))
end {function IsEven}
```

```
function CalcSalesTax isa num (SalePrice, TaxRate isa
                                  in num)
    {Purpose: calculates the sales tax for a given price.

begin
    WholeDollars <- Price DIV 1
    Change <- Price MOD 1
    if (Change MOD TaxRate = 0) then
        Clip <- 0
    else
        Clip <- 1
    endif
    Step <- (Change DIV TaxRate) + Clip
    CalcSalesTax returns (WholeDollars * TaxRate) + Step
end {function }
```

```
function IsVowel isa boolean (ThisChar isa in char)
    {Purpose: returns True IFF ThisChar isa Vowel}
begin
    if (ThisChar = 'A') then
            IsVowel returns true
    elseif (ThisChar = 'E') then
            IsVowel returns true
    elseif (ThisChar = 'I') then
            IsVowel returns true
    elseif (ThisChar = 'O') then
            IsVowel returns true
    elseif (ThisChar = 'U') then
            IsVowel returns true
    else
            IsVowel returns false
    endif
end {function IsVowel}
```

Examples of
procedures

```
procedure GetThreeNums (Num1, Num2, Num3 isa out num)
    {Purpose: obtains three fum values from the user}

begin
    print ('Please input a number value')
    read (Num1)

    print ('Please input a 2nd number value')
    read (Num2)

    print ('Please input a 3rd number value')
    read (Num3)
end {procedure GetThreeNums}
```

```
procedure HighestTwoOfThree (NumOne,NumTwo, NumThree
            isa in num, HighOne, SecondOne isa out num)
    (Purpose:identify largest and second largest
            of 3 unequal number values.}
```

```
begin
    if ((NumOne < NumTwo) AND (NumOne < NumThree)) then
        {NumOne is lowest, so rank NumTwo and NumThree}
        if (NumTwo > NumThree) then
            HighOne <- NumTwo
            SecondOne <- NumThree
        else
            HighOne <- NumThree
            SecondOne <- NumTwo
        endif
    else
        if ((NumTwo < NumOne) AND (NumTwo < NumThree)) then
            {NumTwo is lowest, so rank NumOne and NumThree}
            if (NumOne > NumThree) then
                HighOne <- NumOne
                SecondOne <- NumThree
            else
                HighOne <- NumThree
                SecondOne <- NumOne
            endif
        else {NumThree is lowest, so rank NumOne and NumTwo}
            if (NumOne > NumTwo) then
                HighOne <- NumOne
                SecondOne <- NumTwo
            else
                HighOne <- NumTwo
                SecondOne <- NumOne
            endif
        endif
    endif
end {procedure HighestTwoOfThree}
```

Exercises.   For each of the following, write a module to carry out the indicated task. Each module must be either a procedure or a function as implied by the problem. All parameters should be *in* or *out* parameters as apprpriate to the task.

4.13.   Reading in four pieces of numerical data from the user for use elsewhere in the algorithm.

4.14.   Reading in one piece of numerical data from the user for use elsewhere in the algorithm.

4.15.   Determining the smallest of four numerical values and returning that value.

4.16.   Determing the average of four numerical values and returning that value.

4.17.   Determining whether or not two char values are identical and returning the answer.

4.18.   Returning three numerical values such that they are sorted in ascending order.

4.19.   Returning the largest two of three char values.

4.20.   Deciding whether the value of a given *char* variable is a consonant and returning that value.

4.21.   Determining and returning the winning (high) score of a contest with five contestants.

4.22.   Determining and returning both the winner and the runner up scores in such a contest.

4.23.   Printing the results of that contest showing all five scores.

Input/Output Parameters   *Input/Output* parameters provide two-way communication. They are useful when the calling algorithm wants to send values to a module, have those values transformed, and get the results back. For example, imagine that a calling algorithm wants two numbers to be sorted so that the larger number is first. This might be done via:

```
procedure SortTwoNums (A, B isa in/out num,
                            IsaTie isa out boolean)
{receive two values, returns them in sorted order;
 IFF the values are equal, then IsaTie is true }

var
    Temp isa num
begin
    if (A = B) then
        IsaTie <- true
    else
        IsaTie <- false
        if (B > A) then
            Temp <- A
            A <- B
            B <- Temp
        endif
    endif
end {procedure SortTwoNums}
```

This module will see if the two numbers are out of order. If so, it will swap them. If they are lready in order, they will not be swapped. The end result is that A will hold the larger value and B will hold the smaller value. If they are equal, the boolean will return *true*, if not it will return *false*. If this module was called via:

```
SortTwoNums(X,Y,AreEqual)
```

then the values of X and Y would be sent to the SortTwoNums module, along with the boolean variable AreEqual. Regardless of whether or not they were originally in order, after SortTwoNums executed its steps the larger value will be stored in X and the smaller value in Y, and the AreEqual boolean will indicate if the two values are equal. The first two parameters are *in/out* while the third one is an *out* parameter.

With *in/out* parameters, communication is accomplished in a way similar to the way *output* parameters work: the called module "gets access" to the variables that are passed as parameters. In our SortTwoNums examples, the identifier A is the name within SortTwoNums that refers to the variable known as X to the calling algorithm, and B is the local name for variable Y, just as IsaTie refers to AreEqual.

In fact, the only difference between *output* parameters and *in/out* parameters is that *output* parameters cannot see the *original* values of the variables passed by the calling procedure; *in/out* parameters are free from this restriction: they can see the original and they can modify it. Thus, anytime a variable is passed by the calling algorithm as an *in/out* parameter, the calling algorithm is giving the called module complete access to one of its variables. For this reason, one should not use *in/out* parameters (or *output* parameters) indiscriminantly. They should be used only as needed by the particular requirements of the algorithmic task at hand.

Exercises   4.24. Describe each: "in," "in/out," and "out" parameters and when each should be used.

4.25. What is the difference between actual and formal parameters?

4.26. In the following algorithm, which variables are actual parameters and which are formal parameters?

```
algorithm Calculate_Product

var
     Height1,
     Height2,
     Height3,
     HeightProduct isa num
```

```
{*****************************************}

function MultiplyThree (Num1, Num2, Num3 isa in num)
{ Purpose: takes in three parameters and returns their
      product }
begin
    MutlipleThree returns (Num1 * Num2 * Num3)
end {module Multiply}

{*****************************************}

begin { main }
    Height1 <- 45
    Height2 <- 60
    Height3 <- 49
    HeightProduct <- MultiplyThree(Height1, Height2,
                      Height3)
    print(HeightProduct)
end {Calculate Product}

{*****************************************}
```

For problems 4.4., 4.5., and 4.6., specify whether each parameter should be *in*, *in/out*, or *out*.

4.27.   procedure GetInput (Num1 isa _____ num,
                              Num2 isa _____ num)
                  {Purpose: reads in the two numbers for use
                      by other modules}

4.28.   function Equal isa boolean (Num1 isa _____ num,
                                  Num2 isa _____ num)
                  {Purpose: returns "true" if the two numbers
                      are equal}

4.29.   procedure Increment (Number isa _____ num,
                                  Increment_Value isa _____ num)
                  {Purpose: increments the value of the first
                      parameter by the value of the second one}

4.30. Implement the contents (declarations, if any, and instructions) for the procedure of
      problem 4.4.

4.31. Implement the contents (declarations, if any, and instructions) for the function of problem 4.5.

4.32. Implement the contents (declarations, if any, and instructions) for the procedure of problem 4.6.

4.33. Write an algorithm that uses the modules from problems 4.4 through 4.9 that will do the following: obtain four values from input, determine if any two or more or them are equal, then print out how many of them are (0, 2, 3, or all 4). Your algorithm should consist of whatever variable declarations are needed, along with assignment statements and calls to the relevant modules. Your algorithm should *not* perform any task that the modules can do for it.

4.34. What is wrong with the use of data in the nonsense algorithm, below? (Assume that the modules not provided exist and are correct. Look for multiple problem areas.)

```
algorithm DooWop
var
      ThisVar,
      ThatVar,
      OtherVar isa num

begin
      GetData(ThisVar, ThatVar, OtherVar)
      ShoobieDoo(ThisVar, ThatVar, OtherVar)
      OutputData(ThisVar, ThatVar, OtherVar)
end {DooWop}

procedure ShoobieDoo (A, B, C isa in/out num)
begin
      ThisVar <- ThatVar + OtherVar
end {ShoobieDoo}
```

For problems 4.12 and 4.13, perform a high level design for the specified tasks. By high level design, we mean: show the main algorithm in detail and show the header lines (*including formal parameters*) and *Purpose* comments for each module that the main algorithm uses. *Do not implement* the details of the modules, only the main algorithm. Apply the concept of abstraction, i.e., decompose the problem into distinct logical subtasks.

4.35. Read in an employee's salary, calculate the appropriate state and federal Income Taxes, Social Security, Medicare withholding, and net salary, then print the resulting information. (Details concerning how to calculate each withholding amount can be ignored, as they should be hidden inside modules).

4.36. Read in data concerning number of miles driven, number of gallons of gasoline consumed, total gasoline expenditures, then calculate both *miles per gallon* and *cost of fuel per mile*, and print out the all the information. (Details concerning how to calculate each item can be ignored, as they should be hidden inside modules).

A larger example...

Consider the algorithm **GradeCalc**. Its purpose is simple: based on a student's various numerical averages (exam, quiz, project, and lab) and on the weights assigned to each by the professor, it calculates a letter grade for the course. We could do this without any procedural abstraction, as follows:

```
algorithm GradeCalc
     {Purpose: calculates course grade based on student's
          average for projects, quizzes and lab, and on stu-
          dent's exam score}

const
     {grade factors:                                    }
     ProjFac is .35          {weight of Project Average}
     QuizFac is .30           {weight of Quiz Average}
     LabFac  is .10            {weight of Lab Tasks}
     ExamFac is .25              {weight of Exam}

     {grade thresholds:                                 }
     ACutOff is 90                 {min score for A}
     BCutOff is 80                 {min score for B}
     CCutOff is 70                 {min score for C}
     DCutOff is 60                 {min score for D}

var
     ProjAvg,                 {student's Project average}
     QuizAvg,                  {student's Quiz average}
     LabAvg,                   {student's Lab average}
     ExamScr,                   {student's Exam score}
     CourseAvg isa num        {students combined Average}
     LtrGrd  isa char          {student's Course grade}

begin
     print('Enter your project average:  ')
     read(ProjAvg)
```

```
print('Enter your quiz average:  ')
read(QuizAvg)

print('Enter your lab average:  ')
read(LabAvg)

print('Enter your exam score:  ')
read(ExamScr)

CourseAvg <- (ProjAvg * ProjFac) + (QuizAvg * QuizFac) +
    (LabAvg * LabFac) + (ExamScr * ExamFac)

if (CourseAvg >= ACutOff) then
    LtrGrd <- 'A'
else
    if (CourseAvg >= BCutOff) then
        LtrGrd <- 'B'
    else
        if (CourseAvg >= CCutOff) then
            LtrGrd <- 'C'
        else
            if (CourseAvg >= DCutOff) then
                LtrGrd <- 'D'
            else {CourseAvg < DCutOff}
                LtrGrd <- 'F'
            endif
        endif
    endif
endif

print('Your course final grade is:  ', LtrGrd,'.')

end {algorithm GradeCalc}
```

All the algorithmic steps are provided in a single chunk. There is no procedural abstraction, and understanding what this algorithm does requires that you read and understand the whole thing at once.

Since the problem it solves is so simple, this should not present a large problem in this case. However, remember that this algorithm solves a trivial problem. No single part of it would tax the ability of a bright 10-year-old child. Thus, like all our examples, it is used for purposes of simply illustrating concepts. If we had a reasonably complex example, you would find it much more difficult to grasp the "sense" of the algorithm if were all "glopped together" in a single list of instructions.

To express the same "GradeCalc" algorithm in an appropriately modular way requires that we organize it in terms of the logical subtasks that are required to solve the problem. An algorithm which features appropriate modularity is given below:

```
{————————————————————-}

algorithm GradeCalc
     {Purpose: calculates course grade based on student's
          average for projects, quizzes and lab, and on stu-
          dent's exam score}

var
     ProjAvg,                    {student's Project average}
     QuizAvg,                     {student's Quiz average}
     LabAvg,                       {student's Lab average}
     ExamScr,                      {student's Exam score}
     NumGrade isa num {student's numerical Course grade}
     LtrGrd  isa char    {student's letter Course grade}


begin
     GetData(ProjAvg, QuizAvg, LabAvg, ExamScr)
     NumGrade <- CalcAvg(ProjAvg, QuizAvg, LabAvg, ExamScr)
     LtrGrd <- CalcLtrGrd(NumGrade)
     OutputGrade(LtrGrd)
end {main algorithm}



{————————————————————-}



procedure GetData  (ProjInData, QuizInData,
                    LabInData, ExamInData isa out num)
     {Purpose: obtains grade components from standard input}

begin

     print('Enter your project average:  ')
     read(ProjInData)
```

```
      print('Enter your quiz average:  ')
      read(QuizInData)

      print('Enter your lab average:  ')
      read(LabInData)

      print('Enter your exam score:  ')
      read(ExamInData)

end   {procedure GetData}


{----------------------------------}


function CalcAvg isa num (Proj, Quiz, Lab, Exam
                              isa in num)
    {Purpose: calculates overall course average based on
        exam and averages for projects, quizzes, labs}


const
     ProjFac is .35            {weight of Project Average}
     QuizFac is .30              {weight of Quiz Average}
     LabFac  is .10               {weight of Lab Tasks}
     ExamFac is .25                    {weight of Exam}

begin
     CalcAvg returns ((Proj * ProjFac) + (Quiz * QuizFac) +
                     (Lab * LabFac) + (Exam * ExamFac))
end {function CalcAvg}

{----------------------------------}

function CalcLtrGrade isa char (CourseGrd isa in num)
     {Purpose: converts numerical course grade to a letter
         grade.}
const
     ACutOff is 90
     BCutOff is 80
     CCutOff is 70
     DCutOff is 60
```

```
var
    Letter isa char         (student's Final Course Grade)
begin
    if (CourseGrd >= ACutOff) then
            Letter <- 'A'
    else
        if (CourseGrd >= BCutOff) then
            Letter <- 'B'
        else
            if (CourseGrd >= CCutOff then
                Letter <- 'C'
            else
                if (CourseGrd >= DCutOff) then
                    Letter <- 'D'
                else {CourseGrd < DCutOff}
                    Letter <- 'F'
                endif
            endif
        endif
    endif
    CalcLtrGrade returns Letter
end  {function CalcLtrGrade}


{------------------------------------------}


procedure OutputGrade(OutGrd isa in char)
    {Purpose: output the final letter grade}

begin
    print('Your course final grade is: ', OutGrade,'.')
end  {procedure OutputGrade}


{------------------------------------------}
```

The Importance of Procedural Abstraction

Observe that we have not significantly changed the instructions of the algorithm, only the organization of it. The only changes to the instructions concerned parameters and identifiers. All in all, we did little more than subdivide the program into one high level "main" algorithm and a few "lower level" modules. The impact of these changes is discussed below.

1) Writing
algorithms

Procedural abstraction allows us to effectively subdivide algorithm creation work among different people. For example, each individual algorithm module might be assigned to a different person. This kind of division of labor amongst teams of programmers is standard practice in the software industry.

> ☐ Because each module communicates with the rest of the algorithm only via a clearly defined *interface* of parameters, none of the algorithm writers need to be concerned about the specific code written by others. Instead, all they need to coordinate is the parameters by which the various modules communicate.

They do not even need to waste time trying to agree on identifier names for each piece of shared data. Instead, they can concentrate on the type of data they are sharing, and the number of parameters that are required for the various modules. Once the number and kind of parameters is known, the algorithm writers are free to go off and create their own code as best suits their tasks. Without procedural abstraction, they would be faced with a nightmare of arguments about identifier names, who gets to access which variables and who doesn't, etc. This dramatically increases the opportunity for bad teamwork, wasted time, and errors. The use of distinct modules which communicate only via parameters reduces the number of problem areas and allows everyone to be clear about the interaction of their various subalgorithms.

> ☐ Even when an algorithm is written by single person, these same advantages are important. Over the hours (or days or weeks) it might take to develop an algorithm, the algorithm writer will forget many details and waste a great deal of time recovering forgotten information. Modular design allows the writer to focus his attention on individual modules, and allows him to forget the details of the other modules when he is not working on them.

2) Testing code

The use of parameters to define the interface between modules is particularly valuable when testing algorithms implemented in software. Testing and validation is an important undertaking that is often poorly understood and inadequately performed. The main goal is to demonstrate that the software being tested does what it is supposed to do and that it does so reliably. *This is not a trivial task.* It tends to be complicated and expensive and is a problem that plagues the software industry.

> ☐ The use of parameters to define an interface between modules allows each module to be tested individually without being "hooked up" to the rest of the algorithm. This is valuable as it is extremely difficult (sometimes impossible) to determine what part of a large program is producing a given error.

This module-by-module testing requires temporary algorithms, or "drivers," which send the module appropriate input data, and "stubs," which are temporary modules that receive data output by the tested module. By using *drivers* and *stubs* to test each module individually, problems can be isolated before the modules are combined into a large program. By testing the parts of the algorithm individually, the task of determining the exact causes of an error is made a great deal easier. Determining the cause of an error is the hard part of debugging. Once the cause of an error is known, the needed repair is generally straightforward.

Thus, the "extra" work of testing with stubs and drivers actually saves an immense amount of time. Unfortunately, novice programmers often don't want to bother with it because they naively (and incorrectly) assume that this "extra" work *costs* time. This misperception on the part of novices often results in them spending three or four times as many hours working on a program than is necessary! (Try to remember this when enrolled in a programming course!)

3) Maintaining code When algorithms are implemented as computer programs, those programs must be *maintained*. This includes fixing bugs, refining existing features, and adding new features. Maintenance is very expensive. In fact, *writing* a program is cheap when compared to the costs of *maintaining* it. In the software industry, as much as 90% of the cost of software is due to maintenance.

> ☐ Algorithms that feature procedural abstraction (good modular design and well-defined interfaces among the modules) make the programs which implement them a great deal cheaper to maintain. The programmers who maintain them can more readily identify the parts of the code where changes are required and what the consequences of those changes will be.

Without the use of parameters and the interface specification they provide, the *unintended* consequences of a single change to an algorithm can be nearly impossible to determine. With good modular design, the consequences of changing code in one module can be anticipated by examining the various module interfaces and identifying other modules which can be affected.

4) Reusing logic Frequently, a given task must be performed multiple times within an algorithm.

> ☐ Procedural abstraction allows us to write the algorithm for a given task once, then use it (and reuse it) whenever it is required. This is, quite obviously, far preferable to "reinventing the wheel" each time a given task is called for.

To illustrate how procedural abstraction help us reuse logic within an algorithm, consider an algorithm similar to `GradeCalc`. This algorithm is called `CompareGrades`. It it is for two friends who made a bet about who would do better in the class.

```
algorithm CompareGrades
     {Purpose: accepts grade data as input from Student1,
          then from Student2; determines who wins the bet,
          based on the higher grade}

var
     ProjData,                {Project average from input}
     QuizData,                 {Quiz average from input}
     LabData,                   {Lab average from input}
     ExamData,                  {Exam score from input}
     S1Grade,              {Course grade for Student 1}
     S2Grade isa num       {Course grade for Student 2}

begin   {main}
     GetData(ProjData, QuizData, LabData, ExamData)
     S1Grade <- CalcAvg(ProjData, QuizData, LabData, Exam-
          Data)
     GetData(ProjData, QuizData, LabData, ExamData)
     S2Grade <- CalcAvg(ProjData, QuizData, LabData, Exam-
          Data)
     OutputResults(S1Grade, S2Grade)
end {main}


{————————————————————————-}


{insert algorithm GradeCalc's procedure GetData here}


{————————————————————————-}


{insert algorithm GradeCalc's function CalcAvg here}


{————————————————————————-}
```

```
procedure OutputResults (Student1Grd, Student2Grd isa
                          in num)
     {accepts data from the main algorithm, decides which
         output message should be generated, then prints
         that message}

begin
    if (Student1Grd > Student2Grd) then
        print('Student1 Wins, Student2 pay up!')
    else
        if (Student1Grd < Student2Grd) then
            print('Student2 Wins, Student1 pay up!')
        else {Student1Grd = Student2 Grd}
            print('It's a tie.  Pay the prof!')
        endif
    endif
end   {procedure OutputResults}


{——————————————————————--}
```

Notice that the main algorithm calls both GetData and CalcAvg twice.

> ☐   The Lifespan of Data: One important thing to remember about our modules
> is that they do *not* remember data from one invocation to the next. When-
> ever a module is called, it "does its thing," then finishes, and its data "dies."
> Thus, any data that is not returned to the calling algorithm is lost. If that
> module is called again, it has no memory of the data values it calculated be-
> fore. In other words, each time a module is called, it begins "fresh."

In the example above, the first call to GetData obtains data for Student1, and
the first call to CalcAvg calculates the course grade for Student1. The course
grade for Student1 is stored in S1Grade, as this is where the result of function CalcAvg is assigned.

After Student1's data is processed, the algorithm then processes Student2's
data. The second call to GetData obtains data for Student2 and, via Get-
Data's output parameters, "writes over" the various scores earned by Student1.
The fact that we are "writing over," i.e., losing, the various scores belonging to
Student1 is of no consequence, as the algorithm has already determined Stu-
dent1's course grade, has returned that value to the main algorithm's S1Grade,
and has no further use for Student1's other scores.

After obtaining `Student2`'s data, the algorithm makes its second call to `CalcAvg`. Observe that the actual parameter list used to call `CalcGrade` is no different than the first call with respect to the last parameter in the list. However, the first call to `CalcGrade` returns a value to `S1Grade`, while the second call to `CalcGrade` returns a value to `S2Grade`.

By changing the variable to which the value of the function is assigned, we instruct procedure `CalcAvg` to return its result to a different location. *Observe that this occurs without changing function CalcAvg in any way.* `CalcAvg` is the same, only the variable to which it assigned is different.

This same effect can be achieved with procedures by altering the actual parameter list. Imagine the we have `procedure DoStuff` that features the following header lione:

```
procedure DoStuff (X, Y, Z isa in num, A, B isa out num)
```

An algorithm might call this algorithm twice, as follows:

```
begin
    GetData (A, B, C)
    DoStuff(A, B, C, ThisData, ThatData)
    GetData(D, E, F)
    DoStuff (D, E, F, SomeData, OtherData)
    . . .
end
```

Here we have exploited the *decoupling* between name and data which parameters allow. Using parameters allowed us to have the results of `DoStuff` returned to one pair of variables (`ThisData` and `ThatData`) in the first call and to another pair of variables (`SomeData` and `OtherData`) in the second call. This is a simple example of a *very powerful* principle:

☐ By using parameters to *decouple the name of the data from the data itself*, we can use the same code in various situations within an algorithm, simply by changing the actual parameter list. This is far preferable to rewriting code to suit the various demands of each particular situation.

Had we not used parameters, we would not have been able to do this. Without parameters, we would have had to rewrite the code that calculates whatever is done within `DoStuff`. Perhaps this would have meant redundant code, i.e., two versions of procedure `DoStuff`, one version for each call. Or, perhaps it would have meant unnecessary and convoluted code, i.e., various variables and if statements to make

`DoStuff` send its results to whichever variables should have received it. Either of these alternatives is very messy and is bad practice. By simply using parameters appropriately, we did not have to alter `DoStuff` in any way.

5) Reusing code among different algorithms

In our `CompareGrades` algorithm, we also have an example of how procedural abstraction, and the interface specification it provides, allow us to reuse code among *different algorithms.*

Observe that `CompareGrades` contains three modules. Observe further that two of these three (`GetData` and `CalcAvg`) were lifted directly from algorithm `GradeCalc` *without being changed in any way.* The code was "stolen" from `GradeCalc`, plain and simple. And it works.

This is very good. We want to reuse code whenever it is reasonable to do so. Reusing code is far better than rewriting code in every algorithm. Why "reinvent the wheel" again and again? There is no good reason. It's a waste of time and energy.

Observe, also, that the variables declared in algorithm `CompareGrades` are different than those use in `GradeCalc`. Thus, the actual parameters sent to `GetData` and `CalcAvg` in algorithm `CompareGrades` included identifiers unknown in algorithm `GradeCalc`.

Notice further that this did not interfere in any way with reusing the `GetData` and `CalcAvg` modules. Again, we exploited the *decoupling* of *data* and *name* which parameters allow. It doesn't matter what identifiers are used within the reused modules, nor does it matter what identifiers are used in the new algorithm. The names don't have to correspond. We don't have to go back and edit our code to make them correspond. Instead, we exploit the relationship between the actual and formal parameter lists to make the old code work in the new algorithm.

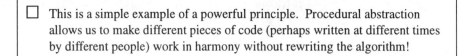 This is a simple example of a powerful principle. Procedural abstraction allows us to make different pieces of code (perhaps written at different times by different people) work in harmony without rewriting the algorithm!

Documenting Modules

Observe that each of our algorithms and modules contains a brief description of what it does. This is given after the header line and before any variable declarations or instructions, contained within braces (i.e., { and }) to signify that these are comments which *describe* the algorithm but which are not part of its declarations or instructions.

Such descriptions are necessary to permit a reader to know what the algorithm is supposed to do. Without them, a reader must figure out their purpose. Thus, they are a required part of algorithms, and all algorithms you submit must contain them.

Experience shows that such descriptions are useful for the algorithm writer as well. Novices typically create their algorithms first and document them last. Research has shown that algorithms are written *faster* when the documentation occurs first. It helps the algorithm writer stay focused on the purpose at hand.

Exercises 4.37. When should you use procedures in your programs? What kind of parameters can be used in the declaration of procedures?

4.38. What makes functions different from procedures? When should you use functions in your programs? What is the only kind of parameter that can be used with functions and why?

For problems 4.16, 4.17, and 4.18, you will design and implement procedures and functions to handle the class information of a university. Use good modularity and documentation in all of your answers.

4.39. Write a module (either a procedure or function) named `GetStudentInfo` that will ask the user for the following information and return their responses to the calling module.

```
SocialSecurityNumber
Age
GradeLevel (should be "F," "S," "J," or "R" for
                Freshman, Sophomore, etc)
GPA
GoodStanding (should be true if their GPA is >= 2.0,
                otherwise false)
```

4.40. Write a module (either a procedure or a function) that will take in a `GradeLevel` (as defined above) and print out "Freshman," "Sophomore," "Junior," or "Senior" depending on the class rank.

4.41. Write a module (either a procedure or function) named `PrintStudentInfo` that will print out the following information:

```
SocialSecurityNumber,
Age,
GradeLevel,
GPA, and
GoodStanding
```

If called via:

```
PrintStudentInfo(1234567890, 21, "J", 3.2, true)
```

your output should look something like this:

```
Student 1234567890 is 21 years old.
Class rank: Junior
GPA = 3.2
GOOD STANDING
```

Recursive Control

As we have seen, procedural abstraction allows us several benefits. Among these is the capability to write an algorithm for a given task only once, then call it whenever it is needed. Our algorithms can trigger any given modular capability whenever conditions call for it. A well designed algorithm will largely consist of a series of calls to procedural abstractions such that the *individual modules "do the work"* while the *main algorithm organizes and coordinates*.

Many tasks are inherently repetitive, including most tasks in which lists of data are processed, e.g., tracking inventory, computing salaries, processing experimental data, calculating grades, and so on. When faced with a repetitive task, we not only want to trigger some modular capability, we want to trigger it *as many times as necessary*. Procedural abstraction allows us to manage repetition via *recursion*.

> ☐ A *recursive module* is one that achieves a repetition of algorithmic steps by calling a "clone" of itself. It does this via a *recursive call*, a call from within a procedure or function in which *its own identifier* is used.

Generally, recursive modules conform to one of two forms:

```
form (1):
    if (terminating condition) then
        do final actions
    else
        take a step closer to terminating condition
        call "clone" of module
    endif

form (2):
    if (NOT(terminating condition)) then
        take a step closer to terminating condition
        call "clone" of module
    endif
```

☐ The *terminating condition* in a recursive algorithm is the condition which stops the module from calling itself again. It is necessary that the terminating condition is eventually reached, else the repetition will go on forever. If, at any given step, the terminating condition is not true, we must do something that will move us closer to it, then call the module again. If we keep getting closer to the terminating condition, then eventually reach it, the recursion will stop, and we will have our solution.

Both forms (1) and (2) contain a test for the terminating condition and the recursive call. The difference between the two forms is that in form (2) once the terminating condition is reached, nothing more is done; the module is finished. In form (1), when the terminating condition is reached there are still some instructions to carry out, but no more recursion is done.

☐ A recursive function will always use Form 1, as a function must always resolve to some value, and thus must have a *returns* statement executed regardless of the path of execution through the function. A recursive procedure may use either form, depending on the particulars of the problem.

To clarify the concept of recursion, let's write a recursive algorithm which will print the integers from 1 through 10. To write a recursive algorithm, we need to extract the steps which are repeated over and over again during the solution process. One step we know will be repeated is the *print* instruction, which needs to be executed exactly 10 times. This gives us a hint as to our terminating condition; it should be satisfied after the number 10 has been printed. Because we want to stop after this has occurred, and have no other tasks to do once that condition is reached, we shall use recursive form (2) for this module:

```
procedure PrintTen (Counter isa in num)
    {Purpose: repeatedly print out value of Counter and
        increments it by 1 until the value exceeds 10}
begin
    if (NOT(Counter > 10)) then
        print(Counter)
        PrintTen(Counter + 1)
    endif
end
```

This module is a *procedure* because it has effects on the outside world, i.e., it prints data to some output device. The identifier of the procedure is PrintTen. It accepts one parameter, which indicates where we are in the process of climbing from 1 to 10. The first call to this module must come from outside of the module and initializes Counter to the value 1, i.e., the main algorithm might feature the instruction:

```
PrintTen(1)
```

Subsequent calls are done recursively, increasing Counter by 1 each time, until its value finally equals 11 and satisfies the terminating condition. Then the module is finished. Let's trace the execution of this procedure:

Which call of module	Parameter received	Test: "Continue recursion if ... "	Test Outcome	Value printed	Parameter passed
First	1	(NOT(1>10))	Continue	1	2
Second	2	(NOT(2>10))	Continue	2	3
Third	3	(NOT(3>10))	Continue	3	4
Fourth	4	(NOT(4>10))	Continue	4	5
Fifth	5	(NOT(5>10))	Continue	5	6
Sixth	6	(NOT(6>10))	Continue	6	7
Seventh	7	(NOT(7>10))	Continue	7	8
Eighth	8	(NOT(8>10))	Continue	8	9
Ninth	9	(NOT(9>10))	Continue	9	10
Tenth	10	(NOT(10>10)	Continue	10	11
Eleventh	11	(NOT(11>10)	Terminate	N/A	N/A

Notice that this procedure will "work" for a variety of initial values, but what will it do?. If the initial call passes the value 3, then it will print out the integers 3 thought 10. If the initial parameter value is 1.4, it will print out the values 1.4, 2.4, 3.4, ..., 8.4, 9.4. In fact, it will print out the the series of all the values from the initial value, incremented by 1, up to but not exceeding 10. It will do this if passed a negative number, and it will do this if passed a number greater than 10. Thus, it seems that we've written a procedure that is more general than it had to be: it will *repeatedly print and increment by one from any initial value up through 10.*

Notice too that we could make this algorithm more general by using a second parameter in place of the literal value *10*. In this way, we could have the algorithm print out numbers to whatever value was specified by the additional parameter, e.g.,

```
procedure PrintIncrements (Counter isa in num,
                              Ceiling isa in num)
    {Purpose: repeatedly prints out Counter and incre-
        ments it by 1 until the value exceeds Ceiling}
begin
    if (NOT(Counter > Ceiling)) then
        print(Counter)
        PrintIncrements(Counter+1, Ceiling)
    endif
end  {procedure PrintIncrements}
```

To print out the numbers 1 though 10, the initial call would be:

```
PrintIncrements(1, 10)
```

while printing the values 7 through 23 would require the call:

```
PrintIncrements(7, 23)
```

So far, we've achieved an algorithm that is general with respect to both starting and stopping values; the only rigid component is the fixed rate of increment, 1. We might make the algorithm more flexible such that it can work with any size increment by adding a third parameter by which the step interval can be passed, e.g.,

```
procedure PrintIncrements (Counter isa in num,
                    Ceiling isa in num, Step is in num)
        {Purpose: repeatedly prints out Counter and incre-
            ments it by Step until the value exceeds Ceil-
                ing}
```

```
begin
    if (NOT(Counter > Ceiling)) then
        print(Counter)
        PrintIncrements(Counter+Step, Ceiling)
    endif
end   {procedure PrintIncrements}
```

Here, all we've done is add a third parameter, Step, which governs the size of the increment. Should we wish to examine the values from 3 to 100 in increments of 1.5, we would make the initial call:

```
PrintIncrements(3, 100, 1.5)
```

which would result in printing:

```
3, 4.5, 6, 7.5, 9, ... , 96, 97.5, 99
```

For another example, imagine that you're trying to hang a picture on your living room wall, and that you want to make sure that you attach it directly to a 2-by-4 vertical stud in the wall. Your walls are covered with thick sheet rock, so the usual stud finder devices don't work. You know where the center of one stud is, and you know that the studs are spaced 16" apart. To determine the location of all the studs relative to the one you've located, you might use a similar algorithm, one in which the recursive procedure also calls another procedure which handles the generation of output, e.g.:

```
procedure StudFinder (Location isa in num,
                      Span isa in num,
                      Spacing is in num)
    {Purpose: calculates the placement of studs at the
        given Spacing across the Span relative to the
        initial Location.  All parameter values are to
        be in inches}
begin
    if (NOT(Location > Span)) then
        PrintStuds(Location)
        StudFinder(Location+Spacing, Span, Spacing)
    endif
end {procedure FindStuds}
```

```
procedure PrintStuds (Location isa in num)
     {Purpose: receives "Location" in inches and prints
          out the appropriate translation in units of
          feet and inches.}
var
     Feet,
     Inches isa num

begin
     Feet <- Location DIV 12
     Inches <- Location MOD 12
     print{Feet, " feet, " Inches, " inches")
end {procedure PrintStuds}
```

The location of your initial stud is 0, the span of the wall is, say, 180 inches, and the stud spacing is 16" on center. Thus, the initial call would be:

```
StudFinder(0, 180, 16)
```

It would print out the values:

```
1 feet, 4 inches
2 feet, 8 inches
4 feet, 0 inches
5 feet, 4 inches
6 feet, 8 inches
8 feet, 0 inches
9 feet, 4 inches
10 feet, 8 inches
12 feet, 0 inches
13 feet, 4 inches
14 feet, 8 inches
16 feet, 0 inches
```

and then terminate.

To see a more complicated (and useful) example of recursion, we can use recursion to create a module, Power, that is an abstraction of exponentiation, i.e., raising some Base value to Exponent power. Our power module will take the two parameters as input data: Base is the base number and Exp is the exponent to which Base will be raised. Since Power is a function, it reduces to the appropriate value each time it is called, and only *input* parameters are used. Here is our function:

```
function Power isa num (Base, Exp isa in num)
    {Purpose: computes the value of Base raised to the Exp
         power.  Requires a non-negative integer for Exp}

begin
    if (Exp = 0) then
        Power returns 1
    else
        Power returns (Power(Base, Exp-1))
    endif
end   {function Power}
```

Notice how compact and neat this function is. It has a simple terminating condition ("is Exp equal to 0?"), executes a single instruction if the condition is met (Power returns 1) or a single instruction if the condition is not met (Power returns (Base * Power(Base, Exp-1))). Yet it will compute the result of *any* base value raised to *any* positive exponent.

There are three important things to notice about this recursive function.

1. Whenever the value of the exponent (Exp) reaches 0, the function reduces to the value 1. This is the terminating condition. When this condition is satisfied, a simple assignment is made to Return and no further recursion is triggered.

2. Whenever the terminating condition is not reached, the function calls itself. In principle, this works the same as if the function had called a different module, i.e., the calling module passes certain information to the module it calls. The only thing odd about a recursive call is that each call invokes a "clone" of the calling module. While the various clones have the same instructions, each clone acts only on the particular data values it receives via parameter.

   In this example, observe that each recursive call is just like the previous one, with one key difference: each time, the value of Exp is reduced by 1. Since each call effectively "shrinks" the value of Exp, we are certain to eventually reach the terminating condition (assuming that Exp was a originally positive integer).

3. As noted above, when the terminating condition is not reached, a new call is made to the function. This new call is executed *before the current call is finished*. This isalways true: *each recursive call cannot complete until the next call is finished!*

Many people find this confusing to understand and keep track of, so we shall "walk through" an example in order to demonstrate a method to help you keep track of the flow of control ...

Using a* stack *to trace recursion In order to trace the execution of a recursive module, we shall utilize a construct called a *stack*.

☐ Stack: The idea of a stack is very simple: it is a pile upon which you can stack things and from which you can only remove whatever is at the top. There are two main stack operations:

Push which adds a new item to the top of the stack, and
Pop which removes the topmost item from the stack.

An item that is on the stack but which is not at the top may be accessed only after first removing (*popping*) each item on top of it, thus making it the top-most item.

An example of a stack is the cafeteria mechanism for storing clean plates: some number of plates are placed on a spring-like device, and the first person through the line takes the top-most plate. The plate that had been below the top plate then itself becomes the top plate and is taken by the next person through, and so on. The key notion here is that plates can only be added and removed from the top.

To keep track of recursion, each time a module is called, we *push* a new *frame* on the stack. The *frame* contains the data values for the module. The first *frame* on the stack will be the algorithm that initiated the recursive call.

Imagine that our recursive `Power` function is called from the main algorithm via:

```
Total <- Power(3,4)
```

We place a frame for the calling algorithm on an empty stack. Since the assignment to `Total`, above, cannot be done until the `Power` function returns a value, this instruction above is "unfinished business," and we label it so. Thus, the stack might look like:

Main algorithm: Unfinished: "Total <- Power(3,4)"

As `Power(3,4)` begins to execute, it gets its own frame *pushed* onto the stack...

Power(1st):   Base = 3   Power=4
Main algorithm: Unfinished: "Total <- Power(3,4)"

As the initial call to `Power` executes, the terminating condition is not met, since the current exponent value is *4*, not *0*. Thus, the *else* clause is executed:

```
Power returns Base * Power(Base, Exp-1)
```

Given the current data values (Base=*3*, Exp=*4*), this is equivalent to

```
Power returns 3 * Power(3,4-1)
```

which is the same as

```
Power returns 3 * Power(3,3)
```

Thus, we have encountered a recursive call. The first call to Power makes a second call to Power. Until that second call to Power completes, the first call also has unfinished business. We record the unfinished business of the calling module in its frame on the stack, then *push* a new frame for the newly called clone of Power :

Power(2nd): Base = 3, Exp = 3
Power (1st): Base=3, Exp=4, Unfinished: "Power returns 3*Power(3,3)"
Main algorithm: Unfinished: "Total <- Power(3,4)"

As the second call to Power executes, the same thing happens all over again: the terminating condition is not satisfied and the *else* clause is executed. The second call to Power makes a third call to Power and is left waiting for the resulting value so it can complete its business. Thus, we update the top frame and push yet another frame on the stack, which now looks like:

Power (3rd): Base= 3, Exp = 2
Power (2nd): Base=3, Exp=3, Unfinished: "Power returns 3*Power(3,2)"
Power (1st): Base=3, Exp=4, Unfinished: "Power returns 3*Power(3,3)"
Main algorithm: Unfinished: "Total <- Power(3,4)"

As the third call executes, the same thing occurs, so we add the appropriate notation to the stack:

Power (4th): Base=3, Exp = 1
Power (3rd): Base=3, Exp=2, Unfinished: "Power returns 3*Power(3,1)"
Power (2nd): Base=3, Exp=3, Unfinished: "Power returns 3*Power(3,2)"
Power (1st): Base=3, Exp=4, Unfinished: "Power returns 3*Power(3,3)"
Main algorithm: Unfinished: "Total <- Power(3,4)"

The same thing happens with the fourth call too....

Power (5th): Base=3, Exp = 0
Power (4th): Base=3, Exp=1, Unfinished: "Power returns 3*Power(3,0)"
Power (3rd): Base=3, Exp=2, Unfinished: "Power returns 3*Power(3,1)"
Power (2nd): Base=3, Exp=3, Unfinished: "Power returns 3*Power(3,2)"
Power (1st): Base=3, Exp=4, Unfinished: "Power returns 3*Power(3,3)"
Main algorithm: Unfinished: "Total <- Power(3,4)"

When the fifth call is made, the value of Exp that is passed to the fifth instance of Power is *0*. Because Exp is *0*, as the fifth call to Power executes, the terminating condition is satisfied. This triggers the *if* clause, not the *else*, and for the first time we do *not* have a recursive call. The fifth call to Power simply assigns the value *1* to Return and then terminates.

With the fifth call finished, the "unfinished business" of the fourth call can be completed: we now know that Power(3,0) has reduced to the value *1*. Thus, we can substitute *1* for Power(3,0) in the frame for the 4th call and *pop* the 5th call off of the stack..

Power (4th): Base=3, Exp=1, Unfinished: "Power returns 3 * 1"
Power (3rd): Base=3, Exp=2, Unfinished: "Power returns 3*Power(3,1)"
Power (2nd): Base=3, Exp=3, Unfinished: "Power returns 3*Power(3,2)"
Power (1st): Base=3, Exp=4, Unfinished: "Power returns 3*Power(3,3)"
Main algorithm: Unfinished: "Total <- Power(3,4)"

This allows the the fourth call to finish its business:

```
Power returns 3 * Power(3,0)
```

which now resolves to

```
Power returns 3 * 1, or 3.
```

This completes the work of the fourth call to Power: it has resolved to the value *3*. Since its work is done, we *pop* it off the stack and are done with it. Its value, *3*, can now be substituted in the "unfinished business" of the third call to Power.

Power (3rd): Base=3, Exp=2, Unfinished: "Power returns 3*3"
Power (2nd): Base=3, Exp=3, Unfinished: "Power returns 3*Power(3,2)"
Power (1st): Base=3, Exp=4, Unfinished: "Power returns 3*Power(3,3)"
Main algorithm: Unfinished: "Total <- Power(3,4)"

```
Power returns 3 * Power(3,1)
```

now resolves to

```
Power returns 3 * 3, or 9.
```

This completes the work of the third call to Power: it has resolved to the value *9*. Since its work is done, we *pop* it off the stack and forget about it. Its value, *9*, can now be substituted in the "unfinished business" of the second call to Power.

Power (2nd): Base=3, Exp=3, Unfinished: "Power returns 3*9"
Power (1st): Base=3, Exp=4, Unfinished: "Power returns 3*Power(3,3)"
Main algorithm: Unfinished: "Total <- Power(3,4)"

```
Power returns 3 * Power(3,2)
```

now resolves to

```
Power returns 3 * 9, or 27.
```

This completes the work of the second call to Power: it has resolved to the value *27*. Since its work is done, we *pop* it off the stack and its value, *27*, can now be substituted in the "unfinished business" of the first call to Power.

Power, 1st call: Base=3, Exp=4, Unfinished: "Power returns 3 * 27"
Main algorithm: Unfinished: "Total <- Power(3,4)"

```
Power returns 3 * Power(3,3)
```

now resolves to

```
Power returns 3 * 27, or 81
```

This completes the work of the first call to Power: it has resolved to the value *81*. Since its work is done, we *pop* it off the stack and are done with it. Its value, *81*, can now be substituted for the original call in the main algorithm.

Main algorithm: Unfinished: "Total <- 81"

```
Total <- Power(3,4)
```

now resolves to

```
Total <- 81
```

With the assignment of *81* to Total, the job is complete.

Notice all the work that was accomplished by an extremely concise module. Remember: the entire function consisted of only a single recursive *if-then-else* statement:

```
if (Exp = 0) then
    Power returns 1
else
    Power  returns ( Base * Power(Base, Exp-1))
endif
```

This very same logic would have worked just the same, regardless of the base integer and the positive exponent integer passes into it... even had we asked it to compute the value of *119* raised to *238th* power! Simply by passing it different parameters, an immense amount of work would have been done.

Food for Thought:

Recursion and the Afrika Corps

In the early years of World War II, the German Army dominated the British and French forces throughout Europe. Yet the most famous German general, the one most respected by his Allied opponents, is the one who suffered the first German defeat. It was against him that the tide turned in favor of the Allies, yet he is regarded highly in military lore. He is Field Marshal Erwin Rommel, known to his British enemies as the "Desert Fox."

By 1940, the Germans had been victorious in battle and had established continental Europe as a fortress. The British elected to attempt their resurgence at a point where the Germans were furthest from their supply sources and weakest in numbers. The site was North Africa.

Rommel was the commander of the German "Afrika Corps" and was thus responsible for holding off the first British offensive of the war. The German Army occupied virtually all of Europe, and Hitler was considering plans for invading England and plans for invading Russia. With troops committed elsewhere and ambitious plans afoot, Hitler left Rommel to "make do" without adequate support in terms of both men and materiel. Rommel rose to the occasion by deploying innovative tactics by which he held off superior numbers of British and, later, American forces for an extended period.

He accomplished this in large part by deploying a *recursive algorithm* to organize and coordinate his troops in battle. Ordinarily, any commander would keep a healthy segment of his forces in reserve. This was deemed necessary because an enemy attack would threaten some portion of his line, and he needed to have reserve troops available to move up from the rear to support his front line troops at the point where they were attacked. Because his forces were so outnumbered, Rommel did not have enough troops to do this. He required that all his forces be committed to battle to have any hope of taking the day. This, of course, left him with a serious problem: how to respond to points of threat when he had no extra troops to deploy?

Rommel's recursive solution was to decentralize control of his forces, giving each local commander the authority to deploy without approval from above, and to specify for those local commanders the recursive algorithm they were to execute. (Because battle is ongoing, there is no terminating condition in it. Rommel *wanted* "infinite repetition.") Here's the logic of that algorithm in our pseudocode:

```
procedure RulesOfEngagement
begin
    look (to your left and to your right)
    if (you see your comrade in trouble) then
        go help him
    endif
    RulesOfEngagement
end {procedure RulesOfEngagement}
```

In battle, this algorithm was deployed at all levels throughout Rommel's army. Commanders of small units in a skirmish would use it to manage their local troop deployment in that skirmish, just as commanders of large battalions would use it manage the fighting in large battles. Regardless of the scale of fighting, the effect was the same: Rommel's troops would converge automatically on the point of most intense fighting!

This convergence of troops to the point where they were most needed did not occur because of a series of orders from the "top command" down to the lowly soldiers. Instead, it happened as a result of a distributed, organic, recursive process: if a given unit was in trouble, its "neighbor units" would come to its aid. And, in turn, *their* "neighbor units" would see their movement and slide over to help them, and so on. In short, it was a self-managed, chain reaction with a powerful result: *wherever* the Allies attacked most strongly, they would soon be facing the brunt of all the German forces in the area.

Rommel eventually lost, but not because he was "out-generaled." He lost because he was eventually overwhelmed by superior forces and a lack of reinforcements and supplies. Despite his eventual defeat, he went home a hero. Later, he committed suicide to save his family after he was implicated in a plot to kill Hitler.

Summary   The goal of *procedural abstraction* is to subdivide complex problems into manageable "chunks." This is accomplished by creating modules such that *each module serves a particular logical purpose and hides the details involved.*

Doing this allows us to solve complex problems by thinking at a higher level of abstraction than would otherwise be possible. Procedural abstraction also allows us great convenience and efficiency by allowing us to reuse modules in various contexts.

There are two basic kinds of modules: *procedures* and *functions.*

- *Procedures* can accomplish a wide variety of tasks, and may have effects on the data of other modules and on the real world outside the algorithm.

- *Functions* are like mathematical functions, i.e., they resolve to a single value and are not permitted to have any other effects.

Procedural abstraction requires that we define interfaces through which modules communicate. Parameters are the means of establishing communication interfaces between modules. There are three kinds of parameters: *input, output*, and *input/output* parameters. For any given situation, one of these three types of parameters is called for, depending on the particulars of the problem at hand.

Modular organization of data and instructions provides a powerful tool for controlling repetition: recursion. Recursive modules allow for a single, simple, and clean decision statement to achieve powerful repetitive effects. Recursive modules generally approximate one of two templates. It is imperative that recursive modules have two attributes:

- It must have a terminating condition

- The terminating condition must eventually be satisfied.

Exercises   4.42. Given the following function:

```
function Unknown isa num (Num1 isa in num)
begin
    if (Num1 = 0) then
        Unknown returns 0
    else
        Unknown returns (Unknown (Num1 - 1) +Num1)
    endif
end {function Unknown}
```

Use an activation stack to trace the execution of this function and report the number to which it resolves when called via:

```
Unknown(4)
```

4.43. Consider the following algorithm and report the exact output that is printed.

```
algorithm Magic
var
    A,
    B,
    C isa num

function Operation isa num (Num1, Num2 isa in num)
begin {Operation}
    if (Num1 > Num2) then
        Operation returns (Num1 * Num2)
    else
        Operation returns (Num1 + Num2)
    endif
end   {function Operation}

procedure Mystify (Num1, Num2 isa in/out num, Num3 isa
    in num)
begin
    Num3 <- Num3 - 1
    Num1 <- Num1 + Num3
    Num2 <- Num1 + Num2
    print ("My numbers are: ",Num1,Num2,Num3)
end {procedure Mystify}

begin {algorithm Magic}
    A <- 3
    B <- 3
    C <- Operation (A,B)
    print ("The values are: ",A,B,C)
    Mystify (A,B,C)
    print ("The values are: ",A,B,C)
    Mystify (C,B,A)
    print ("The values are: ",A,B,C)
end {algorithm Magic}
```

4.44. What is the output from the following program? Trace the execution of this program using an activation stack.

```
algorithm FollowMe
var
    a,
    b,
    c isa num

procedure Normalize (i, j, k isa in/out num)
{ this procedure takes in three parameters and modifies
    them }
begin
    i <- j * k
    j <- k * i
    k <- i * j
    print (i, j, k)
end {procedure Normalize}

function CalculateMin isa num (x, y isa in num)
    { this function returns the smaller of the two pa-
        rameters passed in }
begin
    if (x > y) then
        CalculateMin returns y
    else
        CalculateMin returns x
    endif
end {function CalculateMin}

begin { algorithm FollowMe }
    a <- 1
    b <- a * 2
    c <- CalculateMin(b, a)
    print (c, b, a)
    Normalize(a, b, c)
    c <- CalculateMin(a, b)
    print (a, b, c)
    Normalize (b, c, a)
    a <- c / b
    Normalize (c, a, b)
end { algorithm FollowMe }
```

4.45. Write a recursive module that will do the following:

Read in a number.

If that number is negative, halt.

Otherwise, print the number and make a recursive call to itself.

Explain your choice of either a function or a procedure.

4.46. The Fibonacci numbers are a sequence of numbers defined as follows: For 1 or 2, the Fibonacci number is 1. For a larger number N, the Fibonacci number is equal to the sum of the Fibonacci numbers for N-2 and N-1, i.e.
for $X \geq 3$, Fib(X) = Fib(X - 1) + Fib(X - 2).

This definition gives us::

```
Number:              1  2  3  4  5  6   7   8   9
Fibonacci Number:  1  1  2  3  5  8  13  21  34
```

Thus, the Fibonacci number for 5 is the sum of the Fibonacci numbers for 3 and 4, which means: 2 + 3, or 5. Write a recursive function that computes the Fibonacci number for a given a positive number parameter (which you may name N).

4.47. Write the recursive procedure FindGPA that will find a student's GPA. It will require two parameters to keep track of the total number of credit hours and quality points for the student. The procedure will ask the user if he/she wants to enter another class. If the user enters 'y', the procedure will read in the grade and credit hours for a course, calculate the quality points for the class, update the necessary variables, then repeat. If the user enters 'n', the procedure will print out the student's gpa and terminate.

4.48. Write the recursive function Factorial. This function will receive a integer value that is 0 or greater and will return the factorial of that number.

N! (i.e., "N factorial") = N x (N-1)! for $N \geq 1$
0! (i.e., "0 factorial") = 1

Show the stack trace for this function when it is called by: Factorial(5).

Chapter 5: Tools for "Data Abstraction"

So far, we have only considered atomic data types, i.e., those which can hold only one piece of data at a time. Because it often happens that various pieces of data logically "belong" together, atomic structures are not sufficient for many of our needs. Thus, we require ways to construct more complex data structures from the atomic data types.

When we have many pieces of data that are closely related in some way, it is both logically correct and efficient to organize the data into one single structure instead of having a different variable name for each piece of data. The data structures formed in this way are "composite structures," or "complex structures," containing many cells. You can think of them as being constructed of a group of individual data structures all united under one name.

There are only a few different ways to combine and organize such data. However, we shall soon see that these few tools can be used to construct data structures of infinite variety. Thus, they allow us to design and use whatever data structures are best suited to the problem at hand.

☐ If we organize data properly, we achieve "data abstraction." Just as "procedural abstraction" means that we isolate the details of a given set of logical steps and then refer to it by a meaningful name, "data abstraction" means that we do the same thing with data: we hide the details of how we organize data and then refer to complex logical chunks of data by a single meaningful name. Thus, we can refer to a complex group of data by single name without "getting lost in the details" of how it is organized.

For example, if we wish to keep track of all the students at Georgia Tech, we do not want to fool around with declaring many little variables for each of 12,000 students. Instead, we want to collect together all the data that pertains to a given student into one data structure so that that students' data is grouped together. Furthermore, we would want to collect 12,000 versions of that data structure, one for each student, to give us a single structure for the student body as a whole. In addition, we want to be able to quickly access particular pieces of data for each and every student without undue amounts of searching to find what we're looking for.

> ☐ There are just a few constructs that allow us to group data together. Each has its benefits and its costs, and none is best for all circumstances. Instead, we must consider the properties of both the data itself and of the problem at hand and design data structures which are most suitable for that task.

In the this chapter, we discuss the basic tools for creating complex data structures. Throughout the rest of this course, you'll gain experience and receive guidance in designing data structures which are appropriate to various kinds of problems.

Records

> ☐ We often wish to group data that is of different types, e.g., some data that is numeric, other that is textual, perhaps a boolean, and so on. To group together data of different types requires a *heterogeneous* data structure. Such a data structure is called a *record*.

As an example, consider the following record declaration:

```
EmployeeRecord isa record
     EmployeeNumber isa num
     SocSecNum isa num
     PayRate isa num
     FullTime isa boolean
     Benefits isa boolean
endrecord
```

This structure unites five different *fields* of data within a single data record. The identifier of the record is "EmployeeRecord." In addition, each field within the record has its own identifier: "EmployeeNumber," "SocSecNum," "PayRate," etc.

To refer to the contents of a given field within a record, we concatentate the *record identifier* with the *field identifier*, separated by a period. Thus, to access the employee's Social Security number, we would say,

```
EmployeeRecord.SocSecNum
```

and to access his or her pay rate, we would say,

```
EmployeeRecord.PayRate
```

The period (between "EmployeeRecord" and "PayRate," above) signifies that, after we go to the record specified by the *record identifier* (which precedes the period), we then look *inside that record* to find the field indicated by the *field identifier* (which follows the period). Thus, if we wanted to update the record of an employee who has just changed from part-time to full-time status, we might say,

```
EmployeeRecord.FullTime <- true
```

Creating New Record Data Types

Records give us the ability to group various kinds of data together, but notice the problem they present. If we have a group of 100 employees, we certainly would not want to declare 100 different records! Instead, we would want to create the appropriate *type* of record just once, then declare 100 different instances of it. To solve this problem, we need to be able to *create new data types*.

☐ By creating new data types of our own specification, we add to the *type definitions* which we can use in an algorithm. Once we have created a new data type, we can then create variables of that new data type, just as we can create variables of the atomic types (such as *num*, *char*, etc.).

We create new data types by declaring them, just as we declare variables. Our syntax is similar to that of a variable declaration. Instead of using "is a" or "isa" we use "defines a" or "definesa." For example, to create a new data type, EmployeeRecordType, we would say:

```
EmployeeRecordType definesa record
      EmployeeNumber isa num
      SocSecNum isa num
      PayRate isa num
      FullTime isa boolean
      Benefits isa boolean
endrecord
```

Once a new data type has been defined, we can then use it as the basis for declaring as many variables of that type as we require, e.g.,

```
var
      Employee1,
      Employee2,
      Employee3 isa EmployeeRecordType
```

Following the declaration of these three variables, we have three distinct occurrences of EmployeeRecordType. To access the particular fields within each record variable, we concatenate the identifier for the record *variable* (*not* the identifier for the new record *type*) with the field identifier, separated by a period, e.g.,

```
Employee1.SocSecNum  <- 123456789
```

or

```
Employee3.PayRate  <- 12.50
```

The Difference Between Types and Variables

> ☐ There is a *fundamental difference* between a *type* declaration and a *variable* declaration. Declaring a new (i.e., "user-defined") data type expands our repertoire of available data types, and thus allows us to declare variables of the new type. By itself, however, it does *not* create any variables of the new type. As with atomic data types, we must *explicitly declare* any variables we require.

Because data types are just definitions that can be used to create variables, but are not themselves variables, the scoping rule is different. Recall that variables can be "seen" only within the module in which they are declared, i.e., they are all "local." In contrast, type definitions are "global." This means they can be seen from all modules.

> ☐ *The scope of a type definition is unlimited within an algorithm.* That is to say, *if you define a new data type anywhere within an algorithm, that type definition can be "seen" and used for declaring variables anywhere*, i.e., in the main algorithm or in any of the modules it calls.

Anonymous Data Types

Separating *type definitions* from *variable declarations* is sufficiently powerful that in this course *it is required* when creating complex data structures.

> ☐ If you do not take advantage of this ability to "abstract out" the details of data structure design from the actual declaration of variables, you will be creating inferior data structures which are called *anonymous data types*. The name "anonymous data types" comes from the fact that such poor designs combine the *declaration of a complex variable* with the *definition of a new data type* such that the data type has no identifier and thus is "anonymous."

An example of *poor abstraction* featuring an *anonymous data type*:

```
var
     ThisEmployee isa record
          EmployeeNumber isa num
          SocSecNum isa num
          PayRate isa num
          FullTime isa boolean
          Benefits isa boolean
     endrecord {ThisEmployee}
```

An example of good abstraction with distinct *type* and *variable* declarations:

```
type
     EmployeeRecordType definesa record
          EmployeeNumber isa num
          SocSecNum isa num
          PayRate isa num
          FullTime isa boolean
          Benefits isa boolean
     endrecord  {EmployeeRecordType}

var
     ThisEmployee isa EmployeeRecordType
```

> ☐ Anonymous data types are bad, as they "hardwire" too many details into too many places in your algorithm. Any time you declare a complex variable that *includes* a data type declaration, you are guilty of "anonymous data typing." We consider this a significant shortcoming.

Many programming languages permit such design errors, but this fact should be not considered as an indication that anonymous data typing is permissible. After all, the design of automobiles permits you to drive into a wall at high speed, but that fact does not recommend that you actually do so!

Later in this chapter, we shall see examples that show the kinds of problems anonymous data types cause. For now, remember that we do not permit them.

Exercises   5.1 Declare a record type called `ClassGrade` which will hold the following information about a students grade in a class:

- lab average(a number)

- homework average(a number)

- quiz average(a number)

- whether or not currently grade is passing(a boolean)

5.2. Create a procedure that will read in (from the user) the information for a record of
the type declared in the previous problem, and pass that information out of the procedure. The procedure should only have one parameter. For the boolean value in the
record, read in a character ("Y" or "N") from the user and then determine whether to
assign *true* or *false* to the boolean.

5.3. Create a module that will collect this data for the class as a whole, keeping track of
the class average with respect to labs, homeworks, and quizzes, and a running total
of the number of students who report themselves to be passing or failing. Thus, the
module will accept data for a student and summary data for the class, and will update
that summary data to include the data for the student. Create any additional data
structures required.

Dynamic Data Structures

We've seen how to unite dissimilar data within a single structure by defining record
data types, then declaring record variables of those types. Such structures are *hetero-
geneous*, as they collect data of various types within a single record. This leaves us
with the problem of how to group together many occurrences of data *of the same
type*?

For example, we know how to create records which store various kinds of employee
data, but how do we create a structure that will contain the data for all the various employees of a company? Or, more simply, we know how to create a variable to store a
number, but how can we create a structure in which we can store a *list* of numbers?

> ☐ To store lists of values, we have two choices: *static* structures and *dynamic*
> structures. Static structures are, by definition, fixed in size, while dynamic
> structures grow and shrink dynamically as needed.

For pedagogical reasons, we shall cover dynamic structures first and will wait until later in the chapter to cover static list structures.

Dynamic structures are called "dynamic" because we do not have to specify their size. They grow and shrink dynamically so that they always fit the list data exactly. They are also known as *linked* structures because their elements are "linked together" by *pointers*. You will recall that *pointers* are the fourth of our atomic data types. We have not seen much of pointers until now. This is because pointers are useful primarily for allowing us to create and use dynamic structures and, thus, there's little to say about them until we deal with dynamic data.

There are three kind of dynamic data structures: *linked lists*, *trees*, and *graphs*. We shall discuss each in turn.

Linked Lists

A linked lists is the simplest form of linked structure. It consists of a chain of data locations, called *nodes*, linked together by pointers as in the following drawing:

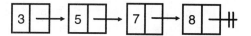

In this case, the nodes hold only one data item plus a pointer. However, nodes can hold multiple different data items in any combination we require. The only stipulation is that all nodes in a given list must have the *same* structure, i.e., they must have room for the same data types. The compartments that hold data inside a node are "fields." The nodes in the list above have two fields : a *number* field and a *pointer* field. Notice that the pointer field in each node points to the next node in the list.

> ☐ The last pointer in the list points to *nil*, signifying that this pointer does not point to anything. A *nil* pointer is always used to mark the end of the list.

Before we go on to more details of linked lists, it may be helpful to present an analogy to help you visualize how linked lists behave. They are quite a bit like trains, actually. Imagine a passenger train with multiple cars. Each car can hold some number of people, and the cars are linked to each other by a coupling which hooks one car to the car behind to it. This is rather like our drawing above: the nodes are are like train cars, our data fields are like the passengers, and the pointers are the couplings. Train cars can be added at the front and the back of the train very easily, and they can be added in the middle by unlinking two cars and linking a new one in between. Again, this is very much like a linked list and is the source of their great value: linked lists can be changed to suit the needs of the moment. Nodes can be added, deleted, and rearranged at will, just as railroad cars can be added, removed or reordered.

In our example, each node consists of two fields: a number and a pointer. Thus, each node itself must be a record, as it contains dissimilar data types. You might expect that nodes are defined in a type definition, e.g.,

```
type
     ListNode definesa record
           Data isa num
           Next isa ptr
     endrecord
```

This is close. The only thing wrong with the above type definition is that a pointer declaration must include a specification of the type of data to which it can point. This is because a given pointer can only point to one type of data. Thus, we do the following:

```
type
     ListPtr definesa ptr toa ListNode
     ListNode defines a record
           Data isa num
           Next isa ListPtr
     endrecord
```

Observe that we first defined ListPtr as a data type: a pointer that can point to a ListNode. Then, we used that new type in defining the **Next** field within List-Node.

In the drawing above, we have a linked list consisting of four record variables, each being of type ListNode and each one thus having both a Data field and a Next field. As drawn above, the linked list is not good for anything. Why? Because we cannot "get at it," i.e., there is no name for the linked list and, without an identifier, we have no way to refer to it. Thus, we need some means of naming the linked list. To name a linked list, we use an atomic pointer variable of the same ListPtr type that we used for defining the Next field, e.g.,

```
var
     ListHead isa ListPtr
```

With *ListHead* pointing to first node in the list (we'll discuss how to arrange this shortly), our list would look like:

ListHead

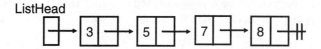

Observe that ListHead is *not* a node. It contains no data and is not, strictly speaking, part of the linked list. Instead, it is a named pointer variable that gives us a way to access to the list.

This is the second use of a ListPtr in the example so far. First we used ListPtr as the *type of a field* within each ListNode, and now we use it as the *type of a named variable* that points to the beginning of the list. We use a ListPtr in these two situations for one reason: both ListHead and the Next field within each node must be able to point to variables of type ListNode.

Using pointers
to access nodes　To illustrate how to use pointers, we shall begin by using the following linked list as an example:

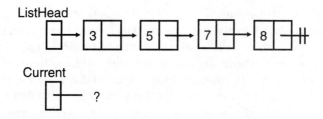

which implies the declarations:

```
type
        ListPtr definesa ptr toa ListNode
        ListNode defines a record
            Data isa num
            Next isa ListPtr
        endrecord
    var
        ListHead,
        Current isa ListPtr
```

Ignore, for the moment, how we created the list and how we arranged to have ListHead point to the list of four nodes. For now, observe that ListHead points to the first node in the list, while Current is pointing to a question mark. The question mark implies that the value of Current is *undefined*, i.e., we have *declared* it as a variable but have not *assigned* any value to it. Pointers, like any other variable, should *always* have some value assigned to them. Thus, if `Current` is not pointing to anything, we should assign it the value *nil*, via,

```
Current <- nil
```

We would pictorially represent the result of this as:

ListHead

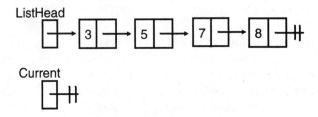

Current

Or, we might assign `Current` to point to the first node in the list via,

```
Current <- ListHead
```

To understand this instruction, let's review what pointers are. Pointers store only the *address* (or *location*) of a node, *not any data values*. `ListHead` points to the first node in the list because it "knows where that first node is," i.e., `ListHead` contains the *address* of that node. By assigning the *value* of `ListHead` to `Current`, we get the *address* from `ListHead` and store a copy of that *address* in `Current`. Thus `ListHead` and `Current` both hold the same value: not a data value but an *address*, i.e., they both now know where the first node is to be found and thus we say that each one "points" to the first node in the list, which we show as:

ListHead

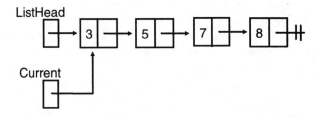

Current

To access the contents of the nodes themselves, we must "follow" a pointer which points to them. To follow a pointer, we use the "carat" symbol (^), which means "follow the pointer and go where it leads." Thus, to retrieve the value stored in the `Data` field of the the first node and store it in *num* variable `SomeNumVar`, we would write:

```
SomeNumVar <- ListHead^.Data
```

This statement is read as "follow `ListHead` to wherever it points; once there, inspect the value stored in the `Data` field and copy that value into `SomeNumVar`."

To store the value 4 in the `Data` field of the first node, we would say,

```
ListHead^.Data <- 4
```

This statement is read as "follow `ListHead` to wherever it points; once there, access the `Data` field and store *4* in it." As a result of this instruction, the list would look like:

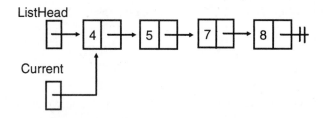

Because `ListHead` and `Current` point to the same node, if we were to now use the instruction,

```
SomeNumVar <- Current^.Data
```

it would result in *4* being assigned to `SomeNumVar`. Because the two named pointers both point to the first node, we could accomplish the exact same thing via:

```
SomeNumVar <- ListHead^.Data
```

To access the second node in the list, we could simply chain together a list of references which points to it. For example, we could assign to `SomeNumVar` the value stored in the second node (i.e., *5*) via

```
SomeNumVar <- ListHead^.Next^.Data
```

which means, "follow the `ListHead` pointer to wherever it points; once there, access the `Next` field; then, follow *that* pointer to wherever *it* goes; once there, access the value in the `Data` field, and copy whatever you find there into `SomeNumVar`."

Similarly, to assign to `SomeNumVar` the data value of the third node, in this case 7, we could write,

```
SomeNumVar <- ListHead^.Next^.Next^.Data
```

We can chain together references to pointers and data fields in whatever fashion is necessary to get to where we want to go. Regardless of the length of the chain of reference, the key trick is to grasp what is meant by the symbols "^." (people often say "up dot" to refer to the *carat* followed by the *period*). "Up dot" means, quite simply, "follow the pointer to the node to which it points, then look in the field..."

Actually, both the "up" and the "dot" each mean something quite specific. The "up" means "dereference the pointer," which is programmer jargon for "follow the pointer and see where it goes." The "dot" means "look inside the field which is specified next." (Note that the "dot" has the same meaning regardless of whether we're using pointers or not, e.g., `ThisEmployee.PayRate` where `ThisEmployee` is a record variable of type `EmployeeRecordType`)

Thus,

```
ListHead^.Next^.Next^.Data
```

means "follow ListHead, then look in the Next field; once there, follow *that* pointer, then look in the Next field that you find there; once there, follow *that* pointer, then look in the Data field."

As you can see, chaining together of pointer references can become confusing and annoying. Fortunately, there is a better way. We can achieve the same effect by changing the location to which a pointer points. Thus, to easily access the second node in the list, we would first write,

```
Current <- Current^.Next
```

This means that we assign to `Current` whatever value is in `Current^.Next`. Since `Current` points to the first node in the list, we know that `Current^.Next` points to the second node in the list. Thus, assigning `Current^.Next` to `Current` results in `Current` pointing wherever `Current^.Next` points, e.g., to the second node. After making this assignment, the list would look like:

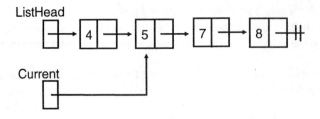

At this moment in time, then, both `Current` and `ListHead^.Next` have the same value, i.e., both of them holds the address of the second node in the list.

Similarly, we can move `Current` to point to the third node in the list by using *exactly the same instruction* again. Because `Current` now points to the second node, we know that `Current^.Next` points to the third node, and assigning its value to `Current` results in:

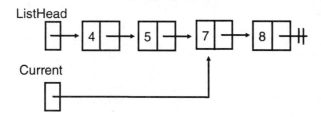

This mode of reference (moving a pointer) allows us to walk through a linked list step by step. For example, if we wished to sum the values stored in a linked list such as the one above, we might do so via a repetitive routine that, on each of its several repetitions, adds `Current^.Data` to the total and then advances `Current` to `Current^.Next` until it reached a value of *nil*.

When manipulating pointers into a linked list, note that it is necessary to be careful about the implications of which pointer we adjust. Observe that, in our examples, we declare and manipulate temporary pointers (such as `Current` or `Temp`). We do so because of the danger in moving `ListHead` itself. We want `ListHead` to *always* point to the first node in the list and must be careful that we do not move it away accidentally. Why? Consider the result if we now executed

```
ListHead <- ListHead^.Next
```

`ListHead` will now point to the second node, while `Current` still points to the third node. By moving `ListHead` "down the list" we have lost our access to the first node. Even though the first node points to the second node, *nothing points to the first node*. This means that we have effectively "lost" the first node in the list. Thus, be sure to move `ListHead` (or whatever you call your primary list-access pointer) only when you intend to change what you mean by "head of the list."

Using pointers to add nodes   A big advantage of linked lists lies in the fact that we do not have to know in advance how many elements there will be in a linked list. This is because we can dynamically create more elements and add them as we go along. We can add a node to our list by creating a new one and inserting it into the list at the end, at the beginning, or at any point in-between.

For example, consider the following linked list:

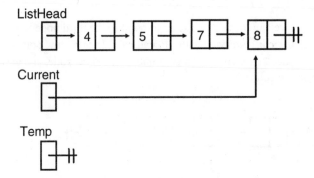

To create a new node, store the value 9 in it, and add that node to the end of the list, we would write,

```
Temp <- new(ListNode)
Temp^.Data <- 9
Current^.Next <- Temp
Temp^.Next <- nil
```

Let's consider what each of these four instructions does. The first instruction,

```
Temp <- new(ListNode)
```

creates a new variable of type `ListNode` and stores its location in `Temp`. `Temp` now points to it. Thus, after it executes, the situation looks like:

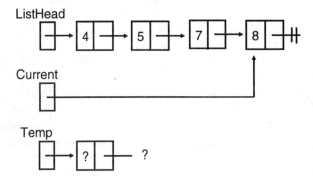

The question marks indicate that the values of both the new node's fields (`Data` and `Next`) are undefined.

The second instruction,

```
Temp^.Data <- 9
```

assigns the value *9* to the Data field of the node is pointed to by Temp, resulting in:

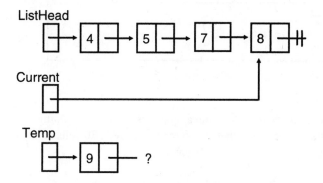

The third instruction,

```
Current^.Next <- Temp
```

connects the new node to the list: Current^.Next had been *nil* but is assigned to point to *whatever* is pointed to by Temp, resulting in:

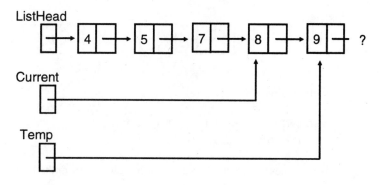

Finally, we assign,

```
Temp^.Next <- nil
```

which gives us:

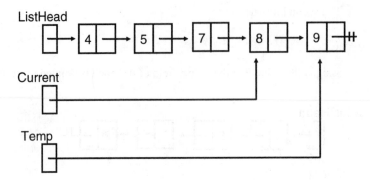

Using pointers to delete nodes   We can also *delete* nodes from a linked list as needed. Doing so means that no space is wasted by variables that are no longer needed. To delete a node, we simply arrange that there is no pointer pointing to it.

(In some programming languages, an automatic process gathers such nodes and returns their space to available memory. This is known as *garbage collection*. In other languages, explicit actions must be taken to free the space used by such nodes. For simplicity, we'll adopt the former convention.)

For example, imagine that we want to obtain the value from the first node in the list below, then delete the first node from the list.

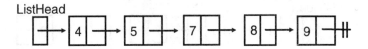

We could do this via,

```
SomeNumVar <- ListHead^.Data
ListHead <- ListHead^.Next
```

The first of these instructions obtains the data value from the first node and stores it in `SomeNumVar`. The second instruction adjusts the `ListHead` pointer by over-writing its contents (i.e., the address of the first node) with whatever address is stored in the first node's pointer (i.e., the address of the second node). If applied to the linked list shown above, these instructions would result in the list as shown at the top of next page.

One great advantage of linked lists is that we can have exactly the space we require at all times. If the list is too big, we shrink it; if it is not big enough, we expand it.

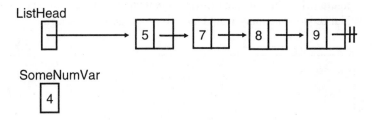

ListHead

SomeNumVar

The list is never to big or too small, and there is never any wasted space. While the particular details of manipulating them may be confusing at first, there is nothing mysterious about them. They provide a very important tool and, with practice, working with them becomes "second nature." This is one of the reasons we introduce you to them early: we want you to gain enough familiarity and competence with them that manipulating them will become almost automatic for you.

The Scope of Linked Data

Earlier, when we gave our rule for the scope of data, we said, *"The scope of named data is limited to the module in which it is declared."* Notice that we said the *"scope of named* data is limited..."* That is exactly what we meant: any *named* variables are limited in scope. Observe however that the nodes in a linked list do *not* have names. The named pointer variables (e.g., `ListHead` and `Current`, which are needed to access the nodes) have names, but they are not nodes. The nodes themselves have no names. Nodes in a linked structure have the same scope as *types* and *constants*:

The nodes of a linked structure are not limited in scope.

Static vs. Dynamic Variables

To understand this, it is helpful to understand something about how and where computers store data. In particular, you should understand the difference between *static* and *dynamic* allocations of memory. Earlier, we suggested using a *stack* to help trace the execution of recursive calls. As each call was made, a frame for that call was pushed on top of the stack and, when each call completed, its frame was popped off the stack. In point of fact, this mechanism is more than just a good way to trace execution; it is how most computers really operate!

Imagine the computer's memory to be a large rectangular area consisting of many individual cells such that each cell has its own address. As a program begins to execute, a frame is pushed onto the stack. Within this frame is where all the *named* variables and constants that are declared within the main algorithm are actually stored. (The more named variables and constants that are declared, the larger this frame will be, as it must be sized to accommodate all the named data that has been declared.) Thus, in the main algorithm included the declaration of the two variables, `ListHead` and `SumNumVar`, as execution begins memory would look like the

figure below left. If `ListHead` were then initialized to *nil* and `SomeNumVar` initialized to *4*, memory would look like the figure below right.

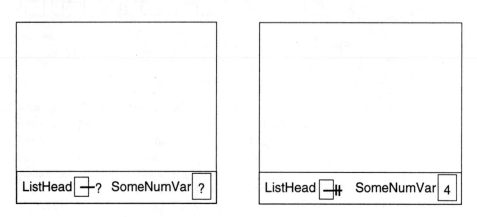

Now, imagine that within the algorithm is a procedure that inserts a new node into
the list. It might look like:

```
procedure AddToList   (Current isa in/out ListPtr,
                       NewNum isa in num)
     {Purpose: inserts a new node, containing the value
         of NewNum into a linked list, immediately after
         the node pointed to by Current; requires that
         Current not be nil}
var
     Temp isa ListPtr
begin
     Temp <- new(ListNode)
     Temp ^.Data <- NewNum
     Temp^.Next <- Current^.Next
     Current^.Next <- Temp
end {procedure AddToList}
```

and the main algorithm might call it via:

```
AddToList(ListHead, SomeNumVar)
```

As this module is called, its frame is pushed onto the top of the stack, and within that
frame is where all its *named* data resides. Thus, after the call, but before the procedure's code has been executed, the stack would look like the figure below left.

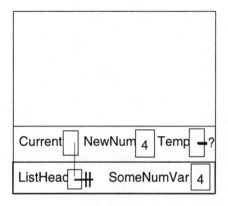 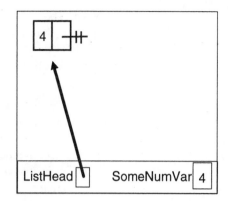

Above left, we see the new frame on the stack for the called procedure, and we see its named variables within that frame. In particular, note that:

- NewNum has received its own copy of the value passed to it via parameter. It gets its own copy because NewNum is declared as an *in* parameter.

- Current does *not* get its own copy of ListHead; instead, it gets access to ListHead itself. This is because Current is declared as an *in/out* parameter, meaning that whatever changes might be made to Current are in fact made to ListHead. As an *in/out* parameter, Current effectively operates as a *pseudonym* or *alias* for ListHead within the called procedure.

- The value of Temp is *undefined*; it has been declared as a local variable within the called procedure and thus does not have any initial value passed to it via parameter. its value is not defined until an instruction within the procedure assigns a value to it.

As the code of AddToList is executed, a new node will be created, its Data field assigned a value, its Next pointer assigned a value, and it will be connected to the list. However, since the new node is not a *named* variable (but rather is *dynamically allocated* and thus is *accessible only via following a pointer*), it will not reside in a stack frame.

> ☐ All *dynamically allocated variables* do not reside in the *stack*. Instead, they reside in another area of memory, in what is called the *heap*.

While real world computer implementations vary, you may think of the *heap* as being at the "other end" of memory from the *stack*, i.e., the stack begins at the bottom and builds upward, while the heap begins at the top of memory and expands downward. The state of memory after `AddToList` has executed, and then popped off the stack, is shown on the right side of the figure (top of previous page). Observe that it has left behind a different data state than it found: there is now a node in the *heap* and `ListHead` points to it.

> ☐ This is the kind of thing that really happens, more or less, when a program is run on a real computer:
>
> As each procedure or function is called, it gets its own *stack frame,* which is *pushed* onto the stack and thus expands the stack upward. As each subprogram completes, its frame is *popped* off the stack, shrinking the stack and freeing the memory that the stack frame had occupied.
>
> As each piece of *dynamic memory* is allocated, it partially fills the *heap.* As each piece of dynamic memory is deallocated, it frees up room in the *heap.*
>
> When the *stack* and the allocated portion of memory in the *heap* grow, in some combination, to the point where they collide with one other, the computer has run out of memory.

This process explains *why* it is that *named* variables declared within procedures or functions do not live for the life of the program. It is because they physically exist within the stack frame for the module in which they are declared. And when that module completes, and its frame is popped off the stack, the physical locations for the named variables get "blown away." The *only* reason that the named identifiers declared within the main algorithm "live" throughout execution is because the stack frame for the main algorithm is created when the algorithm starts and does not get popped off the stack until the entire algorithm completes.

> ☐ As you create algorithms and trace their execution, an awareness of these facts allows you to do just what a computer does. In short, you can follow the creation and reallocation of variables by making sketches of memory, placing *named* (or "*static*") variables in the appropriate stack frame, placing *dynamic* variables in the heap, and updating values in the appropriate locations. Experience has shown that such sketches are invaluable tools for aiding students (and programmers!) in understanding what their algorithms *really* do.

Summary of Linked List Features   Linked lists provide a way to store a *homogeneous* collection of data such that many items of the same type can be associated within the same list structure.. Each item in a linked list is a *node.* Each node consists of *data* and a *pointer.* The data may be simple (such as a number), or it may be a complex structure (such as a record consisting of numerous data fields). The pointer within each node allows the nodes to be connected to one another into a single list, in much the same way that railroad cars are coupled together to constitute a train. Like the cars of a railroad train, nodes may be added, deleted, rearranged, and have their contents changed at will.

The nodes of a linked list are *dynamic variables* which an algorithm may create and deallocate at any time. Thus, a linked list can always be of exactly the right size for any given list of data. Dynamic variables are allocated space in the *heap*, and survive as long as some pointer points to them. In this respect, dynamic variables differ from *static (or named) variables* which come into being only when the module in which they are declared is called, and which are deallocated only when their module completes and has its frame popped off the activation stack.

Because the dynamic variables that constitute a linked list have no identifiers, they can be accessed only by navigating to them from some *named* pointer variable. At least one named pointer variable must exist on the stack and point to the linked list for the list to exist and be accessible. By following a named pointer to the linked list, the nodes of the linked list may be accessed as appropriate to the task at hand.

Traversing Linked Lists   Traversing a linked list means stepping through the list, node by node, to print or process the data contained in some or all of the nodes. A linked list traversal algorithm starts with a pointer pointing to the beginning of the list, allowing us to print or process the data in the first node, then moves the pointer to each successive node in turn. The traversal ends when the pointer points to *nil*, i.e., has the same value as does the last "Next" pointer in the list.

Any traversal algorithm is inherently repetitive, i.e., it must execute an appropriate series of instructions some number of times. As with all repetitive algorithms, this may be accomplished via a recursive routine.

A Recursive Traversal   The purpose of this example traversal is to start at the beginning of the list and continuously print-and-move until we encounter the list's end, at which point we simply stop. Since there are no "terminating steps," we use the second recursive form:

```
if NOT (terminating condition) then
    move one step closer to the terminating condition
    call a "clone" of the recursive module
endif
```

To construct the recursive solution, we need only "plug in" the particulars to this general form. What is our terminating condition? We know that we'll need some temporary pointer variable. We'll call it `CurrentPtr`. Our traversal should terminate when `CurrentPtr = nil`, which will indicate that we're at the end of the list. Thus, our terminating condition is:

```
(CurrentPtr = nil)
```

and we can state our condition for *continuing* the recursion as:

```
if NOT (CurrentPtr = nil) then
```

or, equivalently:

```
if (CurrentPtr <> nil) then
```

"Taking one step closer" to the terminating condition means "printing and moving the pointer." We can write these steps as:

```
print (CurrentPtr^.Data)
CurrentPtr <- CurrentPtr^.Next
```

The former instruction carries out the required action (printing), while the latter instruction "moves us one step closer": `CurrentPtr` is now one position further down the list, perhaps pointing to the next node or perhaps *nil*. In either case, with `CurrentPtr` advanced, we can now "call a clone of the recursive module" via,

```
TraverseRecurse (CurrentPtr)
```

That's all there is to it. The recursive solution is given below.

```
procedure TraverseRecurse (CurrentPtr isa in ListPtr)
begin
    if (CurrentPtr < > nil) then
        print(CurrentPtr^.Data)
        CurrentPtr <- CurrentPtr^.Next
        TraverseRecurse(CurrentPtr)
    endif
end {TraverseRecurse}
```

Observe that the last two instructions before the `endif` can be combined into:

```
TraverseRecurse(CurrentPtr^.Next)
```

Presumably, when this procedure was called, it was passed the value of `ListHead`. Since we do not want to change the value of `ListHead`, we use an input parameter and give that parameter the name `CurrentPtr`. Because the parameter is an *input* parameter, any changes to `CurrentPtr` will *not* affect `ListHead`, because `CurrentPtr` is a local *copy* of `ListHead`'s value.

In effect, we *assume* that our algorithm begins at the head of the list. However, this is determined by the calling algorithm: the traversal will begin at *whatever* location is dictated by the parameter that is initially passed in. Thus, if the calling algorithm sends us a pointer that points to the middle node of the list, then we shall traverse only the last half of the list.

If `CurrentPtr` is not *nil*, we print the data field of the node it points to. Then we move `CurrentPtr` one node closer to the end of the list (the stopping case) and call the procedure recursively. In effect, what we are doing is calling many clones of the procedure, and each one is passed a "list head" pointer to a smaller list. The reason we call it a "list head" pointer (in quotation marks) is that it does not actually point to the first node of the entire list, but rather points to *the first node in the list of nodes that have not yet been visited*. Our algorithm has no way of knowing if anything is to the left of `CurrentPtr`. Hence, each clone 'thinks' that it is getting a full linked list. The process is illustrated by figures *a* through *f* (next page).

- (a) The original list before calling the traversal procedure.

- (b)-(f) The list as the traversal progresses.

- `CurrentPtr` can be thought of as a head pointer to a list that is one element smaller each time the procedure is called recursively. The large "bubbles" enclose the nodes in `CurrentPtr`'s list at each recursive call.

A Recursive Search   *Searching* a linked list to find a particular data value requires modification to the traversal algorithm. We must add a parameter by which the searching routine can receive the *target value* (the value for which it is searching), and we must change the actions we take so that we print messages which indicates whether the search has succeeded or failed. Because there *are* actions to take after the terminating condition has been reached, the first of our two formats for recursion is called for. Also, we must change the terminating condition to stop under either of two conditions:

```
(Current^.Next = nil) OR (Current^.Data = Target)
```

Should these two conditions be *OR*'d into one condition? Are they fine as they are? Or should there be two different tests in different places? Is there any reason to favor one version over the other?

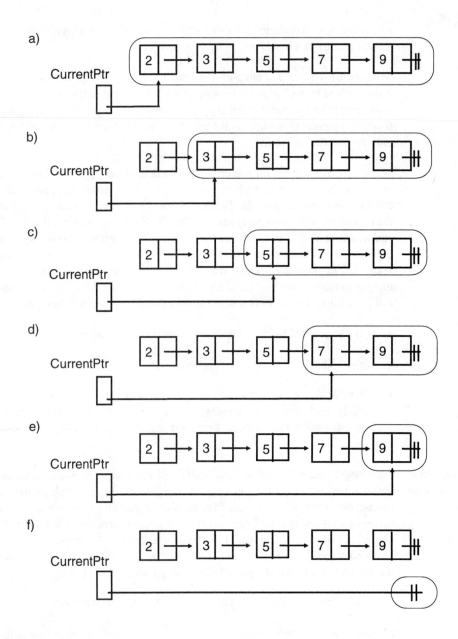

Exercises 5.4. Create a module that will accept a pointer of type ListPtr and will return the sum of the numeric values in a linked list.

5.5. Create a module that will delete the last node in a linked list.

5.6. Create a module that will traverse a linked list of numbers and insert a new node with the value 32 immediately after the first node that holds a value greater than 10. If no such node is found, the module should terminate without doing anything.

5.7. A string is defined to be a collection of characters. We do not know how many characters we want our string to hold, so we need a linked list of characters to hold the string. Declare the data structure(s) necessary to for a linked list implementation of a string.

5.8. Write a recursive module called `ReadString` that will take in a `StringPointer` and will add characters to the end of the string linked list. When it encounters the character '.' (period), the procedure will terminate.

5.9. Write a recursive module ReadStringBackwards that will behave just as the module from problem 5.5 except that it will add each new character to the front of the list instead of to the end. As a result, it will store words backwards.

5.10. A palindrome is a word that is spelled the same forwards and backwards. ('dad', 'mom' and 'sis' are palindromes, but 'bro' is not.). Use the modules you developed in problems 5.4 - 5.7 to create an algorithm that detects if a character string is a palindrome. (Do not re-write the modules that you wrote for those problems, but call them as needed from this algorithm). Your algorithm will:

a) read in a character string (ala problem 5.5);

b) traverse the resulting string, reading each character in it, and copying each character into a reversed string (ala problem 5.6);

c) after creating the two strings, traverse both strings together, comparing each character, until you have determined if the original stored is a palindrome.

Binary Trees

A tree is a data structure that is made of nodes and pointers, just like linked lists. The difference between trees and linked lists is how they are organized. In a linked list, each node is connected to one "successor" node (via a "Next" pointer), i.e., it is *linear*. In a tree, the nodes can have *several* "next" pointers, each pointing to a different node.

The top node in the tree is called the *root* and all other nodes branch off from this one. Every node in a tree can have some number of *children*. Each *child* node can, in turn, be the *parent* node to its children, and so on. Of course, within each node, each of the various pointers requires its own unique field identifier, perhaps "Child1," "Child2," "Child3," and so on. A common example of a tree data structure is the generic "family tree" used in geneology.

The most common form of tree data structure is a *binary tree*. A binary tree is a tree that is limited such that each node can only have two such pointers. This is why it is called a "binary" tree. To distinguish between the two children of a node, they are referred to as the "left" and "right" children. Nodes which have no children, i.e., both child pointers have been assigned the value "nil," are called "leaves." Thus, we have very sensible nomenclature if we just think of a real world tree upside-down: the root is at the top and the leaves are at the bottom. The figure below shows one example of a binary tree.

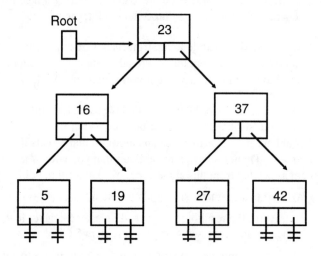

A binary tree implies declarations similar to those of a linked list. For the example shown above, in which each node has only a single numerical data field, the declarations might be:

```
type
    TreePtr definesa ptr toa TreeNode
    TreeNode defines a record
            Data isa num
            LeftChild isa TreePtr
            RightChild isa TreePtr
    endrecord
```

In the same way that successful use of a linked list requires that we always keep a named pointer (perhaps called `ListHead` or some other descriptive name) pointing to the first node of the list, successful use of trees require that we always keep a named pointer pointing to the root of the tree. Without such a pointer pointing to the tree, we have no way to access the tree. (Furthermore, if there is no pointer pointing to the root, a chain reaction of deallocation would automatically result.) Thus, it is imperative that there is always some named pointer (perhaps called `TreeRoot` or `Root`) pointing to the root node of the tree. For tree manipulation purposes, we often use other, temporary pointers so that we do not move the `TreeRoot` pointer away from the root. Thus, we will often have declarations of named pointer variables such as

```
var
      TreeRoot,
      Current isa TreePtr
```

To access various locations in a tree, we use pointers just as we did before, i.e., to access the data value stored in the "left child" of the root, we might say,

```
      Current <- TreeRoot
      Current <- Current^.LeftChild
      SomeNumVar <- Current^.Data
```

The first instruction causes Current to point at the root of the tree. The second instruction causes Current to then point to the left child of the root. Once it points there, the third instruction copies the value of that node into the variable SomeNum-Var.

Trees are invaluable for helping us overcome a universal problem: how to store large amounts of data such that we can combine both:

• fast access to any particular piece of data

• flexibility in terms of adding and deleting data from storage.

Without trees, we often have to choose between speed and flexibility. As we shall see, with trees we often can have both.

Traversing Binary Trees   Binary trees can be used to overcome one of the weaknesses of linked lists: the inability to quickly find a particular node. After all, we want to do more with data structures than just store data in them: we need to be able to retrieve the data as well. With a linked list, finding a value means starting with the first node and examining all the nodes in the list until we find the one we're looking for. Binary trees let us find things faster. However, traversing binary trees is a bit more complicated than traversing linked lists because we cannot merely step through a linear sequence. Trees are not linear and we instead have to navigate through the various branches. For each node in the tree, we must traverse one branch, then return to the root and traverse another branch, and so on until each branch has been traversed. While trees may have any number of branches, the most widely used tree is the binary tree, and we shall confine ourselves to that topology.

Because of the recursively-defined structure of a binary tree, the traversal algorithm is inherently recursive. To see what we mean by "recursively defined structure," think of the three components of a binary tree:

- a root node
- a left subtree
- a right subtree

The left child of the root node is itself the root of the left subtree, and the right child is the root of the right subtree. The same can be said for each and every node in the tree: each node is the root of the subtree below it. Even the leaves of the tree are roots of their own subtree, albeit subtrees which contain no further subtrees.

Tree traversal algorithms exploit this fact. We must first traverse one subtree, then return to the root to traverse the other subtree. An ordering of steps which does this can be recursively called each time a new node is visited.

We can break the original tree traversal problem into three smaller parts:

1) traversal of a single node: the root
2) traversal of the left subtree
3) traversal of the right subtree

Traversing a single node is trivial: we simply visit that node and take care of whatever our business might be (processing its value, printing out its value, whatever). To traverse each of the two subtrees, we simply consider the topmost node of each subtree as the root of that subtree and recursively call the algorithm.

There are three ways to traverse a binary tree, called *InOrder*, *PreOrder*, and *PostOrder*. They are remarkably similar to one another, each containing the same three logical steps, listed above. They differ only in the order in which the three steps are carried out.

The ordering of steps is what gives rise to their names. In the *PreOrder* traversal, the root node of a tree is the first one visited (hence the prefix "*Pre*"), then the left subtree is traversed, and finally the right subtree. In an *InOrder* traversal, the root node is visited after the left subtree and before the right subtree - it is "*In*" the middle. In the *PostOrder* traversal the root node is visited after both the left and right subtrees have been completely traversed - thus the prefix "*Post.*" Because the *InOrder* traversal is used most frequently, we shall concentrate first on the algorithm for it.

(We have used capitalization, e.g., "PreOrder," "InOrder," "PostOrder," to clarify what the words mean. Henceforth, we shall omit the capitalization and use the usual forms: "preorder," "inorder," and "postorder.")

Given the root of a tree, an inorder traversal traverses the left subtree of the root, then visits the root, then traverses the right subtree. In traversing the left or right subtree, the same rule is applied in a recursive manner. The algorithm is as follows. (Note that the numerical labels for each line are not part of the procedure. They are there to facilitate our discussion of the execution of the algorithm.)

```
1 procedure Inorder(CurrentPtr isa in TreePtr)
      {Purpose: performs an inorder traversal on a binary
          tree which stores numbers, printing the data
          value stored in each node}
2 begin
3   if (CurrentPtr <> nil) then
4      Inorder(CurrentPtr^.LeftChild)
5      print (CurrentPtr^.Data)
6      Inorder(CurrentPtr^.RichtChild)
7   endif
8 end {Inorder Traversal}
```

This algorithm looks amazingly simple considering the complicated task it performs: it can traverse any binary tree, regardless of its particular shape, regardless of whether it is balanced or lopsided, and regardless of whether it contains one node or billions of nodes. Thus, it provides a good example of the elegant power of recursion. Let's step through the algorithm, using the *binary search tree* shown at the top of the next page.

Binary Search A *binary search tree*, or *BST*, is a binary tree that has its data values arranged in a
Trees particular way: each node contains a value *larger* than *all* the values in its left subtree and *smaller* than *all* the values in its right subtree. This relationship, between node's value and the values stored in the subtrees rooted by a that node, holds true for each node in the tree. Any binary tree that conforms to this pattern can be called a *binary search tree*.

Given the values stored in this tree, a traversal which outputs the values in sorted order must produce the output:

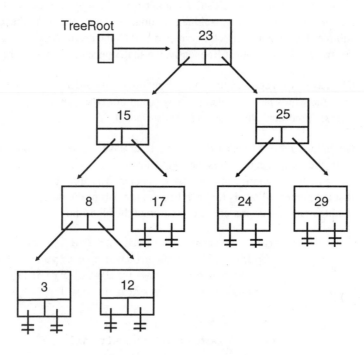

TreeRoot

```
3, 8, 12, 15, 17, 23, 24, 25, 29
```

This is accomplished by an *inorder* traversal. To see how it does it, we shall again use a *stack* to help us keep track of the recursion. (We know that the tree nodes themselves are stored in the *heap*, but we wo not waste the space to show the heap each time, only the stack.) In each stack frame we will keep three pieces of information for each recursive call: (1) the data value stored in the node pointed to by CurrentPtr, (2) the number of the instruction in which the recursive call was made, and (3) the node to which a pointer was passed in the recursive call; we'll indicate this via the data value stored in that node. Since recursive calls are made only in the lines labeled 4 and 6 in the algorithm, each call can only be interrupted by a recursive call in line 4 or line 6.

(Suggestion: it might be best to take scrap paper and copy the algorithm from the previous page *and* sketch the tree shown above. Otherwise you'll either *not* follow our trace of the recursion *or* drive yourself batty flipping pages back and forth!)

The algorithm is initially called via

```
Inorder(TreeRoot)
```

where `TreeRoot` is a `TreePtr` that points to the node containing the data value 23. Thus, the algorithm is initially passed a pointer to the node containing 23. Since that node has a left subtree, whose root is the node containing 15, the algorithm is interrupted by a recursive call to traverse that subtree (line 4). Thus, we put a frame on the stack representing the first call of procedure Inorder, i.e., when `CurrentPtr` points to the root node). In this frame, we record information such as: *the line in which the execution of the algorithm was interrupted by a recursive call*, and *the node to which a pointer was passed to the recursive "clone" of the algorithm*. Thus, with `CurrentPtr` pointing to the root, and a recursive call occurring in line 4 of the procedure, our stack frame might look like:

CurrentPtr points to node w/23; Call: line 4; Passes ptr to 15

The second clone of the algorithm then begins, with the node containing 15 being *its* root. This node has a left subtree also, so the algorithm is interrupted in line 4. A recursive call is invoked on its left subtree, i.e., the subtree whose root is the node containing 8. Thus we put another frame on the stack:

CurrentPtr points to node w/15; Call: line 4; Passes ptr to 8
CurrentPtr points to node w/23; Call: line 4; Passes ptr to 15

The third clone of the algorithm begins, with `CurrentPtr` pointing to the node containing 8. This clone of the algorithm is interrupted exactly as the previous ones were, and the stack looks like:

CurrentPtr points to node w/8;   Call: line 4; Passes ptr to 3
CurrentPtr points to node w/15; Call: line 4; Passes ptr to 8
CurrentPtr points to node w/23; Call: line 4; Passes ptr to 15

The fourth clone of the algorithm has `CurrentPtr` pointing to the node containing 3. As before, it is interrupted inn line 4, and the stack now looks like:

CurrentPtr points to node w/3; Call: line 4; Passes ptr to nil
CurrentPtr points to node w/8; Call: line 4; Passes ptr to 3
CurrentPtr points to node w/15; Call: line 4; Passes ptr to 8
CurrentPtr points to node w/23; Call: line 4; Passes ptr to 15

Here, we find something different. This time, the algorithm is called to act on the tree rooted by a *nil* pointer. As it begins execution, the stack looks like:

| CurrentPtr points to nil |
| CurrentPtr points to node w/3; Call: line 4; Passes ptr to nil |
| CurrentPtr points to node w/8; Call: line 4; Passes ptr to 3 |
| CurrentPtr points to node w/15; Call: line 4; Passes ptr to 8 |
| CurrentPtr points to node w/23; Call: line 4; Passes ptr to 15 |

Because `CurrentPtr` is *nil*, the condition in line 3 fails. Thus, this clone of the algorithm completes its work without doing anything at all. its frame (the top one) is popped off the stack.

At this point, we return to the stack and "wake up" the process represented in what is now the the top-most frame. This is the clone that has a pointer to the node containing 3 as its root. It was interrupted in line 4. Since that call has now finished, it can proceed to line 5 and its `Current^.Value`, the number 3, is printed. The algorithm then proceeds to line 6. This causes the algorithm to be interrupted again, this time by a recursive call which passes the current node's *right* child pointer. Thus, the stack now looks like:

| CurrentPtr points to node w/3; Call: line 6; Passed Ptr to nil |
| CurrentPtr points to node w/8; Call: line 4 Passed Ptr to 3 |
| CurrentPtr points to node w/15; Call: line 4; Passed Ptr to 8 |
| CurrentPtr points to node w/23; Call: line 4; Passed Ptr to 15 |

Once again, we have a stack that is five frames high, and once again the topmost frame has a *nil* pointer as its root pointer, e.g.,:

| CurrentPtr points to nil |
| CurrentPtr points to node w/3; Call: line 6; Passes ptr to nil |
| CurrentPtr points to node w/8; Call: line 4; Passes ptr to 3 |
| CurrentPtr points to node w/15; Call: line 4; Passes ptr to 8 |
| CurrentPtr points to node w/23; Call: line 4; Passes ptr to 15 |

Since the new call is passed a *nil* pointer, the test in its line 3 fails and it completes without doing anything. As a result, the topmost stack frame is popped off the stack, and the fourth stack frame is now the topmost one. It wakes up having completed its line 6 and it continues its execution. After line 6, all that remains is for it to end, at which point its stack frame is popped off the stack too.

Now, the topmost stack frame is the third one, i.e., the one whose `CurrentPtr` points to the node containing the data value 8. It wakes up having completed its line 4. It continues execution to line 5, printing out the value 8. So far, we have printed out the values 3 and 8. Execution then proceeds to its line 6, which is a recursive call to which the right child pointer is passed, e.g.:

| CurrentPtr points to node w/8; Call: line 6; Passes ptr to 12 |
| CurrentPtr points to node w/15; Call: line 4; Passes ptr to 8 |
| CurrentPtr points to node w/23; Call: line 4; Passes ptr to 15 |

The recursive call gives us a new fourth frame on the stack, in which `CurrentPtr` points to the the node containing the number 12. With `CurrentPtr` pointing to that node, the test in line 3 succeeds. Next, line 4 is executed and the recursive call interrupts execution, giving:

| CurrentPtr points to node w/12; Call: line 4; Passes ptr to nil |
| CurrentPtr points to node w/8; Call: line 6; Passes ptr to 12 |
| CurrentPtr points to node w/15; Call: line 4; Passes ptr t/o 8 |
| CurrentPtr points to node w/23; Call: line 4; Passes ptr to 15 |

With the recursive call, a new fifth frame is pushed onto the stack:

| CurrentPtr points to nil |
| CurrentPtr points to node w/12; Call: line 4; Passes ptr to nil |
| CurrentPtr points to node w/8; Call: line 6; Passes ptr to 12 |
| CurrentPtr points to node w/15; Call: line 4; Passes ptr to 8 |
| CurrentPtr points to node w/23; Call: line 4; Passes ptr to 15 |

With `CurrentPtr` having a *nil* value, the line 3 test fails and the fifth frame pops off the stack without doing anything.

This wakes up the fourth frame, which had gone to sleep in its line 4. When it wakes up, it proceeds to its line 5 and prints out the value 12. (Thus far, we've printed 3, 8, and 12) Execution then proceeds to its line 6, which is a recursive call (passing the right child pointer of the node containing the data value 12). This again puts the fourth frame to sleep. Since a *nil* pointer is passed by the fourth frame to the fifth, we once again have a new fifth frame that encounters a failed condition in its line 3, then pops off the stack without doing any work. The fourth stack frame re-awakens having completed its line 6. It then completes its execution and it too pops off the stack.

This wakes up the third stack frame, which had most recently gone to sleep via a recursive call in its line 6. When it wakes up again, there is nothing for it do but finish, so it is popped off the stack as well. Thus, in short order, we've has the fifth, four, and third stack frames pop off the stack. When we return to the second stack frame, we see that it went to sleep in the following state:

| CurrentPtr points to node w/15; Call: line 4; Passes ptr to 8 |
| CurrentPtr points to node w/23; Call: line 4; Passes ptr to 15 |

Thus, when it wakes up, it proceeds to line 5, printing out the value 15. (So far, we've printed out the values 3, 8, 12, and 15.) It then proceeds to line 6, which is a recursive call, passing a pointer to the right child of its `CurrentPtr`, i.e., to the node containing the data value 17. This results in a new third frame on the stack which, in turn, is interrupted in its line 4 giving:

| CurrentPtr points to node w/17; Call: line 4; Passes ptr to nil |
| CurrentPtr points to node w/15; Call: line 6; Passes ptr to 17 |
| CurrentPtr points to node w/23; Call: line 4; Passes ptr to 15 |

The node containing the data value 17 has no children. Thus, we encounter the same series of behavior we saw before: a recursive call, passing the left child *nil* pointer, causes a new fourth frame to be pushed and popped without doing any work; then the value 17 is printed (giving us 3, 8, 12, 15, and 17 so far); then a recursive call passing the nil right child pointer causes another fourth frame to come and go without doing anything.

At this point, we return to the third frame which wakes up, finishes, and pops off the stack. We return to the second stack frame, which also wakes up and finishes. This returns us to the first frame, the original call, which itself had gone to sleep in its line 4. When it wakes up, it proceeds to its line 5, printing out the value 23, giving us the values 3, 8, 12, 15, 17, and 23 so far. After printing out its value, it proceeds to the recursive call in line 6, giving us:

| CurrentPtr points to node w/23; Call: line 6; Passes ptr to 25 |

The recursive call gives us a new second frame, which is interrupted in its line 4:

| CurrentPtr points to node w/25; Call: line 4; Passes ptr to 24 |
| CurrentPtr points to node w/23; Call: line 6; Passes ptr to 25 |

This gives us a new third frame:

| CurrentPtr points to node w/24; Call: line 4; Passes ptr to nil |
| CurrentPtr points to node w/25; Call: line 4; Passes ptr to 24 |
| CurrentPtr points to node w/23; Call: line 6; Passes ptr to 25 |

We get a quick push-and-pop of a new fourth frame (which has a nil pointer and thus does no work), followed by the printing of a data value (in this case 24, giving us 3, 8, 12, 15, 17, 23, and 24), followed by another quick push-and-pop of another fourth frame with a *nil* pointer. The third frame then finishes and pops off the stack, returning us to the second frame. The second frame wakes up after having completed its line 4 and proceeds to print it out its data value, giving us 3, 8, 12, 15, 17, 23, 24, and 25. It then proceeds to its line 6 recursive call, giving:

CurrentPtr points to node w/25; Call: line 6; Passes ptr to 29
CurrentPtr points to node w/23; Call: line 6; Passes ptr to 25

This leads to another new third frame:

CurrentPtr points to node w/29; Call: line 4; Passes ptr to nil
CurrentPtr points to node w/25; Call: line 6; Passes ptr to 29
CurrentPtr points to node w/23; Call: line 6; Passes ptr to 25

As before, a fourth frame (for CurrentPtr's nil leftchild) comes and goes, the value of the current node is printed (giving us the complete set of values in order: 3, 8, 12, 15, '17, 23, 24, 25, and 29), then another fourth frame (for CurrentPtr's *nil* right child) comes and goes.

We have now printed all the values in ascending order. We return to the stack to find that both processes on the stack "went to sleep" in their 6th line. In turn, they each wake up, complete, and pop off the stack. The traversal is now complete.

Whew! All this from a tree containing only 9 nodes! Imagine if the tree had a few thousand nodes! And, remember, all this was accomplished by a simple recursive algorithm containing only one *if* statement, two recursive calls, and a *print* instruction.

The other two kinds of tree traversal are remarkably similar. Preorder traversals visit the root, then the left subtree, then the right subtree. The algorithm is almost identical to the Inorder case, except the order of the instructions is different. But the change is significant! The output from the example tree we used previously will be 23, 15, 8, 3, 17, 25, 24, 29 for the preorder traversal.   The algorithm is as follows:

```
procedure Preorder(CurrentPtr isa in TreePtr)
    {Purpose: performs a preorder traversal on a binary
        tree which stores numbers, printing the data
        value stored in each node}
begin
    if (CurrentPtr <> nil) then
        print(CurrentPtr^.Data)
        Preorder(CurrentPtr^.LeftChild)
        Preorder(CurrentPtr^.RightChild)
    endif
end {Preorder}
```

Postorder traversals visit the left subtree, then the right subtree, then the root:

```
procedure Postorder(CurrentPtr isa in TreePtr)
    {Purpose: performs a postorder traversal on a bi-
        nary tree which stores numbers, printing the
        data value stored in each node}
begin
    if (CurrentPtr <> nil) then
        Postorder(CurrentPtr^.LeftChild)
        Postorder(CurrentPtr^.RightChild)
        print(CurrentPtr^.Data)
    endif
end {Postorder}
```

Searching a Binary Search Tree

Now that we know how to traverse a binary search tree, let's see how to search for a value in one. As with a linked list, the binary search tree the search and traversal algorithms are somewhat different.

The beauty of a binary search tree is that the items in it are arranged in such a way that it makes searching very fast. For any value in the tree, we know that all the values in its left subtree are smaller than the current value, and all values in its right subtree are larger. Therefore, when doing a search, we compare our target to a value in a node, and then move to the node's left or right child depending on the result of the comparison. In a *balanced* (symmetrical) tree, each such decision automatically eliminates approximately one-half of the remaining nodes from the search. This process is illustrated (top of next page) as we search for the value 17.

As we search for 17, we first encounter the root, whose value is 23. Since that value is larger than the target, we narrow our search to the left subtree of the root. Thus, we make a recursive call, passing the root's LeftChild pointer. Our second call thus focuses on the subtree rooted by the node containing 15. Because 15 is smaller than our target, we can narrow our search to the right subtree by making another recursive call, this time passing a pointer to the RightChild of the current node. This call discovers that its CurrentPtr^.Data matches the Target value.

How do we construct a recursive algorithm to accomplish this? First, we determine which kind of module to use. Because we will be printing messages, we know we must use a procedure and, since the printing is something we do *after* reaching the terminating condition, we know that we must use the first of our recursive formats:

```
if (terminating condition) then
    do final actions
else
    take a step closer to terminating condition
    call "clone" of module
endif
```

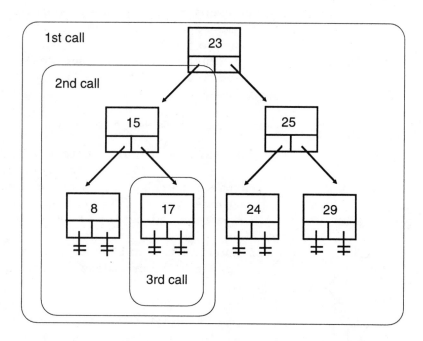

Having made these decisions, we can now begin to fill out the logic of the procedure:

```
if ((value found) or (value not in tree)) then
    print appropriate message
else
    take one step to the right or the left
    make recursive call
endif
```

Notice that both the *if* and *else* clauses must each deal with two possibilities. The *if* clause must print out one of two messages, as appropriate, and the else clause must take one step to either the right or to the left. Thus, both the *if* and *else* clauses of our general format imply there own internal decisions. We might articulate the logic as:

```
{the first part: if terminating condition satisfied)
    if (at nil ptr) then
        print "value not in tree" message
    else
        if (at node containing target value)
            print "value found in tree" message
    endif
```

```
{the second part: taking one step closer}
    if (must search left subtree)
        go to the left
    else {must search right subtree}
        go to the right
    endif
```

From this logic, we can write the algorithm as follows:

```
procedure BSTSearch (CurrentPtr isa in TreePtr,
                     Target is in num)
{Purpose: search a binary search tree for the given
        target value; print out appropriate results
        message indicating if target is in the BST.}
begin
    if (CurrentPtr = nil) then
        print ("The tree does not contain ", Target)
    else
        if (CurrentPtr^.Data = Target) then
            print ("The tree contains ", Target)
        else
            if (CurrentPtr^.Data > Target) then
                BSTSearch(CurrentPtr^.LeftChild, Tar-
                    get)
            else {CurrentPtr^.Data < Target}
                BSTSearch(CurrentPtr^.RightChild,
                    Target)
            endif
        endif
    endif
end {procedure BSTSearch}
```

Exercises   Problems 5.9 through 5.11 refer to the binary tree shown at the top of the next page..

5.9. Is this tree a binary search tree? Why or why not?

5.10. What is the output of an in-order traversal of the tree?

5.11. What is the output of a pre-order traversal of the tree?

5.12. What is the output of a post-order traversal of the tree?

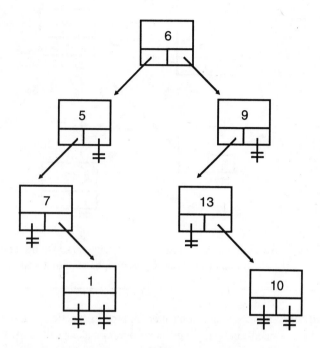

5.13. Draw the binary search tree that would result if we started with an empty tree (Root = nil) and added the following numbers in order:

   7, 4, 8, 10, 2, 3, 9, 23, 20, 18, 12, 1

5.14. Create a module that will determine largest value in a binary tree of negative numbers (*not* a binary search tree). Declare any necessary data structures including the binary tree itself. The module will be passed the root of the tree as a parameter and shall
return the largest value found in the tree. If the tree is empty, then return 0 as the maximum value in the tree.

5.15. Create a module that will locate the largest value stored in a binary search tree.

5.16. Create a module that will traverse a binary tree of numbers and compute the average of the values stored in it.

Graphs

A graph is a data structure that does not have the restrictions of linked lists and trees. Graphs are simply sets of nodes connected by pointers. They need not be linear (as do linked lists) nor do they have to have "parent-child" relationships (as do trees). They may contain any arrangement of nodes and connecting edges. An example:

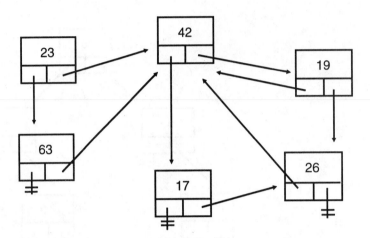

We shall touch on graphs in later chapters. Do not concern yourself about how to create and manipulate them. Instead, be sure that you understand the concept.

Iterative Control So far, we have controlled all repetitive actions via *recursion* whereby we achieve repetition by having a subprogram make a call to itself. A second means of controlling repetition is provided by the "iteration construct," also known as a "loop."

> ☐ To "iterate" means to "repeat," and a *loop* construct provides a way to to effect repetition without making recursive calls.

Unlike many programming languages which feature a variety of rather odd "special case" loop constructs, we use a single, general loop structure. Its form is:

```
begin
    do something
    loop
        step 1
        :
        step n
        exitif (condition)
        step n+1
        :
        step m
    endloop
    do yet another thing
end
```

A loop may appear anywhere within a body of instructions. Our loop construct begins with the word "loop" and ends with the word "endloop." All the instructions in between those two words are part of the "loop body." The execution of instructions proceeds in the normal sequential fashion, from top to bottom. When the algorithm reaches the "endloop" instruction, it *automatically* goes back to the top "loop" instruction, and repeats the block of steps all over again. Notice how indentation is used to show which steps are inside the loop.

In most situations, the repetition must not go on forever. It must end when an appropriate data state has been reached. Thus, the loop body includes an "exitif (condition)" instruction which allows us to break out of the loop when the terminating condition becomes true. The sequence is as follows: starting at the "begin loop" instruction, each step is executed in order. When the "exit if (condition)" step is reached, the condition is tested. If it is *true*, iteration is stopped, and execution resumes at the first step *after the "end loop"*. If the condition is *false*, the iteration continues in sequence until it reaches the end of the loop, goes back to the top, and repeats the entire process again.

Let's look at an example of a loop, one that might apply to Sisyphus in *Paradise Lost*:

```
1.  loop
2.      select a rock
3.      roll the rock uphill
4.      exitif (there are no more rocks at the bottom)
5.      go back downhill
6.  endloop
7.  celebrate
```

Given the algorithm above, what happens? At step 1 he enters the loop. Starting at step 2, he selects a rock and, at step 3, he rolls it up the hill. Then if there are no more rocks to be rolled uphill, the exit condition tested in step 4 is *true*; if so, he skips the rest of the loop, and goes immediately to step 7 to celebrate finishing the job. If there *are* more rocks, however, the exitif condition in step 4 is *false* and he must execute step 5 (go to the bottom of the hill). Then, in step 6, he encounters endloop, which signifies that he must return to the top of the loop and perform the loop sequence all over again.

> ☐ In constructing a loop, the exitif statement can be placed anywhere within the loop body. Where it is placed is determined by the particulars of the repetitive task.

In the example above, we placed the `exitif` test in the midst of the other loop body statements. Often, such placement is appropriate to the problem at hand. Sometimes, however, it is appropriate to place the `exitif` at either the very beginning of the loop body or at the very end.

☐ Placing the "`exitif(condition)`" as the first line in the loop body creates what is called a *sentinel loop* because the test is done before any other instructions inside the loop are carried out. In effect, the `exitif` test serves as a sentinel (or guard) that determines whether or not execution is allowed to enter the loop even one time. Using a structure like this allows the possibility that the loop will be skipped entirely if the condition is *true* the first time it is tested.

```
loop
     exitif (condition)
     step 1
        :
     step n
endloop
```

For example, our rock-rolling problem *should* feature a sentinel loop *if* it might be the case that there are no rocks to begin with.

☐ Placing the "`exitif(condition)`" as the end of the loop body creates a *test-last loop*, because the condition is tested after all other instructions in the loop are carried out. Using this structure guarantees that all the steps in the loop will be executed at least once before the loop is exited. This form is used whenever the statements within the loop body *must* be executed in order to obtain the value that is tested in the *exitif* test.

```
loop
     step 1
        :
     step n
     exitif (condition)
endloop
```

Let's look at the registration algorithm from Chapter 2 one last time. It contains a "test last" loop. If we rewrite it, the algorithm will look something like the following:

```
begin
    Make a prioritized list of courses you want to take
    Start with an empty schedule, i.e., NumOfHrs = 0
    loop
        Choose the highest priority class
        if ((class isn't full) AND
            (time doesn't conflict)) then
                Add the class to your schedule
                Add the hours to the current NumOfHrs
        endif
        Cross the class off your list
        exitif (( NumOfHrs >= 15 ) OR
                (all classes crossed out ))
    endloop
end
```

This loop features examples of two things that are very important.

* First, notice that certain initialization steps were performed before the loop began, e.g., making the list and initializing NumOfHours to zero. Often, some sort of initialization is required prior to the loop so that the loop will begin with appropriate values.

* Second, observe that each pass through the loop took one step towards the termination condition. Sooner or later, any student would either have 15 hours scheduled or would have crossed off all the courses on the list. Thus, this loop is not an "infinite loop" which goes on forever.

When constructing loops, it is imperative that you be careful to insure that both of these things are taken care of: appropriate pre-loop initialization of values, and certainty that the terminating condition will be reached.

Iteration vs. Recursion

☐ In principle, iteration and recursion are equivalent. Anything that can be done with one can be done with the other.

For example, consider our procedure for traversing a linked list and printing out each value stored in the list. We had implemented this with *recursion* via:

```
1 procedure TraverseRecurse (CurrentPtr isa in ListPtr)
2 begin
3    if (CurrentPtr < > nil) then
4       print(CurrentPtr^.Data)
5       CurrentPtr <- CurrentPtr^.Next
6       TraverseRecursively(CurrentPtr)
7    endif
8 end {TraverseRecursively}
```

We can implement the same logic using *iteration* via:

```
1 procedure TraverseIterate(CurrentPtr isa in ListPtr)
2 begin
3    loop
4        exitif (CurrentPtr = nil)
5        print(CurrentPtr^.Data)
6        CurrentPtr <- CurrentPtr^.Next
7    endloop
8 end {TraverseIterate}
```

From "the outside," these two procedures are indistinguishable (except for their names). Each one is passed some pointer value, and it has the effect of printing out all the values in the list. Thus, from external appearances, there will be no way to tell whether the traversal is implemented iteratively or recursively. In both cases, when it is initially called, a parameter (CurrentPtr) gets passed the value of some pointer to the list, presumably ListHead. In both cases, it is an *input* parameter, thus insuring that we do not change the original value of ListHead (or whatever pointer was passed in).

In the iterative version, the first instruction in the loop is the *exit if* test. Why? Observe that the exit condition might be true at the very beginning, e.g., if there is nothing in the linked list, e.g., if

ListHead ──╫─

then parameter passing would give us

CurrentPtr ──╫─

This is equivalent to the initial test in the recursive version which guarantees that nothing else is done if the pointer is *nil*. Thus, in both cases we first check if CurrentPtr is *nil*. If it is, then we must exit immediately, because lines 4 and 5 cannot be carried out: if CurrentPtr is *nil*, then there is *no such thing* as CurrentPtr^.Data or CurrentPtr^.Next. Executing these instructions would be an error (If we tried to access them via a computer program, the program would "blow up," i.e., abruptly stop running without completing its tasks).

In sum, we see a strong similarity between the logic of the iterative and recursive solutions. For most algorithmic tasks,the recursive and iterative implementations will show strong step-by-step similarities.   Given that recursion and iteration are logically equivalent, how do you tell which to use for a given circumstance? There are a few factors to consider:

> ☐ *In practice, you can use recursion to accomplish <u>some</u> things a great deal easier than you can with iteration.*

For example, for both linked lists and trees, a search can be readily articulated using either a recursive or iterative approach. The same is true for linked list traversals. However, for tree traversals there is a very real practical difference. Recall how clear and compact the recursive solution is. The same is not true for an iterative approach. Because a tree traversal "bounces up and down" throughout the tree, its logic is different from the linear paths taken for such searches and for list traversals.

The recursive tree traversal solution *implicitly* exploits the activation stack to keep track of "where it is" in the traversal process. If you were to write an iterative solution, you would not get this "free benefit" that the combination of recursive calls and the activation stack provide. Instead, you would have to code your own *stack* data structure and the appropriate *push* and *pop* routines; you would also have to write code to initialize the stack and to call those *push* and *pop* routines at the appropriate places, simply to *manage* the tree traversal. We get all this "for free" when we use recursion. Thus, while it certainly is possible to do tree traversals iteratively, nobody seems to want to (except for some computing students who want to see what an iterative tree traversal might really look like). As a practical matter, then, virtually all tree traversals are done recursively simply because it is a lot easier that way.

> ☐ *Recursive solutions often present a "clearer, cleaner" articulation of the essential logic than do iterative solutions.*

Not only is it easier to do tree traversals recursively than iteratively, it is also a great deal easier to see the logic in the recursive approach. Why? Because the recursive solution is not cluttered up by `loop`, `exitif`, and `endloop` statements; instead, recursive solutions generally present an easily understood *if then else* format for expressing the repetitive logic. Thus, for many complex problems, recursion has the advantage of providing "easier to understand" solutions. Comparing iterative and recursive solutions to tree traversals will make this point instantly clear!

□ *Recursion implies costs in both time and space that iteration does not.*

Each time a recursive call is made, a new frame must be pushed onto the activation stack, and each time a recursive call completes, its frame must be popped off of the stack. Each of these *push* and *pop* operations takes some small amount of time. In addition, each stack frame also consumes memory. If the execution of a recursive routine features enough recursive calls, then it is possible that memory will be filled, in which case a "stack overflow error" will result and the program will "crash."

As a result of these two concerns, recursion was not popular back when computing resources were rare and expensive. The practical economies of hardware meant that programmers "could not afford" recursion. However, those economies have changed.

□ The modern affordability of both processors and memory means that time and space costs do not matter nearly as much as they once did. Instead, as algorithm complexity grows, the advantage of cleaner logic gains greater importance, especially at the algorithm design stage.

Often, an algorithm will be developed featuring a recursive approach. If time and space concerns do matter, the algorithm can be "translated" into an iterative form.

It is no accident that we introduced recursion first. Experience has shown us that students who learn recursion first can easily pick up iteration later. Unfortunately, it seems that those who learn iteration first often suffer from a mysterious form of "loop-induced brain damage" that makes it difficult for them to master recursion!

□ What matters is that you master *both* recursive and iterative approaches so that you can deploy whichever one is best for a given situation. Often, it doesn't matter which one you use. However, when it *does* matter, it should be the problem at hand, and not your personal bias, that determines which approach you use.

As it happens, iteration goes hand in hand with the data structure we introduce next.

Exercises 5.17. Create a module to traverse a linked list of numbers and compute the sum of numbers stored in it, using iteration instead of recursion.

5.18. Create an iterative (i.e., "loop controlled") module that will search for a given target value in a BST of numbers.

5.19. Create an iterative module that will print out the contents of the string data structure you implemented earlier.

5.20. Create module to read in values from input and construct a linked list of boolean values.

Arrays

☐ Like a linked list, an *array* is a *linear structure*. That is, it is used to store a *list* of data, i.e., multiple values of one type of data. Unlike a linked list, the capacity of an array is fixed, not dynamic. A given array is declared to have some *fixed number* of identical *cells* placed under one structure.

Thus, while we might think of a linked list as analogous to a railroad train, an array is more similar to an apartment house with a fixed number of apartments, each one having its own apartment number. While we can rearrange the contents of the various apartments, we cannot readily modify the location of apartments relative to one another within the apartment building. Arrays feature this same limitation.

Because all the data contained in an array is of the same type, an array (like a linked list) is a *homogeneous* data structure. This is a requirement of arrays: each and every cell in a given array must be of the same data type.

☐ Each *cell* (or *element*) in an array can hold one data item, and has its own address, or *index*, within the array. The *index* of an array cell is the number of its position in the structure. For example, the first cell in the array has an index of 1, the fourth has an index of 4, and so on. This feature gives arrays a benefit that linked structures lack: the capability for *random access* to any item in the list, i.e., we can jump directly to whatever cell index we like.

In this respect, arrays are analogous to CD's which allow the listener to immediately jump to any musical track, while linked lists are analogous to cassette tapes which require that you fast forward through previous songs if you wish to get to a later one.

We define an array data type by specifying the identifier for that type and by giving its dimensions and the type of data it can hold. For example, we might define an array to hold a list of five numbers via:

```
type
    NumArrayType definesa array[1..5] of num
```

Any variable declared to be of this type will consist of five cells which can hold numbers. For example, we might declare two such array variables via:

```
var
    ThisArray,
    ThatArray isa NumArrayType
```

To visualize an array, we draw arrays as a group of cells joined together, with the appropriate indices. For example, the structure of variable ThisArray would be:

```
                     1 2 3 4 5
ThisArray           |_|_|_|_|_|
```

We access the data values stored in an array by referring to the identifier of the array followed by the index of the item we want to access. Thus, to store the list of values 1, 9, 6, 7, 4 in the array variable ThisArray, we could write:

```
ThisArray[1] <- 1
ThisArray[2] <- 9
ThisArray[3] <- 6
ThisArray[4] <- 7
ThisArray[5] <- 4
```

which would give the result:

```
                   1  2  3  4  5
ThisArray         | 1| 9| 6| 7| 4|
```

Having done this, we might then use arrays' random access capability to assign certain values from ThisArray to selective elements in ThatArray via:

```
ThatArray[5] <- ThisArray[3]
ThatArray[2] <- ThisArray[1]
```

which would give us:

```
                   1  2  3  4  5
ThisArray         | 1| 9| 6| 7| 4|

                   1  2  3  4  5
ThatArray         | ?| 1| ?| ?| 6|
```

☐ It is possible to assign the entire contents of one array to another array of the same array type. This is something we could not do in a single operation with a linked list (we'd need a procedure to traverse both linked lists, copying values one-by-one along the way). With arrays, copying can be accomplished by simply referring to the array variables identifiers *without* reference to individual elements.

For example,

```
ThatArray <- ThisArray
```

would result in:

```
                1 2 3 4 5
ThisArray      1 9 6 7 4

                1 2 3 4 5
ThatArray      1 9 6 7 4
```

Arrays are invaluable anytime we need to store or process words. With arrays, we can use single structures, i.e., arrays of *chars* (typically called *strings*), to store words, people's names and addresses, or any other *char* data. For example:

```
const
      MaxStringSize is 20
type
      NameString definesa array[1..MaxStringSize] of
            char
var
      FirstName,
      LastName isa NameString
```

Arrays are valuable because they allow us to group many instances of the same kind of data together under a single name, and to access it rapidly via array indices.

☐ Arrays are *superior* to linked lists in one respect: with arrays, we can instantly access any item we wish, i.e., we have *random access* to any cell in the array without having to traverse the structure.

☐ Arrays are *inferior* to linked lists in another respect: they are *static* structures, which means that we must define their size and structure when we declare them. Once an array is declared, we can manipulate the contents of any and all cells in the array, but we cannot change the size or structure of the array. Thus, if we declare an array to store 100 items and, as it turns out that we need to store only 2 items, we've wasted space; if we need space for 101, we're out of luck.

Traversing Arrays   Traversing an array is typically done with a loop. Here is an example in which we assume the following declarations:

```
const
    MaxArraySize is {some literal num value}
type
    ThisArrayType definesa Array[1..MaxArraySize] of
        num
```

We also assume that the array contains values, i.e., that each of its elements has been initialized to some value.

```
procedure TraverseArray(TrvArray isa in ThisArrayType)
    {Purpose: traverse an array of num, printing out
        all num values in sequence}
var
    I isa num

begin
    I <- 1
    loop
        print TryArray[I]
        I <- I + 1
        exitif (I > MaxArraySize)
    endloop
end {TraverseArray}
```

Searching Arrays   The simplest search of an array is very similar to a traversal, except that the algorithm compares each data element against the target value, and stops when that value is found in the array, e.g.,

```
procedure SearchArray (SrchArray isa in ThisArrayType,
                       Target isa in num)
      {Purpose: determine if Target value is stored in
           SrchArray, print out appropriate message}
var
    I isa num
begin
    I <- 1
    loop
        exitif (( I > MaxArraySize) OR
                  (SrchArray[I] = Target))
        I <- I + 1
    endloop
    if (I <= MaxArraySize) then
        print("Found Target")
    else
        print("Did Not Find Target")
    endif
end {SearchArray}
```

This logic is similar to the previous example, except that the loop has two exit conditions. We will exit the loop when we've reached the end or found the target value.

A More Efficient Search   There is a much more efficient way of searching an array *if* the data in the array is sorted. It is called a *binary search*. This method is useful only when array data is sorted. Let's consider an array sorted in ascending order, as pictured below:

1	2	3	4	5	6	7	8	9
2	5	6	11	15	23	25	42	50

The *binary search* exploits the fact that the values are in sorted order. Because they are sorted, we can always tell whether the target value is to the right or to the left of the value of any given position. If the target value is larger than the value at a given position, then it must be to the right. If so, then we can ignore all the values to the left. Conversely, if the target value is less than the value at a given position, then it must be to the left and we can ignore all the values to the right.

A binary search implements this logic repeatedly until the search is completed. It begins by examining the value located in the middle of the array. If we get lucky and that middle element contains our target, the search is complete. In the more likely event that we have not found our target, we decide to move right or left depending on whether the target item is greater or less than the value of the element. Thus, approximately half of the array is disqualified.

We then move to the middle of the *remaining* elements, and decide again whether to move right or left. With this decision, half of the remaining elements are disqualified. This process is repeats until we either "hit" our target or are left with only one element which is not the target, i.e., the target value is not there to be found.

Before we look at an example, we need to define a convention to use when we have an even number of elements. For an group of N elements, where N is even, the middle element will be defined as the one at the position given by (N/2)+1.

For an example, refer to array[1..9] we drew above, and imagine our target is the number 25, stored in the 7th element of the array. Start looking at the middle element, whose index = 5. Since 15 is less than 25, we must search the right half of the list, i.e., array from positions 6 through 9. According to our convention, the middle element of the right half is at index 8, so we check there for the target. It is greater than 25, so we must now search the remaining two elements (6 and 7). The middle of these two elements is at index 7. Here, we find our target and the search is over.

This process is represented in the diagrams below. The arrows indicate the element that is currently being compared to the target. The rounded box surrounds the array elements that have not yet been eliminated from the search.

(a) At first, the entire array is under consideration.

(b) After comparing the target 25 to 15, we know the result must be to the right of index = 5. The "middle" element of that range is 42, so we compare 42 to 15.

(c) We eliminated 42 and the element to its right, so there are only two elements left. The "middle" element is the value 25, which is our target.

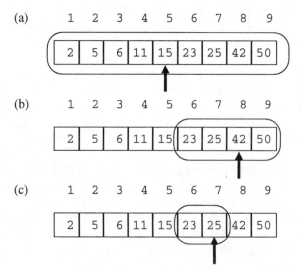

Note the efficiency of this search. With a linear traversal, we would have needed to start at the first element and compare 7 elements against the target. With the binary search we need only 3 comparisons.

Of course, you might well point out that search by traversal would work better if we were looking for the value 5. True enough. Binary search would again require 3 comparisons, while the search by traversal would require only 2 comparisons.

However, remember that a search algorithm must be *general*, i.e., it cannot make assumptions about which value we might be searching for, nor about where in the list of values it might be. Thus, we evaluate the efficiency of an algorithm in terms of its "average case" or "expected case" performance.

Analysis of efficiency will be covered in more detail in a later chapter. For now observe that for a sorted array of size N, a successful search by traversal may require from 1 to N searches, but will (over many trials for various values) traverse *on average* half the list, i.e., approximately N/2 comparisons. This is true regardless of whether the array is sorted or not. In contrast, a binary search exploits the ordering of a sorted array to require approximately logN comparisons. For small arrays such as in our example, the difference is trivial. But what would the difference be for an array of 10,000? For 10,000,000?

You may wonder how we might do a binary search on a linked list. The answer is: we cannot. Why? Because binary search requires that we be able to *calculate* the middle position of a list of numbers, then jump to it. We can do this with an array, as the array indexes give us *random access* capability. But it is impossible in a linked list. We can only move around in a linked list by *navigating* through it via pointers. Linked structures do not provide any way to achieve *random access*. However, a *binary search tree* that is full and balanced can and does offer us the same performance that we obtain from binary search on an array. In fact, it implements the same logic: "go to the middle and then throw out half the values with each access."

Exercises 5.20. Given the following type definition, where MAX is a constant that has already been defined,

```
type
      NumArrayType definesa array [1..MAX] of num
```

write a module that will receive, via parameter, an array called InputArray of type NumArrayType and, using loops, will return the subscript(index) of the smallest element in the array.

5.21. Use an array to implement a *stack* of numbers. Items may only be pushed and popped to and from the top of the stack. Create modules for `Push`, `Pop`, `Is-Full`, and `IsEmpty`.

5.22. Use an array to implement a *FIFO queue*. Item may be *enqueued* only at the end of the queue, and may be *dequeued* only at the head of the queue. As items come and go from the queue, you will be faced with the "wraparound" problem: instead of relocating any values within the queue, use the `MOD` operation to handle wraparound. Create modules for `Enqueue`, `Dequeue`, `IsFull`, and `IsEmpty`.

5.23. Create a different Enqueue module for your queue (problem 5.22) such that it's now a *priority queue*. A *priority queue* is a *FIFO queue* in every respect *except* one: items are not always added at the end of the queue. Instead, items are inserted into a priority queue at a position that is based on their priority: the higher your priority, the closer to the front of the line you get.

5.24. Write a procedure that will convert an array of numbers to a linked list of numbers. This procedure should have two (2) parameters - a pointer to the head of the linked list and an array. Use a loop in your answer - DO NOT USE RECURSION. Assume that the array is already full of numbers - you don't need to read them in. Declare any necessary data types you need to solve this problem.

5.25. Create a module that will take in an array of numbers and create a *BST* of numbers.

The Abstraction Power of Constants

Recall that atomic data structures can be either *variables* (whose value can change) or *constants* (whose value is fixed, e.g., *pi*). Constants are useful tools for abstraction much like user-defined data types are.

In the example above, we defined the size of our various array data types by using a *constant, not a literal value*, for the upper size limit, e.g., we did something like:

```
ThisArrayType definesa array[1..MaxArraySize] of num
```

not:

```
ThisArrayType definesa array[1..20] of num
```

Why did we do this? To understand this, note that `MaxArraySize` was also mentioned in the search and traversal algorithms themselves, e.g.,

```
exitif(I > MaxArraySize]
```

Thus, had we used a literal value (say, the 5) instead of a named *constant*, we would have in effect "hardwired" the size of the array into *both*:

- the array type definition itself, *and*

- the code of *any and all loops* which acts upon *any and all variables* that were declared to be of that array type.

Doing things in this manner is an example of a low level of abstraction, as the details would not be isolated and hidden but instead scattered about throughout *both* the type definitions *and* numerous decision statements. To achieve a higher level of abstraction, we want to *separate* the details of array size from the particulars of *both* the type definitions *and* the control structures.

By isolating array size in a constant, e.g.,

```
MaxArraySize is 5
```

we can write both type definitions and control structures to be *independent of any particular size*. Thus, if we later want to change the array size from 5 to 137, we would need only change the value of one constant, e.g.,

```
MaxArraySize is 137
```

This would give us a new algorithm in which *both* the data structure definitions *and* the details of the *all* control structures' decisions would be *automatically updated* to reflect the modified size.

By using constants in this way, we allow for easy algorithm modification. For example, consider my problem with a credit card company: my last name always has the last character missing. Why? Because their array is too short to accommodate my entire name (and I'm probably not the only one). If they wanted to correct this problem, they *might* have to search through all their software and change the size of many, many array declarations and control structures. However, if they made proper use of constants and data types, they would only have to change *one* constant declaration.

☐ Because of the power of constants to raise the level of abstraction, constants are scoped like data definitions, not variable declarations, i.e., constant definitions can be "seen" by the main algorithm and all its modules.

The "Data Abstraction" Power of Creating New Data Types

☐ The ability to create new data types of our own specification is an extremely powerful tool which has relevance beyond just the creation of particular records, arrays, or linked structures. It is a general principle that we use data types to *raise the level of abstraction of our data structures*. We do so by using data types as building blocks from which we can construct *exactly* what is needed.

We can combine various type definitions, constructing data types from arrays and records in whatever fashion suites us, much like a child builds structures out of blocks. The difference is that they child is stuck with whatever blocks come in the box, while we may *define* whatever size, shape, and structure of "building blocks" we want.

Mixing Atomic and Complex Types

For example, consider the details of a new "EmployeeRecord" data type., below. In it, we combine atomic types (in this case *num*) with *user-defined* or *complex* types (in this case, *strings*) to create what is wanted:

```
const
     MaxStringSize is 15

type
     CharStringType definesa array [1..MaxStringSize]
          of char

     EmployeeRecordType definesa record
          Name isa CharStringType
          SocSecNum isa num
          Salary isa num
          StreetAddr isa CharStringType
          CityState isa CharStringType
     endrecord
```

Notice that we have a *record* type with five fields, and that three of these fields are *arrays*. Thus, we wind up with a type definition such that any variable of type EmployeeRecordType will look like the figure at the top of the next page.

If we wanted to declare three variables of type `EmployeeRecordType`, we might then declare:

```
var
     Employee1,
     Employee2,
     Employee3 isa EmployeeRecordType
```

Name:	array(1..MaxStringSize) char
SocSecNum:	num
Salary:	num
StreetAddr:	array(1..MaxStringSize) char
City/State:	array(1..MaxStringSize) char

This would create three different variables. To access the social security number of Employee1 we would write,

```
Employee1.SocSecNum
```

to access the Salary of Employee3 we would write,

```
Employee3.Salary
```

and to access the third letter in the name of the second employee, we would write:

```
Employee2.Name[3]
```

Employee2 is the record, Name is the field within in that consists of an array of characters, and the *3* specifies the location in that array.

Arrays of Records   Similarly, if we have 100 employees, we could define a data type for arrays of EmployeeRecords via,

```
const
    MaxEmployees is 100
type
    EmployeeArrayType definesa array[1..MaxEmployees]
        of EmployeeRecordType
```

This declaration creates a data type of an array of 100 elements such that each element in the array is an occurrence of the five-field record. We could then declare a variable of this type, via:

```
var
    OurEmployees isa EmployeeArrayType
```

We could then access the social security number of the 14th employee via,

```
OurEmployees[14].SocSecNum
```

OurEmployees[14] specifies the 14th element of the array, the period tells us to look inside that record at that location in the array, and SocSecNum tells us which field inside the record to access. Similarly, to access the fourth letter in the name of the 37th employee, we would write:

```
OurEmployees[37].Name[4]
```

OurEmployees[37] specifies the 37th element of the array, the period tells us to look inside that record at that location in the array, and Name tells us which field inside the record to access. The Name field is itself an array of *char*, and thus Name[4] specifies that we want the fourth letter of that name.

Should we want to print out the entire name of the 23rd employee, we might write

```
begin
    I <- 1
    loop
        print (OurEmployees[23].Name[I])
        I <- I + 1
        exitif (I > MaxStringSize)
    endloop
end
```

Of course, this would *not* be a general algorithm for printing names. To benefit from procedural abstraction, it would be far better to do:

```
procedure PrintCharString (ThisString isa in
                                CharStringType)
    {Purpose: print the contents of a CharStringType}
var
    I isa num
begin
    I <- 1
    loop
        print (ThisString[I])
        I <- I + 1
        exitif (I > MaxStringSize)
    endloop
end {procedure PrintCharString}
```

This procedure could then be called whenever we wish to print out any variable that is of type CharStringType. To print out the name of the 23rd employee, it would be called via:

```
PrintCharString(OurEmployees[23].Name)
```

which passes the appropriate character string to procedure PrintCharString.

If we wished to print out a list of all employees, we might create a procedure such as:

```
procedure PrintEmployeeNames (Roster isa in
                                    EmployeeArrayType)
    {Purpose: traverse Roster, calling PrintCharString
        to print out name of each employee}
var
    J isa num
begin
    J <- 1
    loop
        PrintCharString(Roster[J].Name}
        J <- J + 1
        exitif (J > MaxEmployees)
    endloop
end {PrintEmployeeNames}
```

This combination of records and arrays allow us to take advantage of the power of arrays and loops while dealing with more complicated data structures. Using such a structure, we could calculate and print the total payroll for the company via calling,

```
PayrollSum(OurEmployees)
```

where PayrollSum is:

```
procedure PayrollSum (Roster isa in EmployeeArray)
    {Purpose: calculate then print entire payroll
        employees in Roster}
var
    Payroll,
    Index isa num
begin
    Payroll <- 0
    Index <- 1
```

```
loop
    Payroll <- Payroll + Roster[Index].Salary
    Index <- Index + 1
    exitif (Index > MaxEmployees)
endloop
print("The sum of employee salaries is ", Payroll)
end  {PayrollSum}
```

Records of Records Not only can we combine records and arrays in any combination, we can also achieve important benefits by creating records of records and arrays of arrays. For example, we've seen a linked list that featured only a single data item, a number. Imagine that we don't know how to predict the number of employees that we'll have and thus want a dynamic rather than static structure. We might create the appropriate data structure by using our `EmployeeRecordType` and our previous linked list types, changing only the definition of the node itself:

```
type
    ListPtr definesa ptr toa ListNode
    ListNode definesa record
        Data isa EmployeeRecordType
        Next isa ListPtr
    endrecord {ListNode}
```

This gives us a node that consists of a record with two fields: `Data` and `Next`, just as before. What's different is that `Data` is itself no longer a single data field but is now a record of `EmployeeRecordType`. Given such a linked list, we might calculate our total payroll by modifying our recursive traversal routine. Because there is some final action to be taken upon reaching the end of the list (returning 0 to complete the final recursive call), we require the first of our two recursive templates:

```
function PayrollSum isa num(CurrentPtr isa in ListPtr)
    {Purpose:  traverse list pointed to by CurrentPtr,
        resolve to resulting payroll sum}

begin
    if (CurrentPtr = nil) then
        PayrollSum returns 0
    else
        PayrollSum returns (CurrentPtr^.Data.Salary +
                PayrollSum(CurrentPtr^.Next))
    endif
end {procedure PayrollSum}
```

This routine might be initially called via:

```
Payroll <- PayrollSum(ListHead)
```

In much the same way, we can create the structure for a binary tree of employees by changing the definition of our TreeNode:

```
type
     TreePtr definesa ptr toa TreeNode
     TreeNode definesa record
          Data isa EmployeeRecordType
          LeftChild isa TreePtr
          RightChild isa TreePtr
     endrecord {TreeNode}
```

Given a tree of such nodes, we might print out the names of all the employees by making use of our existing PrintCharString procedure, together with a differ-ent implementation of PrintEmployeeNames. To create the appropriate PrintEmployeeNames, we modify slightly one of our tree traversal algorithms, e.g.,

```
procedure PrintEmployeeNames(CurrentPtr isa in
                                 TreePtr)
     {Purpose: perform inorder traversal of tree of em-
          ployee data, calling PrintCharString to print
          out each employee name
begin
     if (CurrentPtr <> nil) then
          PrintEmployeeNames(CurrentPtr^.LeftChild)
          PrintCharString(CurrentPtr^.Data.Name)
          PrintEmployeeNames(CurrentPtr^.RightChild)
     endif
end {procedure PrintEmployeeNames}
```

Arrays of Arrays   The arrays we've seen so far are all one dimensional arrays (or *vectors*). We can also declare manipulate arrays of more than one dimension. For example, we can create a two-dimensional array (or *table*) as follows:

```
const
     DimensionOne is {some literal num value}
     DimensionTwo is {some literal num value}
```

```
type
    ThisArrayType definesa Array [1..DimensionOne] of
        num
    ThatArrayType definesa Array [1..DimensionTwo] of
        ThisArrayType
var
    TwoDArray isa ThatArrayType
```

These declarations provide us with an array variable that is a *data table*. It is constructed by declaring an array of arrays. That is to say, each element of an array of type `ThatArrayType` is itself an array of `ThisArrayType`. Thus, referencing `TwoDArray[3]` accesses the third element of the table which is itself an array of `ThisArrayType`. To access the 7th element of this array, we would write:

```
TwoDArray[3,7]
```

To traverse such an array, we need to use *nested loops*, i.e. multiple loops nested one inside the other, e.g.,:

```
procedure Traverse2D (Array2D isa in ThatArrayType)
    {Purpose: traverse 2D array of nums, printing out
        each value in turn}
var
    I isa num
    J isa num
begin
    I <- 1
    loop
        J <- 1
        loop
            print(Array2D[I, J])
            J <- J + 1
            exitif (J > DimensionOne)
        endloop
        I <- I + 1
        exitif (I > DimensionTwo)
    endloop
end {Traverse2D}
```

This traversal, which prints each array element, starts at element `Array2D[1,1]`, then moves on to `Array2D[1,2]`, and so on. Once `J` becomes greater than the maximum index of the first array dimension, the inner loop is exited, and the outer loop continues, i.e., `I` is incremented. Then the outer loop (and hence also the inner loop) is repeated, with `J` starting over at *1*. So on the second pass through, we traverse `Array2D[2,1]` then `Array2D[2,2]`, etc. The entire traversal is finished when (`I > DimensionTwo`) and (`J > DimensionOne`).

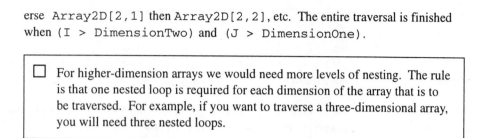

> ☐ For higher-dimension arrays we would need more levels of nesting. The rule is that one nested loop is required for each dimension of the array that is to be traversed. For example, if you want to traverse a three-dimensional array, you will need three nested loops.

Food for Thought:

How Does It Feel to be Dynamically Allocated?

The *dynamic allocation* of memory allows us to write algorithms without making any advance commitment to how much of our space resources we devote to any data structure. This permits our algorithms to use as much memory as needed for a given structure, then *deallocate* it when it is no longer needed.

As a general principle, *dynamic allocation* is "popping up all over" in ways that have nothing to do with computer programming. Modern manufacturing companies no longer want to commit resources in a static way to making a given product. Instead they want flexible manufacturing facilities. For example, automobile manufacturers desire the flexibility to have their production facilities be able to switch over to whatever the hottest selling model is. This is far more efficient than the conventional static allocation of production resources. Why have one plant idle just because it makes a slow seller, while another plant is constantly running overtime? The benefits of dynamically allocating production capability is obvious.

We also see the principle of dynamic allocation being applied in the human arena. There is a growing trend towards using temporary employees in jobs that have traditionally been filled by permanent workers. Why? For the same reason that we don't want to declare an array of 1000 cells if we might only need to store 40 pieces of data. Companies don't want unskilled workers, but they do want the freedom to bring workers on as they need them and to let them go when they don't. Temporary workers can be hired and fired much more easily and cheaply than can permanent employees, and thus offer the same advantages that linked lists offer over arrays.

Before you assume that it's just hard-hearted capitalists that desire dynamic allocation, consider that it's a pervasive theme throughout our society. Until recently, marriages and families were *statically allocated*. Once a couple was married, they were expected by society to stay that way, and the question of whether or not they were happy together didn't really matter much. Similarly, the normal career path of previous generations was static: take a job and "gut it out" until retirement. The question of "satisfaction with my job" just didn't come up very often.

All in all, for better or worse, *dynamic allocation* goes hand-in-hand with freedom of choice, and both the benefits and costs of that freedom come with the territory. Is it better for children to be raised in a stable home? Sure. Is it better to have stable marriages than a series of divorces? Sure. But do you want the benefits of that stability and security if the price is 30 years in an unhappy marriage? Probably not.

The first "high-level" computer languages were COBOL (for business) and Fortran (for science). Neither featured dynamic allocation. The programmer lived with static allocation: he declared his array and lived with the consequences. Just as people lived with their life decisions. Every significant programming language that's been hatched since the early 1970's has featured dynamic allocation. Just as every student who's been born since 1970 has grown up in a world that is shaped by it: dynamic allocation of jobs, of relationships, of future horizons.

This may prove to be one of the more significant evolutionary challenges of modern times, because people have never before had to deal very much with choice. Why? Because there wasn't much of it around. People from previous eras largely had no choice. About their jobs. About where they lived. About how they lived. The college students of today are the first generation that have spent their *entire lives* inundated with it. "What do I want to do?," "Where do I want to live?," "Do I want to have children or not?," "Who do I want to be?." These questions, and others like them, are of the utmost importance to everyone's lives, and surely very few would want to have others taking them away or imposing answers on us. But these *are* largely new questions, ones that your grandfathers and grandmothers probably didn't spend much time wrestling with.

This freedom to choose, this freedom to make decisions that are dynamic, not static, is a new thing in human history. And, like most new things, it is probably both a blessing and a curse. For these questions about our own happiness and satisfaction are precisely the things that help contribute to our unhappiness and dissatisfaction. Yet there is no avoiding them. They are part of modern times.

Perhaps this is why so many people report that life is so complicated, and why young people have so much difficulty "finding their place in the world." Perhaps it's because there's a whole new realm of human experience emerging, a new evolutionary challenge for the human spirit and the human psyche: the challenge of how to live in world where *everything* is dynamically allocated.

Summary   The goal of *data abstraction* is to allow the logical grouping of related data and to separate the means of naming and using data from the low level details of how that data is organized. Well designed data structures feature high levels of data abstraction, which is accomplished via extensive use of user-defined data types and constants. Such structures allow significant modifications to an algorithm's data structures via just a few changes to constants and data types. They also pay big dividends in allowing algorithms to be updated easily and cheaply.

Data structures can be designed and created to fit the data requirements of any particular problem. They can take the form of *static* structures (*arrays*) or of *dynamic* structures (i.e., *linked lists, trees*, and *graphs*.

Linked Lists   Linked lists allow us to collect a list of data that is *dynamic*, i.e., we can change the size of the list at will, and we can rearrange the nodes of the list however we might wish to. Linked lists have the advantage of always being the correct size for the data at hand. The price paid for this is the memory required to store a pointer field for each node in the list. Linked lists also present the disadvantage of requiring traversals to locate data. There is no random access possible with a linked list, and thus we have to examine many items in the list before finding the one we want.

Binary Tree   Binary trees give us all the advantages and disadvantages of linked lists, with two differences. They require slightly more space than do linked lists, as each node requires space for two pointer fields, not one. If they are implemented as a binary search tree, they can be significantly better than are linked lists with respect to the time cost of a search: they are not linear in nature and thus far fewer nodes must be examined before we can locate the one for which we are searching. This benefit is obtained only if the binary search tree is full and balanced, or nearly so.

Arrays   Arrays provide a static way to collect lists of data under a single name. We have to declare the size of an array at the very beginning of our algorithm. This means that we have to know in advance how many cells we will need. Sometimes, it is not possible to know this in advance. In such circumstances, arrays are not the best choice. Arrays also require that we plan for *the maximum possible size*, because an array is "static," i.e., we cannot change the size of the array as we go along. This can be very wasteful, because our array may occasionally be full but often be nearly empty. This is not a problem on paper, but it used to be a significant problem in computer programming. We have a finite number of computer memory cells and, when the cost of memory was high, programmers had to be efficient in using them. Many programmers still believe that efficiency "for its own sake" is important, while others consider the low price of memory and conclude "who cares if we waste it?." However, even if you don't mind wasting memory, the fact that arrays are rigid with respect to size and structure means that they are often not the best choice.

No one structure is best for all circumstances and thus data structures must be designed to fit the needs of the problem at hand. Often, the best structure is one that is constructed from a combination of complex types.

Exercises

Many of the problems below build on the answers to others. Be sure to exploit this fact. Reuse your answers to one question if they will help you answer another question. In such cases, do *not* rewrite your code; refer to any previously written module by calling it with appropriate parameters.

5.26. Design a record type `StudentRecord`, including fields for:

> `Name, Address, Phone, SS#, Major, Class, GPA, and AcademicRecord (a pointer to a linked lists of Terms)`

5.27. Design a data structure, `AcademicRecord`, for student academic performance data, consisting of a linked list of `Terms`, with each `Term` having a `TermIdentifier` (e.g., Fall95), a `TermGPA`, and a `CourseList`. The `CourseList` shall include the courses taken for a given term, including `CourseNumber`, `CourseName`, `Professor`, `CreditHours`, and `CourseGrade`.

5.28. Design a data structure to hold the data for the `StudentBody`, consisting of a *BST* of `StudentRecord`.

5.29. Create a module that will examine the `AcademicRecord` for a given student and determine if that student has ever taken 20 or more credit hours in a single term.

5.30. Create a module that will traverse the `StudentBody` *BST* and create a list SS#'s of all students who have taken 20 or more credit hours in any single term. Students should be inserted into the list in ascending order based on their GPA.

.5.31. Create a module to traverse the `StudentBody` *BST* and create a list of all `Majors` together with the effective GPA of each (e.g., `TotalQualityPoints` earned by `CS` majors / `TotalHours` taken by CS majors).

5.32. Create a module to traverse the `StudentBody` *BST* and collect data on the grades assigned for a given professor. That is, what is the "effective GPA" of students in courses taught by that professor?

Graphical Data Notation

You may expect homework and quiz quetions which require that you represent data declarations and the state of data structures graphically, i.e., by drawing pictures. The next two pages show suggested ways of representing both the declarations of data structures and their data state.

○ atomic data types
▢ user-defined data types

Atomic Data Types

 boolean
ⒸⒸ character
Ⓝ number
○→ pointer

Declaration

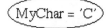
MyChar
ℂ

Usage (shows the value)

MyChar = 'C'

Records

Declaration

StudentRecord

LastInitial	ℂ
Age	N
IsMale	𝔹

Usage (shows the value)

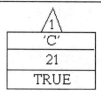

'C'
21
TRUE

Linked Lists

Declaration

ListNode

Data	N
Next	①

Usage

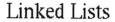
ListHead ① → ◹ → ◹ ⊣

Usage (shows the value)

ListHead ① →

5
①

10
①

Trees

Declaration

TreeNode

Data	N
LChild	①
RChild	①

Usage

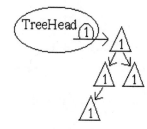
TreeHead ①

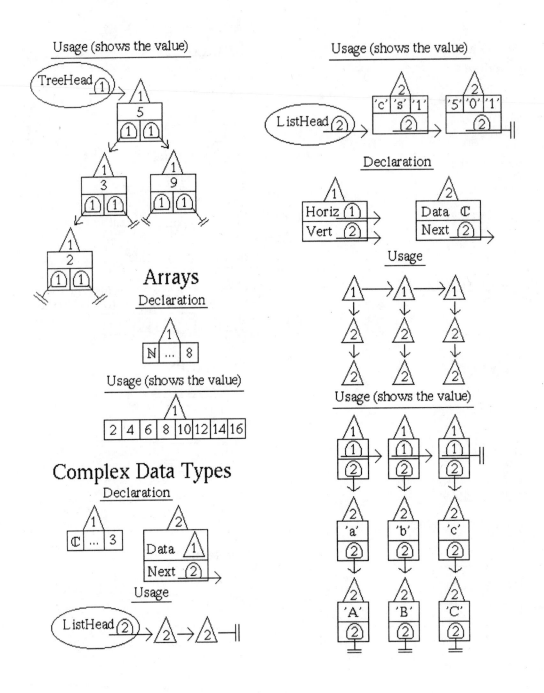

Usage (shows the value)

Arrays
Declaration

Usage (shows the value)

Complex Data Types
Declaration

Usage

Usage (shows the value)

Declaration

Usage

Usage (shows the value)

Chapter 6:   Algorithmic Methods

In many ways, algorithms are like buildings: they require plenty of planning in the design process, they are made from fundamental building blocks (instructions and data, decisions, control structures, abstractions of various kinds, etc., instead of bricks, pipes, and wires), and each is designed to fulfill a very specific function. This chapter will deal with the third property.

Each type of building has its own function and therefore needs an appropriate architecture. The structure built for a hospital would not work well for a shopping mall, and vice versa. Because of this, buildings are not thrown together by whim, but are carefully designed to facilitate their intended function. An architect allows the intended use of a building to dictate its design parameters, rather than beginning with a design and trying to fit it to the building's purpose.

Similarly, when writing an algorithm, it is important to begin by choosing an algorithmic method, or "plan of attack," that is best suited to the problem being solved. Like the architect, we allow the algorithm's intended function to help us in the design process. For example, an algorithm to sort a list of numbers will use a different approach than one to calculate the best route for a salesperson traveling to ten cities. The choice of the algorithmic method is very important, as it influences the efficiency of the algorithm in solving the problem, the amount of computer resources that will be required, and the difficulty of writing the algorithm. In fact, there have been cases where a problem harried scientists for generations, until some daring soul tried a different algorithmic method and showed the solution to be practically trivial using that approach.

You will find that writing algorithms is not a cut-and-dried task by any means. It often takes a good deal of creativity and ingenuity, and it appears to be more of an art than a science. In this chapter, we'll explore four particular algorithmic methods which are commonly used for various kinds of problems. Consider them to be tools which can help you in the design process.

Searches and Traversals

Searches and *traversals* are ways of accessing data contained in structures such as arrays, linked lists, and trees. We saw several examples of such algorithms in the previous chapter. In general, searches and traversals are among the most widely used algorithmic methods. They must be tailored to the particulars of the data structure that is being examined.

- To *traverse* a data structure means to step through the entire structure in an ordered fashion, displaying or acting upon each data element in turn.

- To *search* a data structure means just what you'd think: to examine it to see if it contains a particular "target" value and, if so, to locate the value within the data structure.

The simplest kind of search is merely a traversal in which each data element is compared with a desired "target" value. The traversal ends when the value is located or when the algorithm determines that the value is not there to be found. In addition, as we have seen, there are more efficient kinds of searches that do not require a complete traversal. Such searches exploit the properties of a particular data structure to accomplish a search without looking at each and every value in turn. We shall return to the various kinds of searches and traversals in a later chapter to consider their performance characteristics.

Divide and Conquer

Recall that binary search involves exploiting the organization of data to allow us to "throw away" half of the remaining data at each step. Thus, each step reduces the remaining amount of work by approximately half. This idea, i.e., repeatedly cutting the problem in half, is used in an algorithmic method knows as "divide and conquer." Unlike binary search, which throws away data each time, *divide and conquer* algorithms don't throw anything away. Instead, they repeatedly cut the size of the problem in half *and solve for each half.* "Solving for each half" means cutting each half in half again, in a recursive fashion. Eventually, the problem is broken down into small enough chunks that the solution to each chunk is trivial. Once the trivial solutions are found, the various results are then combined into the solution to the original problem.

Thus, *divide and conquer* is a useful strategy when a problem satisfies three criteria:

- The problem can be easily divided into sub-problems which are smaller versions of the original, each one solvable by the same algorithm as the original.

- There is a terminating condition at which the sub-problems are simple enough to be solved trivially.

- The solutions to the sub-problems can be combined to form a solution for the original problem.

Again, *divide and conquer* algorithms take the original problem and divide it into a number of subproblems, each one a smaller version of the original problem. They then solve each subproblem recursively, and finally combine the subproblem solutions into a solution for the original problem. More precisely, a *divide and conquer* algorithm includes the following three tasks:

1) It divides the problem into a number of subproblems that are smaller versions of the original problem. Usually, we divide each problem into two subproblems, each one requiring half the work of the original.

2) It then attacks each subproblem by recursively calling the divide-and-conquer algorithm to divide each subproblem again as in step 1. In other words, each subproblem is broken in two, then each of those subproblems are broken in two, and so on. The recursive calls end when the subproblem cannot be productively broken in two, i.e., when each subproblem is small enough to solve trivially. When each subproblem is small enough to be trivial, a solution to each one is found.

3) Then, the various subproblem solutions are combined into the solution of the original problem.

To illustrate the divide-and-conquer method, we'll describe the workings of the `MergeSort` algorithm. It is used to sort arrays of numbers efficiently. The three stages of `MergeSort` are:

1) Divide the unsorted array into 2 halves. Now we have 2 subproblems which are one-half the size of the original problem.

2) Conquer the subproblems by calling the `MergeSort` algorithm recursively to divide *each* half-array into 2 arrays. This produces 4 subarrays, each one one-fourth the size of the original array. Recursive calls than divide each of those 4 arrays into 2 arrays, producing 8 arrays each of which is approximately one eight the size of the original, and so on. The recursive calls stop when each subarray contains only one element each and no more division is possible. The solution here is trivial: a one-element array is, by definition, already sorted.

3) With each one-element array sorted, the subproblem solutions are merged together according to the `Merge` algorithm given below.

Merging means "combining two sorted arrays into one larger sorted array." It is very simple. It involves three arrays: the two sorted arrays you wish to merge and a third array into which the resulting larger sorted array is stored. Start at the beginning of each of the two smaller arrays and compare their first elements to each other. Remove the smaller element of the two, and place it as the first element into the third array. Next, compare the first two *remaining* elements, remove the smaller one and place it as the second element in the merged array. Continue the process until all elements have been placed in the merged array. When one of the two smaller arrays runs out of elements, simply place the remaining elements of the other array in their sorted order at the end of the merged array. By the end, the merged array is a sorted list combining all elements from the two smaller arrays. The diagram below illustrates the merge algorithm.

The first values of each subarray (*5* and *3*) are compared. The smaller gets copied to the merged array:

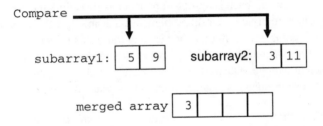

With the *3* copied into the merged array, the *3* is no longer considered for the merge. We then compare the smallest *remaining* values from each of the two arrays, *5* and *11*. The smaller, *5*, goes into the merged array:

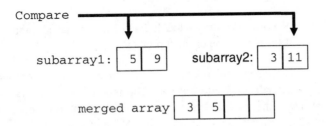

Now the *9* and the *11* are compared, with the smaller one, *9*, copied to the merged array:

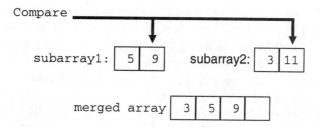

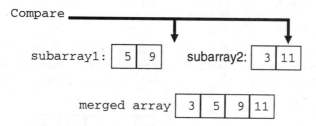

With the left subarray exhausted, the remainder of the right subarray is copied to the merged array, giving:

Now let's look at the `MergeSort` algorithm which uses the three basic steps and the `Merge` algorithm. We will need to pass an array into the `MergeSort` procedure. Since *we want* the array be changed during the sort, we pass it as an *in/out* parameter. We will pass the entire array during each recursive call, and will also pass array indices that mark the beginning and end of the subarray to be sorted. These can be input parameters since we don't have any need to change the original values from which they come.

```
procedure MergeSort (SortArray isa in/out ArrayType,
                     B, E isa in num)
    {Purpose: Sort the array according to the standard
        Mergesort algorithm}
var
    M isa Number

begin
    if (B < E) then
        M <- (B + E) DIV 2
        MergeSort(SortArray, B, M)
        MergeSort(SortArray, M+1, E)
        Merge(SortArray, B, M, E)
    endif
end {MergeSort}
```

`SortArray` is the original array, `B` (for "beginning") is the first index of the sub-array to be sorted, `E` (for "end") is the last index of the sub-array to be sorted, and `M` represents the middle index. If `E` is greater than `B`, we have more than one element in the array and should continue the recursive calls. Otherwise, notice that nothing gets done and the recursion stops. `M` is calculated so that we can split the incoming sub-array into two pieces. Then we recursively call `MergeSort` for the left and right halves of the array. When these halves have been sorted, we will merge them into a larger sorted array using a call to `Merge`. As an example of `MergeSort`, consider the following unsorted array:

```
SortArray = | 5 | 2 | 1 | 7 | 8 | 4 | 6 | 3 |
```

We first call `MergeSort(A, 1, 8)`. Pictorially, the algorithm operates thus as it goes through the divide phase. The level numbers indicate the level of recursion, and the arrow indicates the level of recursion is getting deeper and deeper:

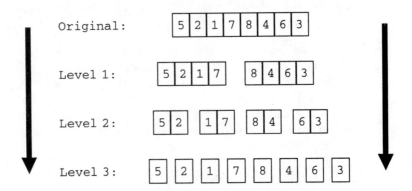

Notice that each sub-array above represents one recursive call. At the first level of recursion, we make two recursive calls - one each for the left and right halves of the initial array, thus creating two arrays of four elements each. At the second level of recursion, we make four recursive calls - one each for the left and right halves of both sub-arrays in the previous level, resulting in four subarrays of two elements each.

After the sub-arrays are all one element large, we begin to merge them and return back through the recursive path. The upward arrow indicates that the algorithm is returning through the levels of recursion:

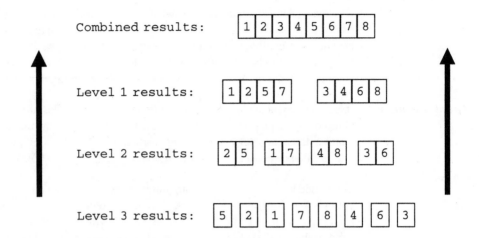

Combined results: | 1 | 2 | 3 | 4 | 5 | 6 | 7 | 8 |

Level 1 results: | 1 | 2 | 5 | 7 | | 3 | 4 | 6 | 8 |

Level 2 results: | 2 | 5 | | 1 | 7 | | 4 | 8 | | 3 | 6 |

Level 3 results: | 5 | | 2 | | 1 | | 7 | | 8 | | 4 | | 6 | | 3 |

Given an array of size N, observe that at each level of recursion, all N items are processed. Thus, for each level of recursion, we do work proportional to N. Furthermore, observe that the *number of levels* of recursion is approximately $logN$. Thus, we have $logN$ passes over the data with N work per pass. Therefore, we say that MergeSort requires $NlogN$ work.

Optimization Algorithms

Optimization problems are those in which the aim is to maximize or minimize a given value. Such problems are important to many people, as they occur in many circumstances, e.g.,

- How can a delivery service cram the most packages into a truck?

- How can a manufacturing facility that produces several products get the most dollar value out the limited number of production hours?

- How can the phone company route phone calls to get the best use from its limited number of phone lines?

- How can a salesperson visit each of the various cities on his route with the least amount of travel time?

- How can a university schedule its classes to make the best use of classrooms with minimal class conflicts?

- How can a student get the highest g.p.a. from a finite number of study hours?

Obviously, there are many reasons why people want to optimize things. Unfortunately, as we shall see in later chapters, many such common and obvious problems cannot be optimally computed in reasonable time. For now, we are concerned with two basic approaches to solving such problems: *approximate solutions* (via "greedy algorithms") and *optimal solutions* (via "dynamic planning").

Greedy Algorithms Imagine that you are led into a room filled with various piles of coins. Each pile contains coins of equal size but which have different values. One pile contains coins worth a dollar, another pile has coins worth a nickel, and so on. Imagine that you are told to fill your pockets with coins of your choice.

You would have no trouble figuring out what you wanted to do: you'd want to fill your pockets with coins of the highest value in order to maximize your gain. If you exhausted that pile, you'd then move to the pile with the next most valuable coins. After grabbing all the coins from that pile, you'd move to the pile of next most valuable coins, and so on, until your pockets were full.

In doing so, you would implicitly be executing a *greedy algorithm*: an algorithm which makes a series of quick "greedy" decisions. It first decides how to obtain the greatest immediate gain. When that decision is carried out, it then makes another quick decision to obtain the next greatest gain, and so on.

The *greedy* method is quite simple and is easy to conceptualize. Hence, the natural instinct is to want to use it for all optimization problems. This is a dangerous instinct, however, because greedy algorithms do not work for many optimization problems. To demonstrate, let's modify our previous example. We specify that only 860 grams of weight can be carried before your pockets break, and we specify the weight and value of the various kinds of coins. Here is a list of the coins' properties:

```
type   value   weight      value/weight
   1   $6.00    500g    .0120 dollars/gram
   2   $4.00    450g    .0088 dollars/gram
   3   $3.00    410g    .0073 dollars/gram
   4   $0.50    300g    .0017 dollars/gram
```

What would happen if we used a greedy algorithm to maximize the amount we carry out of the room? Well, since we want to get the most value for every gram we choose, we would choose the coin with the highest value/weight ratio on each grab. This means on the first grab we will choose a coin of type 1, worth $6. This uses 500g of our 860g limit, leaving only 360g. Of the remaining choices, the only viable one is to take type 4 coin, worth $0.50, for a total of $6.50. This is our final total, because we cannot pick up any more coins and still stay under the 860 gram limit.

Observe that this is not the optimal solution. An solution would specify that we grab a total of $7, by choosing a coin of *type 2* on the first grab and one of *type 3* on the second grab.

A greedy algorithm, then, is *optimal* only when we can optimize the final solution by individually optimizing each step in the solution.

However, a greedy algorithm is often an *appropriate* solution even when it is not *optimal*. Why? Because many optimization problems require immense amounts of algorithmic work to obtain an optimal solution. Sometimes the work is so great that it cannot be reasonably accomplished even with the fastest computer. Other times, the work may be "do-able" but simply not worth the trouble. For example, UPS doesn't want to have to run a complex computer program which requires data about the size, shape and weight of each and every package each time it packs a truck. In practice, UPS will have its trucks packed and on the road before such a program could obtain all the required data and produce a result.

In such circumstances, a greedy algorithm can be used to produce an "approximate solution," i.e., it may or may not produce the optimal result but even if it doesn't, the result may be "good enough" and will likely be better than just random guesses. We'll discuss these kinds of problems in a later chapter.

For now, let's look at a common application of the greedy method: its use in solving what are known as *minimal spanning tree* problems. As an example of such problems, consider the problem of a contractor who needs to construct a telephone network spanning 5 cities. He is given the distance from each city to all the other ones, and the only requirements are:

• Every city must be able to communicate with every other city.

• The construction must use the least amount of cable possible.

This is an optimization problem where the amount of cable is minimized. The contractor does not need to connect each city to every other one directly. That would use too much cable and is unnecessary. Instead, he needs to make sure that there is some path from each city to every other one. A given telephone call might not take the shortest conceivable path, but that doesn't matter. All that matters is that the phone company pays for the least amount of cable.

We use a greedy algorithm to decide which cities to connect with cable. We start with a network that contains no connections, choose the shortest available path, and add it to our network. Then on each later step we choose the next shortest path, chosen from all the cities we have reached so far, and add it - unless it will make a cycle in our network. We do not create cycles because they are inefficient: they add redun-

dant connections between cities that are already linked to the network. Let's walk
through an example using the cities and distances given on the graph below:

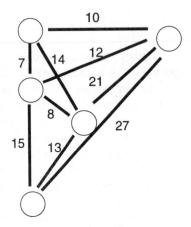

The above figure shows the five cities to be connected by a telephone network. The
distances are marked beside each connecting edge. Now let's look at the steps in
finding the network which connects all cities with a minimum investment in cable.

- In step *a*, we have chosen the shortest path possible, i.e., length *7*, and have
  added it and the cities it connects to our network.

- In step *b*, we have chosen the next shortest path and added it to the network.
  Our choices included the paths of length *10* and *14*, which emanate from the top

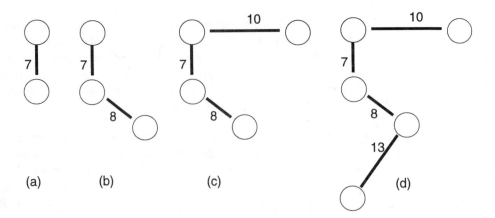

city (or "node") in figure *a*, and *12*, *8*, and *15*, which emanate from the bottom node in figure *a*. Of these, path *8* is the smallest, so select it and add the city to which it goes.

- In step *c*, we have done the same thing. The choices include the same ones as before, less the path of length *8* which has already been added. They also include the paths which emanate from the new node, *21*, *13*, and *14*. The last of these was already among our choices (from the topmost node). Of these choices, the smallest path is length *10*, so we choose it.

- In step *d*, we cannot add the shortest path (*12*) because it would complete a cycle between cities already connected to the network. Instead, we discard that choice and take the next shortest path, whose length is *13*.

Now all cities are connected to the network and there is no need to add any more paths. Thus our solution is complete. Note that a person in any of the five cities can communicate with someone in any other city. Although communication may not be by the most direct route possible, we have used a *greedy algorithm* to achieve our goal of minimizing the amount of cable needed.

Observe that we can view the result as a linked list. A different problem might result in a tree-shaped solution (But *never* a graph. Why?). Also observe that the pertinent information consisted of a listing of the distance of the all the possible edges between the nodes. Thus, an algorithmic solution to this problem might construct a linked list or tree and make its decisions based on values (edge distances and the names of the city on each end of each edge) stored in a table.

Dynamic   *Dynamic programming* is a planning method. Its name has nothing to do with "pro-
Programming   gramming" in the usual sense of the word. Thus, it may be less confusing if we refer
                 to it as "dynamic planning."

Regardless of the name, the idea overcomes the weakness of a *greedy algorithm* approach. *Dynamic planning* laboriously calculates all of the possible solution options, then chooses the best one. Thus, it produces *optimal* solutions, not *approximate* ones. Fortunately, it is a recursive approach, which means that the logic is simple, only the execution is laborious.

To illustrate it, consider the following problem. A traveler is trying to get from point *A* to point *B* by the shortest route. He doesn't care how many cities he encounters, only that his distance is minimized. This problem is known as the "weary traveler" problem. We will consider it using the *directed acyclic graph* of cities shown (top of next page).

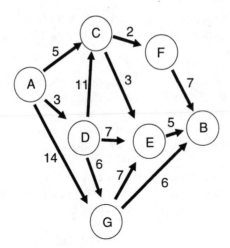

The above figure is a *directed graph* because each edge has a direction, i.e., is a "one way street." It is "acyclic" because, while the edges appear at first to create cycles, the directed nature of them makes it impossible to go around in circles.

Faced with the problem of finding the shortest route from *A* to *B*, we know w hat a *greedy algorithm* would do. Starting at point *A*, it would choose the shortest edge, i.e., the path to *D*. Once at *D*, it would again choose the shortest path (length of *6*) and go to *G* (total travel so far is *9*). Once at *G*, it would again select the shortest path (*6*) and go to *B*, the destination. Thus, a greedy algorithm will plan a route with a total distance of *15*.

However, upon visual inspection, we can see that this solution is not optimal. A total distance of only *13* can be obtained by taking the route from *A* to *C*, then to *E* and on to *B*. The *greedy algorithm* misses this route because the path from *A* to *C* is not the shortest path leaving *A*.

A *dynamic planning* algorithm will discover the optimal path because it does not make any rash decisions. Instead, it considers all the possibilities in a recursive fashion. Given the problem at hand, a *dynamic planning* algorithm will initially decide only that the best path is the shortest one of its three initial choices: traveling from A to B via points C, D, and G. It knows that one of these routes will be best but doesn't know which one. What it does know is:

```
L(A) = Min((5 + L(C)), (14 + L(G)), (3 + L(D)))
```

where L(N) refers to the shortest path from N to the destination. As you can see, it makes use of a Min function which will reduce to the smallest of the values given.

In order to find the shortest path, it is necessary to know the values for L(C), L(G), and L(D). To find out, the algorithm acts recursively to find the shortest path from each of *C*, *D* and *G* to *B*. Thus, it must calculate each of:

```
L(C) = Min((2 + L(F), (3 + L(E)))
L(D) = Min((11 + L(C)), (7 + L(E)), (6 + L(G)))
L(G) = Min((7 + L(E)), (6 + L(B)))
```

Once these values are found, they can be substituted in the L(A) expression and determine the solution. However, to solve these expressions, it is necessary to know the values of L(F), L(E), and L(B). Thus, we must solve for:

```
L(F) = Min(7 + L(B))
L(E) = Min(5 + L(B))
L(B) = 0
```

Since L(B) is quite obviously 0, we can use this use this knowledge to solve both L(E) and L(F):

```
L(F) = 7 via "F to B"
L(E) = 5 via "E to B"
```

We now have enough knowledge to solve L(G) and L(C):

```
L(G) = Min((7 + L(E)), (6 + L(B)))

     = Min((7 + 5), (6 + 0))

     = 6 via "G to B"

L(C) = Min((2 + L(F), (3 + L(E))) = Min((2 + 7), (3 + 5)

     = 8 via "C to E to B."
```

With L(C) and L(G) solved, we can now solve for L(D):

```
L(D) = Min((11 + L(C)), (7 + L(E)), (6 + L(G)))

     = Min(((11 + 8), (7 + 5), (6 + 6))

     = 12 via "D to G to B."
```

We have now solved each component of the original expression, and can now solve for L(A):

$$L(A) = Min((5 + L(C)), (14 + L(G)), (3 + L(D)))$$

$$= Min((5 + 8), (14 + 6), (3 + 12)) = Min(13, 20, 15)$$

$$= 13 \text{ via "A to C to E to B"}$$

Dynamic planning is an example of *divide and conquer* thinking. The routing problem is broken down into each possible route segment. As the distance for each segment is evaluated, its value is stored in an appropriate data structure, then used in calculating the distances for larger route segments, those that pass through one or more points. Eventually, the values for all viable routes are compared, and the optimal one is chosen.

Food for Thought:

The Limit of Imagination

In 1945, Winston Churchill gave a speech in which he coined the phrase "Iron Curtain" to describe the virtual wall of isolation and control that was being placed by the Soviets around Eastern Europe. It may have been the most powerful *Mechanical Model* metaphor ever spoken. A decade later, U Thant, Secretary General of the United Nations, delivered a speech in which he proclaimed the dawning of a New Age, an age which we can see in retrospect as being the age of the *Computational Model*.

Churchill's speech received much more attention than did U Thant's, and his term "Iron Curtain" rapidly became incorporated into everyday language. U Thant's proclamation was hardly noticed. But the Iron Curtain is no more, while U Thant's announcement is becoming more and more true with each passing year.

U Thant announced a watershed change in the very basis of human achievement. He saw quite clearly that things were becoming fundamentally different in a very particular way. Throughout the entire history of human endeavor, he noted, humankind's accomplishment was limited by available physical resources. The question was always, "given the material we've got, what can we make out of it?" U Thant announced that that era, an era that began with the first humans, *was over*.

He was quite clear about the nature of the era that was replacing it. He announced that the essential feature of the New Age is that achievement would be limited primarily by our imagination. Instead of asking, "This is what we've got, what can we do with it?," humankind would instead be asking, "What do we *want* to create, and how do we invent what's necessary to do it?"

In the decades since U Thant's pronouncement, events have proven him correct. Currently humankind is, through computationally-enabled science, going down the road of creation: creating plastic materials that will last for eternity, creating ways to select our own bodily shape and appearance, creating previously unimaginable ways to interact instantaneously with others around the earth, creating new genes to correct genetic flaws and, eventually, perhaps to shape and control the evolution of life itself.

Regardless of whether you see these changes as positive progress or dangerous "meddling with Nature," it is difficult to deny the essential point of U Thant's message from 40 years ago: that human accomplishment is no longer governed by the physical properties of available raw materials; that it instead extends outward from our vision, our intention, our ability to conceive of what we want to create. We can make nearly anything we want. So, what do we want to make?

Twenty five years ago, we put men on the moon and brought them home. Why? Mainly to prove to ourselves that we could do it. Now, we are engaged in exploring frontiers that are much more daring. It's only a matter of time before the genetic code is mapped and manipulable. It's only a matter of time before non-fossil-based energy is both safe and available. It's only a matter of time before the biochemical processes that help govern our thoughts and feelings are well understood. *So what do we want to make?*

The limit is our ability to get the *right conception*, to get the *right idea*, to have the *needed insight*. It's no longer coal we need, it's clarity. Given clarity about what problem we're attacking, we can invent the tools and processes to attack it. *So what are the problems we want to attack?*

This is the main limitation of algorithmic power. *Once we know* what data structure we need to represent some aspect of reality, we can readily create *exactly that data structure. Once we know* the processing steps by which we wish to manipulate that representation, we can implement *exactly those processing steps. Once we know* what we're trying to do, we can do *exactly what we want.*

Algorithmic methods give us the power to manipulate our models, our ideas, our representations *however we wish to.* Computing technologies give us the power to simulate, control, and experiment with *whatever conceptions we might have.* Within certain limits of complexity, the limitations of algorithms are *not in the algorithms.* The limitations are instead in our ability to *properly envision what we're trying to do.* We can implement any logic we want in an algorithm. *So what logic do we want to implement?* U Thant was right. The limitation is no longer in our *stuff*, it's in our *minds.*

Summary

Algorithmic methods provide us with widely applicable solution strategies.

- *Searches* and *traversals* are required with great regularity and, depending on the data structure involved, both iterative and recursive solutions have their place.

- *Divide and Conquer* strategies often provide the most efficient and neat solutions to problems which can broken into discrete subproblems. They are often recursive.

- *Greedy algorithms* provide an adequate optimal solution to some optimization problems and a useful "quick and dirty" *approximate solution* to others. Depending on the particulars, greedy algorithms can be readily implemented iteratively or recursively.

- *Dynamic Programming* (or *Dynamic Planning*) provides a recursive means of exhaustively considering all the options and producing the *optimal solution* to many optimization problems.

Exercises

All of the tree traversal algorithms we discussed are *depth-first*: they begin at the root, go to one child, and continue down a path all the way to a leaf. Only after exploring one subtree do they visit any nodes in the other subtree. Another way to traverse a tree is *breadth-first*. Such a traversal would first visit both children of the root before visiting any grandchildren, i.e., it would make a left-to-right pass through each each level of the tree before going to the next lower level.

6.1. As we have seen, *depth-first* traversals make use of a *stack* to help manage the traversal. In contrast, *breadth-first* traversals make use of a *queue* to manage the traversal. Think about this and explain why a *queue* would be more useful than a *stack* for a *breadth-first* traversal.

6.2. Construct an algorithm for *breadth first* traversal. You may assume that a *queue* data structure exists and you may call Enqueue and Dequeue operations as needed.

Problems 6.3 and 6.4 each require that you implement a *greedy algorithm*. Your solution need not provide optimal solutions, but rather appropriate *greedy* approximate solutions.

6.3. Create a greedy algorithm that solves *bin-packing problems* (such as the example *coins* problem and other problems like it), i.e., problems which involve:

a) Some limited capacity (e.g., how much can you carry, fit, spend, use up, absorb, etc., i.e., "that which limits how much you can do"). In our *coins* example, the limiting capacity was 860 grams.

b) Some number of *kinds* of items, such that each item has:

a *value* (profit), and

a *cost* (how much of the limited capacity is used up by each item of that kind).

In our *coins* example, we had four denominations of coins, each with its own value and weight.

c) A goal of using the limited capacity in a way that *maximizes profit.*

You may assume an unlimited available supply of each kind of item such that profit is limited only by capacity and the particular way that it is used.

6.4. Create a *greedy algorithm* that solves *minimal spanning tree* problems (such as our cable routing problem and other problems like it), i.e.,problems which involve:

a) Some required task such that a solution consists of many possible subsolutions. In our *cable* problem, the required task was connecting all the cities, and the many possible subsolutions were partial cable routings.

b) A cost associated with each possible subsolution. In our *cable* problem, the cost was the distance between various cities.

c) A goal of completing the required task in a way that minimizes cost.

Problems 6.5 through 6.8 refer to the *dynamic planning* approach to optimization. In our discussion of *dynamic planning*, we described the steps involved but did not present either an explicit algorithm or a data structure.

6.5. How might linked lists be used for keeping track of the various nodes, the available paths to other nodes, and the distance of each path?

6.6. Design a data structure that implements your answer to the previous problem.

6.7. How might a *stack* be used to help keep track of which points are on the optimal route?

6.8. Implement an algorithm to do so. You may wish to use a recursive algorithm so that you benefit from the "automatic" *stack* management that the activation stack can provide to recursive routines.

[This page intentionally left blank.]

Chapter 7: Tools for Estimating Cost and Complexity

Algorithms are our creations. The current revolution in science and human understanding is, in large part, due to our ability to do more than create algorithms: our various technologies allow us to *implement* these creations (in computer programs) and *execute* them (by "running" such programs). In short, we not only *create* algorithms, we also can *observe how they perform*.

It is natural and appropriate to be curious about the performance of our creations. For example, automotive engineers certainly want to be informed about the performance of the cars they produce. Furthermore, they do not just "go build a car" in some haphazard fashion, then inquire after the fact about that car's performance. Instead, they *design* their cars to meet various performance-related targets: gas mileage, emissions, acceleration, braking, handling, ergonomics, and so on. Similar concerns apply to algorithms.

> ☐ Despite their abstract nature of algorithms, we want to understand their *performance properties*. Moreover, we *require* knowledge of performance-related attributes if we are to engineer desirable algorithms.

For many programmers, their creation of algorithms has been analogous to building home-made "kit cars," not modern automobiles. They write their programs as best they can, step by step, making changes as appropriate, "making things fit," "making things work," etc. This is the approach followed by early inventors of automobiles. It is entirely appropriate for purposes of the early stages of learning and discovery. But it bears no resemblance to the design and engineering process of modern times.

Not only are modern automobiles designed and evaluated in terms of performance attributes, but many of these attributes are readily understood by non-technical people. For example, nearly everyone understands what is meant by "miles per gallon," "miles per hour," and so on. Furthermore, there are certain levels of performance that are commonly understood to be realistic, while others are not. For instance, what would happen if someone said "I'm an automotive engineer and I have designed a $15,000 car that goes 2000 mph, gets 500 mpg on regular gasoline, and protects its occupants from injury in all possible crashes"? We might expect an average American 10-year-old to know better than to take such claims seriously. In our society, no particular expertise is required to know that such claims are unrealistic.

Similar issues come into play with respect to algorithm performance. To understand the application of computing to the problems of modern times, and to understand what computing can and cannot reasonably do, it is necessary to have a basic foundation in important principles and "rules of thumb," just as an educated car-buyer will know what is meant by "miles per gallon" and will have a general idea about realistic versus ridiculous expectations of performance and fuel economy.

In this chapter, we introduce you to the key measures of algorithmic performance and to the general categories of performance that are considered reasonable. To continue our automotive analogy one step further, we would not expect someone who isn't an engineer to be able predict whether a car gets 27 mpg versus 32 mpg, but we would expect everyone to know the difference in both practical value and "reasonableness" between 25 mpg and 200 mpg. We want to provide you with a similar degree of basic knowledge about algorithmic performance.

Measures of Performance

We are interested primarily in only two aspects of an algorithm's performance: *"How fast will it go?"* and *"What resources does it consume?."* Unlike cars, where motion is produced and fuel is consumed, the key algorithmic measures are *time* and *space*. An algorithm or program uses *time* (i.e., *cpu cycles*) in some proportion to how much *work* it performs, and it uses *space* (i.e., *memory*) in some proportion to how much *data* it manipulates.

> ☐ Remember: the *speed* of a cpu cycle is dependent on the computer, but the *number of cycles required* is largely a property of the algorithm (and the program in which it is expressed).

Thus, we characterize the performance attributes of algorithms as an empirical issue of *time* (or *work*, i.e., number of cycles irrespective of their speed) and *space*.

A Simple Example

For a rudimentary analysis of time and space costs, let's consider an algorithm that makes use of the *if-then-else* construct: an algorithm for a simple calculator. It is specified as having the following behavior:

a) performing the four basic arithmetic operations on two numerical operands,

b) prompting the user to input 3 pieces of data: `Operand1`, `Operand2`, and `Operator`, respectively, and

c) producing the output "`The answer is [answer].`"

d) for simplicity, we specify that it need not cope with the "divide by zero" error.

One such algorithm is provided as *Algorithm 7.1*. It is correct for the specified problem. Assuming that the input values conform to what's expected, it will behave as required by the specification. But how do we evaluate its performance? At the most obvious level, we need to ascertain how much memory it requires for its data ("space") and how many instructions must be carried out ("work").

In this example, the space required is no mystery. We have declared four simple variables and their space is all the data space required. But what about time? Observe that the algorithm contains a sequence of four *if* statements. Each *if* statement requires the test of a condition. If the condition is *true*, then one arithmetic operation and one assignment operation will be performed. Finally, one *print* operation is performed.

Notice that all four *if* statements are evaluated, no matter which operator has been input. When the indicated operation is *addition*, the first *if* statement is executed. Then, even though the tests for the remaining three operations are unnecessary, the program tests for them nonetheless.

Without measuring performance in any way, we can intuitively see that we can improve the efficiency of the program by nesting the *if* statements. Recall that the instructions to be executed in either the *if* or *else* parts of an *if-then-else* statement can be any statement or list of statements. This includes another *if-then-else* statement. By nesting the *if* tests one inside the other, we can keep superfluous tests from being executed. We have rewritten the algorithm (see *Algorithm 7.2*) to take advantage of this.

By nesting the *if* statements one inside the other we have made the number of tests that will be performed dependent upon the input data.

• In the case of an *addition* operation, the first *if* statement is evaluated, the boolean expression (`Operator = '+'`) evaluates to *true*, and the addition operation is performed. The remaining tests, nested inside the *else* clause are bypassed. Thus, when input calls for addition, our new version of the program performs only one test, not four.

```
algorithm Calculator
{Purpose: performs four basic calculator functions, but
    does not handle divide-by-zero error}

var
    Operand1 isa num,                      {the 1st operand}
    Operand2 isa num,                      {the 2nd operand}
    Answer isa num,          {the result of the calculation}
    Operator isa char                         {the operator}

begin                             {read the 2 operands and the
                                  operator from standard input}
    print('Enter the first operand:  ')
    read(Operand1)
    print('Enter the second operand:  ')
    read(Operand2)
    print('Enter the operator:  ')
    read(Operator)
                      {perform the indicated calculation}
    if (Operator = '+') then
        Answer <- Operand1 + Operand2
    endif

    if (Operator = '-') then
        Answer <- Operand1 - Operand2
    endif

    if (Operator = '*') then
        Answer <- Operand1 * Operand2
    endif

    if (Operator = '/') then
        Answer <- Operand1 / Operand2
    endif
                                        {generate the output}
    print('The answer is', Answer,'.')

end {algorithm Calculator}
```

Algorithm 7.1: A Simple Calculator

```
algorithm Calculator
{Purpose: performs four basic calculator functions, but
    does not handle divide-by-zero error}

var
    Operand1 isa num,                    {the 1st operand}
    Operand2 isa num,                    {the 2nd operand}
    Answer isa num,          {the result of the calculation}
    Operator isa char                        {the operator}

begin                          {read the 2 operands and the
                                operator from standard input}
    print('Enter the first operand:  ')
    read(Operand1)
    print('Enter the second operand:  ')
    read(Operand2)
    print('Enter the operator:  ')
    read(Operator)

                        {perform the indicated calculation}
    if (Operator = '+') then
        Answer <- Operand1 + Operand2
    else
        if (Operator = '-') then
            Answer <- Operand1 - Operand2
        else
            if (Operator = '*') then
                Answer <- Operand1 * Operand2
            else
                if(Operator = '/')
                    Answer <- Operand1 / Operand2
                endif
            endif
        endif
    endif                             {generate the output}

    print('The answer is', Answer,'.')

end {end of algorithm Calculator}
```

Algorithm 7.2: A Simple Calculator, Version 2

- In the case of *subtraction*, two tests are executed. The first *if* statement is evaluated, the boolean expression (`Operator = '+'`) evaluates to *false*, and the *else* clause is executed. Within the *else* clause, the second of our *if* statements is executed, the boolean expression (`Operator = '-'`) evaluates to *true*, and the subtraction operation is performed. The remaining tests, those for multiplication and division, are bypassed.

- By the same logic, *multiplication* requires that three of the four tests are performed.

- In the case of *division*, all four tests are executed.

Thus, where our earlier versions of the program guaranteed that four tests would be performed each time, our new version makes the exact number of tests unpredictable. The unpredictability of the amount of work required which we have observed in our `Calculator` algorithm is quite normal.

> ☐ A General Principle:
> It is a *general principle* that we cannot predict the path of execution through a given algorithm. This is a consequence of the fact that flow of control can be altered, based on the decisions made by the algorithm as determined by the value of tested variables. Because an algorithm's path of execution is not predictable, and because different paths may involve different amounts of work, it follows that we cannot predict *exactly* how much work a given algorithm will do.

Measures of work

The fact that the work done by an algorithm is unpredictable does not mean that we shy away from trying to measure it. On the contrary, evaluating and comparing the work required by various algorithms is a very important component of software engineering. In fact, it is only by such measures that we can identify which of various possible algorithms for a given task is preferable.

In general, there are three different metrics by which we evaluate algorithms:

1. *Best Case:* If we consider only the number of tests performed, the best case for our improved `Calculator` algorithm is one test. It occurs when an addition operation is called for.

2. *Worst Case:* Considering only the number of tests performed, the worse case for our improved `Calculator` algorithm is four tests. It occurs when a division operator is called for.

3. *Average Case:* This refers to the amount of work required "on the average." We assume some suitably large number of trials with various input, and determine the mean. In the absence of knowledge about the specifics of the data to be input, we might assume that input is random.

Analysis of work done

Let us now evaluate the work done by our simple `Calculator` algorithm. We will consider the operations visible to us at the level of a high-level language and won't worry about any underlying machine-level detail, i.e., we are concerned here with an algorithm and not a program. We also will ignore the *reads* and *prints*, as they involve dealing with the "outside world" and, for now, we don't know what work might be involved them.

Each *if* statement includes a test that determines if a given condition is *true* or *false*. Each such test involves two steps.

- First, the condition (a boolean expression, e.g. `Operator = '*'`), is evaluated. This evaluation is itself an operation. It always resolves to a boolean value (*true* or *false*), and the boolean result *effectively replaces the tested condition when the test is performed.*

- Secondly, after the boolean expression has resolved to a boolean value, this value is examined to see whether the *if* or the *else* clause is to be executed. This examination of the boolean result (to determine which path execution will follow) is a second operation.

Thus, each *if-then-else* statement requires two operations to determine the flow of control: one operation to resolve the boolean expression to either *true* or *false*, and a second operation to examine this boolean result and select the execution path based upon it.

Apart from the various *if-then-else* statements, our code also includes statements which evaluate arithmetic expressions and assigns the result to the appropriate variable (e.g., `Answer <- Operand1 + Operand2`). These also involve two steps:

- First, the arithmetic expression to the right of the assignment operator is evaluated. It resolves to a value, as determined by the specifics of the operands and operator. The evaluation of our simple single-operator arithmetic expressions requires one operation. (More complex arithmetic expressions would require more operations.)

- Then, after the operation is performed (reducing the expression to a value), the result is then assigned to the variable to the left of the assignment operator. This assignment is a second operation.

Thus, each of the assignment statements in our program involve two operations: the evaluation of the simple arithmetic expression, and the assignment of the result to the specified variable.

Given this, what can we conclude about the work involved in our algorithm? We know that only one arithmetic operation will be performed each time the program is run. We also know that doing this will require two logical operations (one to resolve the value, the other to assign it). Thus, we know that two operations will be performed for any legal input.

We also know that some number of condition tests will be performed, and that each such test also requires two operations (one to resolve the boolean expression to a boolean value, the other to test the resulting boolean value).

Before nesting our *if* statements, the algorithm involved four condition tests each time, resulting in eight operations. In addition, the calculation itself involved two operations, for a total of ten operations. The same number of steps were involved, regardless of the input data. Thus, *best case*, *worst case*, and *average case* all required ten operations.

After nesting our *if* statements, the *worst case* is unchanged. In the worst case, we still have to perform all four tests and one calculation, for a total of ten operations. However, the *best case* is reduced dramatically. In the best case, we will perform only one test and one calculation, for a total of four operations. Nesting also improves the average work considerably. If we assume random input (see sidebar, *The "Random Assumption" About Average Work*), we can expect a random distribution of cases requiring 1, 2, 3, or 4 tests each. This translates to an average of 2.5 tests (i.e., (1+2+3+4)/4) and one calculation, all at two operations apiece, for an average work of 7 operations.

Thus, while the worst case is unchanged, nesting has reduced the best case work by 60% and the average case work by 30%. As you can see, these are considerable improvements. They may or may not be significant, however, as determined by other factors which we will consider later.

As a practical matter, we are usually concerned with average or "expected" work and the worst case more so than the best case. In other words, we rarely worry about things "going right." Furthermore, in most circumstances, we do not attempt to count operations as precisely as we have here. You shall soon see why.

For now, make sure that (a) you understand what we mean by these terms and (b) you can compare the work required by two algorithmic versions of the simple calculator as we have done here.

The "Random Assumption" about Average Work.

In many circumstances, the assumption of random input is a faulty one, and we must be alert to any properties of the data or of the operational situation which will impact what constitutes an "average" case.

For example, we can imagine that a calculator component of a cash register system will not feature a random distribution of operators. When we shop at the grocery store, addition operators predominate. Multiplication occurs only with respect to buying multiples of an item and when computing sales tax. Subtraction occurs only if we hand the clerk coupons, or if an item has been entered erroneously and must be "backed out." Division rarely occurs at all. In such circumstances, the *best* and *worst* cases are unaffected, but we need to consider the *average* case with more care.

In the case of a cash register program, when determining the order in which we want the operators to appear in our code, we clearly would want addition (the most frequent) to appear first and division (the least frequent) to appear last. We might, however, be unsure as to whether multiplication or subtraction should appear second. In fact, we would need some knowledge about which occurs more frequently in the real world.

In either case, the preponderance of addition operations would suggest that the average work in this situation would migrate somewhat towards 4 from the mean of 7 suggested by the assumption of random data.

This kind of phenomena is not limited to the grocery store. In fact, it occurs quite frequently in many things related to "real life." You should be very thoughtful before *assuming* that a truly random distribution of *any* phenomenon will occur.

Exercises: 7.1. Consider Algorithm 7.2. In light of data that shows 60% of operations to be multiplication, 25% to be addition, 10% to be division, and 5% to be subtraction, what is *average* (or *expected*) *work* for *Algorithm 7.2*?

7.2. Given the distribution of operations from problem 7.1, above, modify *Algorithm 7.2* to optimize expected performance. Do so by rearranging the order of operator tests. After optimization, what is expected performance for the modified algorithm?

7.3. The requirements for *Algorithms 7.1* and *7.2* specified that the algorithm need not cope with the possibility of a "divide by zero" error. Modify *Algorithm 7.2* so that it will respond effectively to such an error. You may assume that all other aspects of user input will be legal. In the case where division by zero is attempted, the algorithm shall print a brief error message to the user and prompt the user for a non-zero divisor. Then, evaluate *best case, worst case,* and *average case* work for the modified algorithm. For average work, assume a random distribution of operators and a random distribution of single-digit (0..9) operands.

7.4. You are given an array of ten numbers. Your job is to create an algorithm that calculates the minimum, maximum, and average of these numbers. Your boss has informed you that processor time (i.e., the cost of instructions) is expensive while memory is cheap. Write an iterative algorithm that uses as much memory as desired while keeping the expected work down to a minimum. What is the expected work? How much data space is required?

7.5. You are given the same problem as 7.4, above, except that the economics have changed: processor time is now cheap while memory is very expensive. Write an algorithm that uses as many instructions as desired while using the fewest possible variables. How much data space is needed? What is the expected work?

Increasing the Complexity

The `Calculator` algorithm, above, features unpredictable performance even though we know that input will consist of a certain number of items (2 operands and 1 operator). For most useful algorithms, things are not quite so easy.

Consider, for example, the task of searching a list to see if it contains a particular value. Obviously, we wouldn't want to write special algorithms for a list of 8 items, a list of 213 items, and a list of 1,316,203 items. A useful *search* algorithm will be written so that it is *general*, i.e., it will handle lists of any length. We speak of such algorithms as being designed to search a list of length N, where N is whatever number of items happen to be in any particular list.

Common sense tells us that the amount of work involved will vary based on the size of the list. It will be cheaper to search a list of five items than to search a list of a billion items. In short, common sense tells us that the work we have to do is somehow *proportional* to the length of the list.

In this instance, common sense is correct. In measuring performance, we are generally concerned with *how* the amount of work varies with the data, e.g. the size of the input. Fortunately, as it turns out, we generally don't need to be concerned with an *exact* measure but rather an *approximate* measure of the rate at which the work grows. For example, as the size N of a list grows from *5* to *1,000,000,000*, we want to know *about* how much the required work will increase. To see why we can settle for an *approximate* measurement, let's consider an example.

Let's imagine that we have list of numbers of size *N* and that we must create a search algorithm which will tell us if the value stored in the variable `TargetValue` is in the list. This is all the algorithm has to do: look in the list of *N* items and decide either "Yes, the target value is there" or "No, the target value is not there." How much work will it take to do this?

It depends on two things: *the properties of the data* (i.e., "is the list sorted or not?") and on *the properties of the search algorithm.*

As we saw in Chapter 6, to perform a *linear search* we start at the beginning of the list and work our way towards the end (or vice versa). The search will end when either (a) we find the target value `TargetValue`, or (b) we reach the end of the list without finding the `TargetValue`. If we are reading the values in the list from input, the algorithm might look like *Algorithm 7.3*.

We know that the *if-then-else* will be executed in any case. Thus, the work of the latter part of the algorithm does not vary with *N*. The only thing that varies with *N* is the amount of work we can expect *the loop* to do.

- Regardless of *N*, the best case performance is *1*. This will occur only when we get lucky and the target value happens to be the first item in the list.

- The worst case will be *N* passes through the loop. This will occur only when either the target value is not in the list or it is in last position in the list.

```
begin
   loop
       read(CurrentValue)
       exitif ((CurrentValue = TargetValue) OR (EOF))
   endloop
   if (CurrentValue = TargetValue) then
       print ('the target value is there')
   else
       print ('the target value is not there')
   endif
end
```

Algorithm 7.3: A Simple Linear Search

- The average case is impossible to determine unless we know the probability of the target value being in the list. If we pretend that it will always be in the list (i.e., we only have to verify that it's there), and if we pretend that its position in the list is randomly distributed, then the average case will require approximate *N/2* passes through the loop.

Thus, we can say that:

Best case: 1 pass through loop

Worst case: N passes through the loop

Average case (if the target value is present): N/2 passes through the loop

Observe that we've ignored the work of the *if-then-else* statement. Why? Because it is *constant* regardless of N. It has no effect on the rate at which the work grows with N. Thus, we "throw it out" of our estimate. Similarly, the fact that we're estimating means that we can also throw out *any other* constant or literal factors (we'll see why soon), e.g., the "2" in "N/2." Thus, we say that for linear search, best case is *1*, while both worst case and average cases grow in proportion to *N*. In our "estimation jargon," we denote this by saying:

Best case is "Order 1," which is written *O(1)*

Worst case is "Order N," which is written *O(N)*

Average case is also "Order N"

As mentioned earlier, we generally don't care about "best case," so we refer to linear search as being an "Order N" algorithm. This simply means that the amount of work done by such an algorithm grows at a rate that is more-or-less proportional to N.

Can we do better? Maybe, depending on what assumptions we make. For example, imagine that the numbers stored are the Social Security numbers of students, and that we have them stored in a huge array so that each number is its own index into the array, e.g., if your SocSec# is 123-45-6787, then it would be stored at location 123456787 of the array. This scheme would require an array of one billion elements. To find whether a student is in the class, we need only execute *Algorithm 7.4*.

Given this scheme, the work doesn't vary with *N* (the number of students) at all. We have random access to each number and, regardless of the size of the list, we can do our job with only a single *if-then-else* statement. Thus, we would say that best case, worse case, and expected case are all *O(1)*.

☐ An important distinction!

In our "Big Oh" notation, constant costs are *hidden*. Thus, *O(1)* does *not* mean that only one operation is required. *O(1)* means that work will be equal to *1 * (the constant costs hidden by our Big Oh notation)*.

Remember: with Big Oh, we're concerned with the *rate* of growth. O(1) is our way of saying that the work is constant, i.e., it does not change at all as N grows.

Of course, the problem with our random access solution that utilizes a huge array is its extreme waste. If we have a class of only 25 students, we still require an array large enough to hold the range of possible SS#'s. This means we require a billion cells but use only 25 of them to store data; 999,999,975 of the cells are wasted. We are only using 1/40,000,000 of the space resource our array is occupying, which is obviously absurd. However, it does give us an example of *ideal performance* with respect to work. We'd like to get closer to *O(1)* than to *O(N)* performance, especially when dealing with big lists, but without ridiculous space demands.

We can do better than *O(N)* if we assume that the list is sorted and stored in an array of size N. We have already seen the algorithm in Chapter 6: *binary search*. Recall what the binary search algorithm does: it repeatedly jumps to the middle of the remaining list and makes a comparison with the value stored there. It either finds the target value or determines which half of the list can be ignored. As with the others, best case is *O(1)*; it might get lucky and find the target value on the first try. But what about worst case and expected case?

Consider an example: we have a sorted list of 16 numbers stored in an appr/opriately sized array, and we will assume that we do *not* get lucky and encounter the target value any sooner than worst case. With its first comparison, the algorithm can dismiss half of the numbers, leaving about 8. On the second comparison it can eliminate

```
begin
    if (array[TargetValue] = TargetValue) then
        print ('yes, the target value is there')
    else
        print ('no, the target value is not there')
    endif
end
```

Algorithm 7.4: Random Access to a Large Address Space

half of those, leaving about 4. On the third comparison, it can eliminate approximately half of the remaining 4, leaving 2. On the fourth comparison, it can eliminate half of the remaining two, leaving one. Either the target value will be in that one remaining cell or not. Thus, it takes 4 comparisons to do the work for a list of size 16.

Observe that log_2 of *16* is *4*. (For the mathematically challenged, all we're saying is that 16 is obtained by raising 2 to the 4th power.) Similarly, if the list contained more than 16 elements, but no more than 32 elements, binary search would require about 5 comparisons, i.e., log_2 of 32. (We always assume base 2, but it really doesn't matter which base number system we use: they differ in a constant way and we throw away all the constants). We call algorithms that perform in this way "Order logN" algorithms, which is written as $O(log_2N)$ or henceforth $O(logN)$.

We observe that binary search (*or any algorithm that repeatedly cuts its remaining work in half*) involves work that grows at a rate proportional to *the log of N*, not N. How much better are $O(logN)$ algorithms than $O(N)$ algorithms. As *Table 7.1* shows, for small numbers the difference doesn't amount to much, but as N grows the difference becomes dramatic.

N of no more than:	O(1)	O(logN)	O(N)
16	1	4	16
64	1	6	64
256	1	8	256
1,024 (1K)	1	10	1,024
16,384 (16K)	1	14	16,384
131,072 (128K)	1	17	131,072
262,144 (256K)	1	18	262,144
524,288 (512K)	1	17	524,288
1,048,576 ($1K^2$=1M)	1	20	1,028,576
1,073,741,824 ($1K^3$=1G)	1	30	1,073,741,824

Table 7.1: O(1) vs. O(logN) vs. O(N) performance

This should give you a strong hint as to why we're willing to simplify our estimates by throwing out the constant factors. *Who cares* what they are? Imagine that two algorithms do the same task: the first requires 325 instructions for each pass, while the second requires only a single instruction for each pass. However, the first algorithm is *O(logN)* while the second is *O(N)*. For an N of one billion, the seemingly "expensive" first algorithm would require 325 instructions for each of 30 passes, or

9,750 total instructions, while the seemingly "cheap" second algorithm would require a single instruction for each of one billion passes. Final score: 9,750 vs. 1 billion! In short, for purposes of estimation, we assume that the constant costs don't amount to much in the big picture. Thus, we throw them away in the interest of giving ourselves a "quick and dirty" estimation tool.

Of course, we can contrive a situation where this assumption would be wrong. For example, if the constant costs were one billion, then our estimate would be hiding a considerable cost component! Such an algorithm that offered $O(logN)$ performance would be far worse than many $O(N)$ algorithms *until* N grew to be huge. (How huge?) However, in *most cases*, our assumption is useful. Be sure to remember that it is an *assumption*, one that must be questioned from one circumstance to the next.

☐   Remember!

When we *measure* performance, we care about the *actual time and space resources* used by an algorithm.

When we *estimate* and/or *categorize* performance, all we care about is the *growth* rate of an algorithm's work. We do this by tossing out the constants and paying attention only to the dominant factor, e.g., the way in which growth is proportional to N.

Exercises   7.6. The *exitif* statement is similar to the *if* statement in that it involves the test of a boolean condition to determine flow of control. Consider *Algorithm 7.3*. Observe that the *exitif* test involves two conditions. Based on our discussion of *work* concerning our *Calculator* algorithm (*Algorithms 7.1 and 7.2*), what are the performance costs be for this compound test, i.e., how many instructions will it take to evaluate the *exitif* conditions and decide upon flow of control?

7.7. Given your answer to *7.6*, what are the *actual time and space costs* for *Algorithm 7.3* in terms of N. Be sure to assess the costs for best case, worst case, and average case. For the average case, you may assume that the target value will always be found and that it will randomly distributed throughout the list from one trial to another.

In the previous problems, you assessed actual performance costs. Our *Big Oh* estimates "throw away" much of this information. Since information is being thrown away, it is possible for our *Big Oh* estimates to be deceiving.

7.8. Your manager shows you two algorithms: one is $O(N)$, the other is $O(1)$. He is confused because the $O(N)$ algorithm performs better than the $O(1)$ algorithm for his data set where N = 16K. Upon inspection, you determine that the $O(N)$ algorithm makes exactly N passes through the data and that each pass implies hidden constant costs of 17 instructions per pass. If the $O(1)$ algorithm makes exactly 1 pass through the data, estimate the hidden constant costs (i.e., instructions per pass) that you would expect to find in order to explain its slower performance.

7.9. Same problem as 7.8, above, except that it's an $O(logN)$ algorithm that's being out performed by the same $O(N)$ algorithm. Upon inspection, you determine that the $O(logN)$ algorithm makes 2logN passes through the data. What must the constant costs be per pass to explain its poorer performance?

Performance and Data Structures

We have seen that we can find big performance gains in searching by deploying a $O(logN)$ algorithm rather than an $O(N)$ one. However, our examples of good performance *assumed* that we had the data sorted and stored in an appropriately sized array. How can we make assumptions like that? In truth, we cannot. We can only say that *if* the data is sorted and *if* the data is in an appropriate data structure, then we can get $O(logN)$ performance, otherwise we may have to settle for $O(N)$ performance.

Many times, the data will be sorted anyway due to some other part of the algorithm. Long before the advent of computers, good common sense practices for organizing things dictated that lists of names be kept organized in alphabetical order, numerical identifiers (such as invoices or inventory numbers) be kept in ascending order, and so on. Thus, many times data will be sorted already. If so, then we will exploit that fact. If the data is not sorted, then we have to compare the cost of sorting it and then applying a $O(logN)$ search versus the cost of applying an $O(N)$ search to unsorted data. We'll get to the costs of sorting soon.

With respect to data structures, the problem is that we want an algorithm that is *general*, i.e., will work for whatever size N happens to be. However, we consider arrays to be static, i.e., we cannot make them be general; instead, we have to specify the size of the array in advance. In a given particular situation, this might be done via a constant that determines array size, e.g.,

```
const
    MaxArraySize is 30
type
    ThisArrayType definesa array[1..MaxArraySize] of num
```

In such a situation, we can use MaxArraySize in place of N in our searching algorithm. Or, we might use some variable to keep us informed of how much of the array is being used. Perhaps MaxArraySize is 10,000, yet our algorithm might keep track of how many values have been read in to it and thus "know" that only the first 125 elements are occupied. In this case, we could use that variable in place of N.

However, there is often no getting around the fact that arrays are static and thus cannot support a general "who knows what N is?" algorithm. An array needs to know the maximum possible N ahead of time, and often N is not predictable. This is where a *binary search tree* (*BST*) can be very valuable. A *binary search tree* allows *O(logN)* search performance *if* certain conditions are met.

For any binary search tree that is *full and balanced*, i.e., symmetrical and fully populated, the *height* of the tree is approximately *O(logN)*. For example, a full and balanced tree with seven nodes will have three levels of depth: the root, the root's children, and the root's grandchildren. A search to locate a particular value will have to do at most three comparisons (the root, the appropriate child of the root, and the appropriate grandchild of the root). And, of course, 3 is logN of 8, i.e., of N+1. Thus, a binary search tree *can* give us log(N+1) search performance, which is *O(logN)*, without any advance knowledge of N.

The obstacle to achieving this is that a *BST* may or may not be full and balanced. Observe that we can take the integer values 1 through 7 and build a *variety* of *BST's*. The exact shape of the tree is dependent on the order in which those values arise. For example, if the values arrive in the order, 4, 2, 6, 1, 3, 5, 7, then the result is a *BST* that's perfectly full and balanced as shown in *Figure 7.1*. However, if those values arrive in sorted order, then the tree becomes lopsided and linear, like a linked list that's turned on its side, as shown in *Figure 7.2*.

Thus, to be *sure* that a *BST* will provide optimal performance, we require some algorithm that will *guarantee* that the tree is full and balanced. Such an algorithm will manipulate the shape of the tree as necessary upon the insertion or deletion of nodes. There are a few such algorithms, and each of them has their own costs, i.e., we cannot achieve "guaranteed balancing" for free. We will not concern ourselves with the particulars of such algorithms. However, be sure that you understand what *BST*'s *can* do for us *and* that you understand the *requirements* that must be met for a *BST* to deliver optimal *O(logN)* performance.

☐ A Fortunate Fact:

For *large data sets of randomly arranged data* (unsorted and not ordered in any way), we need not be too concerned about deploying algorithms to keep the tree balanced. *Random* data will usually result in a tree that *is close* to being full and balanced. It will rarely be *perfectly* full and balanced and, on rare occasion, it *may* result in a skewed tree, but *most of the time* random data will produce a nearly optimal *BST*. Thus, for truly random data sets, the easiest course of action turns out to be close to the best!

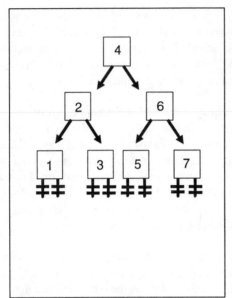

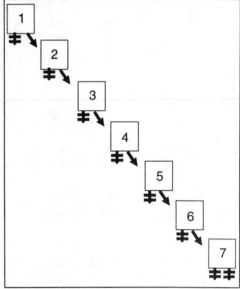

Figure 7.1: A full and balanced BST   Figure 7.2: BST can deteriorate to a Linked List

Exercises   For the problems 7.10 .. 7.14, give the *estimate of worst case* running time (*Big Oh*) of the algorithms described.

7.10. An algorithm searches for the *Max* value in an array of numbers. The size of the array is *N* and the numbers in the array are arranged randomly.

7.11. An algorithm searches for both *Max* and *Min* values in an array of numbers. The size of the array is *N*, and the numbers in the array are arranged randomly.

7.12. An algorithm searches for both *Max* and *Min* values in an array of *N* numbers. The numbers in the array are arranged in sorted descending order.

7.13. An algorithm searches for the *Max* value stored in a full and balanced *BST* which contains *N* nodes.

7.14. An algorithm inserts numbers into a linked list such that the linked list will store the numbers in sorted ascending order. Originally, the list is empty, and the algorithm inserts a total of *N* numbers into the list.

For problems 7.15..7.22, we have two separate data structures to build and use.

- In one case, *N* values must be stored in a balanced *BST*. For each value, the proper *BST* location for the new node must be determined. Once the location is found, a new node is allocated and that node and the new value are inserted into the tree. Then, a special algorithm (it's there, but we don't know the details of how it works) does whatever is required to guarantee that the tree will always be balanced. It does so at a constant cost of B work per insertion.

- In the other case, each value must be stored in sorted ascending order into a linked list.

Thus, we have three algorithms: one that builds an ordered linked list, the other that builds a balanced *BST*, and the "mystery algorithm" that is called by the *BST* algorithm to insure tree balancing.

Give *Big Oh* for each of the following. Be sure to explain your answer.

7.15. Inserting each new value in the *BST* (finding location, insertion, balancing).

7.16. Inserting each new value in the linked list.

7.17. Inserting all N values into the *BST*.

7.18. Inserting all N values into the linked list.

7.19. Responding (via a single boolean result) to single query which asks if a given value is in the *BST*.

7.20. Responding (via a single boolean result per query) to N queries, each of which asks if a given value is in the linked list.

7.21. The total work required to build the linked list, then identify the *Min* value in the list.

7.22. The total work required to build the *BST*, then identify the *Max* value in the tree.

Increasing the Complexity Some More

So far, we've seen the powerful performance gains that can be achieved via an algorithm that is "better than obvious," i.e., improving from the "common sense" linear search, which is O(N), to the more efficient binary search, which gives O(logN). Given the speed of computers, this is the difference between search performance that's "very good" and performance that's "excellent."

Unfortunately, the choices are not always so pleasant. For example, let's consider the task of sorting a list of numbers. Let us assume that we have a list of eight unsorted numbers stored in an array, as shown in Figure 7.3.a. How might we sort them?

☐ Why Sorting?

In reality, you will likely have software applications that are already programmed to perform sorting for you. Why, then, do we insist that you look
at the logic of sorting algorithms? We choose sorting examples because
sorting is a straightforward problem that can be solved via a variety of
different approaches. Thus, it gives us a chance to compare the performance
that *different approaches* offer.

First, let us consider a fairly simple or "naive" sorting algorithm: *Bubblesort*.
Bubblesort works in a simple fashion, as shown in *Figure 7.3*, below.

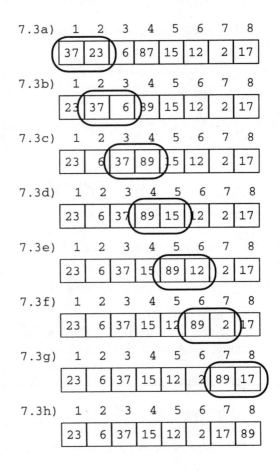

Figure 7.3: One pass of Bubblesort

- The algorithm begins at the leftmost position and compares the contents of that cell (in this case, 37) with the contents of the cell one position to the right (in this case, 23). If those two values are in proper sorted order relative to each other, it leaves them alone; if not, it swaps them. In our example, the values are not in the correct order, so they are swapped, giving the array as shown in *7.3.b.*

- The algorithm then moves one position to the right and repeats the same process, i.e., comparing the values in the second and third cells. In our example, it finds that the 37 and the 6 are not in the proper order, so it swaps them, producing the state of the array as shown in *7.3.c.*

- It then moves one position to the right and repeats the process. In our example, this means that it compares the 37 and the 89, finds that they *are* in the correct order, and thus leaves them alone (*7.3.d*).

- Then, moving to the right again, it compares the 89 and 15; because they are not in the right position, it swaps them, giving the array as shown in *7.3.e.*

This process is repeated until, for an array of *N* items, it compares the values stored at positions *N-1* and *N*, swapping them if necessary. In our example, the final result of this repetitive process would be the array as shown in *7.3.h.*

We might express this portion of the algorithm as shown in *Algorithm 7.5*. Each time through the loop, the variable Index is incremented, thus shifting the algorithm's attention one location to the right. By the time the algorithm stops, it will have performed *N-1* comparisons and somewhere between *0* and *N-1* swaps (depending on the particular values in the list). It will also have guaranteed that the highest value in the list is in the rightmost position.

```
begin
    LastCompareAt <- N - 1
    Index <- 1
    loop
        exitif (Index > LastCompareAt)
        if (SArray[Index] > SArray[Index+1]) then
            Swap(SArray[Index], SArray[Index+1])
        endif
        Index <- Index + 1
    endloop
end {one pass through N}
```

Algorithm 7.5: One Pass of Bubblesort

Notice that our single pass through the array has not sorted the entire list. It has only found the proper sorted position for the largest value in the list, i.e., in the rightmost element. But we don't know about any of the other list values or positions.

To sort the remainder of the list, the Bubblesort algorithm then takes the partially-sorted list (with the largest value now in the rightmost position) and begins all over again. It goes back to the first position, compares the 1st and 2nd values, swaps them if necessary, then compares the 2nd and 3rd values, and so on. In short, it makes a "second pass" through the list, comparing and swapping, just as before. The only difference between this "second pass" and the "first pass" is that the algorithm can stop one position sooner. Because it has already moved the largest value all the way to the right, there is no point in comparing the values at position $N-1$ and N. Instead, the second pass can end after the comparison (and, if necessary, swap) of values in the $N-2$ and $N-1$ positions. After the second pass ends, we know that the *two* largest values are in their appropriate positions at the end of the list.

After the second pass, Bubblesort starts over again and makes a third pass. By now, the two rightmost positions already hold the appropriate values, so the third pass aims to move the third largest value into position. It can end after it deals with the values in $N-3$ and $N-2$ positions. And so on. Thus, we can see that Bubblesort will make $N-1$ passes through the data. We can also see that each pass will require one fewer comparison than the pass before it, i.e., the first pass will make $N-1$ comparisons, the second pass will make $N-2$ comparisons, and the last pass will make only a single comparison. We might express the entire algorithm as shown in *Algorithm 7.6*.

Notice that the algorithm features nested loops. The inner loop governs each pass through the data, while the outer loop governs how many such passes are made. Notice that we have changed the terminating condition of the inner loop. In *Algorithm 7.5*, the terminating condition was (`Index > LastCompareAt`) where `LastCompareAt` had been assigned the value of $N-1$. In *Algorithm 7.6*, the terminating condition is (`Index = RemainingPasses`). This was done so that each "inner loop" pass through the data will stop one step sooner than the pass before. We initialize `RemainingPasses` to N-1, then decrement it after each pass.

☐   Important Note for Novices: If algorithms are new to you, do *not* just glance over this algorithm and continue reading. Instead, make sure that you take scrap paper, draw an array of unsorted numbers, and *trace* the execution of this algorithm on that array. It is imperative that you be able to trace the execution of algorithms, understand their operation, and be able to reproduce their results as you trace them. If you find that you are unable to do this, make sure that you *get help promptly* from a classmate, from a *TA*, or from the instructor.

Estimating Bubblesort's Complexity.

What can we say about its performance? It is "Order what?" In order to estimate "the amount of work an algorithm implies" or "its complexity," examine the algorithm for *repetitive structures*, i.e., loops or recursive calls, that are influenced, directly or indirectly, by N. In the case of Bubblesort, we find such two repetitive structures: the loops that are nested one inside the other. Let's consider each in turn.

The inner loop controls each pass through the list of numbers. Each pass involves some number of comparisons and, if necessary, some number of swaps. Each comparison will have some cost, as will each swap. However, in estimating complexity we are not concerned with these details. We are only concerned with how the work *grows in relation to* N. Thus, we are content to consider the number of comparisons without worrying about their exact cost or about how many of them result in swaps.

How many comparisons will the inner loop do? Well, it changes. On the first pass, it does N-1 comparisons to move the largest value to the rightmost position, on the second pass it does N-2 comparisons to move the second-largest value to the next-to-rightmost position, on the third pass it does N-3 comparisons, and on the last pass it does N-(N-1) or 1 comparison. This is an average of N/2 comparisons. Because we are estimating, we can throw away numeric factors and say that each pass is *O(N)*.

```
procedure BubbleSort  (N isa in num, SArray isa
                           in/out ArrayType)
var
    Index,
    RemainingPasses isa num
begin
    RemainingPasses <- N - 1
    loop
        exitif (RemainingPasses = 0)
        Index <- 1
        loop
            exitif (Index > Remaining Passes)
            if (SArray[Index] > SArray[Index+1]) then
                Swap(SArray[Index], SArray[Index+1])
            endif
            Index <- Index + 1
        endloop {inner loop}
        RemainingPasses <- RemainingPasses - 1
    endloop {outer loop}
end  {procedure Bubblesort}
```

Algorithm 7.6: An Implementation of Bubblesort

We now have an estimate of "work per pass." But how many passes will there be? This is controlled by the outer loop. According to the algorithm as given, there will be exactly N-1 passes. (Can you see why?) We again toss out any specific numeric values and thus say that there will be $O(N)$ passes through the list.

So far, then, we see that each loop involves $O(N)$ work. But what does this say about the algorithm? To answer this, we must notice the *relationship* between the two loops. In this case, they are *nested*, i.e., *each* of the $O(N)$ passes through the outer loop causes the inner loop to do its $O(N)$ work. We have $O(N)$ "inner loop work" that is performed $O(N)$ "outer loop times," which is $O(N)*O(N)$ or $O(N^2)$. Thus, we say that Bubblesort is an "*Order N-squared*" algorithm.

Observe that we arrived at an estimate of $O(N^2)$ complexity because the two $O(N)$ loops were nested one inside the other. The estimate would be very different if they were not nested but instead followed one after the other, as shown in *Algorithm 7.7*.

In this case, we have an algorithm that features a *sequence* of loops each of which is $O(N)$. Since they are not nested, neither influences the amount of work done by the other. Thus, we have N + N work, or 2N work. Of course, the constant factor 2 has no place in our estimates, and so we would say that the algorithm is simply $O(N)$.

The implications of $O(N^2)$ algorithms can be seen in Table 7.2 (next page). Again, for small numbers, the differences between $O(logN)$, $O(N)$, and $O(N^2)$ algorithms don't matter much. However, imagine that you have to process 16,000 numbers (as is a common task concerning the records of many universities, corporations, etc.):

```
begin
     This <- 1
     That <- 1
     loop
          exitif (This = N)
          DoSomeThing
          This <- This + 1
     endloop
     loop
          exitif (That = N)
          DoSomeThingElse
          That <- That + 1
     endloop
```

Algorithm 7.7: An example of sequential loops

- An $O(logN)$ or *"sublinear"* solution would require only about 14 times whatever the constant costs might be,

- An $O(N)$ or *"linear"* algorithm would require about 16,000 times constant costs,

- An $O(N^2)$ or *"quadratic"* algorithm would require about *268 million* times the constant costs.

N of no more than	O(logN)	O(N)	O(N²)
16	4	16	256
64	6	64	4K
256	8	256	64K
1024 (1K)	10	1K	1M
16,384 (16K)	14	16K	(256M) 268,435,456
131,072 (128K)	17	128K	(16G) 17,179,869,184
262,144 (256K)	18	256K	6.8719E+10
524,288 (512K)	17	512K	2.7488E+11
1,048,576 (1M)	20	1M	1.0995E+12
1,073,741,824 (1G)	30	1G	1.1529E+18

Table 7.2

Now, consider a company that must process data regarding more than 100,000 stockholders:

- A *sublinear* algorithm implies about 17 times constant costs,

- A *linear* algorithm implies about 100,000 times constant costs,

- A *quadratic* algorithm requires more than *17 billion* times the constant costs.

I trust that you are beginning to see why we care about estimates of algorithmic complexity!

Of course, you might think, "well, ok, let's just go to work and devise sublinear algorithms to solve all our problems." We'd like to do that but unfortunately we cannot. Nor can we devise linear algorithms for all our problems. In fact, for *many* important problems we cannot devise algorithms that are nearly as good as quadratic algorithms! Why? Because performance is not only a property of algorithms. As it turns out, it is also a property of the *problems* we attempt to solve with them.

Thus, when we think about *searching* algorithms, we can choose between various *O(logN)* and *O(N)* algorithms. In addition, we have certain techniques, e.g., "hashing," that allow us to get closer to *O(1)* performance. But, when we think about *sorting* algorithms we cannot do as well. This is common sense: in sorting, we must deal with each value at least once. In fact, we must deal with each item somewhat more than once. We *cannot* achieve even a linear solution to the sorting problem.

Fortunately, we can do better than $O(N^2)$. For example, recall the *Mergesort* algorithm discussed in Chapter 6. This algorithm repeatedly divides the list of numbers in half, first into 2 lists of N/2 numbers each, then into 4 lists of N/4 numbers each, then into 8 lists of N/8 numbers each, and so on, until each list was of size 1. Let us call this "Phase 1" of the `Mergesort` algorithm. How many passes through the data would be required to accomplish this? Note that each time, the collection of numbers is divided into twice as many lists as before, with each such list being half the size. Does this sound familiar? It should. This repeated pattern of "cutting in half" or "doubling the number" is generally a clue that we're facing an *O(logN)* phenomenon and, indeed, the first phase of `Mergesort` does indeed involve *O(logN)* passes through the data.

Once the list of N numbers has been decomposed into N lists of 1 number, what then? Mergesort proceeds to build sorted lists from the decomposed list. First it "merges" adjacent pairs of "1-item lists" to create N/2 sorted lists, each of size 2. Then, it merges pairs of these N/2 sorted "2-item lists" to create N/4 sorted lists of size 4 each. And so on, each time doubling the size of the sorted lists and cutting the number of them in half. Again, this sounds like *O(logN)*, doesn't it?

In sum, `Mergesort` takes *O(logN)* steps to decompose the original list and *O(logN)* steps to reconstruct it into a properly sorted list. These two *O(logN)* steps occur in sequence, thus giving 2*logN work, which is still *O(logN)*. But this concerns only *the number of passes* through the data. How much work is involved in *each pass*? The answer is *N* regardless of the particulars of each pass, i.e., if the algorithm is merging *N* 1-item lists into *N/2* 2-item lists, it is still dealing with each of N items, just as if it is merging *N/16* 16-item lists into *N/32* 32-item lists. Each of the N values is dealt with (compared, copied, etc.) during each of the *O(logN)* passes. Thus, we can see that `Mergesort` implies *O(logN)***O(N)* work, which is *O(NlogN)*. As it turns out, this is the best that can be accomplished with respect to sorting.

As we can see from the *Table 7.3*, below, while *O(NlogN)* performance is not quite as good as simple linear performance, it is clearly preferable to *O(N²)* performance.

N of no more than	O(logN)	O(N)	O(NlogN)	O(N²)
16	4	16	64	256
64	6	64	384	4K
256	8	256	2048	64K
1024 (1K)	10	1K	10K	1M
16,384 (16K)	14	16K	224K	256M
131,072 (128K)	17	128K	2,176K	16G
262,144 (256K)	18	256K	4,608K	6.8719E+10
524,288 (512K)	19	512K	9,728K	2.7488E+11
1,048,576 (1M)	20	1M	20M	1.0995E+12
1,073,741,824 (1G)	30	1G	30M	1.1529E+18

Table 7.3

In the rest of this chapter, we will have more to say about:

• categories of algorithmic performance, and

• what is realistic performance and what is not.

Each of these topics can be readily mastered *assuming* that you have a foundation in understanding the basics of *Big Oh*. The material we have just covered is truly prerequisite to understanding the next section.

For now, concentrate on understanding what we mean by *O(1)*, *O(logN)*, *O(N)*, *O(NlogN)*, and *O(N²)*. Review the particular algorithms, discussed here. Make sure that you understand how we arrived at our estimates for each one and what the performance implications are.

☐ Keys to Finding *Big Oh*

1. Look for *repetitive structures*. (Remember, *iteration* and *recursion* are equivalent to each other.) It's the repetitions that count. Judge *how* the amount of repetitive work will grow with respect to N.

2. When multiple repetitive structures are present, determine *Big Oh* for each *and* notice the relationship between them ...

3. If the repetitive structures are *nested*, then there is a *multiplicative relationship* with respect to *Big Oh*, e.g., an *O(N)* loop nested inside another *O(N)* loop gives *O(N*N)* which is $O(N^2)$.

4. If the repetitive structures are *sequential*, then there is an *additive relationship* with respect to *Big Oh*, e.g., an *O(N)* loop that is separate from and follows some other *O(N)* loop gives *O(N+N)* which is *O(N)*.

Exercises 7.23. You are given an unsorted list of numbers and are told to find the *mode*, i.e., the number which occurs in the list with the greatest frequency. Create an algorithm that will work for any N. You may use an array type where `constant Max is N`. What is *Big Oh* for your algorithm?

7.24. You are provided with a full and balanced *BST* of numbers and an unsorted list of numbers. Your job is to examine each number in the unsorted list and determine if it is in the *BST*. What is *Big Oh* for the job?

7.25. You are provided the same data as given in problem *7.24*. This time, you are to examine each value in the *BST* and determine if it is in the unsorted list of numbers. What is *Big Oh* for the job?

7.26. For reasons we can't fathom, a robot has been programmed to paint a batch of N used cars the same color. Furthermore, each car will be painted a *different* color than it was before. The robot will grab a bucket of paint and begin painting cars. As it approaches each car, it will first verify that the new color is different from the old color. If the robot discovers that it is using paint that matches the color of the current car, the robot discards its paint bucket, fetches a bucket with a different color, and begins painting all N cars again! What is *Big Oh* for the robot's algorithm?

7.27. The boss wants to snoop into his employee's private lives. You are provided with a database in which employee data records are stored in an array sorted by employee number. Your job is to identify any employees who live together. Imagine an algorithm to do the job. What is its *Big Oh*? How much memory will it require?

7.28. What is your opinion of the ethical implications of the job assigned in 7.27? If you were assigned this job, would you do it? If so, why? If not, why not?

7.29. In your opinion, how should society deal with the ethical issues in question 7.27.

7.30. Imagine that a reasonable person disagrees with your position on question 7.27? What rationale might that person have for disagreement?

The O(logN) Basketball Championship.

Anyone who follows collegiate basketball sees an example of an *O(logN)* algorithm at work each March in the NCAA Basketball Tournament. The tournament is "searching" for a champion. It begins with 64 teams and, with each round of games, half the teams are eliminated. This pattern of cutting work in half with each repetitive pass is the hallmark of *O(logN)* algorithms. As a *O(logN)* algorithm with an *N* of *64*, we would expect the championship tournament to take *log64* (or *6*) rounds of games to "locate" the champion. Indeed, both the champion and runner up play exactly 6 games.

Given its *O(logN)* nature, we can see that by adding one more round of games tournament participation could increase to 128 teams. Two more rounds (for a total of 8 rounds) would accommodate 256 teams. With three more rounds, 512 teams could be accommodated, creating more slots than there are Division I college teams. Thus, with nine rounds of games (instead of the current six), *all* teams could be admitted to the tournament (thus making the basketball season itself entirely superfluous!).

How many rounds would be required to allow participation by 300 colleges and 3000 high school teams?

Reasonable vs. Unreasonable Algorithms

It is often useful to categorize phenomena. So far, we have considered a few algorithms and classified them by their complexity, i.e., $O(1)$, $O(logN)$, $O(N)$, $O(NlogN)$, and $O(N^2)$. We have also looked at the performance implications of each category. We have seen how $O(N^2)$ (*quadratic*) algorithms imply far worse performance than $O(1)$ (*constant*), O(logN) (*sublinear*), O(N), (*linear*), and O(NlogN) (*nearly linear*) algorithms whenever N grows to a fairly large number.

From this, we can say that *for large N*, the performance of certain categories of algorithms is vastly superior to others. Based on what we've done so far, we can imagine that some algorithms might be $O(N^3)$, $O(N^4)$, $O(N^5)$, and so on. We can also reason that $O(N^5)$ algorithms would be worse than $O(N^4)$ algorithms, which in turn would be far worse than $O(N^3)$, and so on. Simple calculation bears this out, as is shown in Table 7.4, below.

N	O(logN)	O(N)	O(N²)	O(N³)	O(N⁵)
4	2	4	16	64	1024
16	4	16	256	4K	1M
64	6	64	4K	256K	1G
256	8	256	64K	16M	1.1E+12

Table   7.4

From this, we can see how much of an impact the performance of a given algorithm has: for an *N* of only 256 items, an *O(logN)* algorithm would require only about 8 times the constant cost, while an $O(N^5)$ algorithm would require about a *trillion* times constant cost. If *N* grows to only 256K, an *O(logN)* algorithm can perform its job in only about 18 times constant cost, while an $O(N^5)$ algorithm would require a "billion billion billion" times constant cost. As you can see, depending on the performance of the algorithm, things can quickly get "out of hand" far worse than has the National Debt.

Now, for the part that many people find hard to believe: things can get *far, far* worse. In fact, all of the categories of algorithms we have discussed so far are considered to be "good" or "reasonable" algorithms. You might well wonder, *"If all of the above are "good," what in the world does it take to be "bad"?*

For an example of a "bad" or "unreasonable" algorithm, consider the solution to the standard "Towers of Hanoi" problem. The problem is quite simple: you are given 3 vertical pegs and some number of rings that are stacked up on one of the pegs. No two rings are of the same diameter, and they are stacked such that each ring has only larger rings below it and only smaller rings above it (like the shape of a traditional wedding cake), as shown in *Figure 7.1*.

The problem simply requires that you move the stack of rings from one peg to another peg with only two constraints: (1) you cannot move more than one ring at a

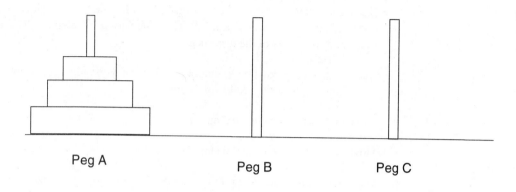

Peg A   Peg B   Peg C

Figure   7.1

time, and (2) you may never place a larger ring on top of a smaller ring. (You may place any smaller ring on top of any larger ring.)

The solution is rather simple from a logical point of view. You can see that each peg works like a stack, and that the problem allows us to "pop" and "push" rings however we like, just so we never put a smaller one on top of a larger one. A rather simple recursive algorithm can solve this problem for any number of rings:

```
procedure TowersOfHanoi (N, A, B, C isa in num)
begin
    if (N=1) then
        print('Move' , A, ' to' , B)
    else
        TowersOfHanoi (N-1, A, C, B)
        print('Move ,' A, ' to ', B)
        TowersOfHanoi (N-1, C, B, A)
    endif
end {Towers of Hanoi}
```

In the algorithm above, N initially refers to the total number of rings, and A, B, and C refer to the three pegs. The two "print" instructions are analogous to a combination of "Pop(from A to X)" and "Push(from X onto B)," Observe that each recursive call does two things:

1. It decrements N, insuring that N will eventually reach 1, the terminating condition, and

2. It passes the three "peg parameters" in a different order, e.g., the first recursive call sends the "peg identifiers" in the order "A, C, B" and the new clone of the procedure will receive them as "A, B, C." Thus, the various recursive calls deal with different combinations of the three pegs.

For example, given the situation as diagrammed above with only three rings on peg A, the algorithm produces the following steps:

- Move the smallest ring to an empty B

- Move the middle-sized ring to empty peg C

- Move the smallest ring from B to C so that it rests on top of the middle size ring.

- Move the large ring from A to the now-empty B.

- Move the small ring from C to the now empty A.

- Move the middle-size ring from C to B so that it rests on top of the large ring.

- Move the small ring from A to B so that it rests on the middle-size ring.

The problem is now solved.

> ☐ Note to novices: Make sure that you step through the execution of the recursive algorithm with diagrams of the pegs and a stack (to keep track of the recursive calls) on scratch paper until you understand it and can get the same results.

Observe that it took seven operations to solve for three rings. What is the relationship between the N rings and the cost in operations? We might wish it the cost was $(2N + 1)$, which would mean that we have an $O(N)$ algorithm. Unfortunately, this is not the case. Instead, we find that the cost is $(2^N - 1)$. For three rings, the cost is 7, for four rings the cost is 15, for five rings the cost is 31, for ten rings the cost is 1023, for for 20 rings the cost is more than a million, for 30 rings the cost is more than a billion, and so on.

Observe that each time we increment the size of N by one, we *double* the amount of work required. This is similar to the relationship between N and work in $O(logN)$ algorithms, but with the log factor going the other way, i.e., working against us, not for us. In *O(logN)* algorithms, incrementing work by one allows us to double N; here, incrementing N by one doubles the amount of work! This is the nature $O(2^N)$ algorithms, and the consequences are not pretty, as we see in *Table 7.5*.

N	O(logN)	O(N)	$O(N^2)$	$O(N^5)$	$O(2^N)$
4	2	4	16	1024	16
16	4	16	256	1M	65K
64	6	64	4K	1G	1.845E+19
256	8	256	64K	1.1E+12	1.158E+77

Table   7.5

For 64 rings, the cost is about 1.845E+17. How large is that? Well, if we could perform a million moves per second, it would take more than *half a million years*. A computer that can execute a million instructions per second, e.g., one *mip*, would take a *several times* longer, as determining each move requires multiple instructions. Graphics routines which draw the movement of rings on the screen would take even longer still. So, perhaps we could use a 1-mip machine to do the job in only about 10 or 20 million years. (The exact factor by which we would have to multiply the "more than half a million years" is precisely the effects of the constants that are "hidden" by "Big Oh.")

As N grows, things get worse in a hurry. For only 256 rings, the cost is a number so large that it features 77 zeros to the left of the decimal. As a point of comparison, consider that scientists believe that the number of microseconds since the *Big Bang* has only 24 digits, and that the number of protons in the known universe has only 77 digits! We're already up to 78 digits and we are only considering 256 rings. What about a thousand rings?

Obviously, $O(2^N)$ algorithms are bad news. They are perfectly reasonable from a *logical* point of view, but are of little to no value from a *practical* point of view simply because we cannot use them for any significant value of *N*.

Observe that this fact will not change with continuing improvements of the speed of computers: in any $O(2^N)$ algorithm, each time we increment *N* by one, we double the amount of work required. Before we can increment *N* very far, we run into problems that cannot be solved by "fast computers." We encounter limitations imposed by the laws of physics. Even if it took zero time to execute each instruction and we could move instructions in and out of cpu registers at the speed of light, the fact remains that *the speed of light is only so fast* and we would quickly encounter an *N* which made the amount of work unreasonable. Thus, while such algorithms may be ok for arbitrarily small values of *N*, as *general* algorithms, their costs are unreasonable *regardless* of the kind of computer we might have or even *imagine*.

In fact, this is the terminology we use for the next level up the ladder of algorithm classification: "reasonable" vs. "unreasonable" algorithms:

- Algorithms which have *N* only as a *polynomial* factor in *Big Oh* are considered to be *reasonable*, including $O(logN)$, $O(N)$, $O(NlogN)$, $O(N^K)$ where *K* is any constant value. There are two mostly-interchangeable names for such algorithms: *reasonable* or *polynomial*.

- Algorithms which have *N* as an *exponential* factor in *Big Oh* are considered to be *unreasonable* and are only useful to theorists in various ways and to the rest of us as points of comparison. There are two mostly-interchangeable names for such algorithms: *unreasonable* or *exponential*.

Keep in mind that these are general categories of algorithms. In a given circumstance, a "reasonable" algorithm might take longer than an "unreasonable" one *if* N is very small. However, as generalizable solutions to particular *kinds* of problems, the *reasonable/unreasonable* (or *polynomial/exponential*) dichotomy is valid and very useful. If an algorithm is reasonable, we might use it; if it's unreasonable, we don't even bother as there's no point in implementing it.

Categories of Unreasonable Algorithms

For a mundane example of another unreasonable algorithm, consider the "bounded tiling problem." You've just bought a house that has an unfinished basement, and you want to put tile on the basement floor. You don't like linoleum, and instead want to spend a little extra and use ceramic tiles that were custom-made by an artist. Part of the appeal is that the tiles are not all identical, but instead feature four designs which cross the tile boundaries, i.e. each edge of each tile contains half of one of four designs. You must match the half of "design1" from one tile with the other half of "design1" from another tile by butting their edges together. There are only four such "overlapping images," but the tiles differ in terms if which half of which image appears at each of its four edges. In addition, the tiles are not perfectly square, and will fit together perfectly only if you don't rotate them, i.e., there is a specified "top," a "bottom," a "left," and a "right" edge to each and every tile. The problem is one of determining whether or not you can arrange the tiles so that everything matches up correctly.

Observe that we are not concerned with trying to discover what pattern will work; we're only concerned with determining *whether or not you can* arrange the tiles so that all their various sides match up so that each half-image is adjacent to its other half. The output is a simple "yes, you can" or "no, you cannot." We will assume that you have N tiles (where N is the square of some positive integer, say M) and that you wish to tile a space is square, i.e., each edge of the square require the SquareRoot(N) or M tiles.

As a particular example, let's assume that you have either very large tiles or a very small room, i.e., you require only 25 tiles cover a square space that is 5-tiles by 5-tiles in dimension. How much work will it take to provide an answer about whether or not you can do it?

There are 25 possibilities to consider for the first tile. With one of the 25 tiles in the first position, there are 24 remaining tiles that might go in the second position. With two tiles selected, there are 23 remaining tiles that might go in the third position, and so on. Of course, it might well happen that you'd get the first 24 tiles in place just fine, only to learn that the edges of 25th tile doesn't match up with edges of its neighbors. In the worst case, we might have to consider *all* the possibilities before being able to answer the question. How many possibilities is that? It's 25! ("25 factorial"), or 25*24*23*...*3*2*1.

Unfortunately, 25! contains 26 digits. At a rate of 1-mip, it would take 470 billion years to obtain an answer, much longer than the time elapsed since the Big Bang. Of course, if we had a machine that could run 1000 times faster, it would only take 470 million years. A machine that was a *million* times faster could give you an answer in only 470,000 years, and a machine that runs a *billion* times faster, could give you an answer in about 500 years. Unfortunately, you'd planned on doing the job next weekend. And, as it turns out, you measured wrong. You don't have a 5-by-5 area; your basement requires a 20-by-20 tile arrangement. Do you know what 400! is?

Just as there are various performance categories within the larger category of reasonable algorithms, e.g., $O(logN)$, $O(N)$, $O(N^2)$, etc., there are various performance categories of unreasonable algorithms. So far, we've seen an $O(2^N)$ and an $O(N!)$ algorithm. We might also imagine a particular $O(N^N)$ algorithm. All are exponential, i.e., unreasonable. The consequences for relatively small N are summarized below in Table 7.6, below.

What does all this mean? Quite obviously, it means that certain computational problems cannot be reasonably solved by general solution algorithms. This, of course, goes against the current assumptions that most people make, i.e., that computers are fast enough to crunch out solutions to any computational problem. Such is, quite simply, not the case; rather, it's a *myth* of the computer age.

N	Polynomial				Exponential		
	$O(\log N)$	$O(N)$	$O(N^2)$	$O(N^3)$	$O(2^N)$	$O(N!)$	$O(N^N)$
10	4	10	100	1,000	1,024	7 digits	11 digits
50	6	50	2,500	125,000	16 digits	65 digits	85 digits
100	7	100	10,000	7 digits	31 digits	161 digits	201 digits
1,000	10	1,000	7 digits	10 digits	302 digits	unimaginable	unimaginable

Table 7.6

This also explains why we're interested in *approximate solutions* to various problems. At first, one might think that approximate solutions are poor solutions, i.e., "why settle for an approximate solution, one that might not give the Right Answer, instead of computing the optimal solution?" By now, the answer should be obvious to you: an approximate solution that will give us an answer that's "not far off" is far better than a solution that takes several million years to obtain! For many problems, approximate solutions are the only ones we can really obtain.

Food for Thought:

How Well Do Your Ideas Perform?

Computing gives us the capability to *implement* and *execute* algorithms. Because of this, we are dealing with a fundamentally different kind of "object of our own creation" than did previous generations of people.

Computing allows us to:

(a) *externalize our ideas* about how things work into algorithms,

(b) *implement our ideas* in computer programs,

(c) *try out our ideas* by running the programs, and

(d) *evaluate the behavior of our ideas* by observing the results.

Do our algorithms behave as anticipated? Do they satisfy what we want them to do? Do they show flaws in our ideas about the phenomena we're trying to model?

If so, can we learn from these flaws to create better models? All these questions, and many more, inevitably arise because we are creating a new kind of human artifact: the specification, implementation, and empirical evaluation of the *behavior implied in our ideas* about various phenomena.

In Chapter 1, we saw that the alphabet gave humankind a means to externalize thoughts, observations, etc., into the written word via an abstract symbol system. Computing takes us to another level: it gives us a way to observe the *performance* of our ideas. To put it another way: the alphabet enables us to externalize our thoughts, and computing gives us a way to externalize the *implications* of our thoughts. This capability provides much of core transformative power that computing provides: via computer modeling and simulation, computing let's us evaluate if our ideas are good enough.

Summary

The performance of algorithms is determined by the resources they consume, *time* (cpu cycles) and *space* (memory). While the speed of a given computer determines how many cycles can be performed in a given amount of time, the number of cycles required is primarily a property of the algorithm.

In general, the exact performance of an algorithm cannot be predicted. This is because algorithms make decisions, sometimes millions of them, and each particular decision can alter the number of subsequent instructions that are executed, as well as the amount of memory consumed. Thus, three measures of algorithm performance are considered: *best case, worst case*, and *average* (or *expected*) *case*. Generally, the *best case* is of little concern.

As a rule, we are concerned with *worst case* and *expected case*, but care must be taken with respect to the latter. The *average* or *expected case* is often difficult to ascertain, as it is often heavily influenced by properties of data that are difficult to know. In particular, one cannot simply assume that truly random data will present itself, so equating *expected case* with what one sees from random data is a dangerous assumption.

Frequently, the performance of an algorithm is tied to the size of the data: the greater the amount of data that is fed into an algorithm, the greater the amount of *time* and *space* resources that the algorithm will require. Because of this relationship between the size of the input and the cost of the algorithm, we are generally less concerned with absolute measures of performance and more concerned the *rate at which costs grow* as a function of the size of the input data.

We express this in "order notation," or *Big Oh*, where:

- $O(N)$ signifies a *linear* algorithm that has cost that grow in direct proportion to input size of N;

- $O(1)$ signifies an algorithm that has only *constant* costs, i.e., changes in input size N do not affect performance at all;

- $O(logN)$ signifies a *sublinear* algorithm, i.e., one that has costs that grow only at a rate proportional to log_2 of N;

- $O(N^2)$ signifies a *quadratic* algorithm, one who's costs grow proportionally to the square of the input size;

- $O(2^N)$ signifies an *exponential* algorithm, one that grows at a rate on the order of 2 raised to the size of the input;

and so on.

Such measures are *estimates*, and are assessed by examining the points of repetition within the algorithm: one assesses the relationship between input and the repetitive steps required by the algorithm, e.g., for an input of size N, a given algorithm will, in the worst case, require $2N^2-2$ time. One then throws out numerical constants, leaving N^2, thus indicating an $O(N^2)$ algorithm.

The various kinds of data structures have certain performance implications. *Arrays* and *linked lists* are both *linear* structures and, thus, many operations on them, such as searches and traversals will be *linear* or $O(N)$. Arrays, however, allow *random access*, which is $O(1)$, while linked lists do not. Thus, access to a given location in an array is constant time, while for a linked list it is $O(N)$ in the general case. Similarly, random access allows us to exploit a *sorted* array to locate a target value in O(logN) time via *binary search*, which linked lists can not support. *Binary search trees* are not linear and can, like sorted arrays, exploit binary search strategies to locate contents in $O(logN)$, but only if they are full and balanced. If not full and balanced, search performance can deteriorate to that of a linked list: $O(N)$.

Algorithms which have performance estimates featuring input size N as a *polynomial* factor are considered *reasonable* algorithms. Those which feature input size N as an *exponential* factor are considered to be *unreasonable*, as their cost is sufficiently prohibitive that they have no practical utility.

Chapter 8: Tools for Verifying Correctness

Bugs and Debugging   During World War II, Navy officer Grace Hopper and her colleagues were calculating trajectories using one of the first computers ever built. At some point, the vacuum-tube behemoth stopped working, and the scientists began an exhaustive search for the source of the problem. After much work, they finally discovered that an insect was stuck in the circuitry of the computer. Ever since then, hard-to-find sources of error in computer programs have been called "bugs."

"Debugging," then, means finding all errors in a program and correcting them. In this chapter we shall focus on some techniques for debugging. These techniques are invaluable to any computer programmer because it has been estimated that over 70% of a programmer's time is spent dealing with errors. In fact, it is almost unheard of to write a program of any size that is completely correct in the first draft. No programmer is expected to write a bug-free first draft, but he is expected to do enough testing that he can eventually detect and correct all of the errors.

Occasionally, a major error escapes detection, often with terrible results. We rely on computers to carry out all sorts of critical tasks, and if a computer is programmed incorrectly there can be dire consequences. For example, consider the "Hubble Space Telescope" project. After the telescope had been launched by NASA, it became evident that there was a problem in the optics. Upon examination, an error was discovered in the computer program that monitored the lens grinding. It was a very small error, and would have been simple to correct - had someone found it in time! This illustrates how important it is for programmers to carefully check their work.

> ☐   There are four types of errors one needs to worry about when writing algorithms: *ambiguity*, *syntactic errors* and *semantic errors* (which are different aspects of *language errors*), and *logic errors*.

Ambiguity   Of the three, ambiguity is the easiest one to eliminate.

> ☐ Ambiguity arises in an algorithm when imprecise or unclear instructions are included. Such instructions yield many interpretations, and will lead to an unpredictable final outcome of the algorithm.

Human beings are quite good at making educated guesses to overcome such ambiguity, but computers are notoriously incapable of doing so. A computer would not be able to execute an ambiguous algorithm. To guarantee that an algorithm written for a computer is sufficiently clear and precise, we translate them from the natural language (such as English) in which they are originally written, to a special language called a programming language.

Programming languages, including BASIC, Pascal, Fortran, and C, have a very limited vocabulary of words and symbols (other than identifiers) that they can recognize. This means that there are fewer ideas that can be expressed in such languages than in English. Programming languages have one great advantage, however; it is much easier for a computer to understand a limited language than a rich one such as English.

For example, let's consider a simple instruction that adds two numbers and places the result in a variable called X. In English, there are a plethora of ways to express this operation:

```
X equals the sum of 2 and 2
X equals the addition of 2 and 2
find 2 plus 2 and place the result in variable X
etc.
```

In the Pascal programming language, however, there is exactly one correct way to express the operation:

```
X := 2 + 2;
```

It is obvious that it is easier to create a computer program capable of understanding this one form of addition instruction rather than the various forms expressible in English.

Language errors   Once we have translated an algorithm into a programming language, another type of error presents itself: language errors.

> □ Language errors fall into two categories: *syntax* errors and *semantic* errors.
>
> *Syntax errors* can be thought of as "typos" or similar mistakes, such as misspellings or using words that are not part of the computer language. For instance, if the language we are using is Pascal, a semicolon is required at the end of most instructions. Leaving the semicolon off constitutes a syntax error. Other examples include using 'x' to indicate multiplication rather than the asterisk '*', and typing a capital letter ('O') where a zero ('0') is called for. Such errors are the kind of things done primarily by novices. Once a person is familiar with the programming language and the symbols on the keyboard, he/she can avoid most syntax errors if careful.
>
> *Semantic errors* are errors in the *meaning* of an instruction. An instruction may be precise and have no typos, and yet may not make sense, or may be illegal in the context in which it appears.

For instance, consider the following:

```
const
     MaxArraySize is 100
type
     NumberArray definesa array[1..MaxArraySize] of num
var
     ThisArray isa NumberArray
     X isa num
     Y isa char
begin
     read(Y)
     X  <- Y
     ThisArray[150] <- X
end
```

According to the syntax of our pseudocode, there are no syntax errors. Each individual symbol is valid, but they are arranged such that their meaning is improper, e.g., after a char value is read into variable Y, the next statement attempts to assign that character value to X, which is a number variable. Then, an attempt is made to assign a value to cell 150 of the array variable ThisArray. We know from the declarations that the type of this array has locations 1 through 100; position 150 simply does not exist. In both of these cases, syntactically correct symbols are used in an improper manner with regard to the meaning they have. These are semantic errors: errors with respect to the *meaning* of syntactically-correct instructions.

☐   Both syntactic and semantic errors are fairly easy to deal with, because the computer itself can detect them. This is accomplished by software which translates algorithms from their human-readable form (written in a programming language and know as "source code") into a binary machine-readable form (appropriate to the computer and known as "object code").

There are two kinds of such special-purpose translation software: *compilers* and *interpreters*. For most programming languages, translation is performed by a *compiler*, which scans the entirety of the source code and produces either a listing of errors (if there are any) or executable binary code (if there are no errors). In the presence of any errors that are detected by the compiler, the program being compiled cannot be run until all the "compile-time" errors are corrected and the source code is successfully recompiled. Often, it takes multiple "compile-repair-recompile" cycles before a programmer can actually run his program for the first time.

The other kind of translation software is called an *interpreter*. Unlike a compiler, an interpreter does not try to translate the entire program and make a list of all the errors in one step. Instead, an interpreter begins to translate-and-run the program one step at a time. Thus, the first instruction is examined and, if correct, it is executed; then the second instruction, and so on. Thus, using an interpreter, if a program is correct except for a single error near the end, the program will appear to run, then abruptly stop near the end and give the programmer an error message.

Regardless of whether translation is accomplished by a compiler or an interpreter, if a statement contains either a syntactic or semantic error that the translation software can recognize, the computer will halt processing and print an error message to the programmer stating in where the offending element resides. The programmer then checks that part of the program for errors and corrects the indicated error or errors. At worst, he may need to consult a language reference manual and/or "play detective" to compensate for the imperfect ability of translation software to correctly identify the cause of each error it finds.

These kinds of errors are *not* the difficult kind. Yet, for novices, they prove to be a big distraction. When novices are introduced to programming, it is usually the case that they spend countless hours "wrestling" with the compiler: writing a poor program, then relying on the compiler to find their errors. Unfortunately, what usually happens is that the repair of some errors makes the program only slightly better and allows the compiler to then find *more* errors that had been effectively masked by earlier errors. The net result is that novices can spend 2 hours *writing* a program but 15 hours *debugging* it. In our experience, it is far better to make sure that novices know how to write decent programs *before* they try to compile them and run them. Then, instead of spending 2 hours writing and 15 hours debugging, a novice might spend 4 hours writing and 2 hours debugging.

Logic errors The third class of errors, called logic errors, are often much more tricky to find than other types of errors, and they plague veterans as well as novices.

> ☐ Logic errors occur when a program is syntactically and semantically correct, but the algorithm itself has a flaw in it.

For example, consider the following algorithm intended to sum the numbers from 1 to 10:

```
algorithm AddOneToTen
var
     I isa num
     Total isa num
begin
     Total <- 0
     I <- 1
     loop
         I <- I + 1
         Total <- Total + I
         exitif ( I >= 10 )
     endloop
end {AddOneToTen}
```

The way that the algorithm is written, it will be understood by a computer and will execute. However, it will give an incorrect result. To see why, step through the loop by hand, using paper and pencil. Notice that the loop begins when I equals *1* and ends when I equals *10*. Also notice that it terminates when the value of I reaches *10*. Thus, it might appear to work correctly. Unfortunately, we have incremented I inside the loop *prior to* its addition to the Total, Hence, our algorithm produces the following result:

$$Total <- 2 + 3 + 4 + 5 + 6 + 7 + 8 + 9 + 10 = 54$$

This is obviously an incorrect answer to the task the algorithm was designed to perform: it fails to add the value *1* to the total.

Observe that there is no single cause of this error. Rather there are two different "possible causes" and thus there are two ways that we can correct the algorithm: we can leave the loop "as is" and initialize variable I to *0*, not *1*; or we can leave the initialization of I alone and move the first in-loop step (which increments the value of I) to the last in-loop position. Many logical errors are like this: it is not "one thing" that causes them, but rather an error-producing combination of two or more statements.

However, without any changes, the algorithm provides a perfectly valid answer to a different question - namely, "what is the sum of the numbers from 2 to 10?" Many logic errors can be looked at in this manner: they result in an algorithm that answers a different question than the intended one. For this reason, such errors are often hard to recognize, because the program appears to work correctly. It is important to check all algorithms carefully "by hand and mind" before accepting them as correct. Do not merely write an algorithm and assume it is correct just because it will get through the compiler, execute and return a result!

Programmers have a phrase that accurately describes the effect of logic errors: "garbage in, garbage out." This states the truth that a computer is only as correct as the program it is running. Even if you write your algorithm carelessly and it contains logical errors, the computer will do exactly what you tell it to do - unfortunately!

To avoid logic errors, it is crucial to thoroughly understand the problem to be solved, and to be clear about what each step of your algorithm is doing.

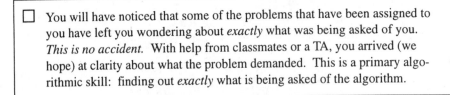

> ☐ You will have noticed that some of the problems that have been assigned to you have left you wondering about *exactly* what was being asked of you. *This is no accident.* With help from classmates or a TA, you arrived (we hope) at clarity about what the problem demanded. This is a primary algorithmic skill: finding out *exactly* what is being asked of the algorithm.

You must get accustomed to *asking questions* about particular requirements, as it will be impossible to create successful algorithms without doing so!

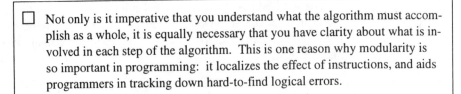

> ☐ Not only is it imperative that you understand what the algorithm must accomplish as a whole, it is equally necessary that you have clarity about what is involved in each step of the algorithm. This is one reason why modularity is so important in programming: it localizes the effect of instructions, and aids programmers in tracking down hard-to-find logical errors.

Recall, for example that the error in our earlier "AddOneToTen" algorithm. It was caused by an *interaction* two parts of the algorithms: the "initialization of I" and the "incrementing of I." Neither of these two parts was wrong in and of itself; the error was caused by the fact that these two parts did not coordinate things properly. Now, imagine that these two lines were not so close together. Imagine that they were spread apart by several pages of other instructions. How long do you think a novice might spend before he found the problem? Modularity (i.e., procedural abstraction) forces us to put things together in small logical chunks which makes each chunk *and* the whole algorithm far easier to diagnose and repair.

One must also examine the kinds of input data that the algorithm will need to handle. An algorithm that works for most input values but fails for one value is like a time bomb waiting to explode. For example, a program that takes the logarithm of an input value N will fail when N is 0... *if* the programmer forgot to check if (N = 0) and deal with it. Imagine the chaos if this system was being used by a national bank when someone input a value of zero and caused the program to crash.

This is not just a hypothetical concern. There have been numerous occasions of this kind of error having disastrous consequences. For example, a few years ago, the entire AT&T long distance telephone network crashed (see *"The Day the Earth Stood Still"* at the end of this chapter), crippling communications throughout the entire North American continent and costing literally billions of dollars. It was caused by precisely such a trivial error. A module within their network control program had the job of making decisions about "what to do next" based on the value it received by parameter. The code was written so that it anticipated all the possible values that were *supposed* to be passed to the module. For years, it worked just fine. Then, one day a value was passed that shouldn't have been ...

At first, you might think that the problem lies with the source of the "bad value." However, such perfection is virtually impossible. What *is* possible is algorithmic means to stop such errors from having bad consequences. In fact, standard programming practice calls for very simple and easy ways of handling such things, i.e., by having a simple "guard statement" in the program that says, in effect, "if a bad value comes in, print the appropriate error message, else process the good values." It is a very *simple* thing to do. But it was not done. And, as a result, we saw the day when the entire North American long distance phone system "died."

To make sure such situations do not occur, programmers create "exception handlers" in their programs and create a series of "test runs" using many different input values. If an input is valid, the program should produce a correct result. If the input is invalid, the program should detect it and handle it in a "graceful" manner, not crash.

☐ Unlike language errors, logical errors can not be detected by a computer. The computer sees only the algorithm, not the original problem. Hence, it cannot detect that the algorithm is unsuitable for solving the problem at hand. It is left to the programmer to demonstrate the correctness of his algorithm.

We shall present a method for doing this, but first let's explore exactly what is meant by correctness of algorithms.

Proving
correctness
Obviously, we want to be able to know that our algorithms are logically correct. But how can we *truly know* that they are? If we want to be sure, we require some means of proving that they are. One such approach comes from logicians, and is based on the fact that an algorithmic problem can be divided into two parts:

(1) The specification of legal input data.

(2) The relationship between the inputs and the desired outputs.

For example, the input might be an integer between 1 and 100, and the desired relationship between input and output might specify that "the output is the square root of the input." For an algorithm to be correct, we would expect that the second criterion must be met when input satisfying the first criterion is entered.

There are two classes of correctness of algorithms: total and partial. Total correctness implies that for all valid input values, an algorithm will reach a stopping point and when it halts it will have obtained a correct result (one that satisfies the second criterion). Partial correctness means that an algorithm will not always halt for legal input values, but when it does, it will have obtained a correct result. Hence, it will not always return a result, but if it does then we know the result is correct. Under what condition will an algorithm be partially correct? Well, if for some input values the algorithm enters an infinite loop, it will not halt. For other values, the algorithm does not loop endlessly, and instead produces a correct result.

☐   Our method for proving correctness of an algorithm is divided into two stages: first we prove partial correctness with the use of *invariants*, and then we prove total correctness using *convergence*. An *invariant* is a statement attached to a given instruction in the algorithm that makes an assertion about the state of the calculation at that point. *Convergence* is a way of proving that the algorithm will always terminate, given valid data.

To illustrate these concepts, let's look at an example. Consider a non-recursive algorithm for calculating exponents. We will limit the valid input data to be any number for the base, and a positive integer for the exponent. Instead of presenting the algorithm in text, we shall use its flow chart diagram in Figure 8.1.

We have attached assertions at certain key checkpoints where we are sure that the data match certain criteria. You can probably convince yourself that these assertions are true for the first iteration, but we need to prove that the instructions between checkpoints do not invalidate the assertions at any time. Hence, we show how we can start at each assertion and, traversing the algorithm, arrive at the next assertion. Notice that from assertion 1 we can only reach assertion 2, from 2 we can reach 2 or 3, and from 3 we can not reach any other assertions. The proof is shown below:

1 -> 2: After carrying out the instructions between assertion 1 and assertion 2, we know that Power = 1, X = base, and N = exponent.

Hence, it is true that Power = X(exponent - N) = X^0 = 1.

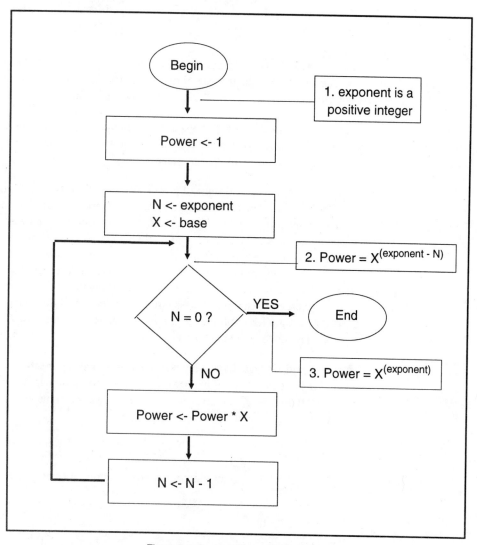

Figure 8.1: An Algorithm with Assertions

2 -> 3: If $N = 0$, and $\text{Power} = X^{(\text{exponent} - N)}$, then

$\text{Power} = X^{(\text{exponent})}$.

2 -> 2: If $\text{Power} = X^{(\text{exponent} - N)}$ and if we carry out the instructions $\text{Power} = \text{Power} * X$ and $N = N - 1$ between successive encounters of assertion 2, then

$$\begin{aligned}
\text{Power}' = X * \text{Power} &= X * (X^{(\text{exponent} - N)}) \\
&= (X^{(\text{exponent} - (N - 1))}) \\
&= (X^{(\text{exponent} - N')})
\end{aligned}$$

Here, Power' and N' are introduced to show that these are updated values of those two variables since the last pass through the loop. This proof has shown that the relationship between N, X and Power is always maintained.

Now we have made our assertions and proven that they are invariant as the algorithm progresses in time. Hence, we call them invariants. Our algorithm is now proven to meet the requirements for partial success.

Now we enter the second stage of proof. We must show that the algorithm is totally correct by proving that it terminates for all legal input values. The only way it could avoid terminating is by iterating through the loop infinitely many times. Hence, checkpoint 2 would be traversed infinitely many times. To show this is impossible, we must demonstrate that there is some variable which converges towards a value which will allow us to exercise the exit condition and drop out of the loop. In the algorithm above, the variable is N, and we must show that it converges to zero. Indeed, this is the case. Each time we pass through the loop, N is decremented. It gets smaller and smaller, until it reaches zero and the loop terminates. Hence, our algorithm is proven to be totally correct.

Notice that if we had allowed inputs such as negative exponents, our algorithm would only be partially correct because it would not terminate for such values; N might start out lower than zero, and each time it was decremented it would diverge away from zero, becoming increasingly negative.

Verification   A simpler alternative to the rigorous approach above is an as-you-go verification method.

☐ When performing this kind of *verification*, one satisfies oneself that each part of an algorithm is correct as soon as it is designed. After all modules of the algorithm have been verified this way, one must be sure to check that the interfaces between modules (the parameters) are not flawed.

For this type of verification, good modularity is essential, as it allows each module to be analyzed separately from the others, instead of treating the algorithm as a huge monolith of complex code.

This is why we emphasize both

- the construction of narrowly focused, task-specific modules;

- precisely defined interfaces between them, with all data passed by explicitly defined parameters.

Such designs *allow* you the chance to create complex algorithms that are correct, maintainable, and extendible. Without these techniques, you have little chance of doing so.

Food for Thought:

The Day the Earth Stood Still

In 1951, the landmark movie (and now a cult film), "The Day the Earth Stood Still" was released. In the film, a pleasant young man from Outer Space arrived on Earth (with his robot) to give Earthlings a strong message. He used his alien powers to interrupt all electrically powered activity, bringing Earthly activity to a standstill. This got him the attention he needed to deliver his message: Spacelings had been observing Earth for some time, and were quite prepared to let us do all manner of stupid things to one another, but the advent of our nuclear capability meant that it was time for us to grow up... or else! Of course, while most Earthlings agreed with this message, there were a few nasty Earthlings in power who didn't appreciate this sort of alien meddling, and so the plot thickened (*"Klaatu berada nikto"*).

In 1989, North America experienced its own version of a day when things stood still. It was "The Day the Phone System Crashed," bringing business in North America to a halt, causing all manner of uproar, and resulting in several billion dollars of lost revenue. American business was not amused.

Witnesses at the AT&T Long Lines control center report an amazing sight. The large electronic map of North America (much like you'd see in a movie "War Room") showed the state of the various sectors around the continent. First, one sector went dark. Seconds later, another sector blacked out. Within minutes, the entire continent went blank, as sector after sector "went down" in a chain reaction.

The entire North American long distance network had crashed. The first job was to get it "rebooted." As it turned out, nobody was quite sure how to do this. Why?

It seems that the network had never actually been started up before! The complex computer-controlled network had *evolved into being* over a period of years, as human-controlled functions were gradually shifted to computer. Thus, there had never been an occasion when the system officially started, which means that it had never before been "off," so no one knew exactly how to turn it on!

AT&T engineers soon figured out how to restart the system (which is why you can call home today), and their attention shifted to figuring out exactly what had happened. And, as mentioned earlier, they found a "bug of omission": the software had failed to anticipate a particular "bad data" state and, though it took years for that data state to occur, when it finally did occur it brought the international communications backbone crashing down. (For those of you with a programming background, the culprit was an "unguarded case statement" in a *C* program.)

This factual story exemplifies one of the chief problems facing us today. We are enmeshed in many *complex interdependent systems*, each with innumerable details, such that the consequences of all the details are impossible to anticipate. This problem shows itself in a couple different ways:

First, it points out the *necessity* to be extremely thorough in creating effective *exception handling*. It's not all that hard to create correct algorithms to do whatever we intend them to do *if only we could count on everything going right*. We cannot. As the saying goes, anything that can go wrong will go wrong. Thus, in addition to the algorithmic necessity to articulate the *intended* recipe of behavior, we must also articulate the behavior of the algorithm for all *unintended* states that might possibly occur! This is a major challenge and demands a measure of thoroughness which no mainstream human activity has ever before demanded. In effect, we must be better at expecting the unexpected than we ever have been before. In practice, this means that a great deal of our software methodologies are focused *not* on achieving what we want, but instead on *avoiding unintended consequences* that we don't want.

Second, it brings into focus the difficulty of making sure our decisions are correct when there are *so many of them* to make. Had the AT&T system had only a few decision points, chances are good that they all would have been appropriately protected. The fact that this one wasn't is primarily due to the fact that it was *one among so many.*

This same problem shows up in people's lives in ways that have nothing to do with software systems. We live in a time when people have an immense number of choices to make, choices about things both important and trivial, that people have never had before. Should you buy this brand of toothpaste or that one? Should you work on your relationship with this person, or end it and pursue a relationship with that person? Is it worth it to repair the old car one more time, or should you get a newer car? Do you give adequate attention to your relationships and let your work suffer, or should you focus on your work and let your relationships slide? Do you save money or do you buy what you want now? Should you rent an apartment or buy a house? Do you watch a show that you're not crazy about on Channel 23 or another show that you're not crazy about on Channel 92? Do you save money but spend energy by eating at home tonight, or do you save energy but spend money by going out? Do you want salad and garlic bread or nachos with cheese? And on, and on, and on. In modern times, the decisions *never stop.* Choices to be made everywhere, so many of them, all the time.

Some suspect that this is one the reasons that people feel so hectic and pressured. At my drive-through bank out in the country, and elderly woman teller I know comments on how *pressed* she feels. "I grew up over there, back before we had plumbing or electricity. Every day, I'd have to walk from here to that blue house to get water from the well. And I don't even want to tell you about going to the bathroom in the winter. But we were done by dark and would sit around and pass the time together. Nowadays, I only work here 'til noon, then I go on home. But by the time I'm done most nights it's *after midnight!. And I don't know why!"*

And neither does anybody else. She used to wash laundry by hand and cook over a wood-fueled stove. All of which was harder and took more time. But she had time and energy. And now she doesn't. She wasn't harried, or pressured, or tense. And now she is, all the time.

Perhaps it's because we spend so much of our lives trying to make the *correct choices.* Perhaps we don't have to spend as much *physical energy,* but perhaps we're spending a ton of *psychic energy,* just trying to make all the decisions.

Summary

The cost of algorithmic errors is enormous. By far the greatest portion of programmer time is devoted to finding and correcting them. Due to this immense cost, increasing effort is devoted to preventing them.

There are four kinds of algorithmic errors:

Ambiguity: the meaning of a statement is unclear or subject to interpretation.

Syntactic errors: the grammar of a statement is illegal in the language.

Semantic errors: the statement is legal syntactically but its meaning is incorrect.

Logic errors: the meaning of one or more statements is clear, and the statements are legal, both syntactically and semantically, but their effect is not correct.

Programming languages, by their nature, preclude ambiguity errors. Syntactic errors and most semantic errors can be detected by software translation tools. Logical errors are the most difficult to prevent and to locate, especially in large complex systems, and are the main source of the huge cost of algorithmic errors.

One approach to the prevention of errors is that of *proving correctness*. The goal of this approach is to logically prove that an algorithm is logically correct with respect to its task. This is done by rigorously articulating the relationship between legal input to an algorithm and the resulting output, and by establishing *invariants* at various key parts of the algorithm. An *invariant* is an assertion about what is necessarily true about the state of computation at that given point in the algorithm. With appropriate invariants established, it is then necessary to logically demonstrate that (a) the algorithmic steps between invariants do not violate the invariants, and (b) the algorithm will terminate for all legal input. This approach is extremely costly and time intensive.

Another approach is as-you-go *verification*. This approach relies on effective modularity and the requirement that each module be individually and extensively tested to *verify* that it performs its designated task. With each module verified, it is then necessary to test and verify that the interfaces between the modules are correct and effective at coordinating their joint effort to accomplish the algorithmic task.

Exercises

Each problem *8.1* through *8.6* has an intended purpose and the corresponding pseudocode solution. It is your task to:

1) Identify all the errors in the given solution. There may be zero, one, or more.

2) For each error, identify what kind of error it is from the list of errors, below, and provide a brief explanation of the error. Your explanation must concisely

describe why/when the error might occur, including all error-producing circumstances not ruled out by the question itself.

3) Make corrections to the pseudocode solution to fix the error. These corrections should only affect one or two lines of code per error. After you have made the necessary corrections, the solution should work perfectly for the problem given. Do *not* completely rewrite the solution algorithm.

Note that a single error in the algorithm may be an example of more than one error type. Give *all* error types that might apply to each error. (Documentation has been intentionally omitted from the problem code, and thus documentation omissions do not qualify as an error in these problems.)

Kinds of errors:

(a) Initialization incorrect

(b) Initialization missing

(c) Using an undeclared variable

(d) Accessing an array incorrectly

(e) Using/calling a function incorrectly

(f) Type mismatch (assigning one type of variable to another type of variable)

(g) Dereferencing (e.g., trying to follow) a *nil* or *undefined* pointer.

(h) Inappropriate kind of parameter (*in, out, in/out*).

(i) Inappropriate kind of module (procedure vs. function)

(j) Failed to increment loop control variable (e.g., `Index` or `Current`)

(k) Logical (algorithm does the "wrong thing" correctly).

(l) Error not listed above (specify the nature of the error).

(m) No error.

For each error that you find, write the line number in which the error occurs in, the letter corresponding to the type of error, and your correction. Use the following type declaration for all the problems (there are no errors in this section):

```
const
    MAX is 10
type
    ArrayType definesa array [1..MAX] of num
    ListPtr definesa ptr toa ListNode
    ListNode definesa record
        Data isa char
        Next isa ListPtr
    endrecord
```

8.1. Intended purpose: A module that counts the number of nodes in a linked list.

```
1: function CountNodes isa char(ListHead isa in
                                 ListPtr)
2: begin
3:   if (ListHead = NIL) then
4:      CountNodes returns 1
5:   else
6:      CountNodes(ListHead^.Next) + 1
7:   endif
8: end
```

8.2. Intended purpose: Return the minimum value found in an array of numbers

```
1: function FindMin isa num (TheArray isa in ArrayType)
2: var
3:    TheMin isa num
4: begin
5:    TheMin <- TheArray[1]
6:    Index <- 0
7:    loop
8:       exitif ((Index + 1) > MAX)
9:       if (TheArray[Index] < TheArray[Index + 1]) then
10:         TheMin <- TheArray[Index]
11:      endif
12:      Index <- Index + 1
13:   endloop
14:   FindMin returns TheMin
15: end
```

8.3. Intended purpose: Create a linked list of 20 nodes all having their data field initialized to the letter 'M'.

```
1: procedure CreateList (ListHead isa in/out ListPtr)
2: var
3:    Current isa ListPtr
4:    Counter isa num
5: begin
6:    Counter <- 1
7:    Current <- ListHead
8:    ListHead <- new(ListNode)
9:    ListHead^.Data <- 'M'
10:   ListHead^.Next <- nil
```

```
11:   loop
12:      Counter <- Counter + 1
13:      Current^.Next <- new(ListNode)
14:      Current <- Current^.Next
15:      Current^.Data <- 'M'
16:      Current^.Next <- NIL
17:      exitif (Counter > 20)
18:   endloop
19: end
```

8.4. Intended purpose: Count the number of A's in a linked list and return that number.

```
1: procedure CountAs (ListHead isa in ListPtr,
                          TheNumber isa out num)
2: var
3:    Count isa num
4: begin
5:    Count <- 0
6:    loop
7:       exitif (ListHead^.Next = nil)
8:       if (ListHead^.Data = 'A') then
9:          Count <- Count + 1
10:      endif
11:    endloop
12:    TheNumber <- Count
13: end
```

8.5. Intended purpose: Create a new node and add it to the end of a linked list. Initialize the newly created node's data field to store the letter 'C'. If the linked list is empty, then have ListHead point to the new node.

```
1: procedure AddEnd (ListHead isa in ListPtr)
2: var
3:    TempNode isa ListPtr
4: begin
5:    if (ListHead = NIL) then
6:       TempNode^.Data <- 'C'
7:       TempNode^.Next <- NIL
8:       ListHead <- TempNode
9:    endif
10:   if (ListHead <> NIL) then
11:      AddEnd (ListHead^.Next)
```

```
12:  endif
13: end
```

8.6. Intended purpose: Sum the values in an array of numbers and return that sum.

```
 1: function Sum isa num (TheArray isa in ArrayType)
 2: var
 3:    TempSum isa num
 4:    Index isa num
 5: begin
 6:    Index <- 1
 7:    loop
 8:       exitif (Index > MAX)
 9:       TempSum <- TempSum + TheArray
10:       Index <- Index + 1
11:    endloop
12: end
```

8.7. Take one "normal" (for you) day, and carry a piece of paper or a small tape recorder with you. Record each time you are faced with a choice (or contemplate one, even if you don't make a decision about it). Record all choice points, no matter how trivial it might be. Do this from the time you wake until the time you go to bed. Do this for just for a single day.

How many choices were you confronted with?

How many of them were trivial "no brainers"?

How many of the trivial no brainers were *truly* automatic decisions. How many actually required a little thought or reflection. Give examples of each kind.

How many choices presented themselves that were not resolvable, i.e., things that bug you in an ongoing way, about which you haven't yet made a clear decision? What were they about? Work? Personal relationships? Your appearance? What?

How many choices did you make without caring whether they were the "right ones" or not? How many choices caused you to really worry about making the "right decision"?

8.8. With respect to whatever you consider to be the important decisions in your life, how many of your decisions do you consider to have been the "right" decision? How many have been the "wrong" decision? In each case, what aspect of your life were they about? For the "wrong" decisions, what was the nature of the error?

Chapter 9: Tools for "Behavioral Abstraction"

From the perspective of having both *procedural abstraction* (to organize instructions into logical "chunks") and *data abstraction* (to allow the logical use of data without concern for its specific implementation in data structures), it's an important step to *behavioral abstraction*. Behavioral abstractions are built from both procedural and data abstractions. They provide the basis for *object-oriented programming* which is the current "state of the art."

The idea of behavioral abstractions is rooted in common sense. Most interesting phenomena in the world can be perceived as combinations of both *procedures* and as *data*. Is a baseball shortstop a "set of procedures" or a "set of data"? Quite obviously, he is both: the "procedures" for fielding and hitting, and the "data" which convey how good he is at these things. Thus, we can conceive of a given shortstop as *a behavioral entity who manifests data via his procedures*. This is what we mean by a *behavioral abstraction*: an entity that "has" both data and the procedures and functions which manipulate that data.

☐ You might think of a behavioral abstraction as a "meta-module," a unit of an algorithm that "has" both procedures and data that are distinct from the rest of the algorithm. They allow us to create abstractions that are superior to what we can create using only procedural and data abstractions alone.

The "Object-Oriented" Paradigm

☐ In our discussion of behavioral abstraction, we will use focus on the *object-oreiented paradigm*. In it, instances behavioral abstractions are known as *objects*. It is the basis for *objected-oriented* design and programming.

The foundation of the object-oriented approach is human, not technical. It comes from the insight that people manipulate objects quite effectively and naturally, without extensive education or training. As the software industry has watched the complexity of its products grow to the point where they are unmanageable, the need for a better approach has become paramount. What is needed is an approach that supports effective "complexity management" through practical means for delegation of responsibility based on contracts of responsibility. This in turn implies an approach that features a *very* high degree of abstraction and a naturally-human means of both communication and manipulation. The *object-oriented* (or *"OO"*) approach is currently viewed as offering the most promise of satisfying these needs.

At its heart, the object-oriented approach implies the exact *opposite* of the traditional view of the programmer as a "clever, solitary hacker":

- The original motivation for hacking came from a very real need to be *clever* in order to overcome the limitations of slow processors and tiny amounts of memory. In contrast, the whole point of the *OO* approach is to exploit the fact that we now have cheap, fast processors and memory in order to make complex software economically viable and technically manageable. We are willing to *sacrifice* both memory and cpu cycles in return for effective solutions to both complexity management and software reusability.

- The traditional image of the clever hacker is someone who is more comfortable alone in his room with a computer than he is with people, i.e., he has technical skills but lacks social know-how. In contrast, the entire basis of *OO* design is social. It is based on communication, delegation, and communication-intensive teamwork among the various members of a society. The "society" isn't composed of people, it's composed of *objects*, i.e., *behavioral abstractions* implemented in software. While undoubtedly a technical enterprise, the foundation of *OO* design is social cooperation among objects, and its origin lies in observations of how people effectively cooperate.

As we delve into objects, it is important to distinguish between programming languages that provide object-oriented capabilities and true object-oriented design. In recent years, the phrase "object-oriented" has become a marketing tool for selling software and training. Many things are sold as providing the "holy grail" of object-oriented features, yet the key to object-oriented design is not in language features or capabilities. The crux of the issue is conceptual, i.e., the approach to system design that is taken by the designer, the eyes through which the analyst sees the problem at hand. Facility with programming languages such as *C++* has very little to do with effective object-oriented design, just as familiarity with drawing tools does not make one a good artist or architect.

We aim to introduce you to basic concepts and constructs in order to give you an introductory foundation. To the extent that you achieve a foundational understanding, you will be well-positioned to build on it, as the demand for *OO* design continues to grow and extend throughout the software industry and beyond.

The Benefits of
the OO Approach

The object oriented approach to software provides three key benefits. Each requires some explanation, some new ideas, and a few new constructs.

- Superior *encapsulation*, such that both data and the operations on data can be better hidden, better controlled, and more cleanly designed and implemented;

- Superior *reusability* of code, such that programmers can better use libraries of existing code rather than writing everything they need for every program;

- Superior *adaptability* of code, such that existing code can be adapted to the job at hand with minimal re-engineering.

Required
Features

For algorithms to be designed and implemented in the object-oriented paradigm, certain constructs and capabilities are necessary as a starting place. Fortunately, by now you are already familiar with most of them:

- Tools for procedural abstraction, as covered in Chapter 4.

- Tools for data abstraction, as covered in Chapter 5

- Algorithmic methods, as covered in Chapter 6

In addition, other capabilities are required. Chief among these are resources that allow intensive communication between an object and the other objects with which it interacts. *OO* provides a more decentralized model of software behavior. As in other examples of modern decentralized management, higher communication costs are implied. In computing, these higher communication costs are acceptable due to the dramatic improvements that have occurred in both price and performance of computing resources. *OO* would have been quite impossible as a mainstream approach in the early 1980's, as affordable hardware could not have supported the higher memory and intra-program communication costs implied by effective *OO* implementations. Thus, not only is OO an idea "whose time has come," it also is an idea whose time *could not have come* earlier.

Achieving
superior
encapsulation

To understand why we need behavioral abstraction to obtain better encapsulation, let's review what we know about procedural and data abstractions to discover where they fall short. Recall that we use *procedural abstraction* to group together the instructions for a given logical task in order to isolate the details of that task inside a module. This allows us to refer to the task by name, send it appropriate parameters, and receive the benefits of that module's work without being concerned about exactly how it does its work. For example, we've seen both iterative and recursive implementations of the Power function. The two version go about their business in different ways, but that needn't matter to the algorithm that might use them. All it "knows" is that it called a `Power` function and received the correct result.

Also recall that we use *data abstraction* to isolate the details of a particular data structure. We saw how we could use type definitions and constants to isolate the specification of the size of an array, thus allowing us to easily modify array size without having to make numerous changes throughout the algorithm. Similarly, we saw how we could "hide" the details of a list of data so that the main algorithm wouldn't have to be changed if we changed the data structure (from, say, a linked list to a tree). We would only have to change the details of the modules which directly access the data, e.g., those that implement the logical operations "Insert," "Delete," etc.

The Limitations of "Procedural" and "Data" Abstractions

Procedural and *data* abstractions leave us with certain things that we can not hide. For example, the main algorithm shouldn't have to know whether data is stored in an array or a linked structure, yet this is something that cannot easily be hidden. In the case of a linked structure, the main algorithm needs to pass a pointer variable which provides access to the linked list or tree. In the case of an array, the algorithm needs to pass the array to whatever modules act upon it. Thus, the structure of data was not truly "transparent," and the main algorithm needed to know "more than it should have" about the implementation of the data structure.

Note, too, that if an algorithm *knows* more than it should, it can also *do* more than it should. For example, we know that a queue is a logical data structure, one that we might implement as an array or as a linked list. We also know that a queue should be operated upon in only certain ways, i.e., *enqueue* to the rear and *dequeue* from the front. However, if other parts of the algorithm know *what* the data implementation is, and know *how* to get to it, then there is nothing to prevent improper operations from being performed. For example, regardless of how well we implement *enqueue* and *dequeue*, there is nothing to prevent another routine from traversing the data structure, sneaking an item into the queue whenever and wherever it pleases and, in doing so, violating the integrity of the queue.

☐ What we want is a means of truly encapsulating both the data and the procedures of *logical entities* so that their specification *cannot* be violated.

Using classes *and* objects *to improve encapsulation*

So far, we have encapsulated data utilizing the data *types* and data *variables*: *types* provide the *definition*, and particular *variables* are instances of a particular type. In the object-oriented paradigm, the term that corresponds to *type* is *class*, and the term that corresponds to *variable* is *object*. Thus, one does not "define an object." Instead, one "defines a class." After a class has been defined, we can declare (or *instantiate*, i.e., "make an instance of") objects of that class, just as we have heretofore declared instances of variables to be of some data type.

Classes differ from types, and objects differ from variables, in some important ways. *Variables* are simply storage locations for data. *Types* give us a way to define the kind of data that we want variables of a given type to store. This *typing* of data helps prevent certain kinds of errors. If a program tries to assign a *char* value to a variable of type *num*, the program is illegal and must be corrected before it can run. This is far better than failing to catch the error, allowing the inappropriate assignment to occur and then being stuck with a program that produces erroneous results.

Classes are similar to *types* in that they provide the definition of data, but they define more than just variables. They define *both* the data abstractions that will be used to store data *and* the various procedural abstractions that are permitted to operate on that data. For example, a *queue class* would consist of both the definition of the data structure used to implement the queue (array, linked list, whatever) *and* the procedures and functions used to implement "queue behavior" (*enqueue, dequeue,* etc.).

In addition to the data typing advantages that we have become used to, classes provide us with a new kind of "security check." Classes *specify* which procedures and functions can access the data. Any instructions that are not included in the class do not have access to the data and thus cannot manipulate it. This allows us to insure that no part of an algorithm can get to data unless it is *supposed* to do so. For example, a *queue class* might define *enqueue* and *dequeue* as the only operations that are permitted on a queue. If so, then it would do us no good to even try to violate a queue by writing `procedure SneakOneIn` to add an item to the head of the queue. Such a procedure could not "get to" the queue data because it was not defined to be part of the class. By *encapsulting* both data and procedureal abstractions together, classes give us the power to control access to data such that only "authorized" procedures and functions are "allowed in."

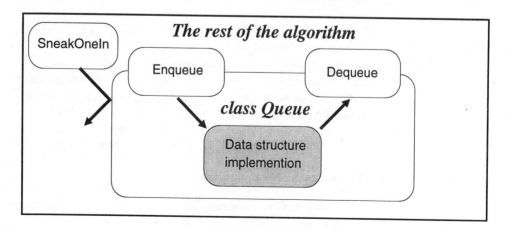

Classes not only allow us to control access to data, they also allow us to control access to the procedural abstractions which operate on that data. For example, imagine that we want to create a *queue* such that the rest of the algorithm can only request *enqueue* and *dequeue* operations. In creating those capabilities, we may find it useful to create additional procedural abstractions. For example, in a class that implements a queue as a linked list, it is useful to have an `IsEmpty` function for use by both the *enqueue* and *dequeue* operations. Yet, let us imagine that we see no reason why the rest of the algorithm needs know about this capability; it exists soley to support *enqueue* and *dequeue* behaviors. We can define the queue class to contain `function` `IsEmpty` such that its existence is unknown to the rest of the algorithm.

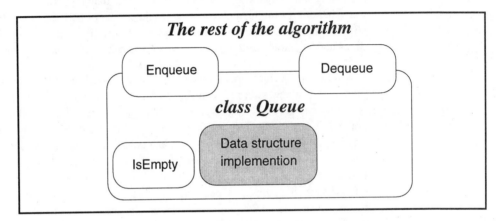

Thus, we can conceive of our *queue class* as having both *public* and *private* features. `Enqueue` and `Dequeue` are *public*, i.e., the rest of the algorithm can "see" them and use them. The data structure itself, as well as any internal modules (such as `IsEmpty`) are *private* and thus cannot be seen or used by the rest of the algorithm.

Classes, then, are more than just data types. They are self-contained modules that can be used by other algorithms. We can implement a *logical* capability (such as a *queue*) as a behavioral entity with its procedures and data united *within* a single *class*. The data is effectively encapsulated within the *class* so that no "unauthorized" code may tamper with the data, and the procedures and functions that operate on that data are effectively encapsulated so that only those that are *public* can be used by the rest of the algorithm. In *OO* jargon, we refer to a class' procedures and functions as its *methods*. We shall henceforth use the term *methods* accordingly.

These are the first three attributes of *classes:*

1. A *class* includes both *data* and the *methods* which can access and manipulate that data.

2. A *class* limits access to its data such that only the *methods defined within the class* can access and manipulate the data.

3. A *class* limits access to its *methods* such that only those that are *public* can be executed by the rest of the algorithm.

The result is a behavioral abstraction which other algorithms may use to achieve the *logical behavior* they want (e.g., managing a *queue*). Those algorithms that make use the *class* have no idea *how* that behavior is actually carried out. The implementation details of both the data and the methods which act on that data are completely hidden from the algorithm that uses the *class*. The "client algorithm" that uses the *class* remains ignorant of the implementation details, and is aware of only as much as it needs to know in order to request the services it desires by calling public methods.

> ☐ The *OO* approach allows us to create *client/supplier relationships*, wherein a *client algorithm* requests service from a *supplier*, with each party having clearly defined responsibilities and expectations of one another. In our example, our *queue class* would be a *supplier* of services to any *client algorithm* that needed to make use of a *queue*.

The Anatomy Once a class is defined, other modules may create and use objects of that class. To ***of a Class*** explicate what a class is, we will "walk through" the sample class definition, below.

```
class Queue
public
    type
        {data type managed by class Queue}
        DataRecType definesa record
                ThisField isa num
                ThatField isa boolean
                OtherField isa char
        endrecord

    procedure Enqueue (NewData isa in DataRecType,
                    Success isa out boolean)
        {
        purpose: add NewData to end of FIFO queue
        precondition: queue exists and is not full
        postcondition: queue exists as before plus NewData
            appended to end of queue
        )
```

```
procedure Dequeue (Served isa out DataRecType,
                   Success isa out boolean)
    {
    purpose: remove item from front of FIFO queue
    precondition: queue exists and is not empty
    postcondition: queue exists as before minus item at
        front; item returned via param Served
    )

private
    type
        {definition of Queue item node}
        QNode definesa record
                Data isa DataRecType
                Next isa QPtr
        endrecord

        {definition of ptr to QNode}
        QPtr definesa ptr toa QNode

    var
        {ptr vars to head and tail of queue}
        QHead isa QPtr
        QTail isa QPtr

    procedure Enqueue (NewData isa in DataRecType,
                       Success isa out boolean)
    var
        Temp isa QPtr
    begin
        Temp <- new(QNode)
        Temp^.Data <- NewData
        Temp^.Next <- nil
        if (IsEmpty) then
            QHead <- Temp
            QTail <- Temp
        else
            QTail ^.Next <- Temp
            QTail <- Temp
        endif
        Success <- true
    end {procedure Enqueue}
```

```
procedure Dequeue (Served isa out DataRecType,
                   Success isa out boolean)
begin
    if (IsEmpty) then
        Success <- false
    else
        Served <- QHead^.Data
        QHead <- QHead^.Next
        if (IsEmpty) then
            QTail <- nil
        endif
        Success <- true
    endif
end {procedure Dequeue}

function IsEmpty isa boolean
    {
    purpose: determines if the queue is empty
    precondition: queue exists
    postcondition: resolves to true if no items are in
        the queue, resolves to false otherwise.
    )

begin
    if (QHead = nil) then
        IsEmpty returns true
    else
        IsEmpty returns false
    endif
end {function IsEmpty}


begin {initialization}
    QHead <- nil
    QTail <- nil
end {initialization}

end {class Queue}
```

Observe that the class includes both a *public* and a *private* section. We'll discuss each in turn.

<table>
<tr><td></td><td>☐ The <code>public</code> section contains everything about the class that the client algorithm needs to know. This is identical to what the client algorithm is allowed to know. Everything that is contained in the <code>public</code> section is visible to any algorithm that uses this class.</td></tr>
</table>

In this example, then, a client algorithm is allowed to know the type definition of <code>DataRecType</code> and the headers of procedures <code>Enqueue</code> and <code>Dequeue</code>. That's all.

> ☐ Observe that there are no variables declared in the <code>public</code> section. This is no fluke. One of our goals is to encapsulate data such that access to it is controlled, i.e., we do not want the rest of the algorithm to have access to our data. Therefore, we *prohibit* variable declarations in the <code>public</code> section

The <code>public</code> section contains that information about the class which the class shares with the client algorithm. Based on the information provided in the <code>public</code> section, a client algorithm can *request services* from this class in exactly two ways: it can ask for an <code>Enqueue</code> and it can ask for a <code>Dequeue</code>. Each operation returns a boolean to the client algorithm which indicates whether or not the requested service was provided successfully.

Furthermore, these operations can be requested only for data that conforms to the definition of <code>DataRecType</code>. <code>DataRecType</code> is provided in the <code>public</code> section because, since the client can request that data be *enqueued* or *dequeued*, it obviously must know the type of data that can be so handled. (Later in this chapter, we shall see that type definitions are often not needed in the <code>public</code> section, but for now you may assume that they are necessary.)

<table>
<tr><td></td><td>☐ The <code>private</code> section contains everything that is needed to implement the class (except what is provided in the <code>public</code> section). The <code>private</code> section includes the declaration of all the class' variables and the implentation details of all the class' methods.</td></tr>
</table>

In the <code>private</code> section we find the type definitions required to *implement* the queue. In the example, the queue is implemented as a linked list, and thus the type definitions for both the list nodes and the list pointers are needed. These are properly *hidden details*. While a client algorithm has a legitimate "need to know" what kind of data the queue will handle, there is *no reason* for the client algorithm to know how the queue is actually implemented. Thus, the details of the data structure (in this case, a linked list) are hidden in the <code>private</code> section.

The `private` section also includes the full declaration of the methods whose header lines were listed in the public section. Again, the variables and code are required to implement the queue, but there is no reason for a client algorithm to be aware of these details. All the client algorithm "needs to know" is *how* it must request service, i.e., it needs to see the header lines for the `Enqueue` and `Dequeue` operations. The details of how these operations are actually implemented are properly hidden in the `private` section.

Additionally, the `private` section includes the declaration of a method (`function IsEmpty`) whose header line is *not* found in the public section. This function is used by both of the public methods, but the absence of the `IsEmpty` header line from the `public` section indicates that no client algorithm can call this method. In fact, clients have no way of knowing that this function even exists. All the clients can do with respect to the queue is make calls to what they see in the `public` section: `Enqueue` and `Dequeue`.

In this class, those two routines bear the responsibility for testing for an empty queue and acting accordingly. Should a `Dequeue` be requested by a client algorithm when the queue is empty, the `Dequeue` operation will return the boolean value `false` to the client, indicating that the `Dequeue` did not succeed. The client algorithm remains ignorant of how this was determined.

If one wished to implement a queue such that client algorithms could themselves request a test for an empty queue, then the header line for `IsEmpty` would need to be included in the *public* section. In either case, the actual implementation of `IsEmpty` would remain hidden in the `private` section.

Scope of Data Within an Class
Observe that the `private` section includes declarations of two global variables (`QHead` and `QTail`). It is obvious that we need to maintain both *head* and *tail* markers for a queue and, indeed, both the `Enqueue` and `Dequeue` procedures contain code that manipulates these variables. It is also obvious that they need to be global, as their values need to live throughout the life of the algorithm. However, observe that these global variables are *not* passed into `Enqueue` and `Dequeue` via parameters. Yet, these procedures manipulate these variables nonetheless.

How can this be? Until now, we have established that *all* data variables that are manipulated by a subprogram *must* be either declared locally within the module or passed to it via parameter. In object oriented programming, however, we make a specific exception to this rule:

> ☐ Within the *private* section of a class, all subprograms may directly access
> any variables that are *declared globally in the private section* without having
> to receive them via parameter.

We make this singular exception for a very good reason. Consider what would happen if we passed QHead and QTail via parameter in the normal way. The header lines of these two procedures would appear as follows:

```
procedure Enqueue (QHead isa in/out QPtr,
                    QTail isa in/out QPtr,
                    NewData isa in DataRecType,
                    Success isa out boolean)

procedure Dequeue (QHead isa in/out QPtr,
                    QTail isa in/out QPtr,
                    Served isa out DataRecType,
                    Success isa out boolean)
```

Notice that the header line of these procedures include not only the identifiers QHead and QTail, but also their data type (in this case, QPtr). Since the client algorithm *must* have knowledge sufficient to call Enqueue and Dequeue, the client would thus have to be aware of *both* the identifiers *and* the data types of our *head* and *tail* markers. Thus, the definition of QPtr would have to move to the public section. In the case of our example, this would be equivalent to informing the client algorithms that the queue is implemented via a dynamic linked structure, which is precisely the sort of thing that we do *not* want client algorithms to know. Thus, passing these variables as parameters would have the unintended and undesired effect of violating the very *encapsulation* of implementation details that we want to achieve.

To solve this problem, we allow global variables declared within the private section to be directly accessible to the code that's implemented in the private section *without* requiring them to be passed as parameters. Observe that this does not *eliminate* scope limits on these variables: since they are all declared and used within the private section, their scope and their usage is still well controlled.

Finally, observe that, at the end of the private section, there is a begin-end block of code (documented as "initialization"). In our example, this code simply initializes the appropriate variables to their initial values. Again, such initialization is an implementation detail that should properly be hidden from any client algorithms.

> ☐ Initialization code is optional, based on the practical needs of the task at hand. If present, any initialization code is executed exactly once each time a client algorithm declares an object of the class.

Contracts We require that each method include documentation that describes the method's *purpose*, its *preconditions* and its *postconditions*. In *OO* jargon, we refer to such documentation collectively as being the *contract* for that service.

If the method is *public*, then the contract must appear in the `public` section, under the method's header line. This is necessary to allow clients to see what the service the method promises to provide. If the method is *private*, then the contract appears there instead.

While documentation is always crucial to effective software maintenance, it is particulary important in the *OO* world. Since the client algorithm, and perhaps its author, cannot "see" the code of the methods, we must provide the client with a specification of exactly what that client can expect each method to do.

Declaring and Once our class is defined, any client algorithm may obtain the benefits of a queue
using Objects without having to implement one. To make use of an existing *class*, the client algorithm need only specify that it is *using* it. By simply including the word "uses," followed by the identifiers of any classes it wishes to use, the client algorithm can make use of whatever code has already been developed. A given client may use any number of classes, and a class may itself use another class. Algorithms which use a class may then declare and use *objects* of that class, much as they might declare variables, e.g.:

```
algorithm DoSomething
uses
    Queue
var
    TempData isa DataRecType
    ItWorked isa boolean
    ThisQueue,
    ThatQueue is Queue
```

With two *queue objects* declared (`ThisQueue` and `ThatQueue`), and with appropriate values stored in record variable `TempData`, the client might request an enqueue.

```
ThisQueue.Enqueue(TempData, ItWorked)
```

This instruction makes a request to *object* `ThisQueue` to *enqueue* the current contents of `TempData`. Since `ThisQueue` is an *object* of the *class* `Queue`, it has the capability to provide that service. Similarly, the instruction

```
ThatQueue.Dequeue(TempData, ItWorked)
```

would call for service to remove the value at the head of the queue `ThatQueue` and return it to the client algorithm by storing it in it in the variable `TempData`. In both cases, the boolean variable `ItWorked` is used to inform the client algorithm whether or not the requested operation was successfully performed.

> ☐ For any algorithm that uses the *class*, simply declaring objects of the *class* provides the power of all the *behavioral abstraction* of that *class*. A client algorithm may include declarations for any number of *objects* of the given *class,* just as it might include any number of *num* or *char* variables. Unlike variables, objects are *protected from direct access*, and can be manipulated by the client algorithm *only indirectly* via calls to the *methods* specified in the class that defines the object.

While the terminology may be new to you, this approach is consistent with the behavior of things in the real world. For example, both "shortstop objects" and "dog objects" are of "classes" that provide a service for "retrieving balls." The actual implementation of how dogs and shortstops carry out the behavior may differ, but they both provide that service. However, the "goldfish class" does not include such a service, so you are unlikely to have much luck getting any "goldfish objects" you may have at home to retrieve balls.

So far, we've seen how an *OO* implementation helps in several ways. It allows us to encapsulate both procedural and data abstractions such that data can be manipulated by *only* those methods that "should" be allowed to manipulate it. Furthermore, the implementation details of how data is stored and how tasks are done are *hidden* from client algorithms.

Exercises   9.1. In Chapter 6, we saw an example of a greedy algorithm that could be used to solve the "minimum spanning tree" problem. Another greedy algorithm that can be used to solve this problem is *Kruskal's algorithm*. *Kruskal's algorithm* is interesting because it is greedy *and* it obtains the optimal solution to this problem.

The logic of *Kruskal's algorithm* is:

- Given a connected weighted graph, sort all of the edges in the graph in ascending order by their weight. Then, starting at the beginning of your sorted list of edges, do the following:

```
    if (adding this edge to your solution would not form a
        cycle in the solution) then
        add it to the solution
    else
        skip it
    endif.
```

- Repeat this step for all edges, proceeding in increasing order of their weight.

Write an algorithm that will read in a set of edges from the user and use *Kruskal's algorithm* to find a minimum spanning tree for those edges. Print out all of the edges from the initial graph, and all of the edges in the solution.

Use the following class in your solution. You should create two objects of this *class*, one for the initial graph and one for your solution. Do *not* write the class. Just *use* it.

```
    class EdgeManager

    type
        Edge definesa record
            EndPoint1 isa num
            EndPoint2 isa num
            Cost isa num
        endrecord

    procedure InitSet

    public
        {this procedure will initialize the set of edges to
            be empty}

    procedure AddToSet(NewEdge isa in Edge)
        {this procedure will add a new edge into the set}

    function DetectCycle isa boolean (EdgeToCheck isa
                        in Edge)
        {this function will return true if adding the edge
            would form a loop in the set, false otherwise}

    procedure PrintOutEdges
        {this procedure will print out all of the edges in
            the set}
```

```
procedure SortEdges
    {this procedure will sort all of the edges}

procedure NextEdge(ReturnedEdge isa out edge)
    {this procedure will return the next edge in the
        set.  the first time you call this procedure it
        will return the first edge, the second time it
        will return the second edge, etc.)

function MoreEdges isa boolean
    {this function will return true if there are any
        more edges to check, false otherwise.}


private
    {you need not be concerned with the private section
        for this problem}
```

end {class EdgeManager}

Achieving Superior Reusability

The existence of a class allows client algorithms to obtain the benefit of the capabilities provided by that class without requiring those clients to contain the code for them, or to even know how the code works. This is a central benefit of the *OO* approach: it allows us to develop and test code separately from the client algorithms, thus supporting the *reuse* of code among various different client algorithms.

Unfortunately, we have yet to overcome an important obstacle that *limits reuse*. Notice that our class Queue is designed to operate only on data of type DataRecType, and that the definition of the fields which constitute DataRec-Type is "hardwired" into the class. Because of this, it is useful only if we need a queue to store items of type DataRecType. If we need a queue to store items of any type *other than* DataRecType, we're out of luck.

Of course, we might find out a way to get around this. For example, if we need a queue to store numbers, perhaps we could do a "cut and paste," creating a copy of class Queue, rename the copy to something like class NumberQueue, then change all the references within that class from DataRecType to num. However, it's usually the case in computing that clever attempts to "get around" something turn out to be messy in the long run. Here, not only would this "clever" process be tedious and error-prone, it would also eventually result in the development of countless "clones" of class Queue, each of which would be identical *except for* the data type (one for DataRecType, one for num, another one for ThatRec, one for

`ThisString`, etc.). Then, if we wanted to change how all our various queues are implemented, we'd have to make those changes in each of the countless copies. We'd soon have a logistical nightmare built upon a series of minor data type differences which have *nothing to do* with the behavior we want from a queue!

Fortunately, there is a better way. Remember that we're *reusability*: we want a way to write and test the code for a queue *once*, and then be able to use it for *whatever type of data* the client algorithm wants the queue to store. In other words, our problem is due to the fact that, in our example, the *class* specifies the type of data that the queue stores when, logically, it should be up to the *client* to say what type of data it it wants a given queue object to manage. This is an example of *incomplete abstraction*.

☐ To properly encapsulate things, it is not enough to prevent the *client* from concerning itself with details that properly "belong" to the *supplier*. We must also prevent the *supplier* from concerning itself with details that properly "belong" to the *client*. In our *queue* example, effective abstraction means that the *supplier* should be able to manage the queue irrespective of the data the client is using the queue to store. Logically *class Queue* has no business caring *what* data is stored. It should only need to know *what to do* with it and be able to make sure that the data is of the type specified.

Using* Generic Parameters *to Improve Resuability   To achieve a higher level of abstraction that supports reuse of code, we make use of a new construct, the *generic parameter.* This construct allows the client algorithm to define the type of data that a particular object of a class will store. When the client declares an object of `class Queue`, it uses the *generic parameter* to pass a type definition specifying the kind of data that is to be managed by the particular object.

Thus, each object serves as a template which manages data of the type specifyied at the time of its creation. For example, within a client we might find:

```
type
    DataRecType definesa record
            ThisField isa num
            ThatField isa boolean
            OtherField isa char
    endrecord {DataRecType}

    StudentRecType definesa record
        StudentName isa NameString
        StudentNum isa Num
        StudentMajor isa DeptString
        StudentGPA isa num
    endrecord {StudentRecType}
```

```
var
    DataQueue isa Queue(DataRecType)
    StudentQueue isa Queue(StudentRecType)
    NumberQueue isa Queue(num)
```

Above, we have moved the definition of DataRecType from the *supplier* class to the *client* algorithm and have also created the definition of StudentRecType. Then, we've declared three objects. Notice the type of each object. Each of the three Queue objects is declared such that its class (Queue) includes a parameter specifying the kind of data which *that particular queue object* will store. All three objects are of type Queue. But each one is different from the others in terms of *what type of data* the queue will store, as specified by the *generic parameter.* DataQueue is declared to be a queue object that will manage data of type DataRecType, object StudentQueue will manage data of type StudentRecType, and object NumberQueue will be a queue of numbers.

In effect, each *object* is being declared to expect a given type of data. The object need not be concerned with what the data type *represents*, only that it will receive data of a *given named type.* Once declared, each of the three queue objects will operate independently of one another (just as three ordinary *num* variables have no bearing on one another).

The client algorithm may then include executable instructions such as

```
    DataQueue.Enqueue(ThisVar, ItWorked)
    StudentQueue.Dequeue(ThatVar, ItWorked)
    NumberQueue.Enqueue(SomeVar, ItWorked)
```

Each of these three instructions is a request to the specified object to provide the service requested, i.e., to enqueue the value of ThisVar on the queue DataQueue, to dequeue an item from queue StudentQueue and store the value in ThatVar, and to enqueue the value of SomeVar into the queue NumberQueue.

For each of these three instructions to be correct, the actual parameter variables must be of the appropriate type, e.g., each of the three instructions require DidItWork to be a boolean, the first instruction's variable ThisVar must be of type DataRecType, the second instruction's ThatVar variable must be of type StudentRecType, and in the third instruction's SomeVar must be of type num.

To make use of the generic parameter, we rewrite the Queue class as follows:

```
class Queue (QType isa type)

public
    procedure Enqueue (NewData isa in QType,
                            Success isa out boolean)
        {documentation as before}

    procedure Dequeue (Served isa out QType,
                            Success isa out boolean)
        {documentation as before}

private
    type
        QNode definesa record
                Data isa QType
                Next isa QPtr
        endrecord

        QPtr isa ptr toa QNode

    var
        QHead isa QPtr
        QTail isa QPtr

    procedure Enqueue (NewData isa in QType,
                            Success isa out boolean)
        {procedure body as before}


    procedure Dequeue (Served isa out QType,
                            Success isa out boolean)
        {procedure body as before}


    function IsEmpty isa boolean
        {procedure body as before}

    begin {initialization}
      {initialization body as before}
    end {initialization}

end {class Queue}
```

Thus, we have a *class* definition in which all references to the type of data stored on the queue is type QType. What is QType? QType is the *formal generic parameter* as specified in the header line of the *class*. Anytime a client algorithm declares an object of class Queue, that declaration must pass an *actual generic parameter* which specifies the type of data which that particular Queue object then treats as QType.

The use of generic parameters to specify data types allows *objects* to be generic data-managing templates. Once a given logical capability is implemented as a well-designed class, objects of that class can be declared to manage data of any type. Thus, code can be reused and programmers need not "reinvent the wheel" whenever they need a given capability for managing data of a different type.

> ☐ Generic parameters allow us to transfer responsibility for determing the kind of data to be managed to the client.

Tracing the execution of object behaviors

In earlier chapters, we suggested that you trace the execution of your algorithms by drawing pictures of its data state. This allows you to see where variables are ("on the stack" or "in the heap"), to create them as the the algorithm allocates space for them, to erase them when they "die," to modify the values stored in them as appropriate, and so on. Such drawings are crucial, as they allow you to *see* the logical effects of what would happen in a computer as your algorithm executes.

Objects present nothing *really* new in this regard, just a new twist. Keep in mind that an instance of all the variables globally declared in a class exist *for each object* that has been created. For example, in our Queue *class* we see that pointer variables QHead and QTail are declared in the private section. These two variables are created for *each instance* of Queue. If the client algorithm creates two *objects* via

```
var
      OneQueue isa Queue(num)
      AnotherQueue isa Queue(char)
```

then both OneQueue and AnotherQueue will each have their own head and tail pointers. In other words, *these two objects each contain their own internal variables*. For this example above, you may *think of* their head pointers as OneQueue.QHead and AnotherQueue.QHead, respectively, and you might use these names as you keep track of their values as you trace your algorithms' execution.

Just remember that you cannot actually *access* them that way. Only those methods defined in the class (such as OneQueue.Enqueue, AnotherQueue.Dequeue, or OneQueue.IsEmpty) may do so. In fact the name, OneQueue.QHead, will never actually appear in any part of the algorithm. The head pointer that will be accessed is determined by the object identifier specified in the call. To apply the En-queue method to OneQueue's internal variables, call OneQueue.Enqueue.

Otherwise, everything else can be drawn just as before. All statically allocated (named) variables exist on the *activation stack* within the *frame* in which they were declared. Whenever that frame is popped off the stack, the named variables "die." All dynamically allocated, i.e., unnamed, variables exist in the *heap*. For example, if OneQueue and AnotherQueue are declared within the client's main algorithm, then their named *head* and *tail* pointers will survive throughout the entire execution of the client algorithm. On the other hand, if they are declared within one of the client algorithm's procedures, then they will "die" as soon as that procedure completes and has its frame popped off the activation stack. In either case, the dynamically allocated nodes which constitute the actual queue itself will live in the heap until such time that no pointer points to them, at which point they are automatically deallocated.

Given the algorithm below, how might we draw its state as it nears completion (after the last instruction within the begin..end block has completed but just before the algorithm ends and all stack frames "die")?

```
algorithm SampleQueueClient
    {purpose: nonsense algorithm to illustrate
              drawing trace of ADT state}
uses
    adt Queue
var
    ThisQueue,
    ThatQueue isa Queue(num)
    Fred isa num
    DidItWork isa boolean
begin
    Fred <- 7
    ThisQueue.Enqueue((Fred+2), DidItWork)
    ThisQueue.Enqueue((Fred+1), DidItWork)
    ThisQueue.Enqueue(Fred, DidItWork)
    ThisQueue.Dequeue(Fred, DidItWork)
    ThatQueue.Enqueue(Fred, DidItWork)
end {algorithm SampleQueueClient}
```

We might draw the final data state as:

```
    [8]———>[7]——||                    [9]——||
```

Main: ThisQueue.QHead—>QNode[8] ThisQueue.Tail—>QNode[7]
ThatQueue.QHead—>QNode[9] ThatQueue.Tail—>QNode[9]
Fred=9   DidItWork=true

Copy *and* **Clone**   There is frequently a need to assign the value of one variable to another, e.g.,

```
ThisVar <- ThatVar
```

Because objects include both data and the operations upon that data, we require some means of requesting that the value(s) of one object be assigned to another object of the same class. We do this via `copy` and `clone` operations. To see why we need two operations, consider that a client algorithm uses our `Queue` class, declares two objects of that class, and manipulates them as shown below:

```
SomeClientAlgorithm
uses
     class Queue
var
     This,
     Thatisa Queue(num)
     Success isa boolean
begin
     This.Enqueue(7, Success)
     This.Enqueue(9, Success)
     This.Enqueue(11, Success)
end
```

So far, the queue object `That` is empty, while `This` has the values *7*, *9*, and *11* stored in it (head to tail). The data state of these two objects might be drawn as:

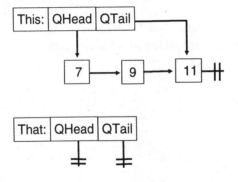

Now, consider that the client's next instruction is:

```
That <- copy(This)
```

☐   The copy operation copies the values of the *internal* variables of one object to another. In the case of pointers, it gives us a copy of the pointers themselves. It does *not* give us a copy of the data to which those pointers refer. Thus, subsequent operations of one object can affect the other object's data.

The result of the copy operation is that internal variables of each object now store the same value. The internal QHead pointers of both This and That point to the node containing *7*, and both QTail pointers point to the node containing *11*.

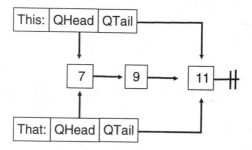

Now, consider the effect if the client algorithm now did:

```
That.Enqueue(2)
```

It would attach a new node containing the value *2* to the end of the linked list. The pointer This.QTail would still point to the node containing *11*, but that node's Next pointer would no longer be *nil*.

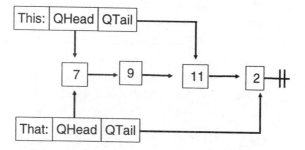

Thus, we now have two different objects, ones that are supposed to feature well encapsulated data, sharing both data and heap memory! While this may be useful for certain tasks, it is also quite dangerous. Can you see why? What would be effects of That.Enqueue(3) followed by This.Enqueue(1)?

☐ If we want a copy of the dynamic data itself, then we use another operation created for that purpose: the clone operation. This operation both copies the internal variables declared within the object itself, *and it also follows any pointers and "clones" any data to which those pointers refer.*

Thus, given our original "7-9-11" list, the operation:

    That <- clone(This)

gives the state:

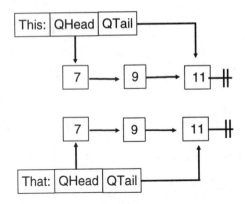

The clone follows the internal pointer variables of This and insures that the internal pointer variables of That point to their own copy of whatever This's pointers referenced. Now, the two objects *each have their own queue* and changes to one will not affect the state of the other.

☐ To prevent *cloning* from having unintended side effects we specify that, as the clone operation follows pointers, it never overwrites anything and instead makes fresh copies of what it finds.

That is to say, clone:

- copies, i.e., overwrites the object's variables such as QHead, QTail, and

- clones, i.e., allocates new nodes and initializes their values to copy the original values, whenever it follows pointers.

The copy operation can be considered to be *shallow* (copying only the object's *internal* variables), while clone can be considered to be *deep* (following pointers and literally *cloning*, not copying, whatever it finds).

Obviously, clone is the safer of the two, as copy allows the possibility of one object's request for service pathologically affecting the state of any another object that is referencing the shared dynamic data. Thus, the copy operation requires explicit notation, e.g.,

```
ThisGuy <- copy(ThatGuy)
```

while the safer clone operation can be denoted in either of two ways:

```
ThisGuy <- clone(ThatGuy)
```

or

```
ThisGuy <- ThatGuy
```

> ☐ The default meaning for the *assignment operator* with respect to objects is the clone, not the copy, operation. Furthermore, because of the risk to data integrity presented by the copy operation, it is reserved for use within the private section of a class. A client may perform clone operations but may not do copy operations.

Exercises 9.2. A *priority queue* is a queue with a somewhat different Enqueue operation. Rather than automatically *enqueuing* each new item at the rear of the queue, a priority queue inserts the new item into a location in the queue as determined by that item's *priority*. Thus, a "high priority" item would likely go directly to the front of such a queue, while a "low priority" item will wind up at the rear. Create a class for a *priority queue*, assuming each enqueued item to have some data field containing a numerical priority associated with it (perhaps in a field named "Priority") such that the smaller the priority rating, the higher the priority.

9.3. Create a class that models the operations of a bank account, including deposits, withdraws, interest accumulation, overdraft protection (with penalty fees), and service charges.

Acheiving
Superior
Adaptability

So far, we have seen one kind of relationship that may exist between objects: *the client/supplier relationship*. A client algorithm requests service which a supplier *object* makes available. Rather than directly manipulating the implementation of a data structure, the client asks the supplier *object* to perform a *logical* operation on it and the supplier takes care of all the implementation-related particulars.

The *client/supplier* kind of relationship is quite natural to people, and many instances of it can be found throughout everyday life. *Objects* often feature this same kind of relationship among themselves. If you grasp the concept and purpose of objects' *client/supplier* capabilities, you're ready to learn more. If not, it's best to review now before proceeding.

> ☐ A second kind of relationship between objects is, in principle, quite simple: one object can be declared so that it *inherits* all the features of another object, then adds some new features or capabilities to it.

For example, if you want a class that provides the capabilities of *priority queue*, and if you already have an object that provides a strict *FIFO queue*, *inheritance* means that you don't have to write the new class from scratch. Instead, you can declare your new class so that it *inherits* all the features of a *FIFO queue*, then redefine the Enqueue service to reflect the capabilities of *priority queues* that are new or different. Thus, you have to write only those portions of the class that are *different* or *missing* from its "ancestor" class.

This has the obvious benefit of saving a great deal of coding. Not only can you easily customize existing code, but this paradigm encourages the development of *libraries* of code. Frequently, programmers discover that the capabilities they want have already been written and tested and are available for use and, if necessary, modification.

Inheriting
and Extending
Behaviors

Given that we have our queue class implemented, imagine that we want a somewhat different kind of *queue*. We want to know how many items are currently stored in the queue. One way to do this would be to have the client algorithm maintain a count, but that would be an example of poor abstraction. The number of items in the queue is properly *a property of the queue* and thus, the queue abstraction should be responsible for keeping track of it.

Without inheritance, either we'd have to revise our original queue abstraction, class Queue (which we might not want to do; perhaps we want clients to be able to declare some queue objects which *don't* keep count) or we'd have to create a whole new abstraction with similar-but-different code (which would result in the same kind of problem that lead us to generic parameters: many similar-but-different classes, such that any improvements to their common components would have to be made to each of the many different classes).

With inheritance, all we have to do is:

```
class CountingQueue (QType isa class)

inherits
    Queue()

public
    function Count isa num
    {
    purpose: indicate the number of items currently
        stored in a FIFO queue object
    precondition: object has been initialized
    postcondition: function Count will resolve to the
        correct num value
    }


private
    function Count isa num
    var
        TempCount isa num
        Current isa QPtr

    begin
        TempCount <- 0
        Current <- QHead
        loop
            exitif (Current = nil)
            TempCount <- TempCount + 1
            Current <- Current^.Next
        endloop
        Count returns TempCount
    end {function Count}
end {class CountingQueue}
```

Observe how little we had to do. All we did was:

- specify that this class inherits from class Queue

- provide the header line and contract for the new capability in the public section (we did this only because we want client algorithms to be able to use it)

- provide the implementation of the corresponding routine in the private section.

We said nothing about data types or Enqueue or Dequeue operations or anything else that a *queue* requires because inheritance made it unnecessary. Since this class inherits from the Queue class, *it gets all that for free.* Our CountingQueue class now includes *all* the features of its ancestor class, including anything and everything that was in its *public and private* sections. In addition, its repertoire of behavior has been expanded beyond that of its ancestor class by the new capability we added. In short, we've managed to build on previous work to cheaply create an enhanced class through inheritance. We call the resulting CountingQueue class a *subclass* of Queue because it inherited features from it (much as we consider dog to be a *species,* and Golden Retriever to be a *subspecies* of dog).

Redefining Inherited Identifiers
We've seen how to extend the capabilities of one class (Queue) by defining a new subclass (CountingQueue) that inherits from the original. Of course, someone might disagree with us about how we've defined our new subclass. For example, you might reasonably say that, for some given problem, Count will be called much more often than will Enqueue and Dequeue and, thus, it makes more sense to always maintain a count rather than traverse the queue and recompute the count each and every time a count is needed. Such an approach would require that we modify the Enqueue and Dequeue services such that they update a counter variable. If we decide to change our implementation of CountingQueue along these lines, we still need Enqueue and Dequeue services, but we need to *redefine* the particulars of what they do. In the object-oriented paradigm, we can accomplish this as follows:

```
class CountingQueue(QType isa class)

inherits
    Queue(QType)

public
    function Count isa num
    {insert contract from previous example}

private
    var
        CounterVar isa num
```

```
procedure Enqueue (NewData isa in QType,
                      Success isa out boolean)
{procedure body modified to increment CounterVar upon
    each successful Enqueue}

procedure Dequeue (Served isa out QType,
                      Success isa out boolean)
{procedure body modified to decrement CounterVar upon
    each successful Dequeue}

function Count isa num
begin
     Count returns CounterVar
end {function Count}

begin {initialization}
     CounterVar <- 0
end {initialization}
end {class CountingQueue)
```

In this example, we still provide client algorithms with a function which returns the number of items in the queue, and we still inherit everything from the ancestor class Queue. "Everything" includes *all* the contents of its *public* and *private* sections. However, in our new subclass, we have *redefined* the particular implementations of of Enqueue and Dequeue so that they maintain the correct value in the hidden variable CounterVar. This is a simple example of another powerful object capability:

☐ We can not only take what we want from ancestor classes and *add* whatever new data structures or services we need, but we can also *redefine* any existing data or methods as appropriate.

This gives us a great deal of power ... which must be used wisely and with care. Keep in mind, that we cannot violate any contracts that we make with clients. Thus, services such as Enqueue and Dequeue must deliver what is promised. In this particular case, our redefinition of these services is acceptable *as long as the new definitions still do what they are supposed to do* from the client's perspective. However, should a redefinition change the service that is provided to client algorithms, then a serious *breach of contract* may occur.

Whenever you create a subclass that redefines an inherited identifier (regardless of whether it be the name of data or the name of a routine, regardless of whether the purpose is to add capability or improve performance) it is *appropriate* to "be paranoid" about changing the functionality provided to the client. The new subclass *must* either:

- honor the contract which its ancestor class has made (as specified in the contract provided in the ancestor's pubic section) or

- provide clients with a new contract, specified in the subclass' *public* section for the redefined service.

In our example, the new definitions are acceptable as long as the *only* meaningful difference in the new behaviors is that the new private variable CountVar is kept up to date. Because this updating of a hidden variable doesn't affect the client in any way, the ancestor's contract will still hold and there is no need to redefine the public section in order to redefine the contract.

Changing Public/Private Status Sometimes it might happen that a subclass might wish to change the *public/private* status of a given identifier. In our Queue example, perhaps a subclass of Queue might want its clients to be able to directly inquire if a given queue object is empty. In the declaration of the class Queue, the function IsEmpty is provided but it is *private* and thus not available to clients. To provide this service to clients, all that's required is that the header line and contract be copied into the *public* section of the subclass. There is no need to redefine the service itself. Just including its header and contract in the *public* section is all that's needed to allow clients to use it.

Of course, just because it's *easy* to make things public doesn't mean that it *should* be done. The key determinant of that question is an analysis of the abstraction itself, i.e., does the client have any *logical need* to call for such a service or is the service an implementation-related detail.

It also might happen that the author of a new subclass might wish to change the status of a previously *public* service and make it *private*. This is a somewhat thornier problem in terms of logic and abstraction. For the most part, we think of subclasses as offering *enhancements* or *specializations* of general class traits, not as *removing* them, just as a subspecies (e.g., a Golden Retriever) generally doesn't lose any basic qualities of its species (e.g., whatever we might mean by "essential dog-ness": has four legs, barks, runs, sniffs, etc.). Similarly, in real life, it is easy to take private information and make it public, but it's just about impossible to take publicly known information and turn it into a secret!

On the other hand, there *are* examples of "birds that don't fly" and "dogs that don't bark," just as there are publicly owned companies that are "taken private" and thus no longer release annual financial reports. So, as in most things, there are exceptions to the rule. If the case calls for removing a capability, (e.g., specifying that an ostrich, though a bird, can't fly) you may do so via *redefinition.*

Simply redefine the `begin..end` block of code such that no instructions are executed in between them, except perhaps for an error message (e.g., "You have asked an ostrich to fly. Ostriches cannot fly!") and provide a new contract which specifies that this service is not available for the given subclass.

☐   Remember!

The power to redefine identifiers provides a great deal of flexibility and power, but this power must be used with care. It is necessary that any new definitions live up to the promises made to clients by its ancestors (in the contracts provided for each service), or else a new contract must be provided in the new object's *public* section. Every class must fulfill its contracts, or the entire basis of the object-oriented approach falls apart.

Deferred Classes   A *good* object-oriented design may identify occasions when it makes sense to create a class that won't do anything itself *except* provide common features for descendant subclasses to inherit. In such circumstances, there may be services and/or data that we *know* are needed among all the subclasses, and thus *should* be specified by the ancestor, but the particulars of the shared items will differ to the point that the ancestor *cannot* implement even an initial version of them. And, since they have not been implemented initially, they aren't there to be redefined.

For example, imagine that we want to create the appropriate classes for representing various two-dimensional geometric shapes, e.g., circles, rectangles, triangles, etc. We might do this by creating a class called `GeometricObjects` which will then have one subclass for each of the particular kinds of figures (`Circle`, `Rectangle`, etc.) Many attributes might be shared, e.g., a list of values which define the figure, the color in which the figure is to be drawn, etc. Yet, certain services, such as the calculation of the area or perimeter, will be dependent on the particular graphical object. Thus, despite the ancestor's knowledge that all its descendants will need to offer the services `Area` and `Perimeter`, and despite its ability to specify contracts appropriate for such services, it will be impossible for the ancestor to define the details of how the area and perimeter are to be calculated. These details *must* be left to the subclasses. In such situations, we make use of the construct *deferred class*.

☐   A *deferred class* is one that specifies the data and the services (and associated contracts) for shared services that its descendants will offer, but which does not implement *one or more* of them. Instead, at the place where we would expect to see the implementation for a given service or data, the declaration is replaced by the word `deferred`.

As a concrete example, let's reconsider our design and implementation of the Queue class and its descendants. The most basic implementation decision is the choice of data strcuture. Shall we implement queues as static (array) or dynamic (linked) memory structures? In the former case, one may typically save time, while the latter may save space. Thus, regardless of how we implement a queue, someone can reasonably claim that we've chosen poorly and are economizing on the wrong side of the time/space dilemma for their particular needs.

One solution is to provide queues for each set of needs: one based on a time-efficient static structure and the other on a space-efficient dynamic structure. In such an implementation, the class Queue would know that each subclass will feature an Enqueue and Dequeue service, and would be able to specify its interface and contract, but would *defer to the subclasses* regarding the actual implementation of these services. Thus, the ancestor class Queue might include the following,:

```
(in the public section:)
    procedure Enqueue (NewData isa in QType,
                            Success isa out boolean)
            {
            purpose: add NewData to end of FIFO queue
            precondition: queue exists and is not full
            postcondition: queue exits as before plus NewData
                appended to end of queue
            )


    procedure Dequeue (Served isa out QType,
                            Success isa out boolean)
            {
            purpose: remove item from front of FIFO queue
            precondition: queue exists and is not empty
            postcondition: queue exists as before minus item at
                front; item returned via param Served
                )

(in the private section:)
    procedure Enqueue (NewData isa in QType,
                            Success isa out boolean)
        deferred

    procedure Dequeue (Served isa out QType,
                            Success isa out boolean)
        deferred
```

Meanwhile, the *private* sections of the subclasses FastQueue and SmallQueue would include the algorithms and data that support the static and dynamic implementations, respectively, for each of these two services.

☐ There is a necessary limitation placed on *deferred classes*. Because they have not specified the implementation of all the behavior they describe, they are of no use for declaring objects. Their only value is in providing a specification of the common basis for subsequent subclasses.

Thus, if we implemented the classes Queue, FastQueue, and SmallQueue as described here, we could declare objects of the two subclasses but could not declare objects of their ancestor. A class which contains even one deferred method or data definition must be considered a *deferred class*, irrespective of how many methods or data items it might completely specify. One deferred identifier is sufficient to prevent us from declaring objects of the class. Yet deferred classes are a powerful tool for allowing code reuse. They give as a way to place shared things together in one place so that subclasses must specify only their differences, not their commonalties.

Summary of the Kinds of Inheritance We've seen three kinds of inheritance relationship among classes. They all allow subclasses to inherit everything that the ancestor class provides, and they all support reuse of existing code. They differ only with respect to the particular details of what traits are inherited and what are not:

- *Extension*: the subclass inherits all traits supplied by its ancestor, then extends or expands the repertoire of behavior by adding one or more new services.

- *Redefinition*: the subclass inherits all traits supplied by its ancestor, then changes what one or more of them mean, in terms of either implementation or functionality, or both.

- *Deferred*: the subclass inherits all traits supplied by its ancestor, but must implement the *deferred* ones before any objects may be declared, as no implementation was provided by the ancestor.

Of course, for a given subclass and its ancestor, you may find any combination of these three kinds of inheritance relations. In a single example, a subclass might implement some deferred features, redefine some other features, and expand its behavior by adding new ones as well.

Resolving Ambiguity Inheritance allows for great flexibility. It also requires that we know how to resolve any ambiguities that might arise. For example, consider that a parent class (Queue) and a subclass (CountingQueue) each have their own definition of what it means to provide the service PrintStatus. For objects that are of class Queue,

`PrintStatus` would print out only those data items of which it has knowledge (e.g., `empty` or `full`), while the subclass might extend `PrintStatus` to output all related information, including both the data defined in the ancestor class *and* the data extensions defined within the subclass (e.g. `empty`, `full` and `count` for objects of class `CountingQueue`).

> ☐ When a method is defined in both a subclass and its ancestor, how do we know which version is used? To resolve any possible ambiguities, we always follow a simple rule: *Each service request is satisfied according to the definition found at the lowest, most-specific level.*

This means that, whenever a service is requested from any instance of a subclass, we first see if that service is explicitly defined (or redefined) for that subclass. If it is, we use that definition. If it is not, we then look to the next ancestor of that subclass and use whatever definition is provided there. If the "parent" of that subclass doesn't explicitly define the service, then we look to the "grandparent," and so on, in a bottom-up fashion. Sooner or later, we will either (a) encounter a definition for that service (in which case we stop looking and use it) or (b) exhaust the "family history" of the class without finding a definition (in which case an error has occurred).

Achieving Polymorphism

We can exploit inheritance to obtain another benefit: *polymorphism*. "Polymorphism" is the ability to take different forms. In the object-oriented context, it means the ability to "change the class of an object to which another object is attached." (*Say what?!?*) To understand what this means, consider the following example.

Imagine that we have a class for managing data about `Vehicles`, and that it is defined to store and retrieve data about each vehicle, including `VIN` (i.e., VehicleIDNum), `Manufacturer`, `Year`, and `Model`. All we expect of this class is that it provides services ("methods") for storing and for returning each of the four pieces of information stored for any object of this class.

Let us assume that the designer of this class determined that it is best to treat each *make* and *model* as a string of characters. Further, let us assume the existence of a `String` class with `Get()` and `Display()` methods. Finally, let us imagine that we are shown the actual implementation of `class Vehicle`:

```
{ ─────────────────────────────────────── }

class Vehicle

uses String

public
    procedure GetData
    { purpose:  get information on the vehicle       }
    { preconditions: none                            }
    { postconditions: Vehicle contains valid data    }

    procedure Display
    { purpose:  display information on the vehicle    }
    { preconditions: Vehicle has valid data           }
    { postconditions: information displayed on screen }

private

    var
        VIN isa num       {variable: VehicleID number }
        Make isa String   {object: Manufacturer data}
        Model isa String  {object: Model type data }
        Year isa num       {variable: Year manufactured}

    procedure GetData

    begin
        print( 'What is the Vehicle Identification
                number?' )
        read( VIN )

        print( 'What make is this vehicle?' )
        Make.Get

        print( 'What is the model type of this
                vehicle?' )
        Model.Get

        print( 'What year is this vehicle?' )
        read( Year )
    end { GetData }
```

```
procedure Display

begin
    print( 'Vehicle:', VIN )
    print( Year )
    Make.Display
    Model.Display
end { Display }

begin { Initialization }
    VIN <- -1 { initialize VIN to dummy value }
    Year <- -1 { initialize YEAR to dummy value }
    {class String responsible for initializing
        "Make" and "Model" string objects }
end { Initialization }

end { class Vehicle }
```

{ —————————————————————————— }

Notice that we do not worry about how the String class will deal with initializing, getting, storing, and displaying strings. As *clients* of the String class, all we care about is the services that it provides us. That is, we take on faith that we can create *objects* of class String and then utilize the String class' public methods Get and Display. The responsibility for these methods falls to the String class, not to its clients.

Imagine further that we have been given the job of creating two subclasses of Vehicle: Car and Truck. Our job is to extend the Vehicle class so that each object of subclass Car stores all the standard vehicle information, plus information about BodyStyle (e.g.. sedan, coupe, convertible, etc.) and NumOfDoors. We might do this via:

{ —————————————————————————— }

```
class Car

inherits
    Vehicle
```

```
private

    var
        BodyType isa String
        NumDoors isa num

    procedure GetData
    begin
        { First get the general vehicle info }
        Vehicle.GetData

        { Then get the additional info specific to cars
            }
        print( 'Enter body style:' )
        BodyType.Get
        print( 'Enter number of doors:' )
        read( NumDoors )
    end { GetData }


    procedure Display
    begin
        { First display info common to all vehicles }
        Vehicle.Display

        { Then print car-specific info }
        print( 'This car is a ', NumDoors, '-door ')
        BodyType.Display
    end { Display }
end { class Car }

{ ————————————————————————————————— }
```

Notice that we do not create any public section for class Car. This is because we inherit the public section from class Vehicle and our extensions to that class do not create any new *public* methods, nor are we making any changes that violate the original contracts. All we are doing is adding to the list of information that an object of class Car will get, store, and display.

Similarly, imagine that we are given the job of creating a class for Truck objects such that each such object will get, store, and display both standard Vehicle data plus GrossWeight. We might do this by:

```
{ ──────────────────·──────────────── }

class Truck

inherits
    Vehicle

private

    var
        GrossWeight isa num { Weight in tons }

    procedure GetData

    begin
        { First get the normal vehicle info }
        Vehicle.GetData

        { Then get the additional info specific to
            trucks }
        print( 'What is the gross weight of the truck in
            tons?' )
        read( GrossWeight )
    end { GetData }

    procedure Display

    begin
        { First display info common to all vehicles }
        Vehicle.Display

        { Then print truck-specific info }
        print( 'This truck has a gross weight of' )
        print( GrossWeight, ' tons.' )
    end { Display }

end { class Truck }

{ ──────────────────────────────── }
```

Above, both Car and Truck classes make use of *inheritance* from their ancestor
class Vehicle. As a result, the two subclasses required us to do only as much programming as needed to specify *the differences* between each subclass and the

ancestor. This "programming by differences" is one common characteristic (and benefit) of the object-oriented programming paradigm.

As a result of our extensions, what do we have? All Vehicle objects will share certain information (and the routines to store and retrieve that information), while each object of class Car will also store and retrieve additional information that is different than that stored for each object of class Truck.

Given this scenario, we can now declare a Queue object to manage information about Car objects and another Queue object to manage Truck objects, e.g.:

```
CarQueue isa Queue(Car)
TruckQueue isa Queue(Truck)
```

If we did this, the CarQueue would not be able to manage Truck objects, and TruckQueue wouldn't be able to manage information about Car objects. Each of the two Queue objects would be able to store information about *only the subclass* that it was declared to manage as specified via the generic parameter.

However, we might imagine a circumstance in which we wanted to manage data about *both* subclasses in a single Queue. Polymorphism allows us to do this. How? By declaring a Queue object to manage data of class Vehicle, e.g.,

```
VehicleQueue isa Queue(Vehicle)
```

A Queue object declared in this way can, quite obviously, manage data about objects of class Vehicle. In addition, it can manage information about *any subclass* of Vehicle, e.g., Car and Truck objects. Thus, at any particular moment, VehicleQueue might store a *FIFO* list containing *any combination* of Car and Truck objects.

Similarly, *any object* of class Vehicle can be used to store and retrieve information about any object of class Vehicle or of any *subclass* of that class. Thus, the object declared as

```
ThisRide isa Vehicle
```

might be used to store data about an object of class Vehicle or of subclass Car or of subclass Truck.

In the event that we had some number of objects stored in VehicleQueue, the instruction:

```
VehicleQueue.Dequeue(ThisRide, DidItWork)
```

would remove *whatever class* of Vehicle was at the front of VehicleQueue and associate it with object ThisRide.

Thus, when we say that polymorphism allows us "to change the class of an object to which another object is attached," we really *are* saying something! In the example above, an *object* (ThisRide) will have its *class* changed (to Car or Truck) based on the class of Vehicle which is dequeued from VehicleQueue.

Everything is an Object

So far, we have seen how objects provide a range of features that support *encapsulation, resuse, adaptabiliity,* and *polymorphism.* What we have only hinted at, however, is the essential difference that object-oriented design implies, namely,

> *Everything* is an object!

In our examples so far, we isolated the data and procedural abstractions pertaining to *a given logical data structure* within a *class* so that the client algorithm can only access data through prescribed services which the *objects of that class* makes available. However, the *client algorithm* itse itself was conventional: it might consist of any combination of unencapsulated constants, data types, variables, and instructions.

In contrast, in object-oriented design, *there are no conventional, unencapsulated algorithm elements.* Each and every supplier *and* each and every client is itself an object of some class. This is an essential feature of object-oriented programming: *each and every element of the algorithm* is an object.

As an example, consider a system that allows car dealerships to place orders for cars and trucks and to find out which of their ordered vehicles have rolled off the assembly line. For the sake of simplicity, we will limit the available options to only those attributes that we have already included in our Car and Truck objects. We will also ignore the way that the factory interacts with this system.

(Obviously, when an order is enqueued onto an "Order" queue, the factory must *dequeue* that order, build the vehicle, and then *enqueue* that vehcile onto a "Built" queue, informing the dealer that the vehcile is ready. The factory view of this process is beyond what we will consider here.)

According to the object-oriented paradigm, what would such an application look like from the dealer point of view? The system itself is quite simple. There are six classes: Vehicle, its subclasses Car and Truck (both of which inherit from class Vehicle), and the Queue class. We have seen implementations for all four of these classes. In addition, we assume the existence of a String class, just as we did in defining the Vehicle class and its subclasses Car and Truck.

Thus, five of the six classes are known to us:

- the Vehicle class provides the data that is relevant to all vehicles, as well as the services which allow this data to be obtained and printed.

- the subclasses Car and Truck inherit from class Vehicle, then add the additional data items that are specific to the subclass. In addition, they redefine the services for obtaining and printing information as appropriate to their extended data.

- the Queue class supports *enqueue* and *dequeue* operations, providing generic queue behavior for whatever data type is specified for a given queue object.

- the String class supports (via unknon means) the ability to Get() and Display() a string.

The sixth class is the only one that is new to us: class Dealership. This class is what is knows as the *root class,* analogous to the main algorithm in conventional design.

The Dealership class is shown below. It includes the declaration of two objects of class Queue which, via generic parameter, are specified as managing items of class Vehicle. Note that Dealership does *not* inherit from any of these classes. Rather, it is a *client* of Queue, i.e., it declares an object of that class and makes use of the services which Queue objects provide.

```
{ ——————————————————————————— }

class Dealership

uses
     Queue,
     Vehicle,
     Car,
     Truck

private

     var
         OrderQueue isa Queue( Vehicle )
         BuiltQueue isa Queue( Vehicle )
```

```
procedure PlaceOrder
{ purpose:  allows Dealership to order a vehicle }
{           for a customer                       }
{ preconditions: OrderQueue exists               }
{ postconditions: information about customer      }
{           request is sent to the factory, or    }
{           an error message is displayed if      }
{           there's no room in the queue          }
var
    NewCar isa Car
    NewTruck isa Truck
    Choice isa char
    Success isa boolean

begin
    print( 'What type of vehicle does the customer
        desire?' )
    print( '(C)ar or (T)ruck: ' )
    read( Choice )

    if( Choice = 'C' ) then
        { They want a new car }
        NewCar.GetData()
        OrderQueue.Enqueue( NewCar, Success )
    else
        { They want a new truck }
        NewTruck.GetData()
        OrderQueue.Enqueue( NewTruck, Success )
    endif


    if( Success ) then
        print( 'Your order has been successfully
            processed.' )
    else
        print( 'We cannot handle another order
            right now—' )
        print( 'business is booming, and we're
            backlogged.' )
    endif

end { PlaceOrder }
```

```
procedure ReadyVehicle
{ purpose:  let the dealer know which vehicles are }
{                assembled                         }
{ preconditions: BuiltQueue exists                 }
{ postconditions: if a Vehicle is ready on the     }
{                  queue, its info is displayed,    }
{                  else an error message is given   }
var
    NewVehicle isa Vehicle
    Success isa boolean

begin
    BuiltQueue.Dequeue( NewVehicle, Success )
    if( Success ) then
        print( 'A new vehicle with the following
            information:' )
        NewVehicle.Display()
        print( 'has just rolled off the assembly
            line. Please' )
        print( 'notify the customer that his or-
            der is ready.' )
    else
        print( 'There are no assembled vehicles
            on the line.' )
    endif
end { ReadyVehicle }




procedure Menu
var
    Choice isa char

begin
    loop
        print( 'Welcome to the dealership.')
        print( ' Choose an option:' )
        print( '(P)lace an order' )
        print( '(G)et the next ready vehicle')
        print( 'provided by the factory' )
        print( '(Q)uit' )
        read( Choice )
```

```
                    exitif( Choice = 'Q' )
                    if (Choice = 'P') then
                        PlaceOrder
                    else
                        if ( Choice = 'G' ) then
                            ReadyVehicle
                        else {have selected invalid option}
                            print ('Please try again!')
                        endif
                    endif
                endloop
                print( 'The dealership has closed.  Goodbye!' )
            end { Menu }



        begin {Initialization }
            Menu
        end { Initialization }



    end { class Dealership }
    { ——————————————————————————————— }
```

Class Dealership serves the role of a conventional "main algorithm." To run the program, the user types Dealership. As Dealership executes, what really happens?

First, the *objects* declared by dealership are *instantiated*. There are two such objects: OrderQueue and BuiltQueue. Each of these objects is created. Where? In the data space in the stackframe belonging to Dealership, i.e., at the bottom of the activation stack. Both of these objects are of class Queue and thus any initialization of them is the responsibility of class Queue. (Inspection of class Queue shoes that the such steps are indeed performed, but the only way we know this is because we have seen the code to class Queue earlier in this chapter. Ordinarily, we wouldn't be able to seethe *private* section of Queue and thus would not know exactly what these steps are.)

Following the instantiation of those two objects, we find the definitions of three private methods within class Dealership: PlaceOrder, ReadyVehcile, and Menu. (All three are *private* and thus cannot be seen by anyone outside of class Dealership.)

Finally, the initialization portion of class Dealership does only a sinlge thing: it calls the method procedure Menu.

This method, Menu, takes effect in the usual way, i.e., it gets its own frame on the activation stack, and its local variables are allocated within that frame. (In the case of Menu, we can see that it requires only a single *char var* named Choice.) It then begins to execute. Examination of procedure Menu shows that it will continuously prompt the user for a choice ("placing an order" or "retreiving data on a built vehicle" or "quitting"). The *quitting* choice is the only one that terminates the execution of the loop, i.e., Menu continues to operate forever unless someone selects the *quit* option. When either of the other two options is selected, either the PlaceOrder or ReadyVehicle methods of Dealership are invoked. In the case of PlaceOrder, a vehicle is *enqueued* on the OrderQueue, while ReadyVehicle causes a vehicle to be *dequeued* from the BuiltQueue. And so on.

Observe that the Dealership's service ReadyVehicle will, when executed, send a request to the Vehicle object that is ready, asking for its Display service. Again, since any particular Vehicle may be a Car or Truck object, and since both Car and Truck classes have redefined Display services, the complete data for each car or truck will be printed without the Dealership having any explicit knowledge of whether it is a Car or Truck object that is responding to the Display request.

In summary, then, we have used a total of six classes: a Dealership class, a Vehicle class and its two subclasses Car and Truck, the Queue class and a String class. Observe that we accomplished the functionality required without having any implementation knowledge whatsoever of the String class. Furthermore, given the existence of the Queue class, and of the Vehicle, Car, and Truck classes, the ordering/receiving functionality of the Dealership required minimal coding. All that was needed was a method for placing vehicle orders, a method for receiving news that a new vehicle is ready, and a menu to control the user interface.

This simplistic example gives just a hint of how powerful processing tools can be built upon other coded abstractions *without knowing about the implementation details* of them. This mode of programming is the current *state of the art*, supporting excellent software engineering practices, especially the extensive reuse of existing code.

Food for Thought

What Science Can't Do (Yet)

In creating behavioral abstractions, we combine a specification of *what an entity is* (its data and structure) with *how it behaves* (its actions). In doing so, we create an algorithmic paradigm that is inherently *social* in nature. Objects *interact* according to how they are defined.

In reaching this point, we have come to a place that touches on many, if not most, of the challenges which both science and society face. It is in the realm of social phenomena that society turns to science for answers and finds little of substance. To date, science has been most successful in understanding and manipulating the *material* world. It has been significantly less successful in understanding and manipulating the world of *human phenomena*. Sociology, psychology, anthropology, management, economics: all these are the new sciences that emerged about the time of electronic media. They are *human sciences* and have been limited in success due to the complex and inherently "messy" attributes that human phenomena present.

As our algorithmic paradigm becomes more and more focused on behavioral abstractions (via the ongoing emergence of the *OO* paradigm), we find ourselves at an important threshold. Such an algorithmic paradigm *means* that our algorithms are based on *social contracts among behavioral entities*. And, as we learn more and more about how to abstract, design, and implement such contracts successfully, we may well get better at being able to abstract and articulate the social contracts that are *implicitly* at work throughout our human world.

We hope this is so, because it is in precisely this arena that our human society faces its pressing dilemmas:

- We seek to understand the workings of our immune systems and our internal "genetic programs." While there is much we do not know, recent research has discovered that these systems involve a great deal of complex interaction among their constituent parts. What are the *implicit contracts* that govern our genetic processes, our biological clocks, our aging mechanisms, and so on?

- We seek a humane society such that fellow citizens do not go without food and shelter. Yet our efforts at social welfare have resulted in unintended consequences that subvert our humane goals. What are the *implicit contracts* that govern human responses to societal systems? How can we support the needy without creating ghettos of dependence which are lacking in hope?

- We seek to educate our populace such that everyone has the basis for a full and productive life. Yet our schools are increasingly unsuccessful at fulfilling their function. What are the *implicit contracts* that determine a student's learning experience? How can we support the need for both knowledge acquisition and critical thinking?

If we enumerate the challenges that our society faces, many of them involve crucial elements of *implicit contracts of interaction* among many entities in a complex system. To date, the human sciences have not achieved scientific rigor such that they produce much in the way of useful information about this kind of phenomena.

As we gain more and more experience with abstracting *explicit* social contracts as the very basis which underlies our algorithmic models, we may be able to better abstract and effectively simulate those *implicit* contracts which are at work in shaping daily human experience. This would seem to be necessary for our human sciences to reach maturity.

Summary

The important idea of behavioral abstraction (which we see manifest in *classes* and *objects*) is the unification of data and the methods which act upon it. By encapsulating both data abstractions and procedural abstractions within a behavioral abstraction, we improve our ability to hide the details of both procedures and data, thus allowing the rest of the algorithm to operate at a higher level of abstraction. Inheritance allows these higher abstractions to be more easily constructed from one another, supporting easier reuse. Utilization of these capabilities permits object-oriented design, in which all abstractions are raised to the level of objects such that an algorithm is a specification of various behavioral entities and how they interact with one another.

Exercises

9.4. Design and implement an *OO* representation of a drive-thru-only bank. Model the behavior of customers and tellers. Be sure to allow for a line of waiting cars.

9.5. Design and implement an *OO* representation of the board game *Monopoly*. You may assume the existence of a random number generator that will serve as dice. You may also restrict the number of properties as you see fit.

9.6. Design and implement an *OO* representation of an airport. Think about this before requesting further specification.

[This page intentionally left blank. }

Part III: The Limits of Computing

[This page intentionally left blank.]

Chapter 10: Concurrency and Parallelism

So far, we have considered algorithms only as if there was a single processor devoted to the execution of a single algorithm. As a practical matter, many computers are used to execute multiple algorithms at the same time. Other computers are designed such that they can devote more than one processor to the execution of a single algorithm. In this chapter, we will introduce the basic concepts that are relevant when we go beyond a simple "one algorithm, one processor" model, and we will consider the implications for algorithmic performance.

Overview:
Concurrency
vs. Parallelism

"Concurrency" and "parallelism" are two terms which become relevant when we go beyond the "one algorithm, one processor" model. They mean quite different things, and it is not unusual to hear them being confused with one another in the general news media. Their respective meanings are given below.

Concurrency

"Concurrency" refers to the execution of multiple different tasks at the same time. For example, at any given moment a time-shared (i.e., multi-user) computer may have a large number of users logged in. In a properly designed and appropriately loaded system, each of these users will have the illusion that the computer is devoted to their job. In reality, the computer is busy juggling various jobs, giving only small "time slices" (small fractions of a second) to each of the many users. In other words, the computer is executing multiple different jobs, or processes, "at the same time."

Notice that I have put quotation marks around "at the same time." This is because we need to be careful about the meaning we attach this phrase. Perhaps there is a single processor that is rapidly taking turns amongst all the users' jobs. Perhaps there are several processors within the single machine such that each processor gives its undivided attention to a single user. Or perhaps each of several processors are rapidly taking turns amongst various users. In the first case (one processor serving several users), the computer is, quite literally, doing only one thing at a time. Thus, strictly speaking, it is *not* doing several tasks "at the same time." However, by rotating its attention among the various users very rapidly, it can give the illusion of doing many things at once. As it rapidly gives service to the various users who are logged in, it spreads its resources (cpu cycles, memory, etc.) amongst the users. It does *not* begin-and-finish one user's job before going on to the next. Instead, it is "in the process" of many jobs at once. We say that such a system serves many users "concurrently."

Concurrency refers to this kind of phenomena (regardless of how many processors are actually built into a given machine): more than one job is being executed at the same time. For a pre-computer example of concurrency, think of your grandmother cooking Thanksgiving dinner: she may have the turkey roasting, and the bread baking, and the beans boiling, all at the same time. Meanwhile, she is busy mashing the potatoes. The preparation of each item on the menu is, logically speaking, a different task. Yet they are going on at the same time, with your grandmother spreading her attention around, monitoring each task as appropriate. In computer jargon, we might think of your grandmother as the "processor" who is "giving service" to multiple "concurrent processes."

Parallelism   Parallelism means something rather different. Where "concurrency" refers to one processor (or more) *sharing attention amongst various tasks*, parallelism refers to the deployment of *multiple processors on the same task*.

For example, science researchers often have reason to analyze large quantities of data and it is sometimes important to analyze the data as quickly as possible. Imagine that a researcher has a huge two dimensional numerical array of C columns by R rows. Imagine further that he has need to find C averages, one for each column's R numbers. With a single processor, an algorithm might sum the R values in the first column, divide that sum by R to find the average for that column, then repeat the same steps iteratively for each of the C columns. With adequate parallel processing capability, a different processor could be assigned to each column. Thus, given C processors, the entire job could be completed in R time, the same time required for a single processor to do "*1/Cth*" of the job.

The crucial quality that defines parallelism is that multiple processors cooperate to collectively do a single job. There are various ways that such cooperation can occur. The number crunching example above is just one such "architecture," one in which each processor shares the same tasks as the others, with each processor focused upon a different subset of data. A real world analogy might be that you want your grandmother to teach you how to bake cookies. As the entire clan is gathering for Thanksgiving, more than one batch of cookies is required. Your grandmother decides that she'll make one batch while instructing you, by both word and example, as you make the other batch. Thus, each of you first makes the cookie dough, each of you spoons it out onto cookie sheets, and so on. In computer jargon, we could say that two batches of cookies are being prepared "in parallel."

Another possible model for parallel processing might occur if, for example, your little brother has insisted on helping make the cookies and your grandmother has decided to keep the peace by giving everyone their own job. Thus, during the first "chunk of time" she has you making a batch of the cookie dough. Then, during the second "chunk of time" (beginning when you say the dough is ready) your grandmother activates two processes: she (a) has your little brother spooning the first-batch dough onto a cookie sheet, and (b) instructs you to take a fresh bowl and make the dough for a second batch. During the third "chunk of time" (i.e., when your brother finishes loading up the cookie sheet and you have the second batch of dough ready), three steps simultaneously occur: (a) your grandmother places the first batch in the oven and monitors the cookies for doneness, (b) your brother is spooning out the second batch onto another cookie sheet, and (c) you prepare a third batch of dough.

Thus, each "processor" (the three people involved) has a different task to complete, with one processor's "output" serving as the "input" to the next processor. We still have multiple processors cooperating on a single task, but this time the work is decomposed such that the various processors depend on one another's' results, and such that their activities must be coordinated. This "architecture" for parallelism is known as "pipeline parallelism," and is the implicit model of the traditional manufacturing assembly line: a job goes down a "pipeline" such that at various points along the way, different processors perform a specific task. Multiple jobs are in the pipeline at the same time, but each one is at a different stage of completion.

Confusion Between the Concurrency and Parallelism

People who don't know much about computational models often confuse the meanings of parallelism and concurrency. This is not surprising, given that the two concepts are both related to the phenomena of having more than one thing happening simultaneously. In fact, for practical purposes of everyday speech, the line between the two can easily become blurred. To see how, return to our example of concurrent processing: your grandmother preparing Thanksgiving dinner.

Let's imagine that your grandfather doesn't have a clue about cooking and, instead of helping, he's "busy" using the remote control to flick between football games. During commercials, he wanders in to the kitchen to smell the food and find out how long until it's time to eat. Since he is oblivious to the particulars of the actual work that's required, all he perceives is that the turkey is roasting in one oven, bread is baking in another, beans are simmering on one burner, while potatoes are boiling on another burner. To him, dinner might mean "one thing" ("time to eat!") more than it means a variety of independent food-prep "algorithms." Thus, from his point of view, he might perceive four different processors (two ovens and two burners) and one task ("make dinner"). From his point of view, we would have multiple processors sharing the work of one task, i.e. "parallelism," not "concurrency."

It might be pointless to use this example to educate him about parallelism vs. concurrency, as his misunderstanding has to do with ignorance of the actual business of cooking, not with any particular terminology. On the other hand, he might easily grasp that cable TV is bringing multiple football games into the house "concurrently," while each play of each game features 11 "parallel processors" per team.

Concurrency

Four Kinds of Concurrent Systems

As we have seen, concurrency refers to the processing of multiple different tasks "at the same time." With respect to computing systems, there are four kinds of concurrent systems. Of these, three have names which include "multi"; these three are commonly confused with one another. All four are described below.

Multiprogramming

"Multiprogramming" refers to a system in which a single processor shares its attention among various users. The original time-shared computer systems found in universities and industry were examples of multiprogramming. In such systems, there is only a single processor and thus only one user's job can receive attention at any given moment. The illusion of simultaneous processing is achieved by the rapid swapping of processor attention amongst the various active jobs.

Multiprocessing

"Multiprocessing" is similar to multiprogramming, with the difference that the computer contains multiple processors. The various processors share a common pool of memory and, since a given pool of memory can respond to only one processor at a time, the various processors access to memory must be coordinated; thus, the systems themselves are more complex. Typically, just as in multiprogramming systems, a processor's attention is distributed in small time slices to multiple concurrent user jobs. Since there are multiple processors, several jobs are being processed at any given moment. Thus, the difference between multiprogramming and multiprocessing is simply that, in the latter, there is more than one processor that swaps its attention among various jobs.

Multitasking

"Multitasking" refers to the ability of a single user to have many jobs proceeding concurrently. Note the difference between "multiprogramming" and "multitasking": the former refers to concurrent processing of "multiple jobs, each one belonging to one of multiple concurrent users"; the latter refers to "multiple concurrent jobs of a single user." Until recently, multitasking was unique to large time-shared systems that would allow a single user to run multiple programs at the same time. In the last decade, however, this capability has migrated to PCs. A PC user can now have multiple "windows" open concurrently with, for example, a word processor running in one window, a spreadsheet in another, a communications package in a third, and so on. The first generations of such systems achieved the illusion of multitasking via swapping the single processor's attention among the various jobs (similar to the idea behind multiprogramming). Later generations of PC hardware and software support true multitasking via processor (hardware) designs that allow the processor to act like multiple independent processors, each one giving its undivided attention to a single task.

Distributed systems   "Distributed systems" refers to systems which do not reside in a single box or at a single location. Instead, they consist of multiple computers, each with its own memory and each with one or more processors, that reside at different sites. Each subsystem, or "node," of the system has its own set of tasks to do, which it does more-or-less independently from the other "nodes" of the system. However, the various nodes communicate with each other to insure the appropriate functioning of the system as a whole. A common example is the reservation systems used by airlines, travel agents, etc. Such a system does not exist in any particular place but instead is literally "distributed" across various sites.

Distributed systems are *not* like a large time-shared system which allows multiple users to log on concurrently. Instead, many computers at different sites processes transactions and interact with a database of relevant information. Even the database itself is likely to be distributed across various sites. Such systems prevent many of the "bottleneck" problems of time-shared systems. However, they introduce greater degrees of complexity. Instead of a single operating system governing a large, complex computer, a distributed system features many independent operating systems and other software which must interact with each other. In effect, there is no one program that is "in charge." Instead, control is distributed to many programs that must cooperate with one another. In human terms, a distributed system is less like a dictatorship (centralized control) and more like a complex society with various competing constituents.

Issues in Concurrency

The move from single processor, single job systems to concurrent systems which juggle various competing demands implies more complexity. Not only might multiple processors need to share a common pool of memory, but mechanisms must support the swapping of processor attention from one task to another. The governing of processor behavior, the swapping of processor attention among various jobs, and the swapping of the various jobs in and out of memory is handled by the computer's operating system. The operating system is, in effect, the first program that the computer runs, and it is this program that allows the computer to run other programs. In concurrent systems, the operating system typically must have capabilities for addressing each of the following three issues.

Protection   With many tasks being processed at once, steps must be taken to insure that one task does not interfere with or contaminate the work of another task. Thus, memory must be partitioned appropriately so that each task's data resides in its own partition. Each task must be prevented from writing data to a memory location that belongs to another task. As tasks come and go, begin and end, the partitioning of memory can become very complicated. As a result there are various "memory management" algorithms which govern how the operating system allocates memory to the various tasks.

Protection is an issue that applies to all other resources as well, e.g., printers, disk drives, modems, etc. For example, if one task has sent text to the printer, all other tasks must be prevented from sending their data to the printer until the task which "has" the printer is finished. In practice, the operating system manages a queue for each resource; only the task at the head of the queue can have access to that resource.

Fairness   "Fairness" has its usual meaning. In concurrent systems, it refers to the need to guarantee that each job gets its "fair share" of processor attention and other resources (memory, disk, printer, etc.). It comes into play when factors of one job affect the resources available to other jobs. For example, imagine that a given concurrent system can handle 10 jobs at a time (this would be a very small system, but it will suffice for our example). What is fair?

At first, it would seem that normal queue behavior would result in fairness, i.e., "first come, first served." This certainly seems fair enough. But... what if ten different users happen to log on, each with their own extremely long job? Imagine that each of these long jobs is 100 times longer than the average job. Thus, under FCFS, these ten users will occupy the system for a time equal to the average load of 1000 users. Is it fair to allow a small number of users to monopolize a shared system? Is it fair that all other users be locked out of the system? What if this policy was applied to the time-shared system you use to submit your assignments? What if the system was tied up for 72 hours straight by a small number of users with big jobs?

So, what might be more fair? Perhaps we could give different priorities to each job based on how much time it's used already. Under such a scheme, new jobs would get a high priority and a big "time slice" of service. Since many jobs are short, we would hope that giving high priority to new jobs would move them through the system rapidly, allowing users to get done and get off, thus making way for new users to login. When faced with a long job, the priority for that job would gradually fall. The longer the job was in the system, the smaller its time slice. In addition, every so often, we would "swap out" the large jobs to disk, effectively making the long jobs take turns with one another instead of monopolizing the whole system.

This certainly seems fairer. We make the long jobs wait a bit, thus allowing fast jobs to get done quicker. In effect, we punish those with huge jobs and reward those with short jobs. We might do this in a way that would encourage those with large jobs to do them at non-peak hours, i.e., let them run faster if they wait til the "dead" hours to run them. This approach would certainly please the largest number of users, and even those with large jobs would agree that it's more fair. But.... how do we insure that the large jobs get *enough* time to finish in reasonable time?

In practice, there is a real danger of having the large (and thus "older") jobs get smaller and smaller amounts of processor attention, to the point where a particularly large job *never* gets finished. This is neither fair to that user, nor is it desirable from the operating system's standpoint. We *want* to get rid of the old, big job. Furthermore, a basic tenet of fairness is that all jobs get to finish in "reasonable" time. There are various proven ways to address this problem, involving various priority levels and queues that are based on priority, not just time of arrival.

Deadlock   "Deadlock" refers to the phenomena of computer systems freezing up because each job is "on hold" waiting for something it cannot have. For example, imagine that we have a concurrent system that can handle only three jobs at once.

Job One wants to print data from disk to the printer. At the moment, it "has" the disk, but is waiting for the printer. It will not give up the disk until it gets the printer and prints its data because, if it were to give up the disk, then getting the printer would do it no good: it couldn't obtain the data it wants to print. However, Job Three has the printer.

Job Two wants to receive data from another source over a modem and write that data to disk. It "has" the modem, i.e., is connected to the other source, but is waiting for the disk. It will not give up the modem until it gets the disk because, if it were to give up the modem, then getting the disk would do it not good: it couldn't obtain the data it wants to write to the disk. However, Job One has the disk.

Job Three wants to print data that it receives over the modem. It "has" the printer, but is waiting for the modem. It will not give up the printer until it gets the modem because, if it were to give up the printer, then getting the modem would do it not good: it couldn't obtain the data it wants to print. However, Job Two has the modem.

Thus, each job is occupying a resource while waiting for another resource to become free. Unfortunately, none of the needed resources will become free, as they are held by another job, which is in turn waiting for another resource. In effect, it is the same problem as traffic "gridlock": a car occupies a space and cannot move until another car moves, but the other cars can't move because they're waiting for other cars, and so on, in a circular fashion.

There are a few policies that can be implemented algorithmically that can prevent deadlock. We might prevent jobs from "holding" resources that they're not actually using. We might establish a hierarchy of resources and implement a rule that only allows a job to hold a "low" resource while waiting for a "high" one, but prevents a job from holding a "high" one while waiting for a low one. As with issues of fairness and protection, there are various strategies and permutations.

Summary   The issues of protection, fairness, and deadlock, each provide a host of problems. Any given solution usually contributes a further problem. The particulars of such algorithms are included in the subject matter of other courses, and are beyond our focus here.

What is important is that you notice that we've got a host of algorithmic problems that are *created* by the fact that we're trying to handle multiple tasks concurrently. Such problems, and their solution algorithms, are "overhead" costs, i.e., they take processor time, they take up memory, yet they don't accomplish any "real work"; instead, they are a "cost of doing business," a price to be paid in order to make concurrency work.

We find many real world analogies. In general, as a system becomes more complex, as it tries to do more and more things, the cost of "complexity management" rises rapidly, often exponentially. More and more resources are consumed by "overhead costs," and less and less resources are available to do "real work." Everyday examples include "large anything": large universities, large charities, "big government," large software development projects, extravagantly staged rock tours, etc., etc.

However, this does not provide any compelling evidence *against* large systems. It only points out that their overhead costs will be high. The other side of the coin is that large systems often can do things that simply cannot be done by small systems.

Distributed systems are, in effect, an attempt to get the "best of both worlds" (the power of large systems with the benefits of small systems) via the connection of numerous small, simpler systems. Each node is notably smaller and simpler than the comparable large system would be. The viability of distributed systems is dependent upon (a) adequate bandwidth (physical capacity for communication) to allow the nodes to communicate effectively, and (b) adequate protocols (rules for communication and interaction) which concisely yet effectively govern the behavior of the various nodes with respect to one another and which guarantee the the "whole job" gets done.

Parallelism   Parallelism refers to the use of multiple processors to reduce the time required to complete a single task. There are a couple of factors that come into play in determining how much parallelism is possible. Properties of the algorithm that is to be "parallelized" typically limit how much gain is possible, i.e., just because we might have a machine with 100 processors, we cannot assume that we can achieve a speed-up by a factor of 100. We shall discuss these factors, show their impact on performance for given algorithms, and utilize a graphical method for representing the parallel potential for a given algorithm. We will also make clear the potential impact of parallelism, both for algorithms in general and for different classes of problems.

An example: Before delving into key issues of parallelism, let's consider an example. Recall that the `Bubblesort` algorithm sorts a list of numbers by repeatedly comparing adjacent values and moving the larger value to the right. In general, it requires N-1 comparisons-and-maybe swaps on the first pass in order to move the largest value to its proper position. With the largest value in place, it then requires N-2 comparisons-and-maybe swaps to move the second-largest value into its proper position, and so on. We have seen that Bubblesort requires O(N) passes of O(N) work per pass, and is thus an O(N^2) algorithm.

Let's now take the idea behind `Bubblesort` (i.e., repeatedly "comparing adjacent values and reordering the pair if necessary") but imagine that we can use as many processors as we want. What kind of performance can we achieve? How might we go about this?

One approach would be to utilize multiple processors such that we can do multiple comparison-and-maybe-swaps at once. For example we might compare the numbers in the first and second positions while simultaneously comparing those in the third and fourth, the fifth and sixth, the seventh and eighth, and so on. In effect, for any even N, we could use N/2 processors to allow us to do N/2 comparisons-and-maybe swaps in one "time chunk."

To see what would happen, let's consider a "bad" scenario for sorting: we wish to sort the numbers into ascending order but the original list has them sorted in descending order. For any even N numbers, this guarantees that we must move each and every number in the list. Below, we show what happens during the first "time chunk." We indicate each of the various processors as dotted lines beneath the pair of numbers that each processor is comparing-and-maybe-swapping, and we then show the resulting state of the list.

```
Original list of 8 numbers
          93  87    74  65    57  45    33  27
N/2 procs: +---+---+ +---+---+ +---+---+ +---+---+
          87  93    65  74    45  57    27  33
List after 1 time chunk
```

Thus, in the first time chunk, we have compared-and-maybe-swapped four (N/2) pairs of numbers.

For the second "time chunk," we might shift our processors over one position, e.g., comparing the values in the second and third positions, the fourth and fifth positions, the sixth and seventh positions, all simultaneously.

```
List after 1 time chunk
        87    93    65    74    45    57    27    33
        +---+---+  +---+---+  +---+---+
        87    65    93    45  74    27    57    33
List after 2 time chunks
```

For the third "time chunk" we might shift our processors back (as the were in the first "time chunk"), and continue in this fashion, alternating which pairs of numbers are compared-and-maybe-swapped, until such time as the entire list is sorted.

In effect, we are having the various processors "vibrate" back an forth between odd/even and even/odd number positions. We show the results of the rest of this "vibrate sort" process, below.

```
List as it
exists after
Time Chunk:

0          93    87    74    65    57    45    33    27
           +---+---+  +---+---+  +---+---+  +---+---+
1          87    93    65    74    45    57    27    33
                 +---+---+  +---+---+  +---+---+
2          87    65    93    45    74    27    57    33
           +---+---+  +---+---+  +---+---+  +---+---+
3          65    87    45    93    27    74    33    57
                 +---+---+  +---+---+  +---+---+
4          65    45    87    27    93    33    74    57
           +---+---+  +---+---+  +---+---+  +---+---+
5          45    65    27    87    33    93    57    74
                 +---+---+  +---+---+  +---+---+
6          45    27    65    33    87    57    93    74
           +---+---+  +---+---+  +---+---+  +---+---+
7          27    45    33    65    57    87    74    93
                 +---+---+  +---+---+  +---+---+
8          27    33    45    57    65    74    87    93
```

By the end of eight "time chunks" the entire list of eight numbers is in the correct sorted order. Thus, in this instance, we have exploited parallelism to reduce the time cost of the sorting algorithm from $O(N^2)$ to $O(N)$.

Product Complexity The example, above, illustrates the first *limitation* of parallelism. Observe that, while we have reduced *time*, we have not reduced the total *work*. True, we can get the job done in only $O(N)$ time. However, we do so at a cost of $O(N)$ work per each time chunk. $O(N)$ work for each of $O(N)$ time chunks still shows a total of $O(N^2)$ work.

☐ A basic principle of parallelism: it *cannot* produce the same results in *less work*. All parallelism can do is transfer the required work to multiple processors such that more work can get done in any given chunk of time. Thus, an $O(N)$ algorithm is still (at best) $O(N)$, an $O(N^2)$ algorithm is still at least $O(N^2)$, and so on. Parallelism does not provide any magic by which total work is reduced; all parallelism can do is shift that work into fewer chunks of time by having multiple processors working at once.

When we considered algorithms and assumed that we had only one processor available, there was no real difference between "time" and "work." Each "time chunk" allowed the processor to do one piece of work, i.e., we could equate "time" and "work." When we introduce multiple processors, we break this 1:1 correspondence between time and work. Instead, we have what is known as "product complexity": "the amount of work per time chunk" multiplied times "the number of time chunks." For any given algorithmic approach to a problem, parallelism may change the required time, but cannot improve on the "product complexity."

This fact allows us to quickly estimate the "ceiling of improvement" that parallelism can provide. For example, imagine that we have an $O(NlogN)$ algorithm that we wish to parallelize. Further, imagine that we have $logN$ processors available. These facts alone are sufficient to let us conclude that the "new improved" parallel version of the algorithm will require *at least* $O(N)$ time. Similarly, having N processors available for an algorithmic approach that is $O(N^3)$ means that we will be able to do no better than $O(N^2)$ time, and so on.

Notice that we have said that the product complexity allows us to quickly gauge the "ceiling of improvement," and that we have used phrases such as "no better than" or "at least" so much work. The product complexity tells us the *best that we can hope for*. How much of this desired gain can be actually achieved is determined by four particular factors, discussed below.

Fixed Number of Processors   Notice that we have casually referred to having N processors or $logN$ processors. In actual fact, the number of processors available is a factor of hardware. Just because N might double, that doesn't mean that we can magically double the number of processors available!

Typically, the number of processors available in a parallel architecture is some power of 2. Thus, we might have a parallel machine that features an array of 16 processors or or 256 or 1024. As time goes by, it is reasonable to expect that the number of processors built in to state-of-the-art parallel machines will grow. But it is absurd to think that this number will conveniently grow with whatever N might be for the problem at hand.

In practice, the number of processors is a *constant*. This means that order of magnitude improvements in processing time are limited to those N where N is no greater than the number of processors available. For all other "inconvenient N," processing time can be improved by no more than a fixed factor, e.g., "twice as fast" or "a thousand times as fast." Such improvements are sometimes quite valuable. In certain situations, they are necessary. But such improvement is something quite different than the order of magnitude improvements required to "revolutionize" computing or to "break the barrier" of problems which are, for practical purposes, too costly to be solvable (more about these in the next chapter.).

Overhead Costs Parallelization does not come free. There must be some way to relate the algorithmic problem at hand to the hardware such that each processor "knows" what to do. And, as we have stressed many times, processors have no sense whatsoever. Thus, there must be some mechanism that allocates the attention of various processors to the appropriate parts of the algorithm and/or subsets of data. So far, we have conveniently ignored this issue.

- For example, in our "vibrate sort," above, we simply assumed that the various processors would compare-and-maybe-swap the "right pair" of numbers, based simply upon what we imagined that we'd *want* them to do. However, we did nothing to make it happen that way.

- Similarly, early in the chapter, we briefly discussed the parallelization of an algorithm for averaging each of C columns of R rows of numbers in a two-dimensional array. In that case, we imagined that each processor would execute the inner loop of the sequential algorithm (i.e., sum a given column of numbers, then divide by R) for a different column. In effect, the outer loop of the sequential algorithm (do the inner loop for each column) was effectively replaced by the multiple processors. Yet, we discussed no means of *making* each processor deal with "its own" column.

In reality, we'd need some algorithmic way to *govern* which processor does what. And, like anything else, this does not come free. The costs associated with instructing the various processors to "do the right thing" depends on the particulars of the parallel processing environment, i.e., it is implementation specific. Thus, there are no general rules of thumb that we can apply across the board. Because the details are implementation specific, and because we are concerned with general principles, for the rest of this chapter we will continue to "wave our hands" at the overhead costs involve. In effect, we will ignore them.

Be advised, however, that they are there and that they can be quite significant. Often, they require that an algorithm be completely rewritten in a programming language designed for parallelism, often by an expensive programmer who specializes in such things. Often times the result will not generalize, i.e., a parallel version of an algorithm designed for one machine with X processors not work on another machine that has Y processors.

One way to think about the costs of parallelization is to imagine real-world, human situations in which things are done in parallel. This occurs whenever an organization has multiple people doing the same thing. Observe that the supervision of such tasks is a primary reason for the existence of "management." Observe, too, that in large organizations (where, presumably, there is a greater deal of parallelization going on) the "management level" has typically grown to be many levels, and that the costs of management has often grown to dwarf those costs which can be rationalized.

With that in mind, let us continue to two issues of parallelization which are indeed properties of the algorithms themselves and not related to either hardware specifics or overhead costs.

Dependencies

By "dependencies" we refer to relationships among various steps within an algorithm such that one step *depends upon* another step for data. For example, consider the following algorithm:

```
begin
(S1)  read(A)
(S2)  B <- A * 3
(S3)  C <- B * A
end
```

The algorithm consists of three statements (labeled *S1* through *S3*). There are two dependencies in this algorithm. First, *S2* assigns a new value to the variable B, based on computation applied to the value stored in variable A. The value of variable A is determined by the execution of *S1*. Thus, *S2* depends on *S1*, i.e., *S2* cannot do its job until after *S1* has done its job.

Similarly, *S3* (which assigns a new value to variable C) depends on both *S1* (for the value of A) and *S2* (for the value of B). Thus, *S3* cannot be executed until both *S1* and *S2* have completed.

From this, we can see that this particular algorithm cannot benefit from parallelization. Regardless of how many processors are available, it will require three time chunks to execute: the first time chunk for *S1*, the second for *S2*, and the third for *S3*. Given an unlimited number of processors, the execution of this algorithm will require the same amount of time as is required given only a single processor.

We represent this state of affairs via a *dependency graph* which shows the various statements of an algorithm. Time is represented in the vertical dimension (rows) and the number of processors in the horizontal dimension (columns). Downward arrows represent the dependencies. Thus, the algorithm above would be represented as:

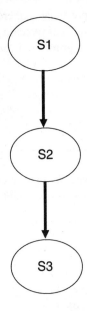

This indicates that three time chunks (vertical rows) are required and that only one processor can be utilized (horizontal columns).

An algorithm of three steps that does not feature any dependencies, such as,

```
begin
{S1}   read(A)
{S2}   B <- B + 3
{S3}   C <- C * 4
end
```

would be represented as:

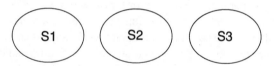

indicating that it could be performed in one time chunk by three processors.

Consider the algorithm:

```
begin
{S1}  read(A)
{S2}  read(B)
{S3}  C <- A * 4
{S4}  D <- B / 3
{S5}  E <- C * D
{S6}  F <- D + 8
end
```

Observe that there are various dependencies involved here: *S3* depends on *S1*, *S6* depends on *S4*, *S5* depends on both *S3* and *S4*, etc. How many processors can we make use of? And how much execution time can we save? Drawing a dependency graph gives us a way to answer these questions:

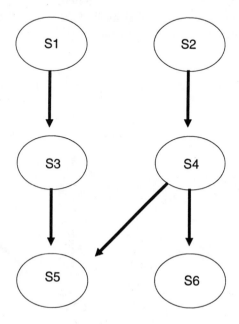

The first two statements feature no dependencies between themselves and thus can occur in parallel (one processor for *S1*, another for *S2*). *S3* is dependent on *S1* and may execute only after *S1* is finished. Similarly, *S4* is dependent upon *S2* and must go after *S2*. *S5* is dependent upon both *S3* and *S4* and must wait for both of them. *S6* need only wait for *S4*. The graph indicates that we can utilize two processors to execute the algorithm in three time chunks (vs. six time chunks using one processor). Several processors would do no good here: the dependencies of the algorithm determine that two processors is the most we can use.

For a more complex example, consider the following algorithm:

```
begin
    I <- 1
    loop
            exitif (I < MaxArray)
    {S1}    read(A[I])
    {S2}    B[I] <- A[I] + 4
    {S3}    C[I] <- A[I] / 3
    {S4}    D[I] <- B[I] / C[I]
            I <- I + 1
    endloop
end
```

This algorithm accesses four different arrays (A, B, C, and D). Each pass through the loop accesses the *Ith* element of each array. For *each pass*, *S2* and *S3* are dependent upon *S1*, while *S4* is dependent upon both *S2* and *S3*. Thus, the dependency graph is:

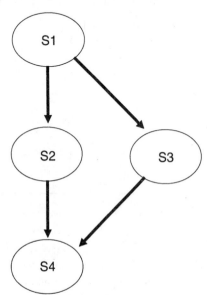

This shows that we can utilize two processors to get the job done in three time chunks. We do not fully utilize the second processor: it is busy only during the second time chunk. Thus, while we double the number of processors, we only reduce our time from four time chunks to three.

Recall that the four steps occur in a loop, and that each pass through the loop references a different index into the four arrays. Since each iteration deals with a different index, we will "wave our hands" and "decree" that we will have different processors deal with each such array index. We are concerned here only with those statements that do "real work" (those labeled *S1..S4*). (We are conveniently ignoring the *exitif* and I <- I+1 statements. These are precisely the statements that any parallel algorithm would need to find some way to replace or otherwise cope with in a real implementation, but don't worry about this aspects now.) In our graph, we refer to the steps in the first loop pass as *S1..S4*, the steps of the second pass as *S1'..S4'* (i.e., "S1 prime"), the steps of the third pass as *S1"..S4"* (i.e., "S1 double-prime"), etc. If MaxArray is *3*, the dependency graph looks like:

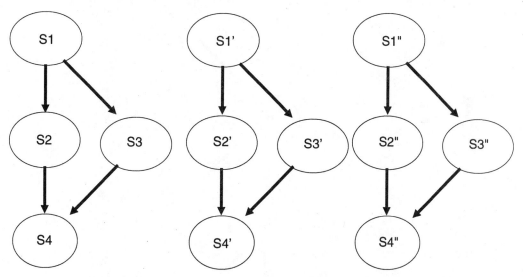

This graph represents that we can complete the work of processing data for our various three-element arrays in three time chunks utilizing six processors. We can generalize this for an array of size *N*: if we have *2N* processors, we can finish the job in only three time chunks. This is tells us the limit of maximum parallelization, given unlimited resources.

Of course, we may have limited resources. For example, what if we were limited to those processors that we could keep fully utilized? (By "fully utilize," we mean that the processors will not be sitting idly by "once the algorithm gets cranked up"; we can tolerate some idle cycles at the beginning and end, however.) By observing the "holes" in the previous graph and by examining the pattern of the per-loop dependency graphs, we can arrive at the graph shown below.

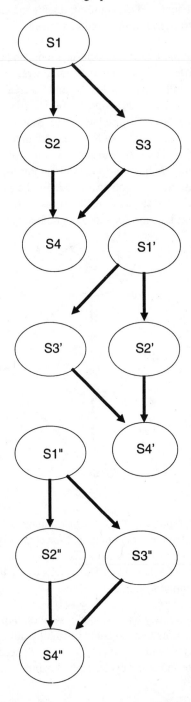

We have created a repeating pattern that keeps both processors utilized. How much time is required for arrays of size *N*? The first pass through the loop completes in 3 time chunks, the second pass completes in 5 time chunks, the third completes in 7 time chunks, the fourth in 9, and so on.

Thus, this graph indicates that we can fully utilize two processors in such a way that we can process arrays of N elements via the given algorithm in (2N + 1) time chunks for any N.

Precedences

"Precedence" relationships are similar to dependencies, in that they refer to the need to *block* the execution of a subsequent statement until a prior statement completes. The reason for this blockage is different however. In a dependency relationship, *S2* would be blocked from executing until *S1* has completed *because S2* needs the data value *produced by S1*. In a *precedence relationship* the blockage occurs because the execution of *S2* would *contaminate* the data needed by *S1*. For example:

```
begin
    X <- 1
    loop
            exitif (X > 3)
    {S1}    read(A)
    {S2}    print(A)
    {S3}    A <- A * 7
    {S4}    print(A)
            X <- X + 1
    endloop
end
```

Observe here that we cannot allow *S3* to execute until after *S2* has executed. Why? It is *not* because *S3* "needs a value" from *S2*; it does not. Instead, *S3* must be prevented from executing until after *S2* is finished because *S3* will alter a value that *S2* must have unaltered. If *S3* executes before *S2*, it will contaminate the data that *S2* is accessing. This is the essence of a precedence relationship: a later statement must be stopped from contaminating the data used by an earlier statement.

A precedence graph is used to show both dependency and precedence relationships. It is identical to a dependency graph except that precedences are also indicated graphically. A *dependency* is indicated (as before) by a downward pointing arrow; a *precedence* is indicated by a downward arrows featuring a horizontal bar, e.g.:

Dependency: Precedence:

Consider the algorithm below:

```
begin
    I <- 1
    loop
          exitif (I > N)
    S1   read(A[I])
    S2   A[I] <- A[I] * 7
    S3   C <- A[I] / 3
    S4   print(C)
         I <- I + 1
    endloop
end
```

At first glance, this would appear to be readily parallelizable, i.e., each pass through the loop deals with a different index into array A and, thus, we might be able to use as many processors as we've got, one processor per index. However, each pass through the loop accesses (writes to and reads from) the simple variable C. Thus, *S3* from the second pass cannot execute until *S4* from the first pass is done, else the wrong value of C will be printed out.

As it stands (see graph, next page), we can utilize no more than two processors; by luck those two can be fully utilized. How much time will execution take for an array of N elements? The first pass is done after 4 time chunks, the 2nd pass after 6, the third pass after 8, and so on. Thus, the parallel version requires $(2N + 2)$ time chunks and can utilize no more than two processors.

Observe that a data structure optimization can make everything run faster. If we declared C to be an array of the same size as A, rather than as an atomic variable, then the precedence would no longer exist. Each pass through the loop could calculate then print C[I] instead of C. Making this change would allow us to process an array of size N in only 4 time chunks given N processors.

For another example, consider the following algorithm. This one accesses eight different arrays of size N.

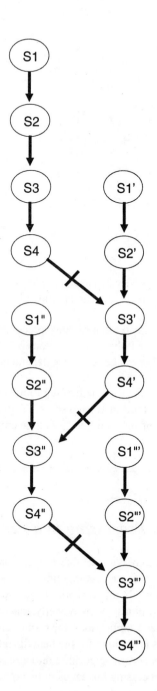

```
begin
    I <- 1
    loop
        exitif (I > N)
S1  A[I] <- A[I] * B[I]
S2  read(B[I])
S3  C[I] <- A[I] / 3
S4  D[I] <- B[I] * A[I+1]
S5  E[I] <- B[I] * C[I]
S6  F[I] <- E[I] * 7
S7  G[I] <- E[I} / 9
S8  H[I] <- C[I] mod 5
        I <- I + 1
    endloop
end
```

In light of the various dependencies and precedences, what degree of parallelization is possible? How many processors can be utilized? What time performance results?

The graph (next page) indicates that we have precedences such that each *S1* blocks the *S2* of the same iteration (why?) and that each *S4* blocks the *S1* of the subsequent iteration (why?). All other relationships are dependencies.

Given this graph, we observe that the first iteration completes in 4 time chunks, the second iteration in 7, the third in 10, and so on. This repeating patterns translates in completion for an array of size N in (3N + 1) time chunks utilizing a maximum of three processors.

Food for Thought:

Distributed Processing in a Free Society

In the recent past, there were considerable expectations that parallel processing would become a dominant force in computing via desktop computers featuring arrays of parallel processors. In this scenario, the array of parallel processors would collectively execute algorithms. More recently, that expectation has changed. Except for certain specialized applications, the cost of creating algorithms for parallel processing architectures is too high for the benefits obtained. (Remember, parallelism cannot turn an *unreasonable* algorithm into a *reasonable* one.) Instead, we can expect to see parallel processing impact us in two other ways, both of which are already well under way.

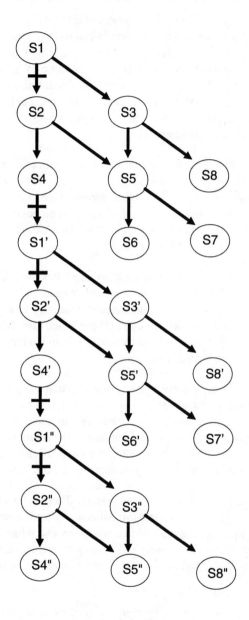

First, we will continue to see the deployment of multiple specialized processors in a computer such that each one has its own special task. There is still a single cpu, but it is supported by other processors that handle specific kinds of work so that the cpu is liberated from handling those tasks. For example, PCs frequently feature video boards that have their own processor so the cpu doesn't have to spend cycles managing the video display. Similarly, there is often another processor to manage data transfer between the hard disk and the computer's RAM. This trend of specialized device processors will continue.

Second, and more significantly, computation will occur concurrently via *distributed systems*. As mentioned earlier, distributed systems spread the work among various sites in such a way that there is no single centralized algorithm who coordinates and controls the others. Instead, multiple distributed processing sites cooperate to make the system work according to protocols which establish how each distributed process may affect the rest of the system.

The latter approach, *distributed systems*, mirrors what we see in society at large. During much of the 20th Century, we saw the dominance of "supergovernments" devoted to centralized control of many aspects of society. Examples range from the Fascist governments of the '30's and 40's (Hitler's Germany, Mussolini's Italy, and Tojo's Japan) to the Russia-dominated Soviet block, to the humane Social-Democratic governments of Northern Europe.

In recent years, the trend has been clearly in a direction away from centralized government management of society. The widespread view is that such governments not only interfere with individual liberty, but are also notoriously inefficient and thus imply huge overhead costs to their cultures. The recent trend has been to reduce government controls in order to allow the more efficient "market forces" to have the freedom to operate without government hindrance

Market forces are, in effect, a distributed system. There is no single centralized algorithm at work to set prices or establish policies. Instead, a multitude of companies operate under the rules of free enterprise, and whatever happens happens. Successful companies prosper and create jobs, while inefficient companies fail and go away. Unlike centralized government control, it is *self-correcting dynamic* process.

As with any distributed system, it presents its own set of problems: What are the rules that govern the behavior of each distributed process? How do want them to behave? Exactly how are they allowed to interact? And so on. As we saw in our discussion of *concurrent systems* (of which *distributed systems* are one example), there are always key issues to be tackled.

Among these issues is *fairness*. Fairness implies the application of some policy of values. Is it fair to let high priority users always get system resources first? Do we want a system that might keep a low priority user waiting forever such that he never gets service? How do we define what fairness means? And, once we define it, how do we implement that definition of fairness in an algorithm?

In fact, we always face two fairness-related questions: "What do we mean by fairness?" (which is a *policy* question) and "How do we guarantee that fairness happens?" (which is an *algorithmic* question). These questions are implicit in *any multi-user concurrent system.*

One of many ways to think about the free enterprise system is as one example of a *multi-user concurrent system.* If we think of it in these terms, these two questions regarding fairness (*policy* and *algorithm*) are among the key issues that our society is forced to confront.

The tension lies in the fact that, while free enterprise is indeed a very *efficient* system, it is not a *moral* system. (Nor is it *immoral*. Rather, it is *amoral*. Morality does not drive it, one way or another. Profitability does.) Thus, we can observe that it was *not* "free enterprise" that eliminated slavery. Or outlawed abusive child labor practices. Or allowed workers to engage in collective bargaining. Or established individual liberty rights. Or insisted on a healthy environment. Rather, it is always *government* that does those things.

By now, it is clear to many that free enterprise provides society with dynamic forces of creativity and growth, while government protects the citizenry from the excesses of an amoral market system. What is unclear is exactly what the interface between them should be. What are the standards of *fairness* and *responsibility* that our society wants its dynamic business forces to honor? And how shall those policies be implemented? And who should be in charge of each?

One of many ways to characterize modern politics is to say that that one political party wants government to be in charge of fairness issues, while the opposing party claims that government an inefficient meddler that should "butt out." In the years to come, you will likely hear much more argument and debate on this. As you listen to that debate, or as you participate in it, remember what the Computing Perspective says: There are *two* questions here, not one. A question of *policy* ("What do we mean by *fair* and *responsible*?") and the question of *algorithm* ("How shall we *implement* our fairness policy?").

Who do you think is best responsible for *fairness policy*? And who should be held accountable for its implementation?

Summary

Concurrency refers to one or more processors giving attention to multiple tasks at the same time or within the same "chunk of time."

- There are four kinds of concurrent systems: *multiprogramming, multiprocessing, multitasking,* and *distributed* systems.

- Three key issues that must be addressed in making concurrent systems work are *protection, fairness,* and *deadlock.*

Parallelism refers to multiple processors working concurrently on the same task.

- *Product complexity* refers to an inherent limitation of parallel performance: parallelism can reduce time, but it cannot reduce work. Product complexity is (*time * number of processors*) = *work*. For a given number of parallel processors, product complexity allows us to estimate the *ceiling of improvement* that parallel processing can provide. Actual improvement is generally less than this ceiling due to various overhead costs implied in managing parallelism.

- Due to the limitation implied by product complexity, parallelism does not allow us to make unreasonable algorithms perform reasonably, nor can it make intractable problems tractable.

- *Dependency* relationships limit the degree to which an algorithm may be parallelized due to the need of a given algorithmic statement to have data that is produced by a previous algorithmic statement, e.g., statement "A" must complete before statement "B" so that it can produce the data that statement "B" requires.

- *Precedence* relationships also limit the degree to which an algorithm may be parallelized due to the need for a give algorithmic statement to complete prior to the execution of a subsequent statement which may corrupt its data, e.g., statement "A" must complete before statement "B" corrupts the data that statement "A" requires.

Exercises

For problems 10.1 and 10.2, draw a precedence graph for the algorithms provided, showing the *maximum number of processors* that can be utilized. The numbers to the left of the loop-body statements are for statement identification purposes. For a second occurrence of a given statement, use X', where X is a statement number; for a third occurrence, use X", and so on.

Note: Read(SomeVar) operations *which act on the same variable* must be sequentialized, e.g., two Read(B[3]) statements cannot execute in the same time chunk.

Two statements *which act on different variables*, such as Read(B[3]) and Read(B[4]), can execute concurrently.

10.1.
```
      begin
         I <- 1
         loop
S1       A[I] <- 2 * I
S2       B[I] <- I + I
S3       C[I] <- A[I] * B[I]
S4       D[I] <- E[I] + (A[I] / 2) + (2 * B[I])
S5       E[I] <- C[I] * C[I]
            I <- I + 1
            exitif (I >= 2)
          endloop
      end
```

10.2.
```
      begin
         I <- 1
         loop
            exitif (I > 2)
S1       Read(B[I])
S2       A[I] <- I * I + 3
S3       D[I] <- A[I] * B[I]
S4       C[I] <- A[I] / 2 + I - A[I+1]
S5       E[I] <- C[I] / D[I]
S6       Read(C[I])
            I <- I + 1
          endloop
      end
```

For problems 10.3 through 10.6, you are given an array of numbers of size M (assume M is very large). Your task is to find the average of the values in the array. Assume each mathematical operation takes one "time chunk" of processor time. Do *not* give *Big Oh* for your answer. You need to report the actual number of "time chunks." Explain your answers.

10.3. How much time is required if 1 processor is used ?

10.4. How much time is required if 2 processors are used ?

10.5. How much time is required if 4 processors are used ?

10.6. How much time is required if an unlimited number of processors are available? What is the maximum number of processors that can be utilized?

[This page intentionally left blank.]

Chapter 11: Hierarchies of Complexity

The Complexity of Problems   In Chapter 7, we considered various performance categories of algorithms, identified each as being reasonable or unreasonable, and considered the implications of performance in each category. Notice that all of this concerned particular *algorithms*, i.e., particular solutions to problems.

Of course, we'd like to have this kind of information about *problems*, not just *algorithms*. If we only have information about *algorithms*, then we can't say very much about what is "do-able" and what isn't. Why? In a given instance, perhaps we're just looking at a poor algorithm and, with a better one, the "hard" problem would become easily solvable. After all, someone might invent a better algorithm tomorrow.

Fortunately, there is much we that do know about the limitations involved in solving various kinds of problems. In fact, we can characterize many kinds of problems in a way that's similar to how we classify particular algorithms.

Recall that we considered three measures of algorithm performance: *best case, average case, and worst case*. Of these, we focus on *worst* case and *average* cases, as they tell us the performance constraints that we'll have to tolerate. We pay rather little attention to *best* case, as we rarely worry about things "going right." For problems, however, it'd be useful to have measures analogous to "best case" and "worst case," i.e., we'd like to know the performance of the best kind of solution we can hope for (even if we don't know what that solution is), and we'd also like to know the performance of the worst kind of solution we might have to tolerate. And, as it turns out, we do have such measures, measures which refer to the *complexity of problems*.

To understand the nature of "problem complexity," it is necessary to understand the meaning of *upper bound* and *lower bound*. Each *problem* has both an upper and a lower bound:

- *Upper bound* refers to what we *know* we can do. It is determined by the best algorithmic solution that we have found for a given problem. For example, we have seen examples of sorting algorithms that are $O(N^2)$ and $O(NlogN)$. While we might implement a sort that is $O(N^2)$ if N is small, we know that we *can* achieve $O(NlogN)$ if we only bother to do so. Thus, we say that sorting "admits a solution" that is $O(NlogN)$. We know of no solution better than $O(NlogN)$. For sorting problems, then, $O(NlogN)$ is the *upper bound*: we know that we don't have to settle for anything worse than $O(NlogN)$ if we don't want to.

- *Lower bound* refers to the best algorithmic solution that is *theoretically possible*. Lower bounds are determined by theoreticians who develop logical proofs about kinds of problems. (Logical proofs are beyond the scope of this course.) For example, any competent theoretician can prove that sorting an unsorted list *cannot* be done in less than $O(NlogN)$ work unless we make assumptions about the particular input data. This tells us that we cannot be sure of doing any better than $O(NlogN)$. Thus $O(NlogN)$ is the *lower bound* for sorting problems.

> ☐ *Upper bounds* tell us *the best we've been able to do so far.*
> *Lower bounds* tell us *the best we can ever hope to do.*

In the case of sorting, both the upper and lower bounds are the same: $O(NlogN)$. There is no *gap* between the two bounds and we thus know that we shouldn't even bother to try to develop sorting algorithms that are better than $O(NlogN)$.

Does this mean that there is no room for algorithmic improvement? No, it most certainly does not. Someone might well invent a better algorithm, but such algorithms will still be no better than $O(NlogN)$. Any improved algorithms can be better only in terms of improving (i.e., reducing) the costs that are hidden by "Big Oh" or in making the algorithm's performance more consistent. In other words, someone might invent a better $O(NlogN)$ algorithm for sorting, but no one will invent an algorithm that is better than $O(NlogN)$. As a result, we can say that the *sorting problem* "is an $O(NlogN)$ problem" or that it "has $O(NlogN)$ complexity."

Be sure that you understand the difference between the terms "upper and lower bounds" and "worst case and best case":

- *Best and worst case* measures refer to the work implied by a *given specific algorithm*. They inform us about how much work that one algorithm will have to do. For a given algorithm, any differences between *best* and *worst* cases are due to properties of the particular *values and/or the ordering* of the input data which is fed into the algorithm. If there is no gap between best and worst cases, then the algorithm is not vulnerable to being affected by particular combinations or orderings of data *values* and thus will perform more-or-less the same each time it is used, depending on the *number* N of input values which it must process.

- *Upper and lower bounds* refer to the *complexity* of a *given kind of problem*, i.e., they inform us about the amount of work that a problem implies. For a given kind of problem, any differences between *upper bound* and *lower bound* are due to discrepancies between *the best algorithm that we've been able to come up with so far* and *the best algorithm that might be possible*. If there is a gap, then someone might invent a new algorithm that lowers the upper bound closer to the lower bound, or someone might invent a better proof that raises the lower bound closer to the upper bound. If there is no gap, then we *know* what the complexity of the problem is, in which case new algorithms may improve the factors hidden by Big Oh, but new algorithms will be not able to change Big Oh for that kind of problem.

Tractable vs.   Now, just as we divided algorithms into categories of *reasonable* (or *polynomial*) and
Intractable   *unreasonable* (or *exponential*), we do the same thing for problems. In fact, we do so
Problems   using the same complexity thresholds:

- Problems that have upper and lower bounds which feature N only as a *polynomial* factor in Big Oh, (i.e., $O(logN)$, $O(N)$, $O(NlogN)$, $O(N^{\wedge}K)$) are considered "do-able" and are called *tractable* problems.

- Problems that have upper and lower bounds which feature N as an *exponential* factor in Big Oh, (i.e., $O(2^N)$, $O(N!)$, $O(N^N)$) are considered "not doable" and are called *intractable* problems.

☐ Terminology:

We use the terms "reasonable" and "unreasonable" to label *specific algorithms*, not kinds of problems.

We use the terms "tractable" and "intractable" to label *kinds of problems*, not particular algorithms.

- Polynomial algorithms are *reasonable*; polynomial problems are *tractable*.

- Exponential algorithms are *unreasonable*; exponential problems are *intractable*.

- We use *reasonable algorithms* to solve *tractable problems*.

- We don't use *unreasonable algorithms* (except for very small N).

- We *don't even bother* to try to develop reasonable algorithms for intractable problems (it's impossible!).

- We do try to find reasonable algorithms which provide *approximate solutions* to "intractable" problems.

Problems that "Cross the Line"

Earlier, we said that problems which have N as only a polynomial factor in *both* their upper and lower bounds are tractable, and that problems which have N as an exponential factor in *both* their upper and lower bounds are intractable.

But what about problems that don't quite fit this dichotomy? What about a problem that has an *exponential upper bound* and a *polynomial lower bound*? Such a problem would be one for which:

- We have found only exponential solutions, i.e., from the standpoint of our algorithms, it *appears to be intractable*;

- We cannot prove the necessity of an exponential solution, i.e., from the standpoint of our proofs, we *cannot say that it is intractable*.

As you might guess, such problems are of great interest to algorithm and theory specialists within computer science. Not only is there a gap between the upper bound and the lower bound, those two bounds are in different categories, i.e., if we look only at the upper bound, we would think such problems intractable, but if we look only at the lower bound, we would think them tractable. Such problems cross the boundaries of our classification system in a way that confounds the experts.

For some such problems, it may be simply a matter of more hard work and/or creative insights by algorithm and theory specialists. Perhaps someone will develop a reasonable algorithm and thus show that the given problem is indeed tractable. Or, perhaps someone will develop a stronger proof, one that demonstrates that the given problem cannot be solved in reasonable time and thus show that it is intractable.

"NP-Complete" Problems

Among the problems that straddle the line between tractable and intractable, we find a very interesting phenomena: a group of many, many problems which share a set of peculiar traits. These problems are known as *NP-Complete*. The traits they share are:

1. Upper bound suggests that the problem is intractable.
2. Lower bound suggest that the problem is tractable.

In addition to the fact that *NP-complete problems* straddle the line, they also share two additional traits:

3. Lower bounds suggest that most such problems can be done in *linear* time, i.e.., $O(N)$.
4. They are *all* reducible to one another.

This last attribute of NP-complete problems is a very powerful one. It means that if we had the ability to solve *any one* such problem in reasonable time, we would be able to solve *all* of them in reasonable time.

Thus, one way to become very famous very fast would be to go home this afternoon and develop a reasonable algorithm to solve any *NP-complete* problem. This would, in effect, lower the upper bound of all such problems down into the category of reasonable algorithms, indicating that all such problems are tractable. It would open the door to practical computational solutions to problems that currently defy such solutions.

Another route to fame would be to jot down a rigorous proof that shows that any one *NP-complete* problem is intractable. This would raise the lower bound up into the category of unreasonable algorithms, this demonstrating that all such problems are intractable.

Either development would resolve the question of whether such problems are tractable or intractable. As it is, we can only *suspect* that such problems are intractable.

There are hundreds of *NP-complete* problems. Examples include:

1. Traveling salesman. Given a weighted graph (e.g., cities with distances between them) and some distance k (e.g., the max distance you want to travel), is there some tour that visits all the points (e.g., cities) and returns home such that distance $<= k$.

2. Three-coloring. Given a graph, can it be colored with at most three colors such that each vertex gets one of three colors and the adjacent areas get a different color.

3. Bin packing. Given N items, each with a profit and a weight, and given some finite weight capacity, and given a desired profit of k, can you select items so that they fit and provide profit of at least k, e.g., *the knapsack problem*.

4. Pert planning. Give a list of actions with constraints as to which actions can/must precede others, can you minimize the total time required, e.g., building the space shuttle.

5. Clique. Given a graph which is not complete and a number k, is there a clique (a set of vertices each one of which is adjacent to the other) of size k.

NP-complete problems are important problems in computer science. They also present significant challenges to those in other fields, i.e., those who want to optimize planning or scheduling.

Oracles and *certificates* are useful concepts when it comes to understanding both NP-complete problems, as well as understanding a class of problems that are *worse* than intractable.

An *oracle* is a mythical and magical "computer talent." Imagine that we are faced with some problem that requires us to make a series of decisions. Imagine further that to solve the problem we must consider a large number of possible actions, i.e., to know whether a given decision is correct, we must follow it through, perhaps making a series of additional decisions, before we can know whether we've made the right original decision or whether we've "gone down a dead end street."

For example, consider a scheduling problem that is *NP-complete*. Imagine that we have N teachers and a specification of the hours during which M classes can be scheduled; each teacher is available to teach a certain number of hours. We want to know whether it is possible to schedule the classes and the teachers such that:

   (a) all the classes are scheduled;

   (b) no two teachers teach the same class at the same time;

   (c) no teacher is scheduled to teach two classes at once.

Some scheduling problems are tractable, but this one is *NP-complete*. It requires that we consider *all* the various scheduling possibilities before we can conclude "no working schedule can be found." If we find a working schedule, then we have shown that such a schedule can be found. We might be lucky and find a working schedule upon our first try, but one might just as well be found only when we consider the very last of all the various possibilities.

To solve the problem and answer the question, we must be prepared to try out all the various possibilities. This requires that we try out *partial* schedules, e.g., schedule teacher A for a certain class at a certain time and teacher B for a certain class at a certain time. If teacher A and B are scheduled to teach the same class at the same time, then we know that this is possibility won't work, that this particular schedule is a "dead end," and thus we don't have to take it further. However, if either the class or the time is different, then this partial schedule *might* work and we thus must continue to evaluate its viability by, for example, adding a particular course for teacher C at a particular time, seeing if that works or not, and so on.

We add more teachers and other classes, step-by-step, until we find that either "yes it will work" or "no it won't." Whenever we add a new element to the schedule, we must evaluate whether "it works so far" or not. If so, we continue with it. If not, then we "back out" of that "solution path" and try another possibility instead. Thus, for a given "partial schedule," we might go all the way down the "tree of possibilities," finding an acceptable choice at each step, only to learn that the very last remaining possibility of class, teacher and time slot won't work. This is very costly to do. The best of known solutions (i.e., the upper bound) is intractable.

Certificates   Observe, however, that for a given input to the problem (teachers, classes, time slots), we don't need to find *all* the schedules that might work, we need find only one to demonstrate that a schedule *can* be found, thus answering the question. If we can come up with a single schedule that does work, then we can quite easily convince someone that a schedule can be found: we simply show them a schedule that does the job!

Such a piece of evidence is called a *certificate*. A certificate is nothing more or less than conclusive evidence that the answer to the question is "yes." A "yes" answer requires only a simple example of a successful solution. Such an example "certifies" that there is a solution, which is why we call any such example a *certificate*. There might be several possible certificates for a given input, but we require only one of them to certify the problem as solvable.

There is no such thing as a certificate which answers "no." The only way to demonstrate a "no" answer is to show that *all* of the possibilities fail.

Oracles   Observe that a certificate is the result of a series of "good" decisions. Each certificate can be thought of as being a list of good decisions; in our example, each decision would be of the form, "schedule teacher X to teach course Y in time slot Z."

Each certificate for an *NP-complete* problem can be made to be reasonably short, with its size bounded by a polynomial N. Most often, certificates to *NP-complete* problems are *linear*, i.e., not just reasonable, but $O(N)$, which is *very* fast.

Thus, if we had some means to "make the right decision" at each decision point, then we could produce certificates in reasonable, usually linear, time. The problem is that we cannot do this, and often must follow a "bad decision path" for some considerable distance before we find out that it leads to a dead end. But, if we had some magical wisdom that allowed us to "see down the path" of a given decision and tell whether it was a good or bad path, then we could develop certificates quite quickly. Thus, if we had some process that had magical powers of foresight, these messy *NP-complete* problems would suddenly become tractable.

We call such a mythical process an *oracle*. As a practical matter, an oracle would be some omniscient process that can give us, in advance, the wisdom of hindsight with respect to a given decision path. In our example, we might ask "should we schedule teacher X for class Y in time slot Z?" An oracle would answer "yes" or "no" to each such question, providing us with the best possible answer.

To put it another way, when faced with a "yes" or "no" question and no basis for rational decision, we might flip a coin. Having an oracle would be like having a "magic coin" that, when flipped, always produces the correct answer. If both possibilities lead to complete solutions, or if neither of them does, then the magic coin behaves realistically, i.e., like a normal, random coin flip.

Thus, by examining the candidate solution provided by an oracle or magic coin, we can readily determine the answer to the problem. If the candidate solution is a successful solution, the answer is "yes, for the given input, there is a solution." If the candidate solution is not legal, then we know that the best possible solution does not satisfy the problem and, thus, that the answer is "no, for the given input, there is no solution."

Neither oracles nor magic coins exist. But we can imagine the effect of them if they did: they could tell us, in advance, whether a decision was good or bad, thus making *NP-complete* problems tractable.

Determinism vs. *nondeterminism*

Algorithms which produce the correct answer via "proper guesses" are known as *nondeterministic* algorithms. They are called *nondeterministic* because there is no way to specify *the basis* upon which to determine the right decision. From a computational point of view, *nondeterministic* algorithms work "by magic."

In contrast, algorithms which produce answers by making information-based decisions at each step are known as *deterministic* algorithms. Any algorithm that can be executed by a computer or (reliably) by people is a *deterministic* algorithm.

For *NP-complete* problems, the best deterministic algorithms are exponential. If we had magical abilities to execute *nondeterministic* algorithms (e. g., oracles or magic coins), then they would be polynomial, often linear. This is where the category of NP-complete problems gets part of its name: "NP" stands for *"Nondeterministic Polynomial,"* i.e., given magical nondeterminism, they can be solved in polynomial time. "Complete" is used to signify that all such problems are reducible to the others, i.e., solve one and you solve the complete set of them.

NP-complete vs. *Intractable* *Problems*

Both *NP-complete* problems and intractable problems feature upper bounds that are exponential, i.e., we are not able to solve either in reasonable time. Of such problems, relatively few are proven to be intractable, i.e., have exponential lower bounds. There are more *NP-complete* problems than there are provably intractable ones.

One example of provably intractable problems is *generalized* chess or checkers (e.g., does Black have a guaranteed winning strategy?). *Generalized* means that we have a different game for each N played on an N by N board; "normal" chess and checkers are not intractable.

Undecidability   So far, we have three categories of problems:

- Tractable problems, those that can be solved in polynomial time.

- Problems, including *NP-complete* problems, for which we have only exponential solutions but for which we can establish only a polynomial lower bound. Our best guess is that these are intractable, but we cannot prove it.

- Intractable problems, those that provably require exponential solutions.

Notice that all three share a common attribute: we *can* develop algorithmic solutions to them. The practical difference between them is that for the latter two categories, our solutions are of no practical value: we can solve these problems but it takes too much time for our solutions to do us any good.

In addition to these categories, we have categories of problems for which no algorithmic solution can be found. In other words, the solutions are not computable *regardless* of the cost.

As an example, consider again the tiling problem we discussed earlier. It was described as a *bounded* tiling problem: we specified that an areas of M by M must be tiled with N tiles, where $N = M^2$. Let us change the problem to ask "for a given number T of *kinds* of tiles, and given some set of restrictions on how these tiles can abut one another (e.g., make their patterns line up), can we arrive at an arrangement that we can use to tile *any* size area?" Thus, instead of asking about a fixed or bounded area as determined by the input, we are now asking about *all* possible areas. In other words, we have removed the bounds on the area. The problem now says, in effect,

```
if (the types of tiles in T can tile any area) then
    print("yes")
else
    print("no")
endif
```

This problem is *undecidable*. There is no way to program any algorithm that can evaluate the condition which determines whether the *if* or the *else* clause should be executed. No answer can be obtained in any finite time. This problem admits no algorithmic solution, period.

For another example of an *undecidable* problem, consider the "word correspondence" problem. In this problem, we are given two groups of words, say, X and Y. By "words," we mean only some string of characters in some alphabet; they do not have to be "real" words. For example, X and Y might consist of the following words from a limited alphabet that contains only two characters, *a* and *b*:

```
Group    1      2     3     4      5
  X     abb     a    bab   baba   aba
  Y     bbab    aa   ab    aa     a
```

Given these word groups, we want to know if we can concatenate the corresponding words from both X and Y such that we produce the same new word from each word group. Given the word groups above, we can accomplish this, as can be seen by concatenating words 2, 1, 1, 4, 1, and 5, which produces the new word *aabbabbbabaabbaba* from both X and Y. However, if we remove the first letter from the first word of each group, as shown below, the goal cannot be accomplished.

```
Group    1      2     3     4      5
  X     bb      a    bab   baba   aba
  Y     bab     aa   ab    aa     a
```

The word correspondence problem is undecidable. There is no algorithm that can distinguish between our two examples of X and Y. The undecidability comes from the fact that there is no bound on the number of words that we might string together.

If we say that we must confine ourselves to choosing a string of 6 or 8 or 73 words to concatenate, then the problem can be decided (at a cost of what Big Oh?). Similarly, if we say that we can choose any number of words but do not have to choose the *same* words or the *same number of* words from each word group, then the problem becomes tractable (e.g., given our second example of X and Y, we can choose 3,2,2 from X and 1,2 from Y and get *babaa* in either case).

A third example of an undecidable problem is the *halting problem*. It states: given some legal algorithm written in some programming language, and given some input to the algorithm, will the algorithm ever reach a stopping place? For example, if the algorithm is,

```
begin
    read(X)
    loop
        exitif (X = 1)
        X <- X - 2
    endloop
end
```

and if the input might consist of any positive integer, we can see that the algorithm will halt if the input is odd and that it will never halt if the input is even. Thus, checking the input to see whether it is even or odd will tell us whether or not the algorithm will halt.

If the algorithm is:

```
begin
    read(X)
    loop
        exitif(X=1)
        if (even(X)) then
            X <- X / 2
        else  {odd(X)}
            X <- 3X +1
        endif
    endloop
end
```

then it is more difficult to say! For example, given the input 3, X takes on the values 3, 10, 5, 16, 8, 4, 2, 1, respectively, and halts upon the next *exitif* test.

If we test this algorithm on any positive integer, then one of two things will happen. Either the algorithm will terminate or else it will produce an erratic sequence of values that shows no signs of either converging or diverging. To date, for any legal input, this algorithm has always terminated, given enough time. Yet no one has been able to *prove* that it will *always* terminate eventually.

In the general case, the halting problem is *undecidable*, i.e., given any finite amount of time, there is no way to tell whether a given algorithm will terminate upon a given input. For any given input, it is easy to tell if it does terminate *if* we observe the termination. The problem lies in trying to determine *when* we can conclude that it the algorithm will not terminate. There is always the chance that, given a little more time, it *might* terminate.

Certificates for Undecidable Problems
Certificates demonstrate the "solvability" of a problem. In the case of *NP-complete* problems, it takes exponential time to produce a solution, yet the solution itself can be verified in polynomial, usually linear time. Thus, for *NP-complete* problems, we do not have reasonable solution algorithms but we do have reasonable-size or *polynomial-time* certificates.

There is an analogous relationship between *undecidable* problems and certificates. While an undecidable problem cannot be solved by algorithmic means, if we imagine having an oracle, we find that *some* (but not all) undecidable problems have *finite* certificates even though there are no finite-time algorithms. In fact, *most* undecidable problems admit finite certificates. We call such problems "partially undecidable."

Some undecidable problems do not admit finite certificates even in the face of magical oracles. Thus, not only are we unable to algorithmically solve them in finite time, we cannot even evaluate whether a given "candidate solution" is correct in finite time. We call these problems "highly undecidable."

Food for Thought:

HAL 9000, Where Are You?

How do we want our computers to behave? The answer is simple: we want them to act like the computers in the movies! Unfortunately, anyone who as ever tried to *actually use a computer* can attest to the distinct lack of intelligence that our computers have. Why is this so?

In truth, it is because we understand *ourselves* so poorly. This fact ties our hands because, quite obviously, the computers in the movies do a remarkable job of communicating with us in our own natural language, and of thinking how we do, only better and faster. This is a widely accepted test of success for artificial intelligence (AI) applications: can an AI program convince a human that its responses come from another human instead of a machine. To actually create computers that act like the ones in the movies, we must develop the ability to abstract our own communication and processing abilities into algorithms.

At present we cannot do this quite because we do not have an *adequate conceptual model* of how we communicate or process information. For several decades now, researchers have attacked these problems without breakthrough success. Work is ongoing, but significant accomplishments remain few and far between.

To date, there are two main approaches to AI: the *rule-based* approach and the *neural network* approach.

- The *rule-based* approach is the older of the two, and strives to discern what processing rules people might be implicitly using when they perform acts of intelligence. Once such rules are articulated, they are implemented in algorithms which then mimic the "intelligent" behavior of people.

- The *neural network* approach is newer, and strives to mirror the processing "hardware" of the human brain. Rather than try to construct *explicit* algorithmics, it instead tries to copy the "architecture of the brain" by creating networks of many processors. Each processor makes only the very simplest of decisions, filtering input and modifying it slightly, but collectively the mass of processors combine to form a response. The goal is to simulate the brain, wherein millions of biochemical synapses lead to a global response.

To date, advocates of both approaches can point to isolated specific successes, but neither approach has demonstrated the achievement for which their proponents had hoped. In both cases, successful results tend to be limited to very narrowly defined topic domains, without much ability to transfer to other domains.

At present, the concerns of researchers in artificial intelligence and psychology overlap in the area of *cognitive science*. This relatively new field is attempting to bring the information-processing paradigm to bear on the problem of abstracting intelligence into algorithms. Concurrently, there is debate about whether the information-processing paradigm is *adequate* to allow us to achieve what we're after. Is it adequate to say that human communication and processing are reducible to "information processing." These questions are a mix of science and philosophy, and there is no clear road map to success.

Thus, we find ourselves limited by our own lack of self-understanding. We don't know enough to know whether or not these problems are tractable or even decidable. It is our knowledge of our own processes that is the limiting factor.

Summary

We have considered four major categories of problems: *highly undecidably, partially undecidable, intractable,* and *tractable*. In addition, *NP-complete* problems straddle the line between tractable and intractable problems. We suspect that they are intractable, but we cannot prove this to be so. If we *pretend* that *NP-complete* problems are intractable, we then have the hierarchy of problems shown on the next page.

We can return to the problem of arranging ceramic tiles to find examples of each of these four kinds:

1. The "fixed width" tiling problem is tractable. You are given as inputs a set of kinds of tiles, *T*, and a number *N*. The task is to determine if a rectangle of size C (some fixed constant and is not part of the input) by N can be formed from T. This problem can be solved in polynomial time.

2. The "bounded" tiling problem is NP-complete and assumed to be intractable. You are given as input a set of tiles *T* square area of size $N = M * M$ and the task is as described earlier. This problem can be solved in exponential time and admits a polynomial certificate.

3. The "unbounded" tiling problem is "partially undecidable." You are given *T* as input and the task is to determine whether *any and all* (i.e., the integer grid) areas

can be tiles within the constraints. There is no algorithm that can solve this problem, but it admits a finite-time certificate.

4. The "recurring" tiling problem is "highly undecidable." You are given T as input and the task is to determine whether T can tile the integer grid such that there is an infinite recurrence of a particular special tile. Not only is there is no algorithm that can solve this problem, there is not even a finite-time certificate, i.e., we cannot even evaluate a candidate solution in finite time.

Much of this material is primarily of interest to theorists. The practical implications are summarized in the diagram below.

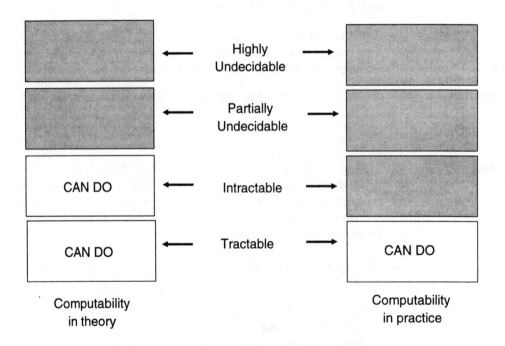

From a practical point of view, *undecidable* and *intractable* problems are equally "bad news." Often, people will refer to problems that are "at least as bad as intractable" (e.g., undecidable problems such as the halting problem) as "intractable." Of course, from our point of view, undecidable problems are *worse* than intractable. When used in this way, the word "intractable" is being used to mean that (for all practical purposes) the problem is not solvable, i.e., it is "exponential or worse."

Appendix: Example Problems and Solutions

Problem: What is the output from the following algorithm?

```
algorithm TraceParameters

  var
    A,B,C isa num

  begin {TraceParameters}
    A <- 2
    B <- 3
    C <- 4
    Calculation (A,B,C)
    print (A,B,C)
    C <- Square(B)
    print (C)
    ProcessNumbers (A,B,C)
    print (A,B,C)
  end {TraceParameters}


procedure Calculation (X isa in num, Y isa out num,
                       Z isa in/out num)

  begin {Calculation}
    Y <- X * Z
    X <- X + 1
    Z <- Y + X
    print (X,Y,Z)
  end {Calculation}


function Square isa num (Value isa in num)

  begin {Square}
    Square returns Value * Value
  end    {Square}
```

```
procedure ProcessNumbers (X,Y,Z isa in/out num)

   var
     Temp isa num

   begin {ProcessNumbers}
     Temp <- X
     X <- Y
     Y <- Temp
     Calculation (Square(Y),Z,X)
   end    {ProcessNumbers}
```

Answer:

```
3 8 11
2 8 11
64
5 32 37
37 2 32
```

Problem:

Write a recursive function to determine if a given input is divisible by 3. Do not use multiplication or division in your solution.

Answer:

```
function Three isa boolean (Value isa in num)
   {resolves to true if 3 is a factor of the number sent in
    by the algorithm.  If there is a remainder, it resolves
    to false.}

   begin {Three}
     if (Value < 0) then
       Value <- -Value          {makes all numbers positive}
     endif
     if (Value < 3) then         {terminating condition}
       if (Value = 0) then
         Three returns true      {remainder of 0 when number
                                  divided by three}

       else
         Three returns false     {remainder of 1 or 2 when
                                  number divided by 3}

       endif
     else
       Three returns Three (Value - 3) {recursive call}
     endif
   end    {Three}
```

Problem: What is the output of the following algorithm?

```
algorithm ArrayTrace
  const
        WIDTH is 3
        HEIGHT is 4
  type
        Array2dType definesa array[1..WIDTH,1..HEIGHT]
                                        of num
  var
        Grid isa Array2dType
        X isa num
        Y isa num
  begin
        X <- 1
        loop
                Y <- 1
                loop
                        Grid[X,Y] <- Calc(Y,X)
                        Y <- Y + 1
                        exitif (Y > HEIGHT)
                endloop
                X <- X + 1
                exitif (X > WIDTH)
        endloop
  end   {ArrayTrace}


function Calc isa num (X isa in num, Y isa in num)
  var
        Temp isa num

  begin {Calc}
        Temp <- X^2
        Calc returns Temp + Y*2
  end   {Calc}
```

Answer:

algorithm ArrayTrace				function Calc			
X	Y	Grid[X,Y]		X	Y	Temp	Calc
1	1	3		1	1	1	3
1	2	6		2	1	4	6
1	3	11		3	1	9	11
1	4	18		4	1	16	18
2	1	5		1	2	1	5
2	2	8		2	2	4	8
2	3	13		3	2	9	13
2	4	20		4	2	16	20
3	1	7		1	3	1	7
3	2	10		2	3	4	10
3	3	15		3	3	9	15
3	4	22		4	3	16	22

Problem:

Declare a data structure that will hold the following data
necessary for a dog show:
1) The show will consist of 50 dog owners who should
   be identified by last name.
2) Each owner can enter as many dogs as he/she wishes.
3) Each dog has a name not to exceed 6 characters.
4) Each dog receives 5 numerical scores from the
   judges.

Answer:

```
const
    NAMELENGTH is 6
    TOTALSCORES is 5
    CONTESTANTS is 50

type
    DogName definesa array [1..NAMELENGTH] of char

    OwnerPtr definesa ptr toa OwnerName
    OwnerName definesa record
        Letter isa char
        NextLetter isa OwnerPtr
    endrecord

    ScoreArray definesa array [1..TOTALSCORES] of num

    DogInfoPtr definesa ptr toa DogInfoType
    DogInfoType definesa record
        Name isa DogName
        Scores isa ScoreArray
        Next isa DogInfoPtr
    endrecord

    OwnerInfoType definesa record
        Name isa OwnerPtr
        Dogs isa DogInfoPtr
    endrecord

    DogShow definesa array [1..CONTESTANTS] of OwnerInfoType
```

Problem:

Write an algorithm that reads in 10 numbers from the user
and calculates the Min, Max, and Average. Processor time is
expensive, memory is cheap. Write an appropriate algorithm
and calculate its costs.

Answer:

We want to make sure that we do the job as fast as
possible. Looking at the problem, it seems that linear is
the best time we can achieve, since we need to look at every
array element in order to find the min, max, and average.
Therefore we should look at O(N) traversal algorithms. The
array is not ordered but that does not affect us here. We
only need one pass through the numbers to calculate all
three, Min, Max, and Average. Here's the code:

```
algorithm MinMaxAve
{ This algorithm calculates the Min, Max and Average of ten}
{ numbers in an array.  We are optimizing for speed, not   }
{ for space.                                                }

const
  SIZE is 10

type
  Nums_Array_Type definesa array [1..SIZE] of num

var
  Min isa num
  Max isa num
  Average isa num
  Total isa num
  The_Nums isa Nums_Array_Type
  Index isa num

begin {MinMaxAve}
  InputData (The_Nums)
  {procedure call to input all data into the array The_Nums}
  {Note: the procedure is not coded here                   }

  { Initialization }
  Total <- The_Nums [1]
  Min <- The_Nums [1]
  Max <- The_Nums [1]
  { Since we have already "processed" the first element of
  { the array, we can start iterating at the second
  { component.
  Index <- 2
```

```
loop
    exitif (Index > SIZE)
    if (The_Nums[Index] < Min) then    {if we have a new min}
        Min <- The_Nums[Index]
    elseif (The_Nums[Index] > Max) then
                                      {if we have a new max}
        Max <- The_Nums[Index]
    endif
    Total <- Total + The_Nums[Index] {adding to the sum}
    Index <- Index + 1                    {move to next element}
endloop

{ Now, to calculate the average from the total above.   }
Average <- Total / NUM_OF_COMPONENTS

print ("The Min is", Min, "The Max is ", Max)
print ("The Average is", Average)

end    {MinMaxAve}
```

ANALYSIS

The runtime of this algorithm is O(N) because of the single loop inside the algorithm body. It goes through each value of the array once. The space costs are 5 variables plus the ten array components.

Problem:

Now, processing time is cheap, while memory is expensive. How would we do the previous task using the minimum amount of memory?

Answer:

Now we want to optimize on space rather than time. Aassuming that we have to have the array of ten variables, let's see if we can have the absolute minimum number of additional variables. One way to do this is to sort the array, which automatically gives us the min and max. To find the average, then, requires only a linear addition of all of the array components.

```
algorithm MinMaxAve
{ This algorithm calculates the Min, Max and Average of ten}
{ numbers in an array.  We are optimizing for space, not   }
{ speed.  This algorithm destroys the original values in    }
{ in the array in order to calculate the average.          }

const
  SIZE is 10

type
  Nums_Array_Type definesa array [1..SIZE] of num

var
  The_Nums isa Nums_Array_Type
  Index isa num

begin {MinMaxAve}
  InputData (The_Nums)
  {procedure call to input all data into the array The_Nums}
  {Note: the procedure is not coded here

  {Sort the array using an existing procedure }
  Bubblesort (The_Nums)

  print ("The Min is", The_Nums[1],
         "The Max is", The_Nums[Num_of_Components])
  {Since the array is sorted we can immediately access the }
  {minimum and maximum components                          }

  { Now calculate the average. Since trying to save space, }
  { we will put the answers in the array itself. This      }
  { destroys the original array.                           }
  Index <- 2
  loop
     exitif (Index > SIZE)
     My_Nums[Index] <- My_Nums[Index] + My_Nums[Index-1]
     {the current array cell takes on the sum of its       }
     {current contents and the contents of the previous    }
     {cell                                                 }
     Index <- Index + 1
  endloop

  {The last array cell now contains the sum of the        }
  {original array contents                                }
  print ("The average is", My_Nums[SIZE] / SIZE)

end {MinMaxAve}
```

ANALYSIS

The runtime of this algorithm is affected by the bubblesort, which we know to be O(N^2). The one loop inside the algorithm to calculate the average is linear, O(N). Therefore, the runtime of this algorithm is O(N^2) + O(N). Since we can get rid of lower-ordered terms, the overall runtime (worst case) of this algorithm is O(N^2). (Had we been concerned primarily with time costs, we could have used a faster sort at the cost of more memory.)

Data space - if we ignore the bubblesort, then we only need the original array space plus the one iterator. In reality, the bubble sort will have two iterators (loop inside of a loop) and a "save" variable for the swapping.

Problem:

Write a class (from scratch) that will implement the behavior of a variation on a queue that allows for the following:
    adding an item to the queue
    removing the first item off of the queue
    removing a selected item from the queue
    printing the contents of the queue
    determining whether an element exists in the queue.
Implement the queue as a linked list. Do not worry about "Success" booleans.

```
class Queue (Qtype isa type)

public

    procedure Enqueue (Data_Item isa in QType)
    procedure Dequeue_From_Front (Data_Item isa out QType)
    procedure Remove_Data_Value (Data_Item isa in QType)
    procedure Traverse_And_Print ()
    function Linear_Search isa boolean (Data_Item isa in
                                             QType)

private

type
    List_Ptr_Type definesa ptr toa List_Node_Type
    List_Node_Type definesa record
        Data isa QType
        Next isa List_Ptr_Type
    endrecord

var
    List_Head, List_End isa List_Ptr_Type
    { Marks beginning and end of list }
```

```
procedure Enqueue (Data_Item isa in QType)
   { This procedure takes a data item and    }
   { puts it at the end of the queue.        }

var
   Temp_Ptr isa List_Ptr_Type

begin { Enqueue }

    if (List_Head = nil then
      {the list is empty, create the first node }
      List_Head <- new (List_Node_Type)
      List_Head^.Data <- Data_Item
      List_Head^.Next <- nil
      List_End <- List_Head
    else
      { The list is not empty, put the node on the end  }
      { of the list. Make sure to move List_End to point}
      { to the new node.                                }

      Temp_Ptr <- new (List_Node_Type)   {create new node}
      Temp_Ptr^.Data <- Data_Item
      TempPtr^.Next <- nil

      List_End^.Next <- Temp_Ptr
              {insert the node after the current last node}
      List_End <- Temp_Ptr
      {adjust the List_End so that it still points to the
        last node}
    endif

end { Enqueue }




procedure Dequeue_From_Front (Data_Item isa out QType)
   { This procedure deletes a data item                  }
   { from the front of the list                          }

begin {Dequeue_From_Front}

    if (List_Head = nil) then
        { The list is empty, generate a message }
        print ("The list is empty")
    else
        Data_Item <- List_Head^.Data    {retrieves data}
        List_Head <- List_Head^.Next    {deletes item}
    endif

end { Dequeue_From_Front }
```

```
procedure Remove_Data_Value (Data_Item isa in QType)
   { This procedure searches through a list for a }
   { data item and then removes it from the list  }
var
      Temp_Ptr, Trail_Ptr isa List_Ptr_Type
begin
      if List_Head^.Data = Data_Item then
      {if the sought for item is the first item in the   }
      {queue, move the List_Head to the next node        }
         List_Head <- List_Head^.Next
      else
        Temp_Ptr <- List_Head
          {We do not want to make permanent changes to    }
          {List_Head - otherwise we will lose the list     }

        loop
           { Stop if we get to the end, or if we find the}
           { data value                                   }
           exitif (Temp_Ptr = nil) OR
                  (Temp_Ptr^.Data = Data_Item)
           { To make sure we can delete the node, we need }
           { to keep a trailing pointer that keeps track  }
           {of the *previous* record                      }
           Trail_Ptr <- Temp_Ptr
           Temp_Ptr <- Temp_Ptr^.Next
        endloop

      { Now, check to see if we found the value.  If we   }
      { did remove it from the list.  If not, then print  }
      { an error message.                                  }
        if (Temp_Ptr = nil) then
          print ("Data value was not found in the list")
        else
          { We found the data value, Delete the node      }
          Trail_Ptr^.Next <- Temp_Ptr^.Next
        endif
      endif
   end { Remove_Data_Value }

procedure Traverse_And_Print ()
   { This procedure prints all the data      }
   { values in the linked list               }

var
      Temp_Ptr isa List_Ptr_Type
begin { Traverse_And_Print }
      Temp_Ptr <- List_Head
      loop
          exitif (Temp_Ptr = nil)
          print ("The value is", Temp_Ptr^.Data)
          Temp_Ptr <- Temp_Ptr^.Next
      endloop
end { Traverse_And_Print }
```

```
function Linear_Search isa boolean (Data_Item isa in QType)
   { This function searches through the list for a specific}
     data value and returns true if that value is found     }

var
       Temp_Ptr isa List_Ptr_Type

begin { Linear_Search }
       Temp_Ptr <- List_Head
       loop
            exitif (Temp_Ptr = nil) OR
                     (Temp_Ptr^.Data = Data_Item)
            Temp_Ptr <- Temp_Ptr^.Next
       endloop

       if (Temp_Ptr = nil) then
            Linear_Search returns false
       else
            Linear_Search returns true
       endif
   end { Linear_Search }


  { Initialization section }
  begin
     List_Head <- nil
     List_End  <- nil
  end

end   { Queue }



{----------------------------------------}
{ Client Routine (conventional paradigm) }
{----------------------------------------}

algorithm Do_Stuff

uses Queue

var

  Number_List isa Linked_List_Queue(num)
  {declaring an instance of the class Queue.  This    }
  {particular queue will contain numbers              }
  My_Data isa num

begin
   { Enqueue a few numbers }
   Number_List.Enqueue ( 42 )
   Number_List.Enqueue ( 101 )
   Number_List.Enqueue ( 99 )
```

```
    { Take the top number off the list }
    Number_List.Remove_From_Front (My_Data)
    print ("The first item on the list was", My_Data)

    { Search for a particular value }
    if (Number_List.Linear_Search (77)) then
        print ("We found it!")
    else
        print ("Dang, it wasn't there.")
    endif

    { Remove a random value }
    Number_List.Remove_Data_Value ( 42 )

    { Now, print out the entire list }
    Number_List.Traverse_And_Print

end   { Main Algorithm }
```

Problem: Implement a Phone Book class.

This contains the object implementation of the Phone Book example.

```
class PhoneBook    { Binary Search Tree version }

public

    {Assume CharStr is defined by another class to hold  }
    {a string of characters                              }

    procedure Lookup(LName isa in CharStr, PNum isa out num,
                     Found isa out boolean)

        {Searches through all records in the database and  }
        {returns the phone number associated with the input }
        {name. Found is returned as false if the number is  }
        {not in the database.                               }

    procedure AddListing(LName isa in CharStr,
                         PNum isa in num)
        {Adds a new name and phone number to the database}

private
  type
    PhoneListing definesa record
        Name isa CharStr
        Phone isa num
    endrecord
```

```
    PhoneTreeRec definesa record
       Info isa PhoneListing
       LChild, RChild isa PTPtr
    endrecord
    PTPtr definesa ptr toa PhoneTreeRec

var
    Book isa PTPtr


procedure Lookup(LName isa in CharStr,
                 PNum isa out num, Found isa out boolean)
begin {Lookup}
    PrivateLU(Book,Name,PNum,Found)
    {PrivateLU is a recursive function and requires that   }
    {Book be passed as a parameter.  So the purpose of this}
    {helper procedure is to take the global variable Book  }
    {and send it as a parameter to PrivateLU               }
end {Lookup}


procedure PrivateLU (Root isa in PTPtr,
                     LName isa in CharStr,
                     PNum isa out num,
                     Found isa out boolean)
begin {PrivateLU}
    if (Root=nil) then   {terminating condition}
        Found <- false
    else {tree is nonempty}
        if (StrLess(LName,Root^.Info.Name)) then
              {in left subtree}
            PrivateLU(Root^.LChild,LName,PNum,Found)
              {recursive call to check left subtree}
        else
            if (StrEq(LName,Root^.Info.Name) then
                {match found - terminating condition}
                Found <- true
                PNum <- Root^.Info.Phone
            else
                PrivateLU(Root^.RChild,LName,PNum,Found)
                {recursive call to check right subtree}
            endif
        endif
    endif
end {PrivateLU}


procedure AddListing(LName isa in CharStr, PNum isa in num)

begin {AddListing}
  PrivateAdd(Book,LName,PNum)
    {PrivateAdd is a recursive function and requires that  }
    {Book be passed as a parameter.  So the purpose of this}
```

```
        {helper procedure is to take the global variable Book  }
        {and send it as a parameter to PrivateLU               }
end    {AddListing}

procedure PrivateAdd(Root isa in/out PTPtr,
                     LName isa in CharStr,
                     PNum isa in num)
        {recursive procedure to add a new record to the BST}

begin {PrivateAdd}
   if (Root=nil) then              {terminating condition}
                       {a leaf of the tree has been reached}
      Root <- new(PhoneTreeRec)   {create a new node}
      Root^.Info.Name <- LName
      Root^.Info.Phone <- PNum
      Root^.LChild <- nil
      Root^.RChild <- nil
   else                    {not at a leaf yet so recurse}
       if (StrLess(LName,Root^.Info.Name)) then
           {add in left subtree}
           PrivateAdd(Root^.LChild,LName,PNum)
           {recursive call}
       else
           if (NOT StrEq(LName,Root^.Info.Name) then
              {check to insure we are not inserting duplicate}
              {add in right subtree}
              PrivateAdd(Root^.RChild,LName,PNum)
               {recursive call}
           endif
       endif
   endif
end {PrivateAdd}

begin {initialization}
   Book <- nil
end {initialization}

end {PhoneBook}


algorithm PhoneBookMaint

uses
   PhoneBook
   CharStr

var
   Name isa CharStr
   Answer isa char
   Number isa num
   OK isa boolean
```

```
            begin {PhoneBookMaint}

              loop
                print("enter name:")
                read(Name)
                print("Add or Lookup [a/l]?")
                read(Answer)
                if (Answer='a') then
                    print ("enter number")
                    read(Number)
                    AddListing(Name,Number)
                else
                    Lookup(Name,Number,OK)
                    if (OK) then
                        print("The number is ",Number)
                    else
                        print("We have no listing for ",Name)
                    endif
                endif
                print("More?[y/n]")
                read (Answer)
                exitif (Answer <> "y")
              endloop
            end {PhoneBookMaint}




            Array implementation of the PhoneBook
            ---------------------------------------------------------

            algorithm PhoneBookMaint { Array Implementation }

            const
              BOOKSIZE is 10000000
              STRSIZE is 30

            type
                CharStr definesa array[1..STRSIZE] of char
                PhoneListing definesa record
                   Name isa CharStr
                   PhoneNum isa num
                endrecord
                PhoneArray definesa array[1..BOOKSIZE] of PhoneListing
                PhoneBook definesa record
                    Info isa PhoneArray
                    NumEnts isa num
                end
```

```
    function StrEq isa boolean (StringA isa in CharStr,
                               StringB isa in CharStr)
      {returns true if strings are identical}

    var
      Index isa num

    begin {StrEq}
      Index <- 1
      loop {character by character comparison of strings}
         exitif (StringA[Index] <> StringB[Index]) OR
              (Index = STRSIZE)
            {exits if A) a character comparison is not identical}
            {      or B) all characters have been compared        }
         Index <- Index + 1
      endloop
      {If we exited the above loop with the final characters   }
      {equal, then the strings are identical}
      StrEq returns StringA[Index] = StringB[Index]

    end {StrEq}


    function StrLess isa boolean (StringA isa in CharStr,
                                  StringB isa in CharStr)
    {compares two strings and returns true if StringA comes}
    {before StringB in alphabetical order                  }

    var
      Index isa num

    begin {StrLess}
      Index <- 1
      loop
         exitif ((StringA[Index] <> StringB[Index]) OR
              (Index=STRSIZE))
            {exits as soon as indication that one string}
            {comes before the other OR exits when end of}
            {string is reached}
         Index <- Index + 1
      endloop
      StrLess <- StringA[Index] < StringB[Index]
    end  {StrLess}


    procedure Lookup(Book isa in PhoneBook,
                  LName isa in CharStr,
                  PNum isa out num, Found isa out boolean)
    {Looks up a name in the database and returns the     }
    {associated phone number.  Found is returned as      }
    {false if the name is not found                      }
```

```
var
  Index isa num
  Done isa boolean {loop control variable}

begin {Lookup}
  Index <- 1
  Found <- false
  Done <- false
  loop
    exitif (Index > Book.NumEnts) OR (Done)
      {exits if A) all entries checked   }
      {        or B) match found          }
    if (StrLess(LName,Book.Info[Index].Name)) then
        {since names are sorted, if we have passed   }
        {the location where the name should be stored }
        {we are done.  Note that Found remains false  }
        Done <- true
    else
        if (StrEq(LName,Book.Info[Index].Name)) then
            {match found}
            Found <- true
            PNum <- Book.Info[Index].PhoneNum
            Done <- true
        else {LName is greater than current Name}
            Index <- Index + 1
        endif
    endif
  endloop
end {Lookup}


procedure AddListing(Book isa in/out PhoneBook,
                     LName isa in CharStr, PNum isa in num)
  {adds an additional person and phone number to the array}
var
  Index isa num
  NewEntry,SaveEntry isa PhoneListing
begin {AddListing}

  NewEntry.Name <- LName
  NewEntry.PhoneNum <- PNum
  Index <- 1
  loop
    if (Index>Book.NumEnts) then
      Done <- true
    else {Index is a valid index}
      Done <- StrLess(LName,Book.Info[Index].Name)
    endif
    exitif (Done)
      {exiting if an empty cell in the array is found or }
      {the correct insertion place has been found         }
    Index <- Index + 1
  endloop
```

```
  {Index > NumEnts OR I indicates first entry >= the given }
  {LName                                                    }

  if (Index>Book.NumEnts) then {new entry goes at end}
    Book.NumEnts <- Book.NumEnts + 1
    Book.Info[Book.NumEnts] <- NewEntry
  else
    {Index is the first entry with name >= the given name}
    if (NOT StrEq(LName,Book.Info[Index].Name)) then
        {insert here if not a duplicate}
      loop {moves each element of the directory down  }
           {to make space to insert the new listing   }
        SaveEntry <- Book.Info[Index]
        Book.Info[Index] <- NewEntry
        NewEntry <- SaveEntry
        exitif (Index = Book.NumEnts)
        Index <- Index + 1
      endloop

      Book.NumEnts <- Book.NumEnts + 1
      Book.Info[Book.NumEnts] <- NewEntry
    else {we have a duplicate - update the phone number}
      Book.Info[Index].PhoneNum <- PNum
    endif
  endif
end {AddListing}



var
  TownBook isa PhoneBook
  Answer isa char
  Name isa CharStr
  Number isa num
  OK isa boolean

begin {main algorithm}

  TownBook.NumEnts <- 0

  loop
    print("enter name:")
    read(Name)
    print("Add or Lookup [a/l]?")
    read(Answer)
    if (Answer='a') then
      print ("enter number")
      read(Number)
      AddListing(TownBook,Name,Number)
    else
      Lookup(TownBook,Name,Number,OK)
      if (OK) then
```

```
          print("The number is ",Number)
        else
          print("We have no listing for ",Name)
        endif
      endif
      print("More?[y/n]")
      read (Answer)
      exit if (Answer <> "y")
    endloop
end   {Algorithm PhoneBookMaint}
```

Here is the BST implementation of the phone book example.
Places that changed from the array implementation (apart
from the Lookup and AddListing modules) are marked with
stars "******".

```
algorithm PhoneBookMaint
{ Binary Search Tree  implementation }

const
  STRSIZE is 30

type
   CharStr definesa array[1..STRSIZE] of char
   PhoneListing definesa record
     Name isa CharStr
     PhoneNum isa Num
   endrecord
   PhoneTreeRec definesa record      *****
     Info isa PhoneListing
     LChild, RChild isa PTPtr        *****
   endrecord
   PTPtr definesa ptr toa PhoneTreeRec *****

{Now Modules and Their Specifications}


function StrEq isa boolean (StringA isa in CharStr,
                           StringB isa in CharStr)
<same as before>


function StrLess isa boolean(StringA isa in CharStr,
                           StringB isa in CharStr)
<same as before>
```

```
         procedure Lookup(Root isa in PTPtr, LName isa in CharStr,
                          PNum isa out num, Found isa out boolean)
begin {Lookup}
  if (Root=nil) then
     Found <- false
  else {tree is nonempty}
     if (StrLess(LName,Root^.Info.Name)) then
        {search in left subtree}
        Lookup(Root^.LChild,LName,PNum,Found)
     else
        if (StrEq(LName,Root^.Info.Name) then
           {listing found -> return phone number}
           Found <- true
           PNum <- Root^.Info.PhoneNum
        else {search in right subtree}
           Lookup(Root^.RChild,LName,PNum,Found)
        endif
     endif
  endif
end    {Lookup}




         procedure AddListing(Root isa in/out PTPtr,
                          LName isa in CharStr, PNum isa in num)

begin {AddListing}
  if (Root=nil) then
     {create new node}
     Root <- new(PhoneTreeRec)
     Root^.Info.Name <- LName
     Root^.Info.PhoneNum <- PNum
     Root^.LChild <- nil
     Root^.RChild <- nil
  else {tree is nonempty; keep going}
     if (StrLess(LName,Root^.Info.Name)) then
        {add in left subtree}
        AddListing(Root^.LChild,LName,PNum)
     else
        if (NOT StrEq(LName,Root^.Info.Name) then
           {checking for duplicate}
           AddListing(Root^.RChild,LName,PNum)
        else {duplicate so update phone number}
           Root^.Info.PhoneNum <- PNum
        endif
     endif
  endif
end {AddListing}
```

```
var
  TownBook isa PTPtr   ******
  Answer isa char
  Name isa CharStr
  Number isa num
  OK isa boolean


begin {main algorithm}
  TownBook <- nil        ******
  loop
    print("enter name:")
    readString(Name)
    print("Add or Lookup [a/l]?")
    read(Answer)
    if (Answer='a') then
        print ("enter number")
        read(Number)
        AddListing(TownBook,Name,Number)
    else
        Lookup(TownBook,Name,Number,OK)
        if (OK) then
          print("The number is ",Number)
        else
          print("We have no listing for ",Name)
        endif
    endif
    print("More?[y/n]")
    read (Answer)
    exit if (Answer <> "y")
  endloop
end {algorithm PhoneBookMaint}
```

[This page intentionally left blank.]

Index

R

S